MAKING MONEY

Paul Clitheroe is a founding director of ipac securities, one of Australia's leading financial planning firms, and has been involved in the investment industry since he graduated from the University of New South Wales in the late 1970s. He has completed the two-year postgraduate course offered by the Securities Institute and is a fellow of that professional body. He was a board member of the Financial Planning Association of Australia between 1992 and 1994; in 1993 he was elected the Vice President and in 1994, the President.

Since June 1993 Paul has been hosting the Channel 9 program 'Money' and since 1999 has been the chairman and chief commentator of *Money Magazine*. Overall, he has been a media commentator and conference speaker for more than fifteen years, and is regarded as a leading expert in the field of personal investment strategies and advice. Paul lives in Sydney with his wife and three children.

Chris Walker is the director of Barrenjoey Communications, a marketing services consultancy. He has an MBA from Macquarie University, and is a senior writer for *Money Magazine*.

Authors' Note

We want to keep this book as relevant as possible. If you have any ideas regarding financial matters that you think should be included in future editions, please write to Paul Clitheroe, *Making Money,* ipac securities, Locked Bag 15, Grosvenor Place, Sydney, NSW 1220.

PAUL CLITHEROE

Written in association with Chris Walker

MAKING MONEY

The 10 steps to financial success

YEAR 2002 EDITION

VIKING

Viking
Penguin Books Australia Ltd
487 Maroondah Highway, PO Box 257
Ringwood, Victoria 3134, Australia
Penguin Books Ltd
Harmondsworth, Middlesex, England
Penguin Putnam Inc.
375 Hudson Street, New York, New York 10014, USA
Penguin Books Canada Limited
10 Alcorn Avenue, Toronto, Ontario, Canada M4V 3B2
Penguin Books (NZ) Ltd
Cnr Rosedale and Airborne Roads, Albany, Auckland, New Zealand
Penguin Books (South Africa) (Pty) Ltd
5 Watkins Street, Denver ext. 4, 2094, South Africa
Penguin Books India (P) Ltd
11, Community Centre, Panchsheel Park,
New Delhi 110 017, India

First published by Penguin Books Australia Ltd 1995
This revised and updated edition published 2001

10 9 8 7 6 5 4 3 2 1

Typeset in 11/13 pt Sabon by Midland Typesetters, Maryborough, Victoria
Printed and bound in Australia by McPherson's Printing Group, Maryborough, Victoria

National Library of Australia
Cataloguing-in-Publication data:

Clitheroe, Paul.
Making money : the 10 steps to financial success.

5th ed.
Includes index.
ISBN 0 670 89295 5 (pbk).

1. Finance, Personal – Australia. I. Walker, Chris, 1954– .
II. Title.

332.02400994

www.penguin.com.au

Acknowledgements

While the basic principles of money never vary, tax, super and other legislative issues always do. The significant changes in the year 2000 with the GST and our tax system, and changes in late 1999 to capital gains tax, meant yet another serious revision of *Making Money*. And this is it, the fifth edition.

As with the previous four editions, my old (and getting older!) university friend Chris Walker has once again put in a significant effort in updating graphs, statistics, legislation and all the other complexities in a book such as this.

Money is never a dull subject, but one of the highlights of the last two years for me was the boom–bust of dot com stocks. I wasn't quite old enough myself to witness the frenzy of one of the gold rushes of the 1800s or early 1900s, but it was fascinating to see first-hand an identical scenario – not about gold, but people rushing towards instant dot com wealth. The end results were the same. Thousands of disillusioned investors, but it is a timely reminder that money rarely comes easily.

In preparing this new edition I would like to thank the research team at ipac securities and my personal assistant Jodie Williamson who co-ordinated their input. Thanks also to Nicola Field for her great help, to Ian Heydon for his work on the Internet chapter, to editor Heather Cam, as well as to Anthony O'Brien, John Ellison, Linda Fischer, Hugo White, Harold Bodinnar, Mike Bartlett, Nicole Raffin, David Wesney, Lisa Morgan, Laura Veltman, David Shirlow and Harold Guberman.

Finally, I would like once again to thank the thousands of 'Money' show viewers and *Money Magazine* readers who continue to share their money experiences with me. Your letters and e-mails have a significant influence on what is in this book.

Paul Clitheroe
June 2001

Contents

Introduction

This book is about building wealth and investing your money wisely. It draws on all the experience that I have gathered in a decade and a half of listening to people's money concerns and giving them advice on how to achieve their goals.

It is not a textbook full of dry academic theory. Nor does it provide 'hot tips' or 'get rich quick' schemes. It will provide you with a practical commonsense guide – in plain English – on how to 'get rich slow', and on how to best invest the money that you have.

I realised many years ago that my clients and people I know rarely became financially comfortable due to a spectacular business success, a 'get rich quick' scheme, gambling or even luck. The huge majority of Australians who are financially comfortable have got there by spending less than they earn year after year, and using their savings to build wealth.

Sounds simple, but I know it isn't easy to do. That's why this book opens with my ten essential steps to growing and protecting your wealth.

For those of you working to improve your financial position, I promise you that by following these steps you can 'get rich slow'. It's not difficult, it just requires some planning. Many people become depressed that it is just too hard to put some money aside on a 'normal' salary. Well, this book is for everyone – not just those earning a high income. I'll show how, for example, saving $1 a day can be turned into nearly $400,000. No miracles here, just a regular savings strategy, time, and the power of compounding returns.

For those who already have some money to invest – savings, an inheritance or retirement money – this book demystifies the world of investment. It explains in a practical fashion how and where to invest, how to manage investment risks and to maximise the return on your money.

I have really enjoyed writing this book – with much help from my old friend, Chris Walker. It contains pretty much all I know about the essentials of investment.

Making Money

My experience as a financial adviser has shown me that money alone does not bring happiness or health. In fact, I've seen all too often the destructive side of money. Its positive side is increasing the options about the type of life you, and those you love, want to lead.

This book will help you to take control of your money – and, therefore, take more control of your life.

CHAPTER ONE

Ten Steps to Financial Security

Money. It seems to be a major issue for all of us in one way or another. During my school days I did odd jobs and picked oranges to give me a bit of pocket-money. During my uni days I was a part-time bartender at the Regent Hotel in Kensington near the University of New South Wales. The long summer holidays were usually spent in my home town of Griffith, again working as a bartender but this time at the Griffith Leagues Club. I'd rather like to pretend that I had a sophisticated plan for the money I earned, but I didn't. It was used to pay – in the main – for activities outside my studies, things at the time that seemed vital, like golf balls, a couple of cheap backpacking holidays or some beer for a party or football game.

No, I didn't save a cent. My only defence (with the benefit of hindsight) is that I was investing in my own education. As I recall, at the time I was simply enjoying my early adult years – and thank heavens I did! One of my central philosophies when it comes to money is to always remember that life is short.

I've now been working in the money business for over 20 years. Four years were spent as an employee of a major financial advisory company and then, in 1983, with four partners, I started up a company – ipac securities – which specialises in investment research and advice for our clients. So, for some 20 years, I've been privileged to meet with a wide range of people to talk about their lives, hopes and fears, and how money relates to all of this.

Without any doubt, meeting with thousands of people, listening and advising, has taught me more about money and real life than anything I ever learnt at university. I've seen first-hand how money can cause real heartache, but I've also seen how it can allow people to live the lives they want to lead and provide security and contentment. My goal with this book is to help you achieve the latter.

Making Money

Wealth builders and wealth protectors

Now, I know that the readers of this book will basically fall into two categories – 'wealth builders' and 'wealth protectors'.

- **Wealth builders:** You are about to start working or, like me, you are still working and trying to build up your wealth. You may have absolutely nothing, or you may be well on your way to having an amount of money that will support you without having to work. You'll be wondering how best to create wealth – buy a house, pay off the mortgage, top up super, or start your own business.
- **Wealth protectors:** You are like my dad or my clients who are using the wealth they have built to provide a satisfying lifestyle. You are concerned about your money not lasting for long enough, having enough income each year, helping or leaving money to the kids, volatile investment markets, confusing legislation and so on.

If you're a 'wealth builder', following my 10 steps to financial security will help you get to where you want to go. If you're a 'wealth protector', most of these 10 steps will still apply, but you should also read my 10 keys to successful investment in Chapter Eleven.

My ten steps to financial security

My real-life money experience has taught me that there are 10 commonsense steps that will really work when it comes to your life and your money.

Step 1. Have a plan

Having a plan certainly sounds sensible; it gives us a sense of direction and provides a path to follow.

Fine, but what should your plan look like, and how do you arrive at one? This is where individual personality comes into it.

Some people have a very clear idea of where they want to be and how to get there, many others don't. But everyone has at least *some* goals, objectives or expectations, dependent to a large extent on their stage in life.

4

So, as the first step in formulating your plan, think about these objectives, and then write them down. You should end up with something like this.

For a young person

- I want to complete my education by doing a three-year apprenticeship. During this time I am prepared to earn little money as I am investing in my skills to allow me to earn a better income later. Completing my apprenticeship is my main objective.
- During these three years I will live at home, and intend to save $50 a week in order to travel to Europe at the end of my apprenticeship. However, I will reassess my plan at that time as I may use the money to buy a car instead, or continue to save to build up a deposit on a home.
- My employer's contributions to super will form a base for my future.

Now while this may seem pretty vague, remember that youth always requires flexibility. It isn't really possible to have a plan at age 18 or 20 that says at age 65 I will:
- have been happily married for 40 years
- have three children and six grandchildren
- own my home
- have an investment property
- be retired.

Life isn't that certain. But as you get older your life becomes more settled and your plans firm up.

For a married couple with young children

- We will continue additional mortgage repayments to pay off the family home in nine years.
- At that stage, we will buy an investment property, start an investment plan or top up super.
- We will have sufficient insurance if one of us is injured, gets sick or dies.
- We will educate our children as well as we are able.
- We will continue to monitor our employers' super and to top this up if our budget allows us to do so. Our target is a 10% contribution each.
- We plan to be financially independent by age 65.

Making Money

For a retired couple

- We wish to leave at least the value of our family home to our children. We have a will lodged with our solicitor.
- We have $250,000 investment money. We plan to use it to give us $20,000 p.a. in income after tax. If doing this reduces the capital that is left to our children, then that is acceptable.
- We will apply for any pension benefits available to us.
- Our investment plan will be one of putting security first. We will avoid high-return/high-risk investments.
- We wish to stay in our home as long as possible. If, for health reasons, we cannot stay at home we will consider living in an environment where help is available.

> **o⊷ KEY THOUGHT**
> Setting objectives is central to a plan. After all, there's not much point in having a plan if you have nothing to aim for!

Once you have set your objectives you have a good reason to draw up a plan – and a reason to stick to it. I'm sure the young apprentice will be much better able to stick to the plan to save $50 a week by thinking about the end objective – the trip, car or home. Trying to save $50 a week for no particular reason does not work for long in my experience.

Now you can start to build your plan – which is how you achieve your objectives. You can get very sophisticated with your planning but, in my experience, commonsense plans work best. Certainly a financial adviser can help you (but you will still need to be able to tell the adviser what your objectives are). The next page outlines an example of a simple plan.

> **o⊷ KEY THOUGHTS**
> - People tend to spend 110% of what they earn.
> - You can't save cash.
> - Being the richest person in the graveyard isn't very clever.
> - People don't plan to fail, they fail to plan.

Objective	Plan
I want to save $50 a week.	Do a budget. Have $50 taken from your pay and transferred to a separate, low-fee savings account without ATM card access.
I want to pay off my mortgage in nine years.	Get your bank to work out how much your repayments need to be. Will your budget allow for this? Arrange to have your repayments increased.
I want a comfortable life in my retirement.	Use your budget to plan how much you need to spend each year. Write down your assets, and what income your assets can generate and for how long. Can you get a pension? What level of risk are you comfortable with? You may find a financial adviser can help you here.

What your plan should contain

1. Your objectives	Be as specific as you can. Set short-term (this year), medium-term (1 to 5 years) and long-term (5 years plus) objectives.
2. Your budget	This is a 'must do' – the vast majority of us won't win Lotto or inherit $1 million. You will only achieve most of your objectives by spending less than you earn.
3. Your current financial position	I own the following assets:

I own the following assets:

Home value	$220,000
Car value	$ 10,000
Bank account	$ 3,000
	$233,000 (A)

I have the following debts:

Mortgage	$150,000
Credit cards	$ 1,000
	$151,000 (B)

I have already built up assets with a net value of: $82,000 (A−B)

4. Important facts	My assets and my life are/are not insured properly. I have a will that reflects my wishes.

Making Money

By working through these four items you have taken the first *key step* to controlling your money.

You understand where you are now. Your objectives tell you where you want to be. Your plan should take you from where you are today, to *where you want to be.*

> ⚬⇥ **KEY THOUGHT**
> You will only achieve your objectives by spending less than you earn.

Step 2. Budget and take control of your money

Chapter Two, 'Your Budget', gives practical details on how to budget and what to do if your budget doesn't work – which, believe me, happens all too often! But, before we go into that, I want to convince you that you *must take control of your money*, and budgeting, leading to saving, is a vital part of the process.

Now, it drives me absolutely nuts when I think that if you are on the average full-time adult income of just over $43,000 p.a., in your working life you will earn about $2 million in today's dollars. If inflation averages 4% this becomes more than $5 million. But how much are you likely to save? If you are like most people, not much, unless you do something about it!

I know life is expensive. And I reckon that you think if you earned an extra few thousand dollars, you'd be okay. But you know what? You probably wouldn't.

Let me explain. I have clients who earn as little as $20,000 and as much as $1.5 million a year. Guess what? They *all* have a problem saving money.

'That's ridiculous,' I hear you saying. How could anyone earn so much money and not have some left over? Well, life is like that – our expectations and our expenditures grow in line with what we earn. We rapidly learn to spend the extra we make. Maybe my own situation is typical.

Back in my university beer-pulling days at the Regent Hotel in 1974–6, I used to earn around $33 for two night shifts (let me remind you a schooner of beer cost only 33 cents in 1974). My family paid my education fees and board at Baxter College at the University of New South Wales, so the $33 was spending money.

And, in those years, I always had some cash in my pocket. Nowadays, I earn a lot more than that but I rarely have spare cash.

Why? Well, there's three young kids' school fees, two cars, better clothes, eating out occasionally, taking holidays and so on. In 1974, my only possessions were jeans, T-shirts and a $120 pushbike. If it was too far for the bike, the bus was fine. My expectations have changed and my basic cost of living has soared.

Believe me, we tend to spend all we earn – and to justify it. But take note that many of us are living well beyond the basics (food, shelter, clothes) and are spending money on things we want (a selection of clothes, cars, holidays, movies, eating out) rather than on what we need.

O— KEY THOUGHT
It's not what you earn that matters – it's how much you spend.

I have financially comfortable clients who have never earned above the basic wage. I also have clients who are nearly broke who earned 20 times the basic wage. What is the single difference? It's simple: my comfortably-off clients consistently spent less than they earned and they saved the rest. They paid off their home, didn't build up credit-card debt, and paid cash for cars, holidays and household goods.

O— KEY THOUGHT
Make a commitment to the concept 'if you can't afford it, you can't afford it'.

I want you to take control of your money because life will be a lot happier if you do. But I don't want you to think you can't afford to have fun along the way. That's silly. I want you to draw up a budget that includes fun things in it. I want your budget to allow you to enjoy your money, yet still enable you to save.

And saving is critical, because if you can save on a regular basis you will become financially comfortable. If you can't, you won't.

Look, I realise budgeting for regular saving is pretty boring, but it's 'getting rich slowly' and it's the only way I know how to *guarantee* that you will actually get there.

Now, if you have already tried a budget and found it doesn't work, don't despair. There is another way of achieving your goals without a budget to help you save. Read about it in Chapter Two – 'The damn budget doesn't work!' (pages 19–20).

Step 3. Save little, save often

I am told on a regular basis 'the stuff you talk about makes sense, but it's all too hard'. But what many people don't realise is that you don't need to save a fortune every week. I'll talk more about this in Chapter Three, 'Savings', but let me entice you with a thought that, on the face of it, may sound incredible.

If you save $1 a day during your working life, how much will you have at age 65? Well, if you can average 10% on your savings (which is quite possible), $1 a day saved from age 18 to age 65 should be worth around $400,000. Two dollars a day is $800,000; $5 a day is $2 million. No miracles, no magic or silly numbers – just a sensible savings strategy and compound interest.

Hang on though – you (like me!) may not be 18. So how does it work for us? Well, when you're older, hopefully you can save more than $1 a day. Let's say you save $5 a day. In 25 years time, it should be worth over $200,000; $10 a day should be worth over $400,000. Even with only five years to save, $10 a day should be worth around $25,000.

Save more if you can and, as you read the rest of this book, I'll answer your questions about where to save – on your mortgage, with investment property, shares or super – and I'll give you lots of practical savings ideas. The point I want to make here is that, while the amount you save is important, it's a *commitment to regular savings* that makes the difference.

Step 4. Avoid punting and silly risks

If there is one thing experience has shown me, it's that risk equals return. Now, low-cost punts like Lotto, a lottery ticket, or a bet on the Melbourne Cup don't worry me at all. These are small things and can be good fun. I lose my money cheerfully, because we don't have a statement in our plan that says 'we plan to become comfortable by winning Lotto'. Incidentally, do you know what your chances are of winning Lotto? Well, it's around seven million to one. I wouldn't count on it!

Humans seem to instinctively want to find an easy way to make money and one that involves little work, like the 'get rich quick' schemes you often see advertised in the papers. The ads use the words 'easy', 'simple', 'no capital required', 'high returns', and 'get rich'. Clearly, the operators of these schemes understand human psychology.

Think about it, though. They want you to pay them to access *their* 'get rich quick' scheme. If it works so well, why don't they use their own scheme to get rich themselves? It's painfully obvious isn't it? The schemes don't work.

Here, I'll take one bet I know I will win. I'll bet you the scheme operator uses your money to do what you should be doing – paying off a mortgage, buying shares or investing in property.

The only way I can see to make money out of 'get rich quick' schemes is to sell them to some mug or, preferably, lots of mugs which, I'm pleased to say, is not in my plan – and I hope it is not in yours.

As an investor you must also be careful when it comes to higher returns than you would normally expect. Do you remember the Estate Mortgage advertisements in 1990? They ran television and print ads claiming very high returns and that they were better than a bank or a building society.

Simple research would have shown you that their returns were up to 5% higher than equivalent investments. This is because they were lending money on high-risk projects. After all, if they were paying investors 17% (given their annual fee was around 2%), then they must have been lending money out at 19%.

Now, if you could borrow from a bank in 1990 at 15%, what sort of people borrowed from Estate Mortgage? As was soon discovered when Estate Mortgage collapsed in 1991, people prepared to pay 19% were borrowers who the banks wouldn't touch – and with good reason, as it turned out. They were high-risk borrowers whose high failure rate ultimately brought Estate Mortgage down. The result was that hundreds of thousands of Estate Mortgage investors lost part or, in some cases, all of their life savings.

The message here is simple. If something offers a higher return it will have a higher risk. Don't get me wrong, though, I'm not against risk. If you take no risk you must expect a low return. Just don't let anyone fool you into thinking you can get a high return with low risk.

Investors should manage risk, not avoid it. As I demonstrate in Chapter Thirteen for instance, shares make a terrific long-term investment, although they are riskier than cash. Over 10 years, they typically earn you around 5% p.a. more on your investment than leaving it in a bank. With cash in a bank, however, your chances of losing money in any one year are zero, while with shares you have around a one-in-four chance of losing money in any one year.

---

o— KEY THOUGHTS

- Risk equals return.
- If it looks too good to be true, it is.
- Don't plan to be financially comfortable by punting.

Step 5. Don't plan to save cash

So, if you don't save cash what are you meant to save – cowrie shells? Not really – unless you live in a tribal community that uses shells as money.

Look at your budget for the *past* year. It may show that you should have saved $2,000 – but where is the money? It's most unlikely to be in your pocket or your standard savings account because, in my experience, Australians can't save cash.

The only way you can save is to put your savings away *before* you spend the cash. So, if you have planned to save around $2,000 a year, based on how you are paid you must plan to save either $38.50 a week, $77.00 a fortnight or $167.00 a month.

It's vital this amount is taken away from you *before* you spend it and that way you won't really notice its absence. So, either have your paymaster transfer it to a separate bank account or increase your mortgage repayments or your super contributions. This way you will 'get rich slow'.

> **◦━ KEY THOUGHT**
> Have your savings automatically 'locked' away *before you spend them*.

Step 6. Plan to own a home debt-free

Now, you don't need any convincing here do you? This is conventional wisdom. Yes, I know renting can be shown to be more cost-effective than home ownership in the short term – but in the long term, home ownership comes out in front.

I also know negative gearing can be a very tax-effective way of buying a property in which you might one day live but, as a general rule, owning your own home and eliminating the debt against it as quickly as possible is a key wealth-creation strategy.

We'll look at this in far more detail in Chapter Six, 'Owning a Home', but let me say again that first and foremost, plan to own a home, debt-free.

Step 7. Super is good – invest in it!

It may take some work on my part to win you over to the line that super is good. You no doubt see it as confusing, ever-changing, overly complex, too restrictive, and loaded with fees. And, yes, you'd be right.

Believe it or not, though, the Government is on the right track with a compulsory super system. Australians are not good voluntary savers which is why many people own nothing at retirement except perhaps their home. And the only reason they own that is because the bank would have taken it away if they had not kept up their repayments.

I believe compulsory and voluntary super is good for us, having as it does so many elements that fit with my ten steps to financial security. It is regular saving; it's tax efficient (really, it is!); it's generally invested in good quality long-term assets (shares, property and fixed interest); and the fact that (like your house) you really can't get your hands on the cash is also a huge plus. As *a part* of your long-term plan, super makes sense.

Making Money

Step 8. Minimise tax

I am always amused when people complain about paying too much tax. On a global scale, we are at the low end of the tax take compared with societies that have a similar standard of living. More importantly, it seems to me that people who pay a lot of tax earn a lot of money. Investors who pay a lot of tax have a lot of investment income.

An easy way to pay less tax is to earn less money. But who wants to do that? In one way, it rather pleases me when my tax bill goes up each year – it means I'm doing better.

Despite this somewhat arcane way of thinking, clearly you should still plan to legally minimise your tax. In other words, I want you to *legally avoid* tax, but *not illegally evade* tax. In Chapter Ten on 'Tax', I cover the basic as well as more complex ways of reducing your tax bill.

The key point is that while you should always try to minimise tax, you should never let tax minimisation strategies drive your investment decisions. For instance, if it is appropriate for you to borrow money for a good investment, go ahead and do it. And if this investment gives you tax advantages along the way, fine, treat that as a bonus, not as the main attraction. If you find yourself or an adviser saying, 'let's negatively gear (borrow money) for an investment to reduce tax', stop. Take a deep breath and think hard.

Don't let me give you the impression that borrowing money to invest is not legitimate; it is. But if the investment is not fundamentally sound you will *lose money you do not own*, outweighing any tax benefits you could ever hope to receive.

> **☛ KEY THOUGHT**
> Focus on investment returns rather than on tax benefits. Tax should not drive your decisions.

Step 9. Protect assets

Now, I'm sure you already understand that you need to insure your home, contents, car and other valuables. This type of insurance is relatively cheap and a 'must have'. However obvious it is, though, I estimate that over 50% of Australians either do not insure assets, or are underinsured.

The other asset you need to protect is *you*. What happens if you get sick, have an accident or, at the extreme end of it all, die? I am a very firm believer in buying as little insurance as you need but, at certain stages of your life, you really need quite a lot. Chapter Eight, 'Insurance', will provide you with the details you need.

Step 10. Take advice if you need it

You'll have to forgive my bias when I talk about the advantages of having a good adviser. I know there are plenty of shonks out there who want to separate you from your money, but there are also a growing number of excellent advisers who are not simply trying to flog you product for commission.

In Chapter Nineteen, 'Choosing an Adviser', I go into detail, but let me say here that you can plan to build and protect your wealth by yourself and you don't need to be Einstein to do it either. Simply following my ten steps and reading this book will give you most of what you need to know – it's just that most of us find it more efficient to do what we do best and to consult others for assistance when we need it.

Even if you do choose to see an adviser you should still work through these ten steps. The best way to use an adviser is not to be totally dependent on their skills but to develop a relationship where you both have an understanding of your plan. Then the adviser can be of great assistance in selecting and monitoring your investments, tax and insurance.

o–– KEY THOUGHT

It's your money. Ultimately *you* are responsible.

Live the life you want to lead

Let me add one final point. It concerns me that a few people I know have reached their financial goals but have developed such squirrel-like habits that they hate spending money on anything. Remember,

Making Money

I believe the value of money is to give you options – *you must plan to have fun along the way.*

I would also hope that one day when you do stop work, you will recognise that part of your hard work was to give you freedom later in life. Unless you have accumulated millions you will then start to eat into your capital. But that's okay – that's what it's for!

> **o⌐ KEY THOUGHT**
>
> It's quite amazing how a little commonsense and planning combine to make you rich – slowly!

So, there you have my ten steps. It's not hard to sit down and use these steps to build your own plan. And, I hope you can see how important it is to have one, no matter how basic.

My 10 steps to financial security

1. Have a plan.
2. Budget and take control of your money.
3. Save little, save often.
4. Avoid punting and silly risks.
5. Don't plan to save cash.
6. Plan to own a home debt-free.
7. Super is good – invest in it!
8. Minimise tax.
9. Protect assets.
10. Take advice if you need it.

Your Budget

Budgeting! The very mention of it makes us wince. Why? Well, I think it's because budgeting confronts us with just how much money slips through our fingers – and with how little we have to show for it. But that's one of its purposes – getting the jolt is good for us.

Budgeting encourages us to take a disciplined approach to spending and saving, enabling us to reach short-, medium- and long-term goals that otherwise might prove unattainable. It helps us find extra money to invest, or to pay for a holiday. *Budgeting is the most important and effective tool for getting our finances under control.*

These are big claims I know, but have you ever heard of a successful business that doesn't have any plans? I'm sure you haven't, because businesses without plans don't last very long. And, in business, at the heart of every plan is a budget.

A business's budget is designed to maintain financial control and to prevent money being wasted. These are the same as your goals, so you have to treat yourself like a business. After all, you generate some pretty big figures too. As I mentioned in the first chapter, the current average adult, full-time Australian wage of just over $43,000 per year multiplied by a working life of 47 years (from 18 to 65) works out at around a hefty $2 million in today's money. Yet, there are many Australians who, after a lifetime of work, end up with little more than the home they are living in – if they are lucky. Having a budget is the first step towards ensuring this doesn't happen to you.

Even people earning very good money never seem to have any. That's because they, like all of us, have a tendency to spend about 10% more than they earn, no matter what their income levels are. I have some very well-paid clients who say the solution to their lack of funds is to earn even more than they presently do. That's wrong. Chances are they will overspend any increased income they receive. In fact, some people who know they will be receiving a pay rise in

Making Money

December start spending more in July just to get used to the feeling of it!

What do I say to these people? I tell them to do a budget, find out where all the money is going and then cut back on the least necessary areas to the point where not only does their income not exceed expenditure, but there's actually something left over to save. This is what budgeting is all about.

> **o⊷ KEY THOUGHT**
>
> A budget tells you where your money is going, where you can cut back, and where you can save.

Whatever you do, don't convert your unspent income into cash and put it in your pocket – because you'll spend it! Saving cash is virtually impossible.

The important thing is to control your own life, which means controlling your money – and a budget is a very important part of the process of making it happen. Here are some aspects to consider.

The discipline has rewards

Most people don't like the discipline of a budget – but it does have its benefits. Without the discipline of a mortgage you would never pay your home off and without the discipline of a budget you would never save. There's a big stick hanging over you with your mortgage (if you don't pay it, the bank takes the house), but if you don't save there's every chance you will retire poor.

Budget for fun

People say that they find the whole idea of a personal budget too restrictive, too ordered, and that it takes all the fun out of life. Well, this is only true if you don't budget for fun – and many people don't. A budget that doesn't allow you to enjoy yourself is completely unrealistic and will be ignored. That doesn't mean all budgets are useless, just that bad budgets are.

Be realistic

Putting together a sensible, real-life family budget that doesn't specify everything down to the last grain of rice (a guaranteed waste of time) is not difficult. In fact, I've made it very easy for you by including a budget guide at the end of this chapter. All you have to do is allocate a couple of hours to work through it. Sit down by yourself or with the family, fill it out as accurately as you can and, please, be realistic.

Be flexible

A budget should be flexible, so don't despair if your circumstances change, rendering your budget inappropriate. You may change jobs, have a baby, receive a rise, or move house. It's not a problem. Just do another budget. Businesses, after all, fine-tune their budgets frequently. Even if there are no major changes in your life I recommend you review your budget every six months.

⚙━ KEY THOUGHT
A budget is not a rigid document designed to make your life miserable. It's a flexible tool designed to make your life better.

'The damn budget doesn't work!'

How often have I heard that a budget doesn't work? In fact, if I had $1 for every time someone has told me that their budget is a disaster, I wouldn't need to do one myself – the money would be pouring in!

I know for some people that a budget just doesn't work and the main reasons I hear are:
- I just can't stick to it.
- Unexpected expenses keep cropping up.
- It's boring.
- My life keeps changing.
- It's just too depressing.
- I'm too tired, or too busy.

Making Money

If you've tried to budget and it didn't work, ask yourself if the budget was realistic in the first place. If you don't think it was, have another go at it.

Let's face it though, for a large number of people, for all sorts of reasons, budgets have not worked and will not work. So what do you do? You stop flogging a dead horse and switch to the pretty simple plan of 'paying yourself first'.

Paying yourself first

With this strategy you only have to make one budgeting decision, which is: what proportion of your income can you save? If you reckon you can save 5% of your income, as soon as you get paid and before you do anything else with it, have it put into your selected savings vehicle. You see, if it gets into your pocket it's as good as spent.

Now, you can take your other 95% and spend it any way you like – but *don't touch the 5%*. That money is your future.

I promise you that after a few months, unless your finances are very tight, you won't miss it. If a pay rise comes along add 1% or 2% to the 5% before you learn how to spend the money.

Before long, you can build up a very healthy savings habit without a budget. But remember, you cannot spend more than 95% (or whatever your chosen percentage is): no abusing credit cards, no personal loans, no other forms of debt.

> **☛ KEY THOUGHT**
>
> A budget is the best option but if it doesn't work for you, use the simple principle of paying yourself first and spending the rest.

Budget planner

The planner's purpose is to show you just how much you are spending, on what, and where opportunities exist to make savings. You might be amazed, for instance, at how much you spend on magazines, tobacco and alcohol. If you cut back on these items, you could probably save yourself hundreds of dollars. Or maybe you could save by not going to the hairdresser so often.

The planner will tell you if you have earned more than you spent, or if you have spent more than you earned. If you have spent more than you earned you will either have to reduce your spending – and now you will have a better idea how to – or you will have to generate more income. On the other hand, if you have earned more than you spent, do something sensible with these savings by putting them into, say, shares, property, managed funds, superannuation, a savings account with no card access, or your mortgage. It's important to get rid of unspent money this way before you learn how to spend it – which never takes long.

Making Money

Money budget planner

HOME	Week	Year
Mortgage Repayments		
Rent		
Local Council Rates		
Water Rates		
Electricity		
Gas		
Telephone/Internet		
Maintenance – Repairs		
Furniture		
Appliances		
Hire Purchase		
Rentals		
Other		
MOTOR VEHICLE		
Registration		
Petrol		
Repairs – Maintenance		
Lease or Loan Payments		
Other		
FOOD		
Groceries – Milk, Bread		
Meat		
Alcohol		
Cigarettes/Tobacco		
Eating Out – Restaurants		
EXPENSES SUB TOTAL		

Your Budget

INSURANCE	Week	Year
House		
Health Insurance		
Home Contents		
Motor Vehicle		
Income Protection		
Death Cover		
Other		
FAMILY EXPENSES		
School Fees		
Child Care		
School Costs		
Pets		
Sporting Activities		
Public Transport		
Subscriptions/Memberships		
Newspapers and Magazines		
Clothing		
Gifts		
Personal Care		
Hairdresser – Barber		
Holidays – Travel		
Entertainment		
EXPENSES SUB TOTAL		

Making Money

HEALTH	Week	Year
Medical Bills		
Dental Bills		
Medicines		
Other		
OTHER FINANCE		
Loan Repayments		
Store Cards – Lay-bys		
Credit Cards		
Superannuation		
Professional Fees		
Donations		
Other		

EXPENSES SUB TOTAL

INCOME

Your After-tax Income

Spouse's After-tax Income

After-tax Income From
Savings Accounts

Other

TOTAL INCOME

LESS YOUR TOTAL EXPENSES

YOUR SAVINGS

Savings

When Frank Sinatra, surrounded by very expensive silverware in the film *High Society*, crooned 'Who wants to be a millionaire? – I don't', he probably wasn't striking too many chords with the audience. Most of them would have been humming along, 'I *DO!*'

Of course, Sinatra could afford to feign such disinterest in money – he was being paid a packet. Because of his great voice he was already a millionaire when he made the movie, and he would have died even richer. But most of us aren't blessed with such a wonderful – and bankable – gift.

Winning the lottery, picking a string of 100-to-1 winners, earning a six-figure salary or pulling off a great business deal – there's no denying that any of these will give your current finances a terrific boost. But, alone, they won't guarantee you'll end up wealthy. And, let's face it, for many people the chance of hitting any of these jackpots is low.

The bedrock of wealth

I have financially comfortable clients who have never earned more than the basic wage and, at the same time, I have clients who have enjoyed enormous incomes during their working lives and yet have retired virtually broke. The basic difference between the two is simple: one lot saved, the others spent. It really brings home just how much *saving is the absolute bedrock of accumulating wealth*.

> **⚬— KEY THOUGHT**
> No other factor is as important in becoming financially secure as saving. It's even more important than investment.

If you are a bit surprised by this, let me clarify what 'savings' means. It's any money that's not spent now but, rather, money put

Making Money

aside to spend next week, next month, next year or in your retirement. In economists' terms it's 'deferred consumption'. This means 'savings' is more than just the money that goes into your piggy bank or passbook savings account, it's also the money that goes into your mortgage over and above the interest charge, into your super, into a sound investment, into a savings plan or term deposit or into a separate account for some special purpose.

Why is saving so important to the creation of wealth? Well, if you save nothing during your working life, by the time you stop working you will have nothing material, regardless of what your income was. It's that simple, and that brutal.

Saving little, saving often

The trouble with saving is that it's not much fun – certainly not as much fun as spending. It requires discipline and commitment, which don't come naturally to most people. So the secret is to find ways of making saving a relatively easy and painless process. Try this simple method on for size.

When you come home from work or the shops go straight to the piggy bank or moneybox and put the loose change from your pocket or your purse into it. When the moneybox is full, bank it into your savings account, pay it into a managed fund, or put it towards your mortgage. Just don't dip into it while it's at home.

You might think I'm joking, but I'm not. This very basic savings technique can generate enormous figures over time.

As mentioned on page 10, if you saved just $1 per day from age 18 you would accumulate around $400,000 after tax by age 65 (assuming 10% annual earnings). If you saved just $2 per day the figure would be $800,000; $5 per day would be $2 million.

This method of accumulating a large sum of money couldn't be easier or less painful, and it illustrates dramatically how powerful a long-term, regular savings regimen can be.

Now, while I reckon that most of us can put aside a few dollars a day without even noticing the absence, I also reckon that most of you reading this book are not 18. Those of you who are older may be thinking you've left your savings run a bit late. You haven't! It's never too late to save, and there is no time like the present to start.

When you are older, and presumably earning a significantly higher income than when you were 18, saving more than $1 or $2 per day shouldn't be all that hard. So, say you are 40 and you save $5 per day, by retirement at 65 you should have accumulated over $200,000. And, if you could save $10 per day it should be worth more than $400,000 by then.

Some of you will be saying that your budget is so tight you can't spare a single dollar to save. Okay, I know that almost everyone goes through some very difficult periods, particularly when there's only one income, kids and a mortgage to meet. But for most people the tough times don't last forever. As soon as they stop you really should grab the opportunity to save.

Let's put our potential to save in perspective. If you were 30 years old on $30,000 p.a. and you expected your income to increase by 7% p.a., by 65 years of age *you would have earned $4.1 million.* If you were 40 years old on $40,000 p.a., given the same growth, you would have earned $2.5 million by retirement. These are huge figures generated from average earnings. Even a small percentage of this saved would produce a very significant sum by the time you stop working. In the light of this, it makes me despair to think how much money passes through people's hands during their lifetimes and how little of it they retain.

The 'power' of compound interest

Let's look at the $1- or $2-a-day savings scheme once again. The reason that savings (and debts) can accumulate so dramatically over longer periods is due to the 'power' of compound interest (which is the method of interest calculation applied to most savings vehicles and applied to most debts).

Compounding is where interest accrues not only against the principal but also against any previously accrued interest. It is, therefore, interest on (principal and) interest. Simple interest is where interest is paid on the principal only.

Over time the difference in the impact of the two methods of calculating interest becomes quite astonishing, as the table on the next page demonstrates.

Making Money

Compound interest

Year	Principal	Compound interest	Year-end balance
1	$ 1,000	$ 1,000 x 10% = $ 100	$ 1,100
2	$ 1,100	$ 1,100 x 10% = $ 110	$ 1,210
3	$ 1,210	$ 1,210 x 10% = $ 121	$ 1,331
10	$ 2,358	$ 2,358 x 10% = $ 236	$ 2,594
20	$ 6,116	$ 6,116 x 10% = $ 612	$ 6,728
30	$15,863	$15,863 x 10% = $1,586	$17,449
40	$41,144	$41,144 x 10% = $4,114	$45,258

Simple interest

Year	Principal	Simple interest	Year-end balance
1	$1,000	$1,000 x 10% = $100	$1,100
2	$1,000	$1,000 x 10% = $100	$1,200
3	$1,000	$1,000 x 10% = $100	$1,300
10	$1,000	$1,000 x 10% = $100	$2,000
20	$1,000	$1,000 x 10% = $100	$3,000
30	$1,000	$1,000 x 10% = $100	$4,000
40	$1,000	$1,000 x 10% = $100	$5,000

Apart from the enormous difference in the final amounts, note how the impact of compound interest accelerates as time goes by – between Years 20 and 30 the compound interest balance grew by $10,721, whereas between Years 30 and 40 it grew by $27,809, almost three times as much.

Here's another example. Let's say that Mary decided to put an annual lump sum into a managed fund earning a real 3.5% p.a. (after fees, tax and inflation). Let's assume that her initial deposit was $3,000 and that this was increased annually by 4% p.a. for inflation. Let's also assume that all earnings were reinvested.

If Mary began this regimen at age 21 and continued it for 15 years, by the time she reached 36 (at which point her final annual contribution would have grown to $5,400) she would have accumulated a total of $107,000.

Now, if at age 36 she left this total amount in the fund, contributing nothing more to it, by the time she was 65 it would have compounded to $869,000.

As a comparison, let's say John *began* the same type of regimen as this (under the same set of assumptions) at the age of 36, at the time Mary stopped. Let's also say his initial annual deposit was $5,400, the same as Mary's final deposit. Significantly, even after making contributions every year until he reached the age of 65 – by which time his final annual contribution would have grown to $16,000 – John would still not have reached as great an accumulated amount as Mary (who had ceased annual contributions at $5,400, 30 years prior). John's total accumulation at age 65 would have been $834,000.

> **⊶ KEY THOUGHT**
> Because it takes time for the power of compounding to really kick in, the moral is: the earlier you start saving, the better.

Tips to help you save

Whatever your overall savings strategy, there are plenty of ways you can reduce your regular level of spending and save without having to live like a monk. Try these.

- Only buy items you need when you need them, that is, don't treat shopping as a hobby or a leisure activity.
- Don't buy something unless you have the money to do so. Just remember the old maxim – if you can't afford it, you can't afford it!
- Pay with cash, not with your credit cards. Credit cards make buying too easy and can be a real debt trap for unwary or compulsive shoppers.
- Don't buy the first thing you see – shopping around is very important.
- Ask for discounts on items like whitegoods, furniture, and even clothes. You'll be amazed how many shops are prepared to bargain and all you have to do is ask – they can only say 'no', and many won't.
- Wait for end-of-year and end-of-season sales before buying.
- Buy next year's Christmas presents at the beginning of the year during the January sales.
- Take advantage of bulk discounts, for example, carton prices on wine and beer.
- Take your lunch to work.

Making Money

- Buy generic (unbranded or in-house supermarket brand) products. The quality may not be as high as some branded products, but for staples like flour, sugar and butter I can't pick the difference.
- Shop in supermarkets rather than more expensive corner stores.
- Be prepared to buy second-hand rather than new goods.
- If you are a smoker, give up. Not only will it save you around $60 to $70 per week (based on a packet a day), you'll feel better and so will everyone around you. Put that $60 to $70 you save into your super – which you'll need to build up because you'll probably live longer!

⌛ KEY THOUGHTS

- Saving is the bedrock of wealth.
- Even a small amount saved regularly will build up over time into something significant due to the power of compounding.
- You can't save the cash that gets into your pocket, so don't plan to.
- You should direct a portion of your income straight into savings before you get your hands on it – which means before you spend it.
- You won't miss what you've never had.
- Establish part of your savings in areas difficult to dip into like superannuation, your mortgage, or at least a separate savings account with no card access.
- Saving requires commitment and discipline, but choosing the right savings strategy can make the process a lot easier and relatively painless.

CHAPTER FOUR

Buying Things

Let me lay my cards straight down on the table (and I don't mean my credit cards). If you want to buy something, try to pay cash. And if you don't have the cash, think again whether you really need to make the purchase. This is a very simple, straightforward philosophy, and, while there are big-ticket circumstances where it's obviously not practicable – such as buying a house, funding an investment or establishing a business – if you stick to it wherever possible you shouldn't get into too much trouble with money.

The reasons to pay cash and avoid debt are clear enough – interest is yet another cost to bear, and entering into debt puts you under a legal obligation to the creditor which can have serious consequences if you can't meet repayments. Namely, the creditor might take your purchase back or, worse still, might take other assets too.

Credit cards

I'll explain how credit cards work for the benefit of the many Australians who don't have any. They are a vehicle for providing instant debt financing up to a predetermined limit which is set either by you or the credit card issuer (a bank, a building society, a credit union, or a credit card company). The whole idea of a credit card is to enable you to buy things at shops and businesses without the need to have the ready cash, or to enable you to receive a cash advance against the card through a bank, a money changer, or an automatic teller machine (ATM).

Whenever you make a purchase or take a cash advance against your card you incur an immediate or deferred interest charge on that transaction. And the way the interest is accrued normally places the card into one of two camps – where interest is charged immediately, or, where you have up to 55 days interest-free before any interest charges kick in. (In the case of cash advances interest always accrues immediately.)

Whether you have a card with up to 55 interest-free days on

Making Money

purchases or one that accrues immediate interest depends upon the policy of the card's issuer and some will offer customers a choice between the two. When you opt for a card with an interest-free period you are more likely to be charged a higher interest rate. Also, the cards with interest-free periods are more likely to attract an annual fee – ranging from around $15 to $50 – than immediate-interest cards on which there is normally no annual fee. Some cards also have nominal transaction fees.

As a card-holder you are sent a monthly statement detailing all purchases and cash advances and any interest that has accrued over the period. You then have the option of paying the account in full or just repaying as little as a specified minimum monthly amount by a specified date.

Clearly it is better to pay the account in full to minimise interest charges, but many people just pay the monthly minimum, rolling over the bulk of the account into the next billing period, which is highly inadvisable. The compounding interest makes buying things on credit very expensive and if you continue to make further purchases with the card you'll find yourself in the grip of serious debt.

Now, it's at billing time you want to pay particular attention to the issuers' policies on interest-free periods. (These can be quite rigorous and, as they vary from one issuer to another, it's a good idea to shop around for the card with the best conditions and rates – though they can be changed at any time.)

When you receive your statement you normally have 25 days (although it may be only 14) to pay your bill. If you have up to 55 days interest-free, this period attracts no interest charges (assuming it started from a $0 balance). If you don't pay the statement out in full some cards charge interest on the outstanding amount taken back to the items' *purchase dates*, not to the end of the interest-free period. What's more, if you buy more on your credit card before you've totally paid the amount already owing you may be charged interest from the date of the new purchases – in other words, no more interest-free period. Your interest-free period on any new purchases may not be reinstated until you have paid fully for all previous purchases.

Most issuers offer their customers a choice of credit cards: Visa, MasterCard and Bankcard. There is really no significant difference between them except that Bankcard is not accepted internationally and is increasingly being overshadowed by the others.

My last word on credit cards is they can be very convenient, they are safer than cash in the event of loss or theft, and they are very useful if you are travelling overseas, particularly in the USA where sometimes only credit cards (not cash) are accepted. The trouble is that they make buying too easy, which erodes your savings and in many cases lumbers you with excessive debt. You must exercise control over your credit cards, rather than the other way around, and you must certainly never delude yourself that having a credit card is the same as having the cash in your pocket!

Charge cards

Charge cards are a variation on the credit card theme and, in Australia, the two best known are Diners Club and American Express (although now American Express also offers credit cards). Where charge cards differ from credit cards is that when you receive your monthly bill you are expected to pay it in full.

Now, because you are supposed to pay your bill in full every month, charge cards officially carry no interest charges. If you do pay it out in full as expected, certainly, there is no interest. However, if you don't pay it out in full, one of a number of unpleasant things will happen to you. Your card will either be cancelled on the spot, or you will be charged very hefty penalty interest rates for a short period up until the time you either do pay it out fully or it's revoked, whichever comes first. In the case of American Express, in early 2001 they charged the greater of $20 or 3% of the amount out-standing per month, equivalent after compounding to a very solid 43% p.a. If this rate of interest wouldn't make you pay up in full, posthaste, I don't know what would. On its standard (green) charge card, American Express also charge a joining fee and annual sub-scription fee ($30 and $65 respectively).

As charge cards will not permit (or severely penalise you) for carrying debt over from one month to the next, it may be that they cause less long-term indebtedness than normal credit cards. Having said that though, some charge cards have no pre-set spending limits – you set your own. So, if self-control is not your strong suit, you could find charge cards the most dangerous plastic of all.

Making Money

Store cards

Store cards are a form of credit card issued by retailers like Myer/ Grace Bros, Target, David Jones and Katies. Hundreds of different retailers in Australia issue store cards which are only for use in their stores.

The good news about store cards is that they attract no annual fees and have a good interest-free period – normally a maximum of either 55 or 60 days. The bad news about store cards is that they usually incur higher interest rate charges than credit cards. A difference of around 5% is not uncommon and it can be as much as 10%. Also, if you don't pay your account in full there are usually no more interest-free days until you do.

Now with some cards, shoppers are invited to buy big-ticket items where they are given, say, 6 or 12 months to pay, interest-free. What's often not pointed out is that if the item is not paid for in full during that period, then interest will be charged on the total price of the item and backdated to the date of purchase, regardless of how much has already been paid off.

Let's say, for example, you use one of these cards (or enter into some other in-house financing arrangement) to buy a $2,000 lounge suite on the basis of it being interest-free for 12 months. Let's also say that after 12 months you only manage to pay off $1,000. Under such an 'interest-free' arrangement you could then find that interest had actually been added to your bill – 12 months' interest in fact, starting at the date of purchase, and on the full $2,000, not on the $1,000 outstanding. To make matters worse, the interest rate would probably be very high – much higher than the average credit card or personal loan rate.

In this example, if the interest rate was 21% p.a. (and higher rates are possible) at the end of 12 months you would owe $1,420 (being the outstanding $1,000 plus 12 months' interest of $420 on the original purchase price of $2,000). And now you would have interest at 21% compounding on this new amount of $1,420 to contend with. Get the picture?!

I should make it clear though that with some stores offering interest-free periods, if, after the interest-free period has expired, there is still an amount owing, interest is only charged on that outstanding amount, not on the full purchase price. The salient point here, of course, is that you must make sure you know what the repayment conditions are and how interest is calculated before you enter into any of these purchase agreements. A bad one, ill-managed, could end up costing you dearly.

Tips on using credit cards

Look, I know that relatively easy access to personal loans and credit cards can be very helpful at times when money is (temporarily) tight or you find yourself in an emergency where you need funds on the spot. But you mustn't let the ease with which you can get access to debt undo you.

Credit cards are particularly hazardous for those who, by their own description, are 'born to shop'. 'Born to stay broke' is more like it. My recommendation to anyone who fits this description is to throw your credit cards away, *now*.

For those of you who do want the convenience of a card, here are some guidelines.

- Shop around for the best card – there *are* differences between them.
- Only keep a minimum number of cards – preferably one.
- Try not to carry any debt from one billing period to another.
- Carry a card that is readily acceptable overseas.
- Try not to use your card, that is, try to pay cash!

Lay-by

Lay-by is an old-fashioned but perfectly acceptable way of buying. It doesn't encourage wild and impulsive consumption – the sort that puts you in the poorhouse – and, if you stick to the rules, you'll pay no interest.

When you lay-by you pay a deposit and the store keeps the item while you pay off the rest of the money in instalments. There's a good incentive for you to pay off your debt because you don't get your purchase until it's paid for!

Terms and conditions vary from store to store, but generally you need a deposit of 10% to 25%. You're then given two to three months to pay the balance, although it can be longer on more expensive items. If you run into financial difficulties most stores will extend the lay-by period by another month or two, however it is advisable to check the store's policy if you can't or don't want to complete your payments. Some stores will keep up to 25% of the cost of the item.

Personal loans

Of the literally thousands of letters I receive, approximately one-third are from people suffering from problems with personal loans. Whenever you contemplate taking out a personal loan, think very carefully why you are doing it because most purchases financed through personal loans leave you with no real asset, only a debt. If, however, after coolly thinking it through, you decide you must have the item, then go ahead and take the loan, but make sure you shop around – interest rates and conditions on personal loans vary considerably.

Always try getting finance from a bank, building society or credit union first as their rates should be significantly lower than those of a finance company, sometimes dramatically so.

Also note if the interest rate quoted to you is a flat rate or a reducible rate. Most loans are reducible, but you can't assume this. A flat rate of 8% from a finance company may look better than a reducible rate of 11% from a credit union – until you realise that an 8% flat rate may be equivalent to a 15% reducible rate in terms of total interest paid over the life of the loan.

The rate of interest offered to you, no matter who the lender is, depends on the lender's perception of the risk of the loan application. The riskier it is perceived to be, the higher the interest rate offered – if, indeed, a loan is offered at all. The factors that go into the lender's estimation of the loan's risk include an appraisal of you the applicant, and of the item you wish to purchase. Loans for second-hand cars, for instance, often attract higher rates than loans for new cars.

The personal information the lender may want will include your employment record, your income, your age, whether you own a home or rent one, what assets you have and so on. The information required about the intended purchase can vary from being quite detailed to none at all.

Personal loans are normally repayable over three to seven years, though it can be longer or shorter. They can be variable or fixed rate and can be secured or unsecured.

Secured *vs* unsecured loans

A secured loan is one where the lender takes additional security over another of your assets – one worth more than the value of the loan. An unsecured loan is one where the lender takes no security other than the item you are buying. Because of the relatively high risk to the lender, unsecured loans are offered at higher interest rates.

In the event you default on a secured loan, the lender has the right to take possession of the secured asset and sell it to recoup the debt. If you default on an unsecured loan, the lender can take back the unsecured item (if it still exists) and sell it. However, if this doesn't cover the outstanding debt, you may be obliged to sell other assets to make good the debt. Of course, the unsecured lender can't take possession of your assets willy-nilly and sell them from under you. Well, not without bankrupting you first! (See Chapter Eighteen for more on bankruptcy.)

Borrowing on the house

There is another way of structuring a personal loan, and that is by having the amount you wish to borrow added to your mortgage, thereby taking advantage of mortgage interest rates which are traditionally the cheapest form of debt. So, if you wanted to borrow $10,000 for a holiday (which is not recommended!) you could 'put it on the house' by increasing your mortgage by $10,000. Hey presto! – here's your low-interest financing. The big problem with this, though, is that the $10,000 holiday could end up costing you a small fortune.

Let's say you had a $100,000, 25-year mortgage and you added $10,000 to it at the end of Year 1. Assuming an average 10% interest rate throughout the life of the loan and adjustments to the payments to repay the loan in the original term, it would add $16,421 in interest repayments to your mortgage over the remaining 24 years. It would certainly want to have been a damn good holiday at that price!

Look, if you have to borrow money it's obviously best to do it at the lowest interest rate possible. But don't fool yourself by borrowing money to buy things like a holiday (which is worth nothing the moment you get back), a stereo, clothes or furniture (which are practically worthless after three to five years). Unless you are very disciplined, using your home loan to buy consumer items is crazy – you may still be paying a fortune for the items 25 years later and long after they have turned to dust.

Cash is king

No matter what type of loan you use it's important to realise there's a big price penalty you pay for debt financing. A hi-fi system priced at $5,000 bought with a personal loan at a reducible interest rate of 15% p.a. over five years would cost you $7,137 ($2,137 in interest). With cash, on the other hand, it would cost $5,000 at most, probably even less with the discount cash can often attract.

When you take out a personal loan

Avoid taking out a personal loan to finance consumption if at all possible. But if you must, make sure you can comfortably answer the following questions before you sign up.

- What is the interest rate?
- How long will it take to pay the loan off?
- What will be the total cost of the loan?
- Can I afford the weekly repayments?
- If I get a wage rise can I pay the loan off faster?
- Are there any penalties if I fall behind with my repayments?
- Do I really need this item?

Seeking help

If you find yourself in trouble with personal debts, the following organisations are great places to start to seek help:

ACT – Care Financial Counselling Service (02) 6257 1788

NSW – Wesley Mission Financial Counselling, c/- Credit Line (02) 9951 5544, 1800 808 488

NT – Anglicare Northern Territory Financial Counselling Service (08) 8985 0000

QLD – Financial Counsellors Association of Queensland (07) 3257 1957

SA – Norwood Community Legal Service (08) 8362 1199

TAS – Anglicare Financial Counselling Service (03) 6223 4595

VIC – Financial and Consumer Rights Council (03) 9614 5433

WA – Consumer Credit Legal Service (08) 9481 7665 or Credit Care (08) 9212 1921.

KEY THOUGHT

If you want to buy something try to pay cash.

CHAPTER FIVE
The Job Market

I know that some readers of this book will have a secure job (whatever that means), some will be approaching retirement and others will be retired already. So you may be wondering why a chapter on the job market has relevance for you.

Well, from a purely vocational perspective it may not. However, from an investment point of view you could find it of value – by identifying the expanding and contracting areas of the economy.

For most of us, our ability to earn an income is easily our most valuable asset and its absence would make life look very different indeed. It is important to remember, though, that the job market of today won't be the job market of tomorrow.

Pretty obviously, our population is getting older. We are having fewer children (1.8 per Australian-born female on average), living longer (average life expectancy for women is 81.5 years and men is 75.9 years) and retiring earlier. (*Source*: ABS, 1998.) This, to me, is a fascinating indicator to where future employment will lie. Into the next century, the growth areas for employment and, therefore, the ones that I am focussing on as an investor, are based on what I believe our ageing population will need.

For starters, there will be heightened demand for carers for nursing homes and retirement villages. For those who decide to stay in their home for as long as they can, this will also provide a boon for the domestic-help industry. Likewise, you don't have to be Nostradamus to see that there will be an increase in the demand for medical nursing staff. It's also expected that the baby-boomer generation could boost the local tourism industry as they have time, and more importantly, the money to travel when they retire.

Information technology

It probably comes as little surprise that many pundits rank technology and communications as the number one growth area, with the service industries – particularly finance and banking – not far behind. Despite the so-called 'tech wreck' in early 2000, the larger technology companies such as Telstra and Optus have continued to grow, thus creating jobs. This trend is set to continue.

On the flip side, there is some uncertainty about the future profitability of some smaller technology companies. You need to keep in mind the relative 'newness' of many of the smaller players operating in this field. These companies, especially start-up dot com businesses have not returned the expected profits. Only time will tell how many will survive in the short term, let alone going on to become viable in the long term. However, the current assessment of the IT industry indicates rapid change, with ongoing new developments, leading to growing employment opportunities. Overall, the future for the technology sector looks good, although it might take some time before the industry settles down completely post the 'tech wreck'.

The services sector

The services sector is ranked just behind IT and telecommunications as a future growth industry. It covers a broad range of vocational areas such as community services; wholesale and retail trades; public administration and defence; finance, property and business services; and recreational services. In recent years careers in sales have been particularly popular, with industry forecasts suggesting that growth in this area will continue.

The good news for people looking to enter sales is that many workers can match their skills and experience to work in it. This area also experiences high employee turnover and, according to the Department of Employment, Workplace Relations and Small Business's *Job Futures Report*, projected jobs growth in sales exceeds the national average.

Over recent years, telemarketing and call centres have also experienced major growth and this trend is expected to continue as demand for these services grows. The upshot of this is that good sales people and telemarketers should have little problem finding work. Another good thing about sales is that the skills can be learnt and developed on the job and generally require little formal training.

The services sector is also playing a major role in changing the traditional way we work. Companies in this sector are now leaning towards more flexible staffing arrangements and working conditions including contracting, part-time work and casual employment, as well as outsourcing.

In the past, people grew their own vegetables and tended sheep to provide wool for clothes, now we simply throw our groceries into a supermarket trolley, or even order them online. The next step could see us outsourcing all of those mundane domestic tasks (like ironing, cooking and cleaning) that all too often otherwise don't get done!

Researching employment opportunities

Whether you're trying to change jobs or fast-track your career, I strongly urge you to take some time to research the job market to pinpoint the 'growth industries'. With the work landscape constantly changing, it's even more important that you get the right qualifications, skills and experience to make yourself more employable and take advantage of careers that offer solid opportunities in the future.

I know it might be stating the obvious, but it's really important that you plan your career carefully. It makes sense not only to find a job in an area where there is growth potential (such as IT or banking), but to also seek out a progressive company that has a commitment to training and career progression.

So where do you begin your research? A good starting point is the *Job Futures Report* that I've already mentioned. (You will find it at www.dewrsb.gov.au.) It predicts that the jobs with the best prospects will be the 'professional' occupations such as computing; business/information; sales/marketing and advertising; health; social welfare and accountancy/auditing. These generally require you to have a degree or higher qualification. Other jobs, such as carers/aides that don't call for the same level of training, also have strong growth prospects.

Job security follows job satisfaction

It is a generally accepted view that the services sector will continue to employ more people at the expense of other industry sectors. And it's not just the most likely scenario painted for Australia – developed, industrialised countries all over the world are moving towards being service-based economies.

So, from the point of view of job security, the service sector is where anyone planning their next career move really ought to look. However, there is more to career choice than job security.

Don't get me wrong – job security *is* important, but it shouldn't be your sole motivator. Finding a vocation you *like* should be top priority. After all, you spend half of your waking life at work so you may as well enjoy it!

And the clincher is that finding a job you like will actually produce its own job security. How? Well, if you genuinely enjoy your work you are more likely to excel at it than someone who doesn't – and that's the best job security you can have. I also believe that people who like their work have a much better than average chance of making good money from it – again, because people who like their work generally do a better job than those who don't.

Personal qualities in employment

Listed below are some fundamental personal qualities that all employers value and will be particularly important in the future employment scene. The more endowed you are with them, the greater your chances of success in whatever area of employment you choose.

- Creativity – the fountainhead of success and the one human characteristic that no amount of brilliant technology will ever be able to replace (at least I pray not!).
- Adaptability – a willingness and ability to learn new skills and to adapt old skills to new situations.
- The ability to communicate well, and to understand easily.
- Commitment and a willingness to work hard.

If you had to distil all this, I think it would ultimately come down to having the right attitude towards the job – one that's fundamentally and genuinely positive. Employers are more likely to be influenced and impressed by this than by any other attribute you might have.

Coping with rapid change

If you find changing jobs difficult, then do it slowly. It's important that you know your strengths and try and be flexible. Even if you have suffered a redundancy (one of the less desirable effects of constantly changing workplaces), there are steps you can take to safeguard your chances of remaining employable.

When it comes to employment diversity, it's definitely a case of 'times have changed'. Most employers now expect to see candidates who have moved between careers and industries. To some employers, a diverse employment background demonstrates flexibility and the capacity to adjust to a new role, company culture and different management practices. The days of 'jobs for life' are well and truly behind us and changing jobs is no longer seen as a way of committing employment harakiri. Taking the occasional risk and branching out into new areas can also add to your value as an employee. Likewise, working overseas or making lifestyle changes can reveal a candidate's enthusiasm for new challenges and the ability to take decisive action.

More and more people have taken the jump into freelancing, working from home or subcontracting as an alternative way of working. Some people refer to this as 'creating your own job', and in fact for many, particularly older workers, this might be their best option. A word of advice, though, think carefully before jumping head-first into the unknown, into a total career change – it can backfire.

At the same time, never take too lightly the value of experience. Experience is crucial in establishing and maintaining useful contacts and industry-specific knowledge. Job candidates that can move straight into a role because they already have the required skills and information are valuable. One way of making a career change is by moving into a job that shares some common ground with your existing occupation. This is a lower-risk option that allows you to explore new career options by combining your old skills with new skills. For example, a writer could move into publishing or a politician could move into used car sales.

Education – stick with it

The surest way of maximising your chances of being able to adapt in this changing world is by investing time and energy in your own education – and to continue this process throughout your life. What's more, it doesn't much matter if you forget some of what you've learnt or can't use it directly in your work. The beauty of ongoing education is it keeps your skills up to date, your mind alive and trains you to think, to question, and to find solutions to problems.

Also, by completing an educational course you achieve something tangible and have a document to prove it. Not only does this boost your self-esteem, confidence and skills levels, it demonstrates to an employer that you have the grit and ability to see something you've started through to a successful end, a quality all employers value and seek.

To improve your skills or find out about vocational training, a phone call to your local TAFE college (or the TAFE course info line: 13 16 01) will give you a good idea of the courses on offer and commencement dates.

Look up the *Yellow Pages* under 'Business Colleges' for courses in fields such as travel, technology, business studies, personnel consulting, hospitality, marketing, secretarial or public relations.

If you are interested in a university course, go to the Universities and Admissions Centre for NSW and ACT (UAC) web site at www.uac.edu.au and follow the links to the Tertiary Admission Centres for the other States, which in turn provide links to universities in your State or Territory.

Job searching

When hunting for a job, your first port of call will probably be the classifieds section of the major metropolitan newspapers such as the *Sydney Morning Herald*, the *Age* or *The Australian*. Local papers also carry job advertisements. If you are open to the possibility of relocating, you might like to consult regional classifieds or ads from interstate newspapers.

Another great way to look for jobs is via the Internet. Some handy web sites to search include:

- Australian Careers Directory: www.detya.gov.au
  This features a comprehensive list of links to other sites which you can use to search for jobs. There are also links to overseas job sites.
- Seek Communications: www.seek.com.au
  This site will email you jobs suited to your requirements. It can also help you to create a resumé online.
- The Monster Board: www.monster.com.au
  Abiding by the principle that practice makes perfect, this site features a virtual interview page asking some questions that are sure

to test the most experienced of interviewees. This site also lets you search for jobs overseas.

- Job Network: www.jobnetwork.gov.au
  This site matches employers with job candidates. If you don't have access to the Internet you can ring the Job Seekers' information line on 13 62 68 or the Employers' information line on 13 17 15.
- New Apprenticeships Centres: www.newapprenticeships.gov.au or phone them on 1800 639 629.

Steps to boost your employment prospects

- Present yourself professionally and be on time for your job interview. First impressions are critical.
- Forget ten-page resumés. Your resumé needs to be concise and easy to read, while providing a snapshot of your achievements, not merely a list of all your jobs. It's also crucial that you adapt your resumé to match individual job descriptions and keep it brief, ideally no more than three pages. Be sure to explicitly deal with *all* selection criteria covered in the advertisement.
- Do your research on the company and the people interviewing you.
- Show prospective employers that you can use technology and send online job applications when email addresses are provided.
- Prepare yourself for any psychological tests that you are required to do. You can research the standard tests on the Internet or at your local library.
- Be prepared to showcase your skills in the interview, to market yourself effectively without lapsing into cheesy self-promotion.
- Persistence brings rewards when job hunting. But remember, there is a fine line between persistence and annoyance, so tread carefully.
- Rehearse for interviews. (Not *The Sound of Music*!)
- Be proactive and ask questions about the job. This shows that you've done your homework and are truly interested in the position.
- Be confident and personable. Make eye contact with the interviewer, offer a firm handshake, smile and speak clearly. Consider using an icebreaker by commenting on something in the room at the start of an interview. Speak confidently and coherently, listen and resist the impulse to interject, and try to present a self-assured, relaxed image.

CHAPTER SIX

Owning a Home

During your lifetime you are presented with the opportunity to sink your money into an untold number and variety of investments. And, like most people, you are bound to ignore virtually all of them. This isn't because you necessarily think they aren't any good, but mostly because you have plenty of other things to do with your money – like paying the bills – and, if there's anything left over, taking a holiday or simply going out.

Another reason you probably ignore these investment offers is the uneasy feeling they give you – not so much due to their merits or lack thereof, but to an uncertainty on your part about their very nature. About how they actually work and, more to the point, about how they make your money grow. Would you want to invest, for instance, in shares, bonds, exotic horticultural crops, or feature films if you didn't really understand what makes them tick?

Generally, you pass up such investment opportunities (even if they're worthwhile) because they are just a bit too intangible. They're not as easy to understand as bricks and mortar. When you buy a home you can see it, smell it and feel it.

There are plenty of good reasons to own your own home, and not all of them are about money. Home ownership gives you a degree of psychological security – even when the mortgage is killing you! It makes you the king or queen of your own domain, and there's no landlord to tell you to get out. When you own your own home, you can create the environment you want – you can decorate it any way you like, you can rip out walls, put in a pool or dig up the garden.

Buying a home is definitely an investment that I recommend most Australians make. But this isn't to say that renting doesn't have its benefits – it does, so long as you don't rent forever!

Making Money

To rent or to buy?

With most of our cities sprawling, residential property close to the city centres is becoming increasingly expensive. Home affordability is spreading outwards and for those who work in the cities and don't want to commute long distances from an outlying suburb or satellite, or for those who simply like living near the 'action', long-term renting close to a city or town centre will become more common. Most renters, however, do aspire to own their own home one day, and with good cause.

Look at it this way. Every dollar you pay in rent goes into someone else's pocket. It temporarily buys you a place to live, but gives you little financial benefit in the long term. If you have to pay to have a roof over your head, you may as well pay the 'rent' to yourself – which is a less painful way of looking at your mortgage.

Now, not everyone agrees with me on this. Some financial commentators, such as economic forecaster Phil Ruthven of IBIS Business Information, reckon that renting makes more economic sense than buying. Indeed, Ruthven claimed on the 'Money' show that many Australians would be around $300,000 better off every 20 years by renting a home rather than owning one.

His and others' arguments are based on the fact that residential property generally appreciates relatively modestly over the long term. They point out that other assets such as shares and commercial property have historically performed better and are likely to continue to do so. They also note that the mortgage repayments on the home you are buying are likely to be significantly higher than the rent you could expect to be paying for it.

The proposition is you would be much better off in the long run if you paid a relatively modest rent rather than a relatively high mortgage, and then invested the difference between these two amounts in assets that appreciate better over the long term than residential property, such as shares.

This argument has merit, particularly when you look at comparative investment returns. Over the very long term, ipac securities' research indicates that residential property has generally appreciated from 1% to 3% per annum above inflation. It also indicates that commercial property over the very long term has averaged from 3% to 5% above inflation and shares have averaged 5% to 9% above inflation.

Now, while I think Ruthven and others are technically right, I have a fundamental problem with their point of view. While it may be that renters are more likely to have more disposable income than home buyers to invest in higher yielding assets like shares – at least in the early years – the question I have is: will the renters actually invest this extra money wisely, or blow it? Given our poor track record as savers I suspect, for many, the answer is the latter.

Under most mortgages, most of us keep up our regular repayments not because we're diligent, conscientious savers who like doing it, but because the lenders carry a big stick. If we don't pay our mortgage, they'll take the house back. This is about as strong an 'incentive' to save/invest as you're going to get.

But as a long-term tenant, after paying the rent, what's the likelihood of then religiously putting aside a fair bit more to invest each week, every week, for up to 25 years with nothing other than a good sense of economic responsibility to drive you? I reckon for most people it's next to nil.

My great fear is that if you do rent and you don't invest the difference between it and a (higher) mortgage, at retirement you will end up with no house and no money.

The other problem I have with the argument for long-term renting is that it hinges on the assumption that the average renter will always have more money than the home buyer in his or her pocket at the end of the week to invest. This certainly may be true for the earlier years, but not for the later ones. Rents rise with inflation, whereas inflation eats away the real cost of a mortgage. A fortnightly mortgage repayment of $600 might seem like a lot now, but it won't in 15 years, particularly compared with what rents are likely to be then.

Now, if you turn your properties over quite often, say every eight years or less, then long-term renting *is* likely to prove a better financial proposition than buying. Frequent buying and selling generates excessive transaction costs, including stamp duties, legal fees, agent's fees and removalist's costs, which, even under the best of circumstances, can effectively mean thousands of dollars down the drain.

Consider investment analyst John Ellison's economic analysis of renting versus buying that follows on page 51. This contrasts the relative financial position of someone buying a home to another person renting the *same* home. The point of the exercise is to find out who would be better off financially over time: the buyer or the renter.

The inputs used reflect typical and real market conditions in early 2001, and take a conservative medium- to long-term outlook.

Property value	$250,000
Deposit	$ 40,000*
Loan	$210,000
Average interest rate on loan (variable)	7%
Term of loan	25 years
Inflation	2%
Rental income	5% of property value
Annual property price growth	4.5% p.a.
Rent, Year 1	$12,500 p.a. (indexed)
Insurances, rates and maintenance and other outgoings Year 1	$3,750 (indexed)
Purchase costs	$12,500
Return on a fixed interest investment	6% p.a.*
Owner's marginal tax rate	31.5% (includes Medicare levy)

* The analysis includes an after-tax calculation of the interest income *foregone* by the buyer on the $40,000 deposit, assuming this money could have been earning 6% in a fixed-term investment over the years rather than being sunk into a home.

Using these figures, the bottom line is that on a year-by-year (non-cumulative) basis, the buyer would be worse off than the renter of the property for the first year only, getting ahead in the second year by $1,400.

More interesting and relevant however is the cumulative result, that is, the total, carried-forward value of the buyer's losses in relation to the renter's gains over the years. Cumulatively, the buyer would be worse off than the renter of the same property for five years, getting ahead in the sixth year by $6,300.

Here are the actual results from Years 1 to 25, with all figures being from the *buyer's* perspective and financial position in relation to the renter's.

Buyer's financial position vis-à-vis renter of the same property (to nearest $00)

Year	Annual gain+/loss−	Cumulative gain+/loss−
1	−$12,700*	−$ 12,700*
2	+$ 1,400	−$ 11,300
3	+$ 2,500	−$ 8,800
4	+$ 3,700	−$ 5,100
5	+$ 5,000	−$ 80
6	+$ 6,300	+$ 6,300
7	+$ 7,800	+$ 14,000
8	+$ 9,300	+$ 23,300
9	+$10,800	+$ 34,100
10	+$12,500	+$ 46,600
15	+$21,800	+$136,700
20	+$31,300	+$273,500
25	+$43,300	+$464,800

* The Year 1 amount is very high due to the one-off purchase costs of $12,500.

This analysis indicates two important points about the relative merits of buying and renting. Firstly, and quite convincingly, a buyer will be better off than a renter over time and, under this particular set of conditions, not too long a time. Secondly, once the buyer is in front of the renter the gap in their respective fortunes widens dramatically in the buyer's favour, as both the final annual and cumulative figures for Years 10 to 25 clearly show.

Now, while this model was designed to reflect reality as closely as possible at the time of writing, you need to be very aware that all analyses of this nature depend on their inputs. Change just one element and the whole picture changes. If, for instance, the loan was not as large as it is here, or the average interest rate was lower, the buyer's relative position would improve. If the property appreciated at a faster rate, the same thing would also happen. Conversely, if the rent was lower or the size of the home loan was greater, the renter's relative position would be improved.

As a matter of curiosity, this rent versus buy model was run under a number of different scenarios, to find which inputs affected the outcome most – and as anticipated, changes to the rate of capital growth had the greatest impact. In other words, if the property's annual price growth accelerated or slowed, it would improve or worsen the buyer's position relative to the renter's more dramatically than anything else.

Finally, note that this model does not take into account property selling costs. These can include large fees to agents of more than 2% of the sale price, as well as legal fees and possibly advertising charges, all of which favour a renter's relative financial position. That said, even with these real and quite substantial costs factored in, if you buy in a good location at a fair price for the long term, owning a home debt-free remains a very sensible goal.

⊶ KEY THOUGHTS

Plan to buy a property to live in because:
- Buying is economically more beneficial in the long term than renting.
- Paying off a home is a great way to force you to save. After all, if you don't pay the mortgage, the bank will sell the house!
- Yes, there is an argument for renting, but you'll need to be very disciplined about putting aside and investing the money you save in the early years.
- In the long run, well-selected property should continue to increase in value.

Buying the right property

The property you buy to live in should satisfy two criteria – it should suit your own needs and it should have certain physical characteristics which will appeal to future property buyers. I am assuming that at some time you will sell your house and move to another which most people do. Therefore, the house you buy should be like any other major asset you hold – it should be reasonably easy to sell.

For a start, buying a home, like selling one, doesn't happen overnight. In fact, it can take seemingly forever if you allow it to. But the way to reduce the time and the inevitable anxiety generated by the whole process is to do your homework well and to follow a few simple steps.

Look at what's sold

Before you get into a real-estate agent's car to go house hunting, get in your own car and drive around the area you are interested in. Look for properties with 'For Sale' signs out the front, with and without 'Sold' stickers on them. Note any properties that interest you and pay particular attention to those that have sold. This is because it's the selling price of properties, not the asking price, that sets the market. Then phone the estate agencies concerned and find out the asking prices of those for sale and, more importantly, the selling price of those that have recently sold.

You won't be able to inspect the sold properties, but looking at them from the outside, talking to the selling agent and to neighbouring residents about them will start to give you an idea about the real level of the local market. It will give you a more accurate picture than you'll get from the asking prices.

Check the selling prices

Next, contact the local council to see if it will allow you to inspect its register of property transfers. These list the addresses, prices and transaction dates of all sales in the local area. Note that some councils will give you free access to this information, some councils will charge you for it and others won't allow you to look at it at all.

If you can get access to local council property transfer records, look for the sales in your target price range and locality. Jot down the addresses and then go and look at these properties from the outside. Many of the properties you'll see this time will have had the signs taken down or may not have had a sign to start with.

You can also find out the most recent sale price of any property in your State's land title office. The fees for this service and the procedure vary from State to State, but, to give you an idea of costs, the South Australian Land Title Office will give you the last sale price of a property if you provide them with an address and $4.20. Getting the same information in Victoria will cost you $11.80, and in Queensland, $10.

In New South Wales, residents of Sydney, the Blue Mountains and the Central Coast can request a report of the past 12 months' residential property sales in their postcode area from Australian Property Monitors, by phoning 1800 817 616. In Victoria, the same applies for residents of the Melbourne metropolitan area. This report lists addresses, type of dwelling, number of bedrooms, some features, selling agent, date and method of sale, and selling price. At $43.95 the report's not cheap, but it could pay for itself many times over.

Inspecting properties

By now you should have finished your homework and should be ready to do some real inspecting. By this, I mean visiting properties during 'Open for Inspection' times and going over them with a fine-tooth comb, both internally and externally.

It also means going with a number of real-estate agents to be shown what's available. If your experience is anything like mine, you will be taken to more properties than you really want to see, including some that fall completely outside the guidelines you specified. Don't despair – many people fall in love with a house that's nothing like the one they had in mind. If this happens to you, pause for a moment and coolly establish that the home satisfies your practical needs, that it's sound and that you can afford it. Then think about it some more!

My advice is to look and look and look. Buying a home is as much an emotional decision as it is a rational one, and when the initial rush of blind infatuation with your new love cools you'll start noticing a few shortcomings, so I urge you to keep as level a head as possible. Make sure you take your time, inspect plenty of properties, get a good idea of what you really want and of local values before you commit yourself. You are, after all, about to make what is likely to be the biggest financial investment of your life – for a long time, one that will probably own you more than you own it!

The buying process

Let's say you've now found your dream home. Before you part with your money, you have to verify that the property is structurally sound and you have to look at the contract to make sure there are no peculiar conditions that apply to the sale.

Sometimes both written building and pest reports are attached to the contract which will save you this outlay. When they aren't and you are serious about the property, I strongly recommend you have them done even though it's at your own expense. These inspections could save you from making a very big and expensive mistake.

There are numerous small companies that do building inspections and pest reports. A written building report for an average home will cost around $250 and a pest report about $100 to $150. Look in the *Yellow Pages* under Building Consultants and phone around for quotes – prices do vary.

Negotiating a price

As a general negotiating stance, try to convey the impression that you aren't as keen on the property as you really are. If you are seen to be completely hooked, your protestations about the price being too high will fall on deaf ears.

Having an agent involved in the negotiations will probably work to your advantage. This may surprise you, because an agent is paid by the vendor and is legally and morally obliged to get as high a price as possible for them. While aware of their obligations, the stark reality is that if the real-estate agent doesn't sell, they don't eat. The agent's self-interest will mean, in many cases, that they will apply just as much if not more pressure on the vendor to drop the price – known in certain circles as 'crunching the vendor' – as they will apply on you to raise it.

So what sort of money do you offer? As a rough rule of thumb the asking price of a property will be 5% to 10% higher than the vendor is prepared to take. I stress, however, that this is not always the case. If you have done your homework you should know if the asking price is close to the mark or completely ludicrous – which is more likely to be the case where there is no agent involved.

If you think the asking price is fairly realistic, offer 15% less. On a house with an asking price of $200,000, for example, this would be an offer of $170,000. If you think the asking price is way over the top, offer 30% less or simply walk away. If you think it's under-priced, try to knock 5% off for luck, but, if the vendor won't listen, just go ahead and pay it.

Negotiations can go on for days, sometimes weeks, with offers and counter-offers flowing backwards and forwards. If you're dealing direct with the vendor, the sale may not be as protracted as through an agent, but the principles of negotiation are just the same. Just remember that the longer the process takes the greater the danger there is of someone else jumping in and snatching the property from under you.

○━ KEY THOUGHTS
- Work out what you need, want and can afford.
- Do your homework about the market.
- Look at as many properties as you can.
- Have the contract checked, and obtain building and pest reports.
- Closely inspect the property you like on different days and at different times of the day.
- Don't pay more than you can afford.

Maintaining your home

It should be pretty obvious that there isn't much point going out and buying a home if you aren't going to look after it properly. Your home is, after all, probably your major asset: you want to protect its value because when it comes time to sell you'll want to get the best possible price you can. You'll also feel a lot happier living in a home that's well-maintained and where everything works than living in one that's falling down around your ears.

The key thing about maintenance is that you have to carry it out on a regular and disciplined basis. This enables you to catch most small and relatively inexpensive problems before they turn into large and expensive ones. It's the same logic as having your car serviced regularly.

Naturally, the age of your home and its building materials will largely determine how often you should give your home an overhaul. Old timber houses require much more maintenance than new brick houses, for instance, but as a general guide, give your home a good inspection once a year to make sure everything is in good order.

Be particularly on guard for pests, remembering that pest inspection is usually a job for the professionals – they're the ones with the experience and the licence to use the chemicals necessary to rid the house of its timber-eating tenants. A pest inspection should be done about once every two years depending on the timber content of your home and the amount of timber, both green and dry, in your locality.

Since maintenance is one of those things you shouldn't cut

corners on – because it will cost you dearly in the long run – I recommend you regularly put some money aside into a separate maintenance account to meet those inevitable bills. This is particularly important if you live in an old house and even more so if you live in a timber one which, if nothing else, will need painting on a regular basis.

Maintenance checklist

These are some of the things to look out for – some will entail getting into the roof and under the floor:
- blocked gutters and downpipes
- cracks in the roofing, ceiling, flooring, walls, tiling and paths
- crumbling putty around windows
- damp in ceilings, walls or flooring
- deterioration of wiring
- evidence of animal activity under the house, in the roof or in the walls
- cavities (where possums or rats could get in)
- jammed windows and doors
- leaking taps, pipes and toilet cisterns
- loose tiles and grouting
- mould
- peeling paint
- peeling wallpaper
- rust
- water damage in cupboards around kitchen sink and vanity basin
- water lying in gutters
- watermarks on ceilings or walls
- wood rot.

Moving, renovating and overcapitalising

Let's say you've been living in your home now for five or six years and, while it has been doing the job well enough, the kids have reached an age where it would be better if they had their own bedrooms. Perhaps you wouldn't mind a room to retreat into yourself. Maybe the house needs major repairs or perhaps you simply don't like its look any more. So, what do you do, move or renovate?

Making Money

Well, you have to consider this with both your head and heart. If you're thoroughly tired of the place you're in and feel like something different, I recommend you listen to your heart and move – even though moving is an exasperating and quite an expensive process. A change of scenery can be revitalising. But if your heart is not really pushing you to move, your head will be saying 'Moving's a nightmare! – Stay, and fix the place up'.

Moving

By choosing not to move you will be spared some major (and unavoidable) expenses including:
- estate agent selling fees
- stamp duty
- solicitor's fees
- removalist's charges
- building and pest inspections
- searches, surveys
- electricity and phone connections.

The costs of moving

Consider the costs of moving from say, a two-bedroom $150,000 house to a three-bedroom $250,000 house:

Estate agent fees (2.5%, negotiable)	$ 3,750
Stamp duty	$ 8,175*
Solicitor's fees	$ 2,300
Removalist's charges	$ 2,000
Building and pest inspections	$ 350
Searches, surveys	$ 330
Electricity and phone connections	$ 300
Total	**$17,225**

* An average figure derived from varying stamp duty rates across Australia

Renovating

If you renovate, you will be up for some fixed costs as well as any number of variable costs depending on how elaborate the renovations are. The unavoidable fixed costs you'll face are: council fees and the preparation of preliminary plans – and you will need to allow at least $2,000 for these.

Variable costs can include builder's fees and materials, architect's fees, storage fees and bank fees for extending your mortgage. Of course, building costs vary significantly depending on the design of your home, your choice of materials, site accessibility, method of construction and your own level of involvement – which you should try to maximise. Doing as much work as possible yourself will save a lot of money because paid labour is generally as great a building cost as materials. (I have to admit I'm not really much of a home handyman so I know this advice is easier to give than take!)

Take note that if you intend to do many or all of the renovations yourself that some States and councils require you to get an owner-builder's licence. This is designed to protect future buyers of your home against unsatisfactory work – and as an owner-builder you are required to take out insurance with your State's statutory building authority to cover faulty workmanship. (See page 62 for contacts.)

On average, current residential (non-project) building costs are around $8,500 per square (approximately 9.3 square metres, exactly 100 square feet), with kitchens and bathrooms being much higher. This figure assumes you do no work yourself and I expect it to be a fair guide for some time.

Average building costs (March 2001):

- It normally costs between $700 and $1,100 per square metre to build a non-project home (approximately $6,500 to $10,200 per square).
- To build a project home normally costs from $530 to $770 per square metre (approximately $4,900 to $7,200 per square).
- Renovations are generally more expensive than building from scratch because of the additional time and costs involved in demolition and reconstruction. Renovations normally range from $700

to $1,400 per square metre or from $6,500 to $13,000 per square.

■ Renovating a kitchen normally costs between $12,000 and $19,600, a standard bathroom renovation normally costs between $8,800 and $15,500, and a laundry upgrade generally costs between $4,600 and $5,800.

(*Source*: Cordell Building Information Services.)

Make sure that before you start you get quotes from a number of builders and play them off against each other. Don't be afraid to say to a builder that his quote sounds a bit high and ask him if he could do better. Many builders are prepared to negotiate on price, especially during slow times.

In our example on page 58, moving from a two-bedroom house to a three-bedroom house cost around $17,000. Ignoring the other qualities of the new house this effectively meant that acquiring an extra bedroom cost about $17,000.

With the basic fixed costs of renovating being at least $2,000 and the costs of moving being around $17,000, the home-owner could have spent around $15,000 on actual renovation works to end up with the same level of expenditure ($15,000 + $2,000 = $17,000). At an average renovation cost of around $10,000 per square, the $17,000 spent on moving could have funded around one and a half extra squares being added to the original house.

To put this into perspective, the size of a bedroom in most new houses is around one square. Therefore, the original two-bedroom house could have been converted into a three-bedroom house for a lesser cost than moving to the other three-bedroom house, assuming the added bedroom was around one square, costing about $12,000 all up. In this example, renovating would have provided better value than moving – which is often the case.

When trying to choose between the two options bear in mind that moving costs involve sliding-scale fees dependent on the value of the properties you are buying and selling. Also, and most importantly, be aware that the average building cost of around $5,700 to $8,700 per square and the average renovation cost of around $10,000 per square are both *very rubbery* figures. The cost of building can range from a rock-bottom minimum of around $4,900 per square to, well, the sky's the limit, particularly if you want wall-to-wall Italian marble and gold-plated taps.

Another thing to bear in mind about renovation is that a lot of people renovate their properties just before putting them on the market in the hope it will lead to a much better price and a faster sale. This may not happen. Firstly, unless you renovate sensibly you may not get your costs back and, secondly, there are a significant number of buyers who are actually looking for unrenovated homes. They want a place they can do up themselves and put their own mark on and, hopefully, add value to.

Overcapitalising

The big danger with renovating (apart from getting entangled with a dodgy builder – do choose carefully!) is overcapitalising. This occurs when the cost of renovating exceeds the market value it adds to a property. When a modest home is renovated to the point where it becomes the best in the street, odds are it's been overcapitalised and the value of the house may only rise by about half the cost of the renovations.

If you find you have overcapitalised, your options are limited and not very appealing. You can sell and recoup only a part of the cost of the renovations – in other words, take a loss. Or you can hang on to your home and wait for inflation to raise overall market values to a point where they finally catch up with your outlay. This could take a long time in the low-inflationary times we're living in. Whichever way, overcapitalisation will prove costly.

Also, be aware that the value you add to your home by renovation depends on more than just the cost of the renovations. It depends on how well they are done and how much is done. It also depends on the age and style of the original home, its locality and, most importantly, its position.

Generally, home improvements that are more likely to add *more* value to your home than they cost include new kitchens and bathrooms/ensuites, extra bedrooms and/or a study, better garaging, enhanced indoor or outdoor entertainment areas, fresh painting, new floor treatment (carpeting, tiling or varnishing), and improved landscaping and gardens.

Home improvements that are more likely to add *less* value than they cost include saunas, spas, and a second storey, with swimming pools often being the least value-adding of all. You may also find it difficult recouping the cost of new plumbing, rewiring, new roofing or expensive fittings.

Making Money

If you're not sure how much value renovations will add to your home and you're worried about overcapitalising, get advice from some real-estate agents or from a qualified valuer – and do it before you spend too much money. Certainly do it once preliminary plans have been drawn up and costs estimated and well before you start knocking out walls! Also, remember those home-buyers out there looking for a home to renovate. If you want to sell your home and it needs upgrading, offering it *as is* could save you a lot of time, effort, worry and expense, as well as completely eliminating any risk of overcapitalising.

Seeking help

If you are planning to build your own home or are wanting to engage a builder, your State or Territory's builders' licensing authority can provide information on whether the builder is licensed, when they were first registered and whether they are still registered.

ACT	ACT Building Control Office (02) 6207 6262
NSW	Building Services Corporation (Department of Fair Trading) (02) 9895 0111
QLD	Queensland Building Services Authority (07) 3225 2800
SA	Office of Consumer and Business Affairs (08) 8204 9644
TAS	There is no licensing board as builders don't need to be licensed to operate in Tasmania.
VIC	Building Practitioners Board (03) 9285 6400
WA	Builders Registration Board of Western Australia (08) 9321 6891.

For more information and for referrals for builders in your State or Territory, contact the Master Builders Association:

ACT	(02) 6247 2099
NSW	(02) 8586 3555
QLD	(07) 3404 6444
SA	(08) 8211 7466
TAS	(03) 6223 2377
VIC	(03) 9411 4555
WA	(08) 9322 5133.

Selling

Selling, like buying a house, takes some time and effort and can be a similarly testing experience. At times you'll probably wonder whether the house is priced realistically, the right method of selling is being used, the agent is on the ball, the market has gone into a freak slump, or if a buyer will be found before your hair falls out. There are ways of making the process easier.

Pricing

There's an old real-estate saying – 'every property is saleable at a price'. So, even if the house 'would suit a handyman', the property is still saleable as long as it's priced appropriately.

Most sellers think their home is worth more than anyone else does. This is because it's special to them – often their blood, sweat and tears have gone into it. Try not to fall into the trap of allowing your sentiments to inflate your property's price. Most buyers will value a property on their perception of its intrinsic merits and shortcomings and not on the fact that you have spent weekends sanding back and varnishing the beautiful bathroom door. They probably won't even notice it!

What they will notice is the price, and arriving at a realistic one that reflects current market values takes some time and effort on your part.

- Start by obtaining a number of market appraisals from local real-estate agents who are actually making sales. 'Sold' signs will indicate their strike rate. Appraisals are free and take around half an hour, and agents are more than willing to provide them.
- Average out the suggested values to give yourself a guide. Don't automatically accept the highest appraisal. Some agents provide deliberately inflated appraisals to win listings – it's a fairly common and particularly irritating practice that invariably leads to vendor disappointment.
- Go and look at comparable local houses or units being offered for sale and, most importantly, those that have recently sold.

Making Money

Should you use an agent?

The next thing to do is decide whether you put the property in the hands of an agent (normally one of those who has already appraised it) or whether you sell it yourself. If you have priced your property realistically, and you have time during the week to show prospective buyers through it, and you are prepared to advertise it adequately, there's no reason why you shouldn't try to sell it yourself and save what can be a significant agent's fee. (These vary from State to State and are increasingly open to negotiation – but work on an approximate range of 1% to 3% of the property's value.)

The reality is most vendors don't price their properties realistically – they are usually too expensive – and they don't have the time to show prospective buyers through because many of the genuine buyers are not weekend window shoppers. Also they're often reluctant to spend much on advertising. The result is a slow sale or no sale. An even more distressing scenario for a private seller is discovering too late that the house was underpriced. Employing the services of a real-estate professional is therefore the right move in most cases, making sure, of course, that you negotiate a fair selling fee first.

Choosing an agent

Choosing the right real-estate agent is like choosing any professional in whose hands you rest your fate. The key things you are looking for are integrity and ability. Unfortunately, real estate is one of those industries with more than its fair share of dubious practices and the last thing you need as you go through the rigours of selling is to be in the clutches of a dud.

So how do you find a good agent? The best way is the same way you find most good professionals – through personal recommendation. It simply involves you asking around. If this method fails, have three or four local agents appraise your property. Choose one who has been making sales, who has drive, who seems genuine and who you think you can get on with.

Generally, don't bother with agents outside your area. Local ones have the best idea of local values and are the best placed physically to show potential buyers through the property. This might seem like stating the obvious, but it's remarkable how many people engage agents outside the area simply because they have a high profile or are 'fashionable'. You don't need this. What you do need is someone who is close at hand and on the ball to efficiently service the job.

Selling by auction

After you've chosen an agent, the next question is: should you sell your property by auction or by private treaty? Most agents associated with the large, franchise real-estate groups push auction pretty vigorously – generally more so than independent agents. This is partly explained by the franchise networks having well-established auction procedures and regular auction dates in place, and a culture which they describe as 'auction oriented'.

The advantages of selling by auction

- If there is more than one buyer at the auction, competitive bidding can lead to a higher price being paid than under the lower pressure of the private treaty method.
- Sale by auction generally requires a 10% non-refundable deposit being submitted by the buyer on the day, meaning that there is less likelihood of the buyer dropping out of the sale than under private treaty where there may be a cooling-off period.
- Auction is the best way of establishing the market value of, and hopefully selling, genuinely unique or special properties where, under conditions of competitive bidding, the property's 'difference' can achieve a premium price.

The disadvantages of selling at auction

- Under longstanding tradition, where properties are being sold by private treaty (simply being offered 'for sale'), real-estate agencies normally foot the bill for their advertising. Consequently, the ads are likely to be relatively modest, though definitely not necessarily ineffective. However, by some strange convention – for which there is no convincing explanation – under *auction* it's the *vendor* who normally pays for a property's advertising campaign.

  These auction-advertising campaigns can run into thousands of dollars depending on the property, the locality and the persuasiveness of the agent. Auction advertising campaigns in excess of $5,000, some times well in excess, are now commonplace. In suburban newspapers particularly, real-estate advertising in recent years has become increasingly grandiose, if not completely over the top, with (often completely unjustified) half- and full-page colour ads now quite commonplace. And 'Why not?' ask the agents. After all, they're not footing the bill. Not only that, and most importantly, these mega-ads have the agents' names and logos emblazoned all over the place, which effectively promote the estate agencies themselves, not just the properties – all at vendor expense. Is it any wonder, therefore, so many agents push auctions *as a matter of course*, even where there is no compelling advantage to the vendor in doing so?

- The intensive advertising/marketing period under auction is relatively short – an average of three to four weeks of inspections prior to the auction day. This may be too short a time to find that special buyer who will really fall for your home and pay top dollar for it.

- Under normal market conditions, average auction clearance rates – those properties that actually sell on or before the day of the auction – only hover around 50% or less. During recessionary times, average clearance rates are lower. If you fail to sell at auction on the day it can have a very demoralising effect on you which may be capitalised upon by the agent where he heavily pressures you to drop the price. A consequence of this is that you could end up accepting less for the property than is really justified.

- Some agencies levy non-refundable auction-marketing charges of up to around $1,000 – and sometimes more – whether or not the sale is successful on the day of the auction or afterwards. This money goes towards costs like auction room rental, the auctioneer's fees, signboard and pamphlets.

I need to point out here that selling 'by auction' involves more than just trying to sell a property under the hammer. It can be sold beforehand, during and after the actual auction, but trying to sell the property on the day is still very much the focus of the whole marketing exercise. This is because it's believed that the auction is where the highest price is likely to be obtained.

Private treaty

Selling by private treaty – where a property is simply offered 'for sale' – can take longer than auction as it's not such a hot-house, time-specific approach. This often slower method can provide more time to find that 'top paying' buyer who has really fallen for the place. Private treaty also tends to be less traumatic than auction, and, as noted on page 65, is often cheaper as there are usually minimal or no advertising charges levied on the vendor.

Private treaty penalises the buyer far less than under auction if they want to back out of the sale, which vendors and agents rightly see as a major comparative weakness. Under auction the buyer generally loses 10% of the value of the property if they do not proceed with the sale after successfully bidding, whereas they can walk away from a private-treaty sale after placing a deposit and lose as little as 0.25% of the agreed purchase price. Clearly, the number of buyers who renege on a sale under private treaty is much higher than under auction.

Under private treaty, whatever you do, don't give your house to a number of agents to sell. An 'open listing' – where more than one agency exists – almost guarantees the property won't be properly advertised. The reason is that agent A who advertises the property is loath to see agent B (who hasn't advertised it but with whom the property is also listed) selling it to B's buyers excited by A's ad. The upshot is that no one advertises it properly for fear of giving the opposition a free kick, which doesn't do the vendor any good at all.

An 'exclusive listing' – where there's only one agent authorised to sell the property, normally for a specified period of, say, a month or two – gives the agent real incentive and a fair go at selling the property. And if it isn't marketed well, the agent loses the listing at the end of the exclusive period.

If you do choose private treaty, I recommend an exclusive listing. But beware – once you sign an exclusive listing, only the agent you have given it to is entitled to sell the property. This not only excludes all other agents – it also excludes *you*. So if you find a buyer, you must still pay the full commission to the agent whether they have anything to do with the sale or not.

Overall, unless you have a genuinely unique property with a value that's hard to gauge, private treaty is probably the way to go. It's

Making Money

less expensive, less traumatic and works just as well as auction –
which, I sometimes suspect, is pushed hard by real-estate agents too
often for their own interests rather than for those of their clients.

For further information

If you need information or help on any real-estate matter, a call to
the Real Estate Institute is a good starting point:

ACT	(02) 6282 4544	NSW	(02) 9264 2343
NT	(08) 8981 8905	QLD	(07) 3891 5711
SA	(08) 8366 4300	TAS	(03) 6223 4769
VIC	(03) 9205 6666	WA	(08) 9380 8222.

CHAPTER SEVEN

Mortgages

There is little doubt that taking on a mortgage or, more to the point, paying one off, shapes our adult lives enormously. While it's the ticket that enables us to enjoy all the benefits of home ownership, it can also be the millstone that binds us to a dreary job and an irritating boss that we otherwise wouldn't put up with. Like a marriage, a mortgage is a major commitment, and possibly an even more scary one. If you don't play your cards right, it can last for all of 25 awful years.

Actually, mortgages need not be too painful. What you have to do is make sure you find the right one to start with, and then pay it off as quickly as possible. This will save you many thousands of dollars and much heartache in the process.

Getting the best mortgage deal

One of the biggest changes in managing our money has been in how we deal with our banks.

Younger readers may find it hard to believe, but most Australians today aged over 30 will at some stage or another have had the humiliating experience of begging the bank manager to lend them money. Until the mid-1980s the bank manager held all the aces. Competition between lenders was low as deregulation (which took place in 1983) had yet to create effective new entrants to the home loan industry. So, to get a loan we would meet with our manager to plead our case.

I suspect it's had a lasting effect on me, because I'll certainly never forget my first home loan application. It was 1983 and I was just married. Vicki and I had found a small but comfortable semi on the lower North Shore of Sydney for what seemed to be the reasonable price of $90,000. We had saved a deposit of over 10% and I had been banking with a major Australian bank since I was a youngster. We were both in stable employment, so it was with a sense of confidence we met with our bank – only to be knocked back!

Making Money

The reason? Well, our savings history was not long enough. By spending one salary and saving the other we had built up our deposit in under a year which apparently was not good enough. Luckily though, by then building societies were growing in strength and we had a far more productive meeting with a manager of what was then the St George Building Society (now a bank). He explained with some delight that they picked up lots of good new business because of the attitude of the banks.

This was my first experience in shopping around for a home loan – simply because I was forced to do so.

When we changed home in 1987 I shopped around very aggressively, no longer looking for someone who would lend us the money we needed, but asking for their best deal. To my surprise, things I thought were not negotiable, such as fees and interest rates, were in fact quite flexible – if you asked.

And that really is the most important advice I can give you when it comes to getting the best deal. You must shop around and you must play one lender off against another, just as if you were buying a car.

You don't need these people as much as they need you. Their business is selling you money. It's up to you to buy at the best price and, in the case of money, the best price means the lowest fees and the lowest long-term interest rate.

For Australians used to begging to the banks, this is all a bit different. But the key to getting the best mortgage is doing some upfront research, followed by some good old-fashioned haggling.

Now don't feel too guilty about beating your bank manager around the head to get the best deal. As you can see in our daily papers, the banks are still making profits measured in the billions – just make sure you make the smallest possible contribution to their profit!

⊶ KEY THOUGHT

To get the best home loan deal you must do your research, shop around and play one lender off against another. Remember, they are fighting for market share and they need your business.

What's on offer

Despite the large number of home loan providers and variability in home loan rates, mortgages are quite basic products with a fairly limited number of variations. These are the options from which you can choose:
- interest-only loans
- principal and interest loans
- variable rate loans
- fixed rate loans
- mortgage offset accounts
- combination of fixed and variable rate loans, known as split loans (including capped rate loans)
- equity credit loans (including redraw loans and revolving lines of credit).

All of these loans can range in duration from 10 to 30 years, with 25 years being the standard term.

Interest-only *vs* principal and interest

With an interest-only loan, your regular repayments are comprised of nothing other than interest charges. You do not repay any of the principal (or 'capital') at all. I can't recommend interest-only loans to the average home-buyer because at the end of the loan period, you still have all of the principal to repay!

Interest-only loans – which have smaller repayments than principal and interest loans – are really designed for investment purposes. They enable you to hang on to a property which, during the term of the loan, hopefully generates some rental income and undergoes capital gain.

Interest-only loans often involve selling the property to repay the principal – which is not what the average home-owner has in mind.

If you are buying a property with the intention of turning it into your home and living in it for some years, you should take out a principal and interest mortgage. This way you are repaying the debt and, at the same time, increasing your equity in the property. At the end of the loan period you will own the property outright.

Making Money

Variable rate *vs* fixed rate

A variable rate loan is one where the rate of interest you pay on your mortgage can be raised or lowered by the lender at its discretion. The changes to the interest rate you are being charged, in turn reflect changes to the official level of interest rates set by the Reserve Bank of Australia.

When the official interest rate changes it does so in response to pressures applied by a wide range of local and international economic and political factors – which could range from a boom in Australia to a crash on Wall Street, to a war in the Middle East. Clearly, many of these influences are beyond the Government's control and cannot be predicted. This means no one, not even the experts, can be sure how interest rates will move in the coming years.

Do you remember, for instance, how high home loan interest rates climbed during the late 1980s? In June 1989 the major banks were charging 17% on home loans. On a $100,000 mortgage over 25 years this meant a minimum monthly repayment of $1,438. Compare this with a minimum monthly repayment of $740 on the same loan with interest rates at only 7.5%. If you have a variable rate loan you must be prepared for the possibility (inevitability?) that interest rates could rise during the long course of your mortgage.

The alternative is a fixed rate mortgage which you enter for a specific period, commonly one to five years. This means that whether market rates go up or down, your rate remains the same and you know exactly what your regular repayments will be.

You can agonise forever about which is the best option and you'll find that interest rate predictions are notoriously inaccurate. Even the best-informed people get it wrong. A friend of mine, a financial director in a major Australian company, took out a fixed rate mortgage in 1990, locked in at 15% for three years. He then sat by, scratching his head, while standard variable (bank) home loan rates dropped 15 consecutive times to a low of 8.75% in September 1993. His decision to take a fixed rate loan could not have been more ill-timed – and he is a financial professional!

I do realise this isn't very comforting for the average home-buyer. What should you do? Well, pretty obviously if you think interest rates will fall you'd go for variable; if they are likely to rise you'd fix your loan. The trouble is you can easily make the wrong call, so my advice is that if you can afford the mortgage repayments at the current rate, but would be in great difficulty if rates increased by more than say 2%, I advise you take a fixed loan for three or four years. At least this way you know you will be able to afford your mortgage for that time.

On the other hand, if your finances aren't so tight, I'd still be going for a variable rate loan as I write this in early 2001. Having said that, and given that interest rates have a disconcerting habit of frequently moving in the opposite direction to the experts' predictions, it is a fact that present interest rates are at historically very low levels, with arguably little room for further downward movement but lots of room for upward movement. As things, including interest rates, don't go down and stay down forever, I'd suggest you keep your eyes on the economy and watch for rising inflation, as that is the best signal for rising interest rates.

Another thing you will want to consider with variable and fixed rate loans is the facility to make extra repayments. With variable rate loans you are entitled to make additional payments in order to pay your mortgage off faster. This isn't generally the case with standard fixed rate loans, where payments over and above the regular minimum repayment are not normally accepted. You need to think carefully about this before you sign anything, as the ability to make extra repayments is very beneficial as we'll see later.

Split and capped

For those of you who want to take an each-way bet on interest rates you have the option of a 'split loan'. These are loans that are part fixed and part variable, in almost any ratio you wish. With split loans it doesn't matter so much which way the rates go – you'll win a bit, lose a bit either way. The real benefit of this unusual structure is that you can make extra repayments towards your loan, as part of it is variable (remembering that fixed rate loans normally don't allow extra repayments).

Then, there are capped rate loans. These usually feature a very low introductory rate lasting for the first 6 to 12 months, then reverting to the standard variable rate. With these loans the interest rate you are charged during the introductory period cannot exceed, but can be less than, the capped rate (though it rarely is).

Making Money

Capped rate loans might appear attractive at first glance but really they are little more than marketing gimmicks. Generally, the capped rate period is too short to be of any value. Sure, the honeymoon period is better than nothing, but it should not be the sole determinant for giving your mortgage business to the lender offering it.

You may be borrowing money for 25 years, so look at the cost over the full 25 years, not just the six months or one year 'special offer'.

Longer *vs* shorter term loans

Whether you choose a 15- or 25-year loan depends simply on what you can afford. The longer the term, the less your monthly or fortnightly repayments will be, however, the longer the term the more you end up paying and the longer you will have the weight of a mortgage around your neck.

If you take out a $100,000 mortgage at 7.5% over 15 years, your monthly repayments are $930, and during the full term of the loan you will pay back a total of around $167,000. However, if you take this mortgage out over 25 years, your monthly repayments drop to $740, but the total amount you will end up paying over the full term rises to almost $222,000 – around $55,000 more than for the 15-year loan.

Clearly, the less time you take to pay your mortgage off the better, so my advice is to take out as short a term loan as you can realistically afford.

Home equity financing

Not so long ago, home equity financing was the new kid on the block in the area of mortgage-based financing. Basically, it's a flexible form of borrowing secured by the equity you have in your home, and its popularity continues to grow. Effectively, it allows you to treat your home as a 'bank', or rather as a store of wealth that you can deposit money into or draw money against via your mortgage.

The most common and straightforward version of this principle is the *redraw loan*. This was an enormous novelty, but a redraw facility is now a feature of many standard variable loans. Generally, it allows you to take back any money you have put into your mortgage over and above the minimum level of repayment due at any point in the loan's life. An example is the Westpac Options mortgage, the first redraw loan offered in Australia. With this you are required to make a regular repayment that will see the loan paid out in a specified time, say 25 years. However, any extra you have put into your mortgage over and above your minimum repayment schedule you can take back, or 'redraw'.

The structure of this and similar loans is clever in that it forces you to pay off your mortgage whilst enabling you to make extra repayments, effectively earning the current mortgage rate on the extra deposits, risk-free and tax-free. The key benefit is, of course, access to the excess money you've paid at no cost (apart from a possible withdrawal fee). If you need money, this facility makes getting your hands on your money cheap and easy. It can also save you having to formally borrow money via a personal loan.

The problem with redraw loans is that by allowing you to draw money back out of your mortgage, it will take you longer to pay it off. Therefore, you will end up paying more total interest over the life of the loan than you would if you just left that money alone. Clearly then, redraw loans require a certain discipline on your part, an ability to resist the temptation to dip into the honey pot. In addition, loans with redraw facilities often have a higher interest rate than the 'no frills' loans without it. These objections aside, however, a redraw facility can be very useful when you do need money for a worthwhile purpose, and redraw mortgages provide an excellent no-risk, no-tax place to park your savings.

The other main type of home equity financing is where you're effectively granted a *line of credit* against the equity you have in your home (which is the difference between how much the property is worth and how much you still owe on it). These types of mortgages are also sometimes called 'equity overdraft loans', because you are effectively being granted an overdraft secured by your home, at lower than standard overdraft rates. Many home lenders offer such loans at an interest rate that is increasingly the same as, or a few ticks higher than, the standard variable rate.

An example is the NRMA Building Society's 'Equity Credit' mortgage which, whilst designed to enable you to buy a home, gives you the power to indefinitely draw money against it. It allows you to keep dipping into the equity you have in your home up to a predetermined limit, theoretically forever. With this and similar loans there is no principal repayment schedule. However, you do have to make at least interest payments, which reduces the possibility of your debt level getting out of hand – a danger with such mortgages.

The money you draw against your home equity can be used for whatever purpose you like, be it business or pleasure. You certainly don't have to justify the withdrawal to the mortgagee, only to yourself. It's a very accessible form of finance – too accessible, some might say. If you are not disciplined enough, there is a real danger of dipping heavily into your home equity and still having a substantial debt outstanding against it, say, 25 years on. At least with a 'standard' redraw loan, after 25 years or less, your mortgage is fully paid out.

Now, there is a recent variation on this theme where all your income goes straight into your line of credit mortgage, where you pay all your bills out of the mortgage via your credit card and, in the process, knock years off your loan. It sounds puzzling, I know, but it actually can work so long as you're a disciplined budgeter and saver.

Modern mortgages

What normally happens is that when you get paid – weekly, fortnightly or monthly – you then pay your mortgage and spend much of the balance of your pay. Frankly, this is pretty inefficient if you have a mortgage. By now you know that if you put extra into your mortgage you can save thousands of dollars over the term of the loan.

And that's the marketing opportunity many lenders have spotted in their never-ending quest for greater market share. They will argue that you should change your mortgage into a *line of credit* – this is a bit like an overdraft – and that your pay should go straight into your line of credit and then you only draw out the amounts you need to spend. An advanced version of this strategy is to use a credit card with 55 days interest-free to pay for all your spending and bills and then to draw down on your line of credit to pay it off in full before the due date.

So what on earth is this all about? I think the best way to explain this one is with an example. Firstly, we'll need some assumptions, let's say:

- you have a mortgage of $100,000
- you earn $2,500 a month after tax

- your mortgage repayments are $700 a month
- your budget shows you need $800 a month for regular expenses and $600 a month for bills
- you save the remaining $400 a month.

With a line of credit, on pay day your entire $2,500 goes into your loan, immediately reducing it to $97,500. It's a bit of a long shot, but if you can use a 55-day interest-free credit card to pay for all of your personal spending and bills, your loan will remain at $97,500 for up to 55 days.

More importantly, even after you've spent your $800 on regular expenses and $600 on regular bills and paid this into your credit card, your $400 of savings is already in your mortgage. This means you have a better chance of not spending it! Well, that's the idea, at least, and frankly, the principle is very sound. You can save thousands of dollars with this type of loan as it does oblige you to budget and save.

I think that most mortgages will work like this in years to come as the concept it's based on makes so much sense. However, if you are thinking of switching – and probably incurring refinancing costs in the process – please be careful, because while the idea of putting your pay straight into your mortgage and using the 55-day interest-free credit card all sounds pretty smart, this is not the bit that produces the biggest savings; it's the fact that you are being *obliged to save*. Every dollar you earn is going straight into your mortgage and every dollar you spend is coming straight out of it. If this doesn't make you stop and think twice about how much you're spending and encourage you to save more, I don't know what will – and *big savings* are exactly what make this type of mortgage work.

Now, if you are already a good and disciplined saver, the costs of switching into such a mortgage may not be worthwhile. By being a good saver you'll knock your conventional mortgage off quickly enough anyway. However, if you're *not* a good saver and could do with a loan that will encourage you to become a better one, and/or you don't already have a home loan and/or you'll incur little or no refinancing costs getting into one of these loans, my advice is to check them out. Talk to some of the many lenders, including banks and building societies, who are offering this product, noting that the way these loans are structured can vary significantly between lenders, particularly when it comes to the method of repayment.

So do shop around. But whichever one takes your fancy, all lenders will run the numbers for you at no cost, and at that price it's very cheap to see if you could benefit from what I think is fundamentally a good concept.

> **⊶ KEY THOUGHT**
>
> With this new type of mortgage it's the fact that you leave your savings in the mortgage that really makes the difference.

The benefits of competition

That there are so many different types of loans available and a wide divergence in interest rates is a result of greatly increased competition in the home-lending industry since the early 1990s.

As with my own experience described earlier, not so long ago the banks had home lending pretty much to themselves. You went to them cap in hand and all they offered you – if anything – were the same small range of loans at the same rates that moved up or down at the same time. There were no innovations like redraw facilities or offset facilities, no extended banking hours, and no one to come to you at your convenience. But, there were hefty loan application fees, heavy early payout fees, a heavy attitude and, most importantly, high interest rate margins (the difference between the price banks 'pay' for their money and the price at which they 'sell' it to you).

Then came the new breed of lenders, spearheaded by Sydney-based mortgage manager Aussie Home Loans. In early 1992 it burst onto the scene in a blaze of publicity offering home loans 0.5% lower than the major banks' standard variable rate. What followed, as they say, is history.

Aussie Home Loans, soon joined by other mortgage managers and ultimately by insurance companies, continued to undercut the banks – who largely continued to ignore them. But with falling market share the banks were belatedly forced to fight back and are now offering mortgage products as diverse and competitively priced as the new army of non-bank lenders. Indeed, as I write in early 2001, Aussie Home Loans, the one that started it all, has its standard variable loan rate of 7.2% bettered or equalled by plenty of different lenders.

Based on ABS figures, in December 1999 non-bank lenders (including permanent building societies) accounted for around 17% of the total home lending market, with much of this being attributable to mortgage managers like Aussie Home Loans. It's a remarkable market share given their virtual non-existence a decade ago, and all of us with mortgages have been beneficiaries. Today, there are some 150 financial institutions offering home loans around Australia and, as far as I am concerned, the more the merrier!

What to look for in a mortgage

Apart from the obvious feature, namely, having as low a rate as possible, these are the things you should look for when shopping for a mortgage, regardless of what type or which lender you prefer.

Low fees and flexibility

When you apply for a mortgage you may be up for an administrative charge known as an *application* or *establishment fee*, though due to increasing competition, not all lenders charge them. Where they do exist they cover the cost of:

- preparing the loan application and any supporting documents
- obtaining details of the Certificate of Title
- attending the settlement of the property
- lodging documents at the Land Titles Office.

The application fee may or may not include the lender's solicitor's fees and valuation fees. However, it *does not* include Government charges such as stamp duty on the mortgage or charges by the Titles Office.

Application fees are a growing area of negotiation between lender and borrower. They can range from $0 to $800 on a $100,000 loan, and average around $600. When you are applying for a loan ask for a discount in this area – you might be pleasantly surprised.

You might also be up for a *valuation fee* – the cost of having your property professionally valued. Like establishment fees these fees can vary tremendously, for example, on a $180,000 property the valuation fee would range from $0 to $400, averaging around $150. Presently, however, most lenders are not charging valuation fees.

There may be times when you are late with your regular mortgage repayment. Most lenders have a *late payment penalty* which is where you are charged a higher rate of interest on the overdue amount. The penalty rate is usually around 1% above your normal rate, though it can be several percentage points higher or a flat fee.

A *redraw fee*, usually of about $50, may apply to 'no frills' (lower interest rate) loans, whereas more expensive 'bells and whistles' type loans tend to offer this facility free of charge. You may also find that a minimum withdrawal applies, usually between $1,000 and $2,000.

Finally, most loans attract *ongoing fees*, usually payable monthly, ranging up to a total of $150 per year.

Refinancing and switching fees

Two other fees you need to investigate are the early pay-out penalty fee when you refinance with another lender and the switching fee (usually $250 to $300) when you change from a variable to a fixed rate loan, or vice versa, with the same lender. Refinancing from one mortgage to another can be an expensive business, depending on the policies of the lenders involved and the current level of interest rates.

Let's say you're thinking about refinancing your mortgage with another bank because it's offering you a better deal. Lenders don't like losing customers, so to discourage you from taking your business elsewhere they may charge a significant exit penalty fee which can be up to three months' interest charge. On the other hand it may be just a flat fee or, increasingly, nothing at all.

On top of this, refinancing from a (higher rate) fixed loan into a (lower rate) variable loan can be very expensive if there is a significant difference in the interest rates of the two loans. The lender will calculate how much revenue they will forego by you switching to a (lower) variable rate loan, and this you will have to pay, in addition to any other fees, before being able to proceed. Of course, it may be worth your while wearing this impost if you think variable rates will fall further. However, if you think they will remain static or indeed rise, there is no point refinancing.

☛ KEY THOUGHT

Remember, it's not the end of the world if you take the wrong mortgage. You can always bail out and refinance elsewhere.

A good mortgage

Look for the following features in your mortgage:
- consistently competitive rates
- flexibility – about exiting, early pay-out, switching to a different mortgage or 'portability' (being able to switch the loan from one property to another)
- low or no application fees (including low or no valuation and mortgage documentation fees)
- low or no ongoing fees
- low or no exit/early pay-out penalty fees
- low or no switching fees (from variable rate to fixed rate, or vice versa)
- ability to make additional repayments
- interest-offset facility
- redraw facility
- written in plain, easy-to-understand English.

Note, the more features a mortgage has, the more expensive it's likely to be. Don't pay for a 'bells and whistles' mortgage with a vast range of features and a high interest rate *unless you are going to use them.*

Mortgage checklist

Here are most of the questions you will need to ask prospective lenders, so take a copy of it with you when you go shopping for a mortgage.
- What are the differences in features between the different rate loans you offer?
- What is your variable rate now?
- What was the rate six months ago?
- How is your variable rate set?
- What are the terms (duration) of your mortgages?
- What are your fixed rates over one to five years?
- What happens to the loan at the end of the fixed term?
- Can the rate be refixed then?
- What is the capped rate?
- For how long is it capped?
- What happens at the end of the capped period?

- Do you have split loans?
- What are the maximum and minimum ratios between the fixed and variable components on your split loans?
- What are the terms of the split loans?
- What is your equity credit rate?
- Do your equity credit loans have a fixed repayment schedule?
- How does this work?
- Can I switch from an equity credit to a variable/fixed rate loan or vice versa?
- Can you switch between fixed and variable loans or vice versa, and between 'premium' and 'standard' loans and vice versa?
- What are the switching costs?
- What are your ongoing (monthly) fees?
- What is your application fee?
- What is your valuation fee?
- What is your mortgage documentation fee?
- Are there any other up-front fees?
- What is the exit fee?
- What is the early pay-out fee?
- Can I make additional repayments?
- Do you have redraw and interest-offset facilities?
- What is the late payment penalty?
- Can I see a copy of your mortgage document?
- How long will it take to arrange finance?
- Is there anything else I should know about your home loans?
- What do you recommend?

When looking for a mortgage, take your time, shop around and ask plenty of questions. Don't sign any mortgage contract without fully understanding what it all means and what it legally binds you to. If you're not satisfied with what's on offer (or with the mortgage you already have), go elsewhere.

To make your mortgage shopping easier, independent researchers Cannex conduct a quarterly review of many of the hundreds of mortgages available, and give each one a star rating. The results are displayed on their web site located at www.cannex.com.au. The monthly *Money Magazine* lists the top five mortgages and other rates from the major lenders, whilst many newspapers also regularly provide a breakdown of the most competitive mortgages available.

The benefits of extra payments

Let's assume you borrow $100,000 to buy your home and it's to be repaid over 25 years, with an average annual interest rate over the life of the loan of 7.5%.

Look at the table below and see how much you save and how much time is shaved off the term of the mortgage by paying an additional $25 and $100 per month over and above the standard repayment set by the lender. As you can see, the amount of time cut off the loan and the size of the savings made by these additional repayments are quite extraordinary. And when you remember that all these savings are totally tax-free, it becomes clear just how smart making extra repayments really is.

$100,000 loan over 25 years at an average interest rate of 7.5%

Paying the minimum repayments	$740 per month
Term length	25 years
Total interest paid	$121,638
Paying an additional $25 per month	$765
Term reduced to	22 years and 9 months
Total interest paid	$108,833
Saving	$12,805
Paying an additional $100 per month	$840
Term reduced to	18 years and 3 months
Total interest paid	$83,932
Saving	$37,706

(*Source*: National Australia Bank.)

Adding a bit extra to your regular repayments is one way of paying your mortgage off earlier, but there are some other ways, as outlined on the following pages.

Making Money

Fortnightly repayments

■ Pay your mortgage repayments fortnightly instead of monthly. To be specific, pay *half* your monthly repayments every fortnight. This simple change in repayment frequency can save you a small fortune and cut years off the loan. With a $100,000 loan over 25 years at 8.5% per annum, paying your mortgage fortnightly would save you almost $37,000 and reduce the life of the loan by six years and six months.

How does it work? Well, when you pay half your monthly repayment every fortnight, you end up repaying the equivalent of 13 monthly instalments per year, not 12. It's this extra month's worth of instalments that makes all the difference. The key is that paying fortnightly really does not seem any more painful than paying twice as much monthly, particularly if you time your repayments to the day you are paid.

Interest-offset accounts

■ Running an interest-offset account is a way of using your savings to offset the interest you pay on borrowings – in this case a mortgage. For example, let's say you have a mortgage of $150,000 with interest charged at 7.5%, and an offset account (a deposit) with a balance of $15,000. Instead of receiving interest on the deposit of $15,000 and paying interest on the full balance of the mortgage, interest of 7.5% is charged only on the *first* $135,000 of the mortgage ($150,000 less $15,000) and no interest is paid on the deposit.

This has significant tax benefits, since as far as the Tax Office is concerned, you have not received the interest on your deposit, and so it is not included in your taxable income. This means you are getting the full benefit of the return on your deposit without losing up to half in tax, and it certainly helps to pay the mortgage off sooner. On the downside, most lenders charge a slightly higher interest rate on mortgages offering this offset facility. On balance though, if used as intended, the slightly higher rate of some offset mortgages is chickenfeed compared to the savings you can make.

Lump sum payments

- Lump sum payments on your mortgage can also dramatically accelerate its reduction. Let's say you put $5,000 towards your $100,000, 25-year, 7.5% p.a. mortgage at the end of the mortgage's first year.

  The $5,000 lump sum payment would reduce your mortgage by a mighty three years and three months and knock almost $24,000 off it. However, if you were able to put $10,000 into your mortgage you would wipe five years and ten months off the term and save almost $42,000! (*Source*: National Australia Bank.)

  Consider putting your tax refunds, share dividends or similar large payment straight into your mortgage account if possible. No other investment will provide the fabulous result of strong tax-free returns without any risk attached (because you are effectively investing in your own home).

How extra payments work

All the methods of paying off your mortgage faster and saving thousands of dollars in the process are facets of the one basic strategy, namely, putting more money into your mortgage over and above the minimum monthly repayment required by the lender.

But why do these extra payments, even when they are quite small, have such a major impact? The answer is really quite simple.

In the early years of your mortgage most of your repayments go towards reducing the outstanding interest, not the principal. That's why on a 25-year, $100,000 loan at 7.5%, after one year you still owe $98,535, after two years $97,193 and three years $95,369. (*Source*: National Australia Bank.)

Now, if all you do is pop just an extra $100 into a $100,000 loan this $100 is immediately deducted straight off the *principal*, so the amount you owe now is $99,900.

However, your regular repayments are calculated on a debt of $100,000, so not only does your extra $100 help, but importantly, *it does not reduce your regular repayment*. This double effect – the extra money and the normal repayment, really get stuck into reducing the amount you owe.

CHAPTER EIGHT

Insurance

Insurance is all about protecting what you have now and what you would like to have in the future. But, as you go through life, the protection you need for the present and your future changes. The key to insurance, therefore, is being attuned to these changes, to make sure you always have the right sort and in just the right amounts. It's a waste of money having too much, but you can't afford to have too little.

What I'll look at in this chapter are the types of insurance relevant to your journey through life, showing when you need what protection, and how much.

Insuring your possessions and you

First up, there are two fundamental areas of insurance – your possessions and yourself. Most people don't question the need for insuring their assets – whether it's their home and its contents, their car, boat or jewellery – and to varying degrees most people do insure these things.

Considered less important by many people (and incorrectly so) is personal insurance – this includes your life, income and health. The reality is that at certain times in your life these insurances are at least as important as the insurance on your possessions, arguably even more so. Yet it is an area where many are underinsured, based on the assumption that 'it won't happen to me' – but unfortunately it can, and sometimes it does. So you need to be prepared.

Shop around, read the fine print

Now, when you decide to buy insurance, regardless of what sort it is, there are two important steps to take. The first is to make sure you shop around thoroughly. This is because there are significant differences in the premiums (prices) and conditions of the policies offered by the various insurance companies. The second, which follows from this, is to make sure you know exactly what each policy covers, or, more to the point, what it doesn't. If this involves quizzing the insurance salesman or broker closely and reading through the policy (as boring as that may be), do it. It's your life, health, income or your possessions being insured, so it's up to you to make sure the cover is right.

Insurance checklist

Apart from the obvious questions about the premium, the other questions you need to ask before you buy include:
- Is there an excess (an initial amount you pay in the event of a claim)?
- Are there no-claim bonuses (where the premium reduces over time if you make no claims, particularly common with car insurance)?
- Is there a waiting time for benefits?
- Are there any discounts (for example, for a fitted car alarm with car insurance, for non-smokers with life insurance, for people aged over 50 with household insurance)?
- What are the exclusions of this policy and under what conditions will the insurer not pay a claim?
- What proportion of claims does the insurer pay?
- How long does it take to process a claim?
- Can I have a copy of the policy to read?

You also need to pay close attention to the way insurance companies *define* things. With income/disability insurance, for instance, the definition of what a 'disability' is varies, with enormous significance in the event of a claim.

Choose a reputable insurer

The company behind the policy is also important. Some insurance companies have a reputation for paying more readily than others. When you see a hitherto unknown insurance company burst onto the scene with a glitzy advertising campaign saying they have the lowest premiums and the best service in town, beware. It may turn out that they will also be the hardest people in town to get any money out of.

In the event that you do have to claim, you don't want the added stress of having to go into battle with your insurer for the cover you thought you had been paying for. Give your business to a company that's well established, enjoys a good general reputation, that people you know have had trouble-free claims against, or that has been recommended to you – and if that means paying a bit more, let me tell you, it's worth it!

Be accurate and honest

Another thing you must be careful about with insurance is to ensure you are accurate and honest when filling out the proposal or application form. If, when you make a claim, the insurer discovers a pertinent fact was incorrectly entered or not entered at all they can legally refuse the claim.

Under the *Insurance Contracts Act* you have a 'duty of disclosure' to tell the insurance company 'every matter which you know or could be reasonably expected to know is relevant to (the insurance company's) decision to accept the insurance risk'.

Please don't try to fudge on this and when you make a claim don't fudge on that either! If the insurance company suspects a phoney or exaggerated claim, you can get set for a long delay until settlement, and possibly even legal action.

Now, let's look at the insurances you'll need as you travel through life, beginning with the ones that protect your material assets.

Household insurance

Home building insurance covers your home against an array of calamities including damage or destruction from fire, wind, hail, earthquakes, vandalism (other than by tenants or people you've invited), water, riots and so on, *but normally excludes damage by flood*. (Note that some insurance companies, including NRMA and AMP, now offer cover against flood damage, but at a much higher premium than for standard home insurance.) Contents insurance simply covers what's inside your house (and, in some cases, outside it) against the same calamities, as well as covering them against theft. The key thing with both types of insurance is to check carefully what is and isn't covered, by reading the policy closely.

Household insurance policies come in different forms. Firstly, you can insure your home and/or its contents on separate policies, or you can have a combined house and contents policy. Buying a combined policy is generally cheaper than buying two separate ones.

Secondly, you can choose between an indemnity policy and a replacement/reinstatement policy. Indemnity policies allow you to insure your home and/or contents for their value, minus an amount for depreciation based on the home or item's age and condition.

The increasingly common replacement/reinstatement policies, on the other hand, allow you to insure your home and/or contents for the full cost of totally rebuilding your home and/or replacing your damaged or stolen contents with – in most cases – new items of an equivalent standard. (This can be a problematic area and it's one where you really need to check the fine print. Some replacement policies may not, in fact, fund the replacement of all old items with new items. For instance, some insurers will not replace damaged carpets older than five years with new carpets.)

Replacement policies have higher premiums than indemnity policies because they cost the insurance companies more, but I recommend them nonetheless. The depreciation factor with indemnity policies means that money will have to come out of your own pocket to restore your property to its former state, and that can be a killer in the event of a major claim.

Most contents policies only pay a maximum amount for each item in your home, normally between $1,000 and $2,000. So if you have a piece of jewellery worth, say, $5,000 or a painting worth $10,000 you would need to list each item separately and probably pay an additional premium.

In the event of a loss, the claim should proceed more smoothly if you can easily prove the existence of the destroyed or stolen items. This proof ideally takes the form of receipts or valuations but photos are also helpful, particularly in the case of stolen jewellery. They also give the police a much better chance of recovery, as does engraving items (such as stereos) with some identification.

Insurers will generally not require you to prove the prior existence of stolen items, but they can if they wish, and without proof the claim can get messy. Of course, any proof you had may have disappeared as well – that's why it's a good idea to keep photocopies of documentation in a safe place other than your home. Around Australia you will find services that will do this documentation and take photos for you. The cost is typically $150 to $250.

Another good way to assist you in the event of a claim is to record a home video of all your household contents *in situ*, including close-ups of serial numbers and purchase receipts where possible. Not only will this help establish the prior existence of any stolen or damaged goods with your insurer, it will also remind you of what you actually had before the claimable event.

Underinsurance

Underinsurance is one of the great financial hazards. Let's say you have a replacement policy on your home, and your home is destroyed by fire. The policy will cover the costs of replacing the house, *but only up to the value for which the original one was insured*. If the destroyed home was underinsured you will have to dip into your own pocket to rebuild another as valuable.

Most people underinsure out of ignorance of their property's current replacement value; others, foolishly, do so to save a few dollars on insurance premiums. And while the consequences can be clearly catastrophic, underinsurance is surprisingly widespread. When the Ash Wednesday fires raged through Victoria in 1983 around 40% of damaged or destroyed homes were found to be underinsured. When Newcastle was struck by earthquake in December 1989, 60% of homes were found to be underinsured, and these by an average of around 30% each (where the maximum insurance pay-out only met around 70% of the total damages bill). When a major hailstorm hit Sydney's eastern and southern suburbs in April 1999, around 40% of homes damaged were underinsured by 30%. In fact, one in eleven (8.5%) homes was not covered by building insurance at all!

According to the Insurance Council of Australia, the average national level of underinsurance on Australian houses is around 30% of their real and total replacement value. On household contents the average national level of underinsurance is about 40%. Items that householders perennially undervalue and hence under-insure are record, CD and book collections, clothing, tools and goods in storage.

Most people do not realise they are underinsured until they claim, and undervaluation is generally the cause of the problem. An effective way around this is to have a registered valuer or registered builder value your house (and contents) for insurance purposes. The valuation normally costs around $300, and it remains valid up until the time you make any capital changes to your property (the valuation is indexed for inflation on your policy).

If you choose to value your home yourself – which you are perfectly entitled to do – make sure you allow for expenses such as the removal of debris from the site, architect's fees and other contingencies. Normally you would add somewhere between 10% and 20% to the replacement building cost to cover these. Also, take into account the potential costs of relocation and temporary accommodation that can arise from a claim, or consider the loss of rent that may arise from damage to an investment property. Most home insurance policies can provide adequate cover for all these eventualities, so make sure you choose one that does.

What it costs to insure your home and contents

Here are some sample premiums per annum for home and contents insurance based on a house with an insured value of $150,000 and contents of $30,000.

City	Insurer	House	Contents	Combined
SYDNEY – Baulkham Hills	NRMA	$259	$233	$489
MELBOURNE – Glen Waverley	RACV	$251	$187	$304
PERTH – Kingsley	AMP	$358	$280	$575
BRISBANE – Kedron	NRMA	$173	$147	$304
ADELAIDE – Modbury	SGIC	$254	$192	$413
HOBART – Kingston	TGIO	$184	$165	$349
Quotes as at February 2001.				

Public liability

Household insurance frequently includes a public or legal liability component, generally up to a limit of $10 million. This covers you for the accidental death or personal injury or damage to property suffered by another party for which you may be held legally liable due to your negligence. This, of course, excludes damage caused deliberately or injuries that occur as a result of motor vehicle accidents which are covered by compulsory Third Party Insurance.

Car insurance

There are three types of car insurance, as listed below.

Compulsory Third Party

Compulsory Third Party (CTP) is the insurance you have to pay when you register your car. It insures you (the driver) or anyone else driving your car against any claim for personal injury brought by another person or their family for any injury or death caused to them by your car, assuming your car was at fault.

This insurance does not cover you against any damage your car may cause to property – so if you ran into someone's Rolls Royce and you were at fault, your compulsory Third Party Insurance would not cover the bill.

From late 2000, the CTP and registration requirements in New South Wales and Queensland were split. The insurance companies manage CTP for the State governments and the relevant government transport authorities are responsible for registration. If you live in New South Wales for example, you'll receive your registration papers from the Roads and Traffic Authority (RTA) and your CTP premium from the insurance company of your choice. In the other States, drivers pay a single sum covering both registration and CTP requirements.

CTP premiums are calculated in a number of ways depending on your age, the age of your car, and which State you live in. For more specific information on how much you can expect to pay, I recommend you call the organisation appropriate for your State or Territory.

ACT	NRMA Insurance Ltd	(02) 6240 4700
NSW	Motor Accidents Authority	1300 137 131
	www.maa.nsw.gov.au	
NT	Motor Accident Compensation	(08) 8946 2261
	www.tiofi.com.au	
QLD	Motor Accidents Insurance Commission	(07) 3227 8088
	www.maic.qld.gov.au	
SA	SGIC	(08) 8233 1188
	www.sgic.com.au	
TAS	Motor Accidents Insurance Board	(03) 6336 4800
	www.maib.tas.gov.au	

VIC	Transport Accident Commission	(03) 9663 7500
	www.tac.vic.gov.au	
WA	Insurance Commission of WA	(08) 9264 3333
	www.icwa.wa.gov.au	

Third party property

Third party property insurance costs up to around $250 p.a. and protects you against claims from a third party for damage to their property caused by your car (assuming it was at fault) whether or not you were driving. Some third party property policies also offer limited cover for damage to your car if you can prove someone else was at fault. The NRMA, for instance, will pay you up to $3,000 for damage done to your car assuming it was not at fault. Anyone who drives is crazy not to have at least this level of car insurance.

Comprehensive

Comprehensive car insurance covers damage not only to anyone else's property but also to your car, up to an 'agreed value', which is theoretically your car's current market value including all added options and registration costs.

Most comprehensive car insurance carries an excess – where you pay an initial proportion of the claim out of your own pocket regardless of who is at fault – as well as an additional excess if the car is driven by a high-risk category driver, such as a male under 25 years old.

Your car insurance also generally accumulates no-claim bonuses, rising over some years to a maximum of 60% – which represents a major discount. (An example of how this works is: with one major car insurer it takes five years to build your no-claim bonus [NCB] up to 60%. If you make a claim and you can prove the accident wasn't your fault, you'll retain your NCB. If it was your fault or you can't prove it wasn't, your NCB may be as much as halved. A second claim may see your NCB reduced to zero.)

The idea of the excess and the no-claim bonus is to discourage you from making small claims. The cost to you of paying the excess and increased premiums over the coming years needs to be calculated before you claim for any minor damage. (Your insurer will do this calculation for you.)

Making Money

Car insurance premiums are calculated taking into account many variables such as the car's market value, its make, its type, the age and sex of the driver/s, whether the car is for private or business use, where you live, if the car is garaged or parked on the street, whether it has a car alarm and so on. Exotic and powerful sports cars, particularly turbos, are especially expensive to insure.

It's very important to shop around for car insurance. There can be an enormous difference in premiums between insurers due to the different ways they measure risk. But remember there is more to insurance than just the premium. Make sure you compare conditions and exclusions, and pay particular attention to the treatment of no-claim bonuses. Most importantly don't get involved with an insurer with a reputation for being a difficult payer.

Insurance for other material items such as boats, motorbikes, aircraft and so on work along similar lines. An insurer assesses the risk based on a number of variables and offers you a premium.

Life insurance

'Life insurance' is actually a misnomer – it should really be called 'death insurance' because death is what you are insuring against. More to the point, you are insuring against an untimely death. There are two types of life insurance – term and whole-of-life (or 'endowment') insurance – which I'll compare later.

Who is life insurance for? Well, it's a product designed for anyone with a family, dependent relatives or debt. If you die and your life is insured, your beneficiaries receive a lump sum pay-out.

In the case of families it makes sense that both parents are insured even if they don't both work. Too often the economic worth of the child-rearer's work is overlooked. Both professional childminding and housekeeping are expensive services and it makes sense to insure the housewife's (or househusband's) life at a similar level to the breadwinner's.

So, how much should you insure your life for? Well, many insurance agents suggest a reasonable figure is 10 to 15 times the annual expenditure needs of your dependants. Others say anywhere between three to ten times your annual salary in addition to an amount necessary to cover your debts is appropriate.

Let's look at my situation. A wife, three children, school fees, bills, and it's my income that makes it all tick over. If I got run over by a bus, without life insurance it could cause my family real problems. So I have term insurance to provide an amount of money that will take care of them all until the kids have at least finished their education.

How did we work out how much we need? Well, it's quite simple really. Our budget identifies our yearly spending and our 'balance sheet' (our list of assets and liabilities) shows us what we have and what we owe. I carry enough insurance to pay out our debts and establish sufficient capital to provide for my family and the kids' education, with a balance to help my wife rebuild her future.

As a rule of thumb, the following guide will help.

How much capital do you need?

The approximate amount of capital required to provide $5,000 of income per year is:

$22,000 if the income is to last for 5 years
$41,000 if the income is to last for 10 years
$56,000 if the income is to last for 15 years
$68,000 if the income is to last for 20 years.

Note that these figures assume you use up all your capital. In other words, if you wanted an income of $30,000 per year (that is, $5,000 x 6) to last for five years, you would need $132,000 ($22,000 x 6) to provide it, and at the end of the five years there would be nothing left. You would have spent the lot!

Also note these figures assume you invest your capital in a diversified range of assets generating historically standard returns. However, these figures are simply a guide and cannot be guaranteed.

Whole-of-life insurance

Whole-of-life insurance (WOL) is structured on the understanding that you contribute towards it for virtually the whole of your life. The premium doesn't change as you get older (apart from indexation), and is determined by the age at which you sign up. The idea is you stop contributing towards the policy either when you die or when the policy matures, which is normally at age 60 or 65.

WOL has an agreed pay-out to your beneficiaries in the event of your death and also has an investment or savings component which part of your premium goes towards. If you are still alive when the policy matures, it is wound up and you receive a lump sum pay-out which is the return on the investment portion of your premium.

WOL policies can be cashed in prior to maturity, however, you will only recoup the full amount of annual premiums paid in after around five to ten years of contributions. If you cash in (or 'surrender') the policy before this, you will get back less than you have put into it. While things are improving, sales commissions and insurance company costs can see many WOL policies having no surrender value for their first three years.

Term life insurance

Since WOL policies have been falling out of public favour, insurance companies have promoted term life policies which insure against death only and have no investment component. This has substantially reduced the cost of obtaining death cover and presently term cover is very keenly priced. (Indeed, term insurance is one of the few products to have come down in price during the past 15 years.)

The cost of term life insurance, for someone with a good health record, depends on your age, sex and whether you are a smoker. Through one major insurer, for example, a 30-year-old non-smoking male will pay just over $1 per $1,000 of cover per year. A 30-year-old male smoker, on the other hand, will pay $1.85 per $1,000 of cover per year. (If smoking doesn't kill you, its costs will!)

A 30-year-old female non-smoker will pay 97 cents per $1,000 of cover per year and a smoker will pay $1.65 cents for the same cover. Commonplace to all insurers is an added standard annual policy fee (in this case $50.00) which does not vary, regardless of the amount insured, your age, sex or whether you smoke.

While other insurers' premiums are comparable to these, it is worth shopping around, as you will see from the tables on the following pages. You also need to look for certain features in your policy, such as the option of renewing the policy regardless of changes to your health. Some companies, for example, guarantee that a policy, once accepted, will be renewable to age 70 or older at the appropriate premium level. Another feature to look for is the ability to link the amount insured to the Consumer Price Index. This ensures that the level of cover is maintained in real terms.

Term life insurance annual premiums for $200,000 sum insured

		MLC	AMP
Male non-smoker		$	$
Age	20	331	385
	30	173	213
	40	223	273
	50	483	628
	60	1,606	2,184
	65	3,022	3,881
Male smoker			
Age	20	364	553
	30	286	369
	40	427	555
	50	1,011	1,444
	60	3,004	3,625
	65	4,944	5,843
Female non-smoker			
Age	20	184	193
	30	163	193
	40	195	221
	50	379	569
	60	949	1,145
	65	1,707	2,016
Female smoker			
Age	20	241	325
	30	231	329
	40	337	471
	50	714	1,280
	60	1,877	2,567
	65	3,459	4,129

(*Source*: AMP and MLC.)
Quotes as at March 2001.

Making Money

Term *vs* whole-of-life

Some people will still tell you that whole-of-life (WOL) insurance is better than term life insurance because it provides a fixed price for your insurance (that is, the annual premium does not increase as you get older), and it has an investment component. In my opinion these arguments don't stack up.

Consider this: a healthy, 32-year-old, non-smoking male taking out life insurance with a death cover of $200,000 through one of the major Australian life offices would pay an annual WOL premium of around $4,200 based on policy maturity at age 65.

The cumulative amount of premiums paid by this policy holder between ages 32 and 65 would be around $140,000. If the policy was surrendered at age 65 it would be worth around $290,000. But I don't believe roughly doubling one's money over 33 years is such an impressive investment result.

The same individual taking out $200,000 death cover through term insurance at age 32 would pay very much less per year as the table on the previous page indicates.

Okay, the annual WOL premium remains constant meaning WOL is relatively cheap in our later life but most of us need high levels of insurance in our thirties and forties (when term cover is cheap) and none in our sixties (when term cover is expensive).

As far as the savings/investment component of WOL goes, you would be far better off investing the savings differential between it and term premiums in other investments such as shares, property, super or accelerated mortgage repayments which show much better long-term returns.

You may find those who argue for WOL have a personal financial interest in the matter, namely that sales commissions on WOL are much more lucrative than the amount earned on term insurance.

•─ KEY THOUGHT

When young, put your money into savings. When married and with a family, take plenty of term death cover. With the kids at work, retain your death cover and establish an investment portfolio. When older, build up your contributions to your investment fund and reduce or eliminate your term insurance.

Income (disability) insurance

Income insurance, also known as disability insurance, protects what is probably your most valuable asset – and if you think that's your car or your house, think again. Unless you've retired, chances are your most valuable asset is your *ability to earn an income*.

Let me illustrate this. If you are 30 years old on $30,000 p.a. and you expect your earnings to increase by 7% per year, you will earn $4.1 million in total income by 65 years of age. If you are 40 years old on $40,000 p.a., given the same growth, you will earn $2.5 million by retirement.

But, while virtually no one would buy a new car or house without immediately insuring it, surprisingly few people take action to insure their income against an inability to work due to illness or injury. This is despite income/disability insurance being widely available at a reasonable cost, and also being fully tax deductible.

Many people don't take out income insurance partly due to believing they are unlikely to be disabled. Perhaps rightly, if you're only thinking about permanent disablement that is. But temporary disablement is common.

A 25-year-old male, for instance, has around a 24% chance of becoming disabled for some period in his life by age 65. If he is disabled for more than three months, then the average duration as claimed for insurance is 2.2 years.

If you're a young professional worker, the odds are greater than even money that you'll be disabled for three months or more before the age of 65. If you're an industrial worker, the likelihood of disablement for some period is much higher still.

Many of us take out life insurance policies to financially protect our dependants against our untimely death, yet we have an eight to nine times greater likelihood of being seriously injured during our working lives than being killed. Surely then, there is a case for taking out income insurance too.

The idea of income insurance is pretty straightforward. You can insure yourself for up to 80% of your income in the event of sickness or an accident rendering you incapable of carrying out your normal work duties. So if, for example, your annual income was $35,000 you could insure yourself for a yearly amount of $28,000 (80%). This benefit would be paid to you until the expiry of the agreed term, or until your recovery allowed you to return to work.

Making Money

Like life insurance, you should have income/disability insurance if you have a job, unless someone else will take care of you if you get sick or injured – with the possibility of it being until you die! Premiums vary depending on your age, sex, occupation and whether or not you are a smoker. Another determinant of the premium is how long you wait for the insurance payments to kick in after you fall ill or the accident occurs. The usual range of waiting periods is 14, 30 and 90 days. The longer the waiting period you opt for, the lower the premium. You can also vary the length of time the benefit is paid to you, from two years through to a maximum term of up until age 65. Clearly, the longer the term the higher the premium.

Income insurance costs

The annual premiums shown below are for income insurance where the benefit is 75% of gross income, payable to age 65 and indexed for inflation.

The premiums include stamp duty and policy fee, and are for the standard income insurance policies offered by the two companies. All policies are guaranteed renewable.

1. Male doctor aged 45; non-smoker; $6,250 gross income per month; 30-day waiting period.
2. Female real-estate agent aged 35; smoker; $3,750 gross income per month; 14-day waiting period.
3. Male plumber aged 50; smoker; $3,437 gross income per month; 30-day waiting period.
4. Female nurse aged 30; non-smoker; $2,500 gross income per month; 30-day waiting period.
5. Female hairdresser aged 50; non-smoker; $2,500 gross income per month; 14-day waiting period.

	AMP	MLC
1.	$1,727	$758
2.	$3,273	$915
3.	$4,833	$2,144
4.	$872	$644
5.	$6,458	$2,761

(*Source*: AMP and MLC.)

Note: Aspects of cover may vary between insurers.

Quotes (all for top-range cover) as at March 2001.

A vital thing to check before you go out and sign up is how each insurance company defines 'disability'. This can be critical in the event of a claim. You will come across three broad definitions:

- an inability to perform your normal occupation (due to illness or injury)
- an inability to perform each and every duty of your normal occupation
- an inability to perform each and every duty of *any* occupation for which you are reasonably qualified by your training, education and experience. Be wary of this one. The insurer would not consider you could work as a lawyer, for instance, if you were an office clerk (pre-claim), but they may think you could work as an office clerk if you were a lawyer (pre-claim), and terminate payments as a result.

The common and reasonable definition of disability is one that means your insurer will compensate you if an illness or accident renders you unable to perform your normal duties or to work at all.

In some cases the definition of disability is modified after you have claimed for a minimum period (usually two years), so that the payment stops if you are able to undertake a job which you are qualified to do, but which might not necessarily be your usual occupation.

What to look for

The sort of income protection policy I recommend you take is one:
- with an unambiguous definition of 'disability' – being, an inability to perform normally your usual occupation
- where the benefits are indexed in the event you are disabled for a long time
- where the policy cannot be cancelled by the insurer, no matter how often you fall ill or for how long.

Whatever you do, make sure you shop around. Premiums vary significantly as do policy conditions – which you must make sure you fully understand.

Total and permanent disability cover

Some people confuse income/disability insurance with total and permanent disability cover (TPD) – which is often an add-on to life insurance. As its name implies, TPD covers you only in the event of *total* disability caused by accident or injury, rendering you incapable of work (and probably much more) for the rest of your life.

A six-month waiting period normally applies to TPD. Not only that, up to age 50 you are 30 times more likely to be disabled for three months than to suffer a TPD-qualifying disablement.

Another area of confusion that arises in connection with this area of insurance is how it fits into the protection offered to you by worker's compensation insurance.

Worker's compensation

Everyone in paid employment must be covered by employer-paid worker's compensation, but this insurance only covers you for accidents that happen while you're at work or travelling to and from work. It does not cover you for accidents that occur at home nor does it cover you for non-accident related illnesses.

Worker's compensation will provide you with your salary or a proportion of your salary for up to six months and will pay any medical expenses up to a point. There are set guidelines for benefits such as what type of treatment is acceptable; how many hours of physiotherapy you get; what sort of rehabilitation and so on.

Worker's compensation certainly has its place but income/disability insurance extends your protection.

Trauma insurance

Also known as 'crisis insurance' or 'vital cover' insurance, trauma insurance pays you either a lump sum or a monthly benefit in the event you experience a major physical trauma. The conditions that qualify you for a pay-out generally include heart attack, heart disease involving bypass surgery, stroke, malignant cancer (excluding skin cancers other than melanoma), chronic kidney failure and any disease requiring an organ transplant.

Trauma insurance generally doesn't cover you for a medical condition resulting from an accident – you need income insurance for that. Some life insurance policies have a trauma insurance component, or you can buy it as a stand-alone product.

Private health insurance

When Medicare was introduced in 1984, 63% of Australians had private health cover. However, from there on we began to abandon it (why bother with health insurance under a free medical system?) to the point that by the end of 1988, only 30% of Australians were privately insured. But in the last few years, the downward trend has been reversed, and as I write in early 2001, the national level of private health coverage has climbed to 45.4% (*Source*: Private Health Insurance Administration Council.). Three major government initiatives have primarily brought this around: the Medicare levy surcharge; the 30% Federal Government health insurance rebate; and Lifetime Health Cover.

Medicare levy surcharge

The Medicare levy surcharge was introduced in July 1997. This is an additional 1% levy on your total taxable income, over and above the current, universal Medicare levy of 1.5%, payable by higher income earners who *do not* take out health insurance.

The surcharge is levied on individuals without health insurance earning more than $50,000 or on uninsured couples/families earning more than $100,000 (with the threshold rising by $1,500 for each child after the first).

Many high earners would find it comparable or even cheaper to pay health insurance premiums than to pay an additional 1% tax, and would be crazy therefore not to have it.

Federal Government's 30% rebate

The Federal Government's 30% rebate on private health insurance took effect from January 1999 and it is offered to all people with health insurance, regardless of their level of income. You can receive the rebate in one of three ways: by having your premiums reduced 30% by your fund; by claiming it through your tax return; or by receiving a direct payment through a Medicare office.

After the introduction of the 30% rebate – which simply made private health premiums 30% cheaper – private health insurance coverage began to increase significantly.

Making Money

Lifetime Health Cover (LHC)

In July 2000, the Federal Government introduced Lifetime Health Cover (LHC). Under this scheme, if you took up hospital insurance by 1 July 2000, you locked into the lowest base rate premiums offered by an insurer for as long as you remain insured – indeed, for the rest of your life, if you wish.

However, if you missed that date (and this applies to anyone contemplating taking out health insurance now) you pay an extra 2% loading on the insurer's base premium, for every year over 30 you are aged. Therefore, if you were to take out health insurance now aged 38, you would pay a 16% loading on the base premium, being 8 (years over 30) x 2%. The maximum loading a person can pay under this scheme is 70% – for people joining at age 65 (people born before 1 July 1934 pay no loading).

If you already had health insurance or took it up by 1 July 2000, and you were over 30, well then, regardless of your real age, you are treated under LHC as a 30-year-old and pay no loading. Age 30 becomes your 'certified age at entry', and for the purposes of this scheme you will remain '30' forever, *so long as you stay insured.* Similarly, if you join a health fund now – and you're actually 43, then 43 becomes your 'certified age at entry', with its 26% loading – and you'll remain '43' forever with the 26% loading for as many years as you remain insured.

What do you get with private health insurance?

Firstly, let's deal with what you don't get. Contrary to a widespread misconception, health insurance does not cover the cost of going to your doctor, at his or her surgery. Private health insurance, more commonly referred to in the past as private 'hospital' insurance, is actually about covering most or all of the costs (for most procedures) arising from going to hospital or from receiving treatment in an approved medical day centre.

As a privately insured patient, Medicare and your fund between them should cover all private hospital accommodation charges to the level of comfort you've insured for, theatre fees (unless it's for a procedure specifically excluded from the cover), medication, medically required ancillary costs and the costs of surgically implanted prostheses. However, with normal health insurance you will have to pay any difference between the Medicare Schedule doctors' fees and what the doctors actually charge – which can be a lot higher. In addition, depending on what type of health insurance you buy, you may have to pay an excess and/or a 'co-payment', which is a daily contribution towards the hospital treatment charges.

Health insurers are now offering what is often called 'no gap' insurance, which is designed to cover that (sometimes yawning) gap between the doctor's schedule fee and the actual fee they charge. Clearly, no gap insurance costs more than standard (with gap) health insurance, but be aware that these policies only provide expense-free private hospitalisation *so long as you go to hospitals and use doctors with which the fund has 'no gap' agreements*. In other words, even with so-called 'no gap' health insurance, if you exercise your choice to use the doctor and/or hospital you really want, you could find yourself facing a 'gap' after all, unless the fund has a 'no gap' agreement with them.

It's worth knowing that if you go to a public hospital as a 'public' (uninsured) patient, Medicare covers the full cost of accommodation and treatment by hospital-appointed doctors, including medication, pathology and X-rays. Conversely, as a public patient going to a private hospital, you would be up for some very significant fees.

Choosing the right insurance policy

With around 50 registered health funds nationwide, offering some 500 different products, it's impossible to compare their offerings in the space of this book. Having said that, private health insurance policies can generally be broken into four main camps.

1 *Policies that cover all procedures in most hospitals*
   If you're going to have health insurance, these are the best ones to have, as health insurance should be just that – insurance. Whilst certain medical conditions are relatively uncommon, particularly amongst the young, you never know what might strike you down – and no one's invulnerable. The drawback of these policies is usually the cost – they're the most expensive, unless you choose an excess. And the higher the excess you choose, the lower your premium.

2 *Policies covering all procedures but restricting the hospitals that you can go to*
   The same applies as above, but check which hospitals you are

Making Money

fully covered in – ideally, good ones that are close to you. Also check how much you're going to have to kick in if you go to a hospital that's not on the list.

3 *Policies that cover most hospitals and may or may not charge an excess, but also add a co-payment for each day you are in hospital*
Make sure you know exactly what the co-payment is, and be aware it is payable on top of any excess that may apply.

4 *Policies that exclude or pay lower benefits for some services – commonly called 'exclusion' products*
Many people are attracted to these due to their lower cost, but what they don't realise is that the cost reflects the lower benefits for the things that most people are likely to claim for.

Health insurance brokers

One way to make the job of picking a health policy easier is to go through a health insurance broker. Free of charge, they should suggest a number of policies for you to consider. Just satisfy yourself that they're not pushing a particular product or products because of more favourable commissions.

Failing that, get some brochures from some health funds that have financial agreements with hospitals near to you or with hospitals you would be happy to go to, pour yourself a very strong drink, and get down to what can be the mind-boggling job of comparing the various policies on offer before you.

Illness and injury – what are the odds?

Age	Heart disease	Cancer	Stroke	Injury and poisoning
0–24 years	391:1	530:1	2,228:1	190:1
25–45 years	201:1	92:1	1,111:1	162:1
over 45	15:1	24:1	59:1	148:1

With odds like these, the question is: can you afford *not* to have personal insurances such as life, health, income and trauma at certain ages in your life?

(*Source*: Australian Health Insurance Association, 1998.)

Mortgage insurance

Mortgage insurance can be worthwhile, but there are two types and you have to be sure you have the right one. One type is designed to protect the *lender*, not you, in the event you can't meet the repayments and the property is repossessed. This is the type of insurance most banks insist you take out if you are borrowing more than 80% of the property's value, or, in the case of some building societies and mortgage managers, more than around 70% of the property's value.

Under this insurance, if, when the lender sells your property it doesn't recoup the full amount of borrowings still outstanding against it, the insurer will make up the difference to the lender. When you are obliged to take out this insurance as a condition of receiving a home loan, you are effectively buying insurance for the lender. I stress, you receive no protection whatsoever from this type of mortgage insurance.

The other type of mortgage insurance, which is voluntary, is designed to protect *you*. It is sometimes distinguished from (lender protecting) mortgage insurance by being called, confusingly, *mortgage protection* insurance.

This insurance is designed to keep up your mortgage repayments in the event an accident or illness prevents you from being able to work and earn an income. Of course, if you had income protection insurance – which I recommend to most people – you would probably not need mortgage protection insurance.

Travel insurance

Travel insurance is a product that I recommend to all travellers, particularly if you are going overseas. What happens, for instance, if you end up in an American hospital and are presented with a pile of notoriously expensive US medical bills? What happens if your $1,000 camera gets ripped off in Bangkok or you cancel your trip due to illness and face a loss of deposits and cancellation fees? Travel insurance is designed to recompense you for these and many other similar dilemmas that commonly befall travellers.

There can be tremendous variation in the specific cover offered by the various travel insurers, therefore I suggest you compare at least three or four different policies before you put your money down. Read the fine print closely, note what is and what isn't covered, and make inquiries about how and when you can make a claim and how and when you will receive payment. And remember, there is much more to selecting an insurance policy than going for the one with the lowest premium. It's the nature of the protection the policy provides that matters.

Travel Insurance

Offered through	Top cover $	Medium cover $	Budget cover $	Australian domestic $
Thomas Cook	416	376	264	152
NRMA	485	372	265	188
ANZ	381	321	233	131

Notes:

1 Premiums are based on family cover for around 30 days.

2 The benefits are not the same for each insurance package.

3 Top cover is generally advised for North America, Japan, Europe, Africa, South America, India and the Middle East; Medium cover for UK, Ireland and most of Asia; and Budget cover for Australasia, Indonesia and the Pacific region.

Quotes as at February 2001.

Disputes

Insurance is an area with virtually unlimited scope for disputation between the insured and the insurer. However, disputes can be minimised if you:

■ select a reputable insurer
■ keep proof of your belongings' existence and condition
■ don't fudge on the proposal or the claim
■ ensure you buy the right insurance policy to start with.

Despite your best intentions and planning, you may feel you are being hard done by, in which case I recommend you contact the General Insurance Claims Review Panel on 1300 363 683 or the Life Insurance Complaints Service on 1800 335 405 or (03) 9629 7050.

☗ KEY THOUGHTS

- Insurance is a fundamental component of wealth creation. It protects the assets you have now and therefore helps secure the future. It is not a luxury, it's a necessity.
- Being overinsured or having the wrong insurance is a waste of money, and being underinsured is false economy and downright dangerous.
- To make sure the insurance you do have is sufficient and appropriate to your present stage in life, I recommend you contact an independent insurance broker or financial planner for an assessment of your insurance position.
- Remember, there is no point working hard over the years to accumulate wealth if, through inadequate insurance, you expose yourself to losing it in a flash!

CHAPTER NINE

Superannuation

Raise the topic of superannuation next time you have a few friends around for a barbecue and you'll get a range of reactions. Some people will look at their watches and ask 'Is that the time?', some will pour themselves extremely large drinks, some will slip into a type of coma, others will become completely absorbed by a spoon or salt shaker, and a few will say 'I think super is okay because people keep telling me it is, but I'm not really sure why.' The majority will tell you that it is confusing, keeps changing and is all too hard.

Well, I'm one of those people who keeps saying super is okay, and what I am going to try to do here is explain why. And I hope as you read this your mind won't drift off to a palm-fringed beach on a tropical island. Bring it back here if it does, because, confusing as super may be, it's worth knowing about. Indeed, if you play your superannuation cards properly, you will actually be able to accompany your mind to that tropical paradise when you retire, as well as doing many other things you have only dreamt about during your working life.

What is superannuation?

Basically, superannuation is designed to provide for us financially in retirement. It's built up over our working lives from contributions made by our employers and, hopefully, topped up out of our own pockets. It's also taxed lightly – both to encourage our active contribution towards it and to increase the size of its pay-out at the end.

That's the good news. The bad news is that it's confusing, your money is locked away for a very long time, and the Federal Government continually fiddles with the rules. While this may bring us no joy, the fact is, we need super.

Consider this: in 2001 we have around six people in the work force for every person in retirement. That's a large pool of taxpayers from which to fund the aged pension. But because we are living longer and having fewer children, by 2030 there will be only three people working for every retired person.

Let's look at it another way. Today we have around 2.3 million Australians aged 65 or more. In 19 years' time, when I reach 65, there will be just under 4 million of us! Already pensions are a major funding burden, accounting for more than 30% of the Federal Budget, so can you imagine what it's going to be like then? Either taxpayers in the future will have to be taxed to within an inch of their lives if the aged pension is to remain at its present (modest) real level, or (far more likely) the pension will fall.

But 'What about the value of the family home?', I hear you say. Who cares about a pension if you're sitting on good real estate? Okay, but do you really want to find yourself at retirement with no option but to sell the home you're perfectly happy living in and don't wish to leave? And after you've sold and put aside sufficient proceeds to live off comfortably for the rest of your life, you will be faced with taking a very substantial downgrading in the type of housing or the location you can afford. No, relying on the value of your home is not the way to plan for your retirement.

A comfortable retirement can only be funded by a separate nest egg of investments, which has been built up for that purpose during your working life. And your success in building up a suitably sized nest egg will depend on your success as a saver. The reason is very clear. If you don't save, you don't invest, and if you don't invest you will have nothing (apart from your home) to retire on.

The problem is, however, that we are not good savers. Certainly earlier generations who lived through tougher times were much better at it than we are. Indeed, Australians now are among the worst savers in the world – currently we only save around 4% of what we earn (down from 11% in the late 1970s). That's why, I am sure, the Government has decided to force us to save, and the way they have chosen to implement this is through compulsory superannuation.

The key word here is *compulsory*. If there was only voluntary superannuation there's little chance we'd contribute enough for it to do what it is supposed to do – provide for a comfortable retirement and head off a society increasingly burdened by taxation to pay for the aged.

Making Money

What is a super fund?

Super funds come in two basic forms.

Defined benefit funds

With defined benefit funds your final pay-out is 'defined' by a set formula. For example, you may get four times your salary if you retire at 55, five times at age 60 and so on. You know in advance what you will get.

These were once quite common in public sector super funds and with some larger companies. The advantage of defined benefit super-annuation is certainty about the size of your payment upon retirement or leaving the company. The bad news is that it may be less attractive if you don't stay with the one company until retirement. I know many people who feel trapped by this type of super. The end benefit is so attractive, they just can't afford to leave. Low motivation is bad for the employee and employer and what a sad situation it is, because no one wins. These people wait for 5 o'clock so they can go home, and long to retire.

With defined benefit funds, how the investments in the fund perform is of no interest to you. Your end benefit is paid anyway (unless your company goes broke and defrauds the super fund). Your employer will be very interested in investment performance though because the better the fund does, the less he has to put in! You may have seen very public arguments about 'surpluses' of defined benefit funds. A surplus means simply that your super fund has more money in it than it needs to pay out to its members in entitlements. Often employers will try to reclaim this surplus, and employees fight to hang onto it.

Providing the surplus is accurately measured, I have no doubt who it should belong to – the employer. They guarantee the member will receive a set benefit and dips into the company coffers if the money is not there. So, given the employer must meet any shortfall, I have no doubt any surplus, if it occurs, also belongs to them.

Accumulation funds

Accumulation funds are becoming increasingly common and are also very simple. Whatever you or your employer puts in, plus investment earnings, less expenses, is yours.

While with defined benefit funds you concentrate your attention on the documentation describing your end benefit and don't worry about investment, with accumulation funds you do worry about investment and you need to ask lots of questions. With accumulation funds what you get is determined by what goes in, but the expenses of the fund and, in particular, the performance of the investments it holds, are critical to what you end up getting.

> **Things you should know about your accumulation fund**
> - How much is your employer putting in?
> - How much do you have today?
> - Where is the money invested?
> - What are the fees and charges?
> - Do you get any insurance cover, if so how much?
> - Can you add your own money to your employer's super fund?
> - Do you have any choice about how the money is invested?
>
> If you don't know the answer to these issues – ask! No reputable employer would not want to answer these questions.

Compulsory employer contributions

The Superannuation Guarantee legislation sets out the compulsory employer contributions to your super fund to the year 2003, expressed as a percentage of your gross income. Employers' contributions are calculated on the first $27,510 per quarter, or $110,040 p.a. of an employee's earnings (indexed 2001/02 amounts). Here are the percentages for each year:

1997/98	6%	2000/01	8%
1998/99	7%	2001/02	8%
1999/00	7%	2002/03 (and beyond)	9%

Making Money

The Liberal Government scrapped the proposed compulsory *employee* contributions which were set to start in 1997. This would have seen us reach a minimum compulsory super contribution of 15% by the financial year 2002/3. Why they got rid of an opportunity to get us to a decent minimum contribution level is completely beyond me!

The fact is, with a contribution level of around 15%, my children's retirement would be taken care of.

However, if you reckon that 15% would have been too ambitious a target and not achievable, think again. Take our near neighbour, Singapore. The combined contributions of employee and employer total 40%. The story in Spain is similar with combined contributions ensuring that 46% is invested in retirement savings. At the other end of the spectrum, plenty of other countries such as France, Belgium and Italy have contributions between 15% and 20%.

Despite the recommendations of various industry bodies and experts, it appears that the Federal Government is going to stick to its ambition of 9% compulsory super by 1 July 2002.

Choice of super investment options

Now, here's some good news. Most super funds have started to offer a choice of investment strategies. By this I mean you get to at least choose whether your money is invested conservatively in a capital stable fund (usually around 70% fixed interest and 30% shares), rather more aggressively in a balanced fund (a mix of fixed interest, property securities and shares), or more aggressively still in a growth fund (pretty much all shares). It's important that we have a choice – it's our money – and that we make the right choice.

Let me make this clear. A young employee of, say, 25, earning the average wage, would be some $500,000 worse off over 40 years at work by investing in a capital stable fund rather than a growth fund – and half a million dollars is a lot to give up. The fact is, while the more aggressive (higher risk) investment options will see you losing money in quite a few years, over the decades you'll be well in front.

I'll certainly be keeping my super in a growth strategy right up to my retirement. These days we retire, on average, for around 20 years, and if my money is going to last, I'll need to keep it exposed to growth assets throughout my lifetime.

It was proposed that from 1 July 2000 all employees, both new and existing, would be offered a choice of funds. This would require your employer to offer you a minimum of four funds to choose from. At the time of writing in March 2001, the date for commencement of this proposal has been deferred and is in the hands of the Government. Now, some people will whinge about having to make such a choice, but if you've read this book you'll know more than enough about choosing a fund that's right for you. It's a bit like picking a mortgage. Think about what features you want and check out the fees and charges. And, finally, if your boss won't give you any investment choice in the company fund, you can give it the flick and go for a fund that does give you the flexibility you want.

In a nutshell, choice is good for consumers – so embrace it!

The basic issues

When it comes down to it you only need to understand the *basics* of super (and, unless you are going to make super your hobby, I'd stick with the basics). Your car runs perfectly well without you understanding the operations of its electronic ignition or what its catalytic converter actually does, and my advice is to take the same approach to super. The rapidly changing minute detail of superannuation you should leave to your super fund administrator, company or personnel adviser. However, you *do need* to know about the investment performance of your fund and you *should* know about the following.

- How do you contribute?
- How much money can you put in?
- What happens to your contributions?
- How much should you contribute?
- How do you get your money out?
- Rolling over your benefits.

How do you contribute?

Employer contributions

Your employer will put an amount in for you under the Superannuation Guarantee scheme, unless you fall into one of the categories where your employer can ask for an exemption. The most common exemptions are listed on the next page.

Making Money

- You are aged 70 or over.
- You are aged under 18 and working less than 30 hours a week.
- You are earning less than $450 per month.
- You already have more than you are entitled to in super under the pension Reasonable Benefit Limit (see page 118, 'How much can you have in your super?').
- It's worth noting that the Government introduced a proposal to allow employees earning between $450 and $900 a month the option of choosing between the Super Guarantee Contributions and the equivalent in salary and wages (for employees under 18 the upper limit is set at $1,800 earned over two months). This 'opting out' proposal was to have begun way back in July 1998, but the commencement date has been deferred each year and at the time of writing in March 2001, is yet to be determined.

Your own contributions

The second way you can put money in is to add your own money to your employer's contribution. This can sometimes be done with what is called *salary sacrifice*. A salary sacrifice is typical industry jargon meaning that you choose to take less salary and have the amount you don't take added to your super. On the face of it this may sound silly, but it is actually a very smart move. Why? Well, like your employer's contributions which go into your super with only 15% *contributions tax* taken out, your salary sacrifice contributions are also taxed at only 15% (providing you earn less than $85,242; for those of you who earn more than this, I'll cover the new surcharge on page 127).

To illustrate – if your personal tax rate is 30%, $1 of salary less income tax leaves you with only 70 cents in your pocket for investment in some other (non-super) area. However, $1 going into your super, less the 15% contributions tax, gives you 85 cents invested in your name. In this case you're 15 cents or about 21% better off for every dollar that's invested in super rather than in some other asset and this benefit increases as your income – and personal tax rate – rises. It's a very good deal.

Now, if your employer's fund won't let you make a salary sacrifice, you can put in after-tax money (that is, money after your normal income tax has been taken out). Please note that most employers do let their employees salary sacrifice! For those of you covered by the Superannuation Guarantee, you won't generally be able to claim a tax deduction on your own contributions made out of your normal after-tax income. These contributions for which no tax deduction is allowable are called *undeducted contributions*.

Having said this, there are circumstances under which you may be entitled to a few small tax concessions if you 'top up' your employer's contributions made under the Superannuation Guarantee. Firstly, if your assessable income is less than $27,000 you can get a tax rebate of up to a maximum of $100 on your contributions. Secondly, if your assessable income is between $27,000 and $31,000 a maximum rebate of up to $100 is also available, but this reduces by 25 cents for every dollar of assessable income over $27,000. Lastly, if your assessable income is more than $31,000 you are not entitled to any tax rebates on your super contributions.

The good news is that the contributions tax does not apply to the contributions that you pay into your employer's fund out of your own after-tax income. And while your contributions are in the super system, a maximum rate of tax of 15% is charged on their investment earnings – which is a real advantage for the majority of working Australians.

Okay, but what if you are self-employed or an employee *not* covered by the Super Guarantee? In this case you get a tax deduction for either the lesser of your 'maximum deductible contribution' (which is explained below); or the first $3,000 you contribute, plus 75% of everything over $3,000.

Be aware that you don't have to put your extra contributions into your *employer's* fund. You can use what is known as *personal super*, offered by banks, building societies, fund managers and insurance companies. The personal super fund is 'yours', meaning it goes from job to job with you and you can choose your own investment options, but a note of caution – some personal super funds have very high fees and life insurance companies are the worst offenders here. Plans offered by banks tend to have lower fees – so shop around carefully!

How much money can you put in?

You, or your employer, can put quite a lot of tax-advantaged money into super. Money on which you or your employer can claim a tax deduction is limited by your *maximum deductible contribution* (MDC) which is age determined. The MDC limits for the financial year ending in June 2002 are:

Age	Maximum (tax) deductible contribution (indexed)
Under 35	$11,912
35 to 49	$33,087
50 and over	$78,054

For the purposes of most readers of this book, you can put as much of your own money that you *do not* claim a deduction on (undeducted contributions) as you like. However, if you are thinking of doing this please get expert advice as every case requires an individual approach depending on your personal circumstances.

How much can you have in your super?

The limiting factor to how much you can have in super is related to a dreadful piece of jargon called Reasonable Benefit Limits (RBL). Since 1 July 1994, this has been based on a flat dollar limit which is indexed to weekly earnings every year on 1 July.

For the financial year ending in June 2002 the RBL for a lump sum is $529,373, and the RBL for a pension is $1,058,742 (where you can take $529,373 as a lump sum and $529,373 as a pension).

Any amount you have above the new RBL levels, plus adjustments for wage increases, is called an *excess benefit*. Excess benefits when taken as a lump sum are taxed at the highest marginal rate plus the Medicare levy. Sadly, I doubt many of us will have such a 'wonderful' problem. Remember, an excess benefit means you have more than $529,373 (indexed) in super if you want it all as a lump sum, or more than $1,058,742 (indexed) if you want 50% as a lump sum and 50% as a pension.

What happens to your contributions?

In a *defined benefit fund*, as we discussed earlier, it does not really matter to you how the underlying investments perform – so long as your employer has the money to pay you when you leave or retire.

If you are employed by a shonky outfit whose boss has gone bankrupt two or three times and you are in a defined benefit fund, then I'd be very nervous. In reality, though, defined benefit funds are usually offered to employees by Government bodies and large companies and are therefore normally safe.

For those of you in an *accumulation fund* what happens to your money is of vital importance – investment earnings minus fees equals what you get!

Let's follow your money through the superannuation system and look at *deductible contributions* first. Remember a deductible contribution (one on which a tax deduction is allowable) is usually put in by your employer under the Superannuation Guarantee and some employers will put in more than they have to. You may be putting extra in by salary sacrifice or, if self-employed, you may be making deductible contributions to a personal superannuation fund. (Please refer to the chart on the next page.)

What happens to your *undeducted contributions*, which is money you put in and get no tax deduction on, is the same as what happens to deductible contributions, except there is no contributions tax or surcharge.

Your own contributions will pay a maximum 15% annual tax on the taxable earnings of your super, but remember this is a very attractive rate. If, for instance, you were earning over $6,000 p.a., you would be paying a higher rate of tax than 15% on any other (non-superannuation) investment income you received. Indeed, if you were earning over $20,000 p.a. you could be paying up to 30% tax on any (non-superannuation based) investment income you received. Once you earn over $50,000 your tax rate jumps to 42%, and above $60,000 it jumps to 47%.

The chapters on investment will give you the information you need to know about making the right investment decisions for your super money, but I want you to consider the following issues.

- Money in super is your money. Understand what's happening to it.
- Ask your employer about your ability to choose investment options.
- For those of you more than five years from retirement, super is a long-term investment. I recommend you consider choosing an investment option that holds long-term growth assets like shares. (Yes, they are more risky in the short term but in the long run will show better returns.)

Making Money

The following chart shows what happens to your superannuation money.

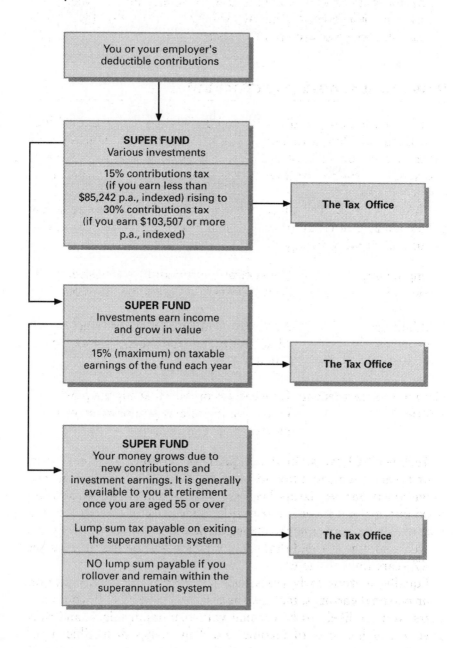

☞ KEY THOUGHT

I cannot stress how important it is that you understand how your super fund is investing the money, what the fees are, how it is taxed and how much you have in super.

How much should you contribute?

This is where theory and reality collide. The theoretical, ideal lifetime financial plan is to buy a home; contribute enough towards super to give you 75% of your final salary each year in retirement, and acquire a significant level of other investments such as property, cash or shares.

This is all very well of course, but the reality is that very few people manage to do all three. With this in mind, my general advice about contributing to super is:

Young people (under 25)	Concentrate on building a deposit for a home. Do not add to employer super.
Middle ages (26 to 45)	Accelerate your mortgage repayments. Make additional super contributions if possible.
Planning for retirement (46 to 65)	Concentrate on building super up as kids leave home and you pay out your mortgage.

Technically, I can argue that super is your best asset – better than your home – due to its tax advantages. Unfortunately, this all falls down when our regulators keep stuffing around with the rules. By maximising your super contributions later in life, you reduce the risk of being disadvantaged by rule changes. It would be a brave 18-year-old who decided that super was going to be their main asset in 47 years time at age 65.

Equally, in your early years you may be on a lower tax rate on your personal earnings, making super less tax effective. In your later years, you are likely to be earning your maximum salary, and thus paying a higher level of income tax. This makes deductible super contributions (even with the maximum super contributions tax of

Making Money

30% for high-income earners) and the 15% tax rate on super invest-ment earnings very attractive.

This is not to say, though, that starting super early is not a good idea. If you start contributing at age 18, you would need to put in around 12% of your salary to have 75% of your final salary in retirement. You might think 12% sounds like a lot, but if you start contributing to super later in life it will cost you much more than 12% for the same end benefit, as the table below shows.

Percentage of salary that would need to be put into super to give you 75% of your final salary each year in retirement commencing at age 65			
Males aged	% of gross salary into super	Females aged	% of gross salary into super
25	16.3	25	19.9
35	24.2	35	29.5
45	40.3	45	49
55	89.0	55	108.3

I suspect you're wondering why females need to put in more. It's simple. Women live around four to five years longer on average than males and, therefore, need their money to last longer.

☞ KEY THOUGHT

Even if you think that it's too hard to put such a high percentage of your salary aside and feel like giving up – don't. These numbers reflect the 'perfect' world. Remember, even $1 a day saved every day is worth real money over 10, 20 or 40 years.

How do you get your money out?

Since 1 July 1999, all employer and employee contributions to super are 'preserved'. This means we can't get our hands on it until we reach a certain age – depending on when you were born this can vary from 55 to 60 as the following shows.

- If you were born before 1 July 1960, your preservation age is 55.
- If you were born between 1 July 1960 and 30 June 1961, your preservation age is 56.
- If you were born between 1 July 1961 and 30 June 1962, your preservation age is 57.
- If you were born between 1 July 1962 and 30 June 1963, your preservation age is 58.
- If you were born between 1 July 1963 and 30 June 1964, your preservation age is 59.
- If you were born after 1 July 1964, your preservation age is 60.

Prior to July 1999, your super was considered to be preserved if the contributions were:

- made under the Superannuation Guarantee (employer's contribution)
- member-financed contributions
- company contributions made after 1 July 1996
- made to a personal super fund before 1 July 1994
- a deductible contribution made to super after 1 July 1994.

Not only did fund members have a preserved component of the super, but there were 'restricted non-preserved' or 'unrestricted non-preserved' segments as well that depended on the nature and timing of the contribution.

Restricted non-preserved benefits generally include any member contributions, voluntary employer contributions (prior to 22 December 1986 for private sector funds and 1 July 1990 for public sector funds) and any earnings on these amounts prior to 1 July 1999. Generally, you had to leave your job to access these benefits, either by cashing in the super, or rolling it over into another super fund.

According to the Australian Prudential Regulatory Authority (APRA), the Government body responsible for regulating superannuation, a member's unrestricted non-preserved super benefit can be accessed by an employee at any time and is the sum of:

- certain Eligible Termination Payments (ETPs – more on these later) that are not sourced from a super fund, approved deposit funds or deferred annuities (more on these later also). These are usually paid out by an employer when the member's employment is terminated;

Making Money

- unrestricted non-preserved benefits rolled over into the fund;
- any preserved and restricted non-preserved benefits where the member has fulfilled a condition of release which has no cashing restrictions;
- investment earnings on the above before 1 July 1999.

As I said earlier, any contributions made into super after 1 July 1999 are preserved. Fortunately, this law is not retrospective and does not affect the status of any non-preserved super you had prior to this date. Any non-preserved super can still be cashed in, in accordance with the super fund's governing rules. If you are not sure what component of your super is preserved or non-preserved, I suggest that you contact the manager of your super fund.

With all super benefits now deemed preserved, it's really very difficult to get your hands on it until you reach the preservation date. About the only way you can access it before you reach the preservation date is to obtain the approval from APRA based on incapacity to work or severe financial hardship. For more information on the early release of superannuation benefits, contact APRA on 13 10 60, or go to their web site located at www.apra.gov.au.

Please note, the hardship provisions were significantly toughened in 1997 and it's now much harder to access your super benefits before the preservation date.

Cashing in your benefits

When you cash in your benefits, your payment, called an *eligible termination payment* (ETP), is broken up into various categories. The main ones are:

- your *pre-1 July 1983 component*
- your *post-30 June 1983 component*
- your undeducted contributions
- your excess component (excess benefits).

Luckily, your super fund administrator will do this for you, but it is worth knowing that with your 'pre-' and 'post-' component, the administrator will look at your total days of work while in the super fund. Let's say you have worked 7,000 days: 3,500 were pre-1 July 1983 and 3,500 were post-30 June 1983. Your split between pre- and post- is the same, so 50% will be called pre- and 50% post-.

Now, let's look at how lump sum tax is applied if you take your money out of the super system.

ETP categories	Lump sum tax rates on withdrawal
Undeducted contributions	This is the bit you put in after 30 June 1983 and received no tax deduction for. The lump sum tax rate is zero.
Excess benefits	Bad news here. On withdrawal from super you pay the highest personal rate of tax (47%), plus the Medicare levy.
Pre-1 July 1983 component	95% is tax-free and 5% is added to your income for the year and taxed at your marginal tax rate, plus Medicare levy.
Post-30 June 1983 component	This bit is broken into two bits – money on which the 15% contributions tax has been paid, and money on which the contributions tax has *not* been paid.

Age	Lump sum tax payable on post-June 1983 *taxed* component	Lump sum tax payable on post-June 1983 *untaxed* component
Under 55	20%	30%
Over 55, $0 to $105,843*	0%	15%
Over 55, $105,843* plus	15%	30%

* The $105,843 is the 2001/02 amount and it is indexed to weekly earnings each 1 July.

Do-it-yourself super

If you are running a business, do-it-yourself super (DIYS) is an option you might have considered. DIYS simply means that you establish your own super fund and invest (within reason) where you choose.

It sounds great, but there are a few drawbacks. Firstly, it will cost you around $1,000 to set up the fund. Then it's likely to cost you another $1,000 a year in accounting, auditing, ASIC lodgement fees and general running costs.

In addition, I see DIYS funds making some shocking investment decisions. For instance, many DIYS funds like the sound of owning a holiday home for the use of the fund members. However, not only is this generally an awful investment, but you're likely to get your tax deductible contributions knocked back. Investments in a super fund must be genuine and appropriate to fund your retirement – and this eliminates the boat, the holiday home and the racing greyhound.

If you are going to go for DIYS, then I'd recommend you have at least $100,000 in the fund and that you set up a sensible investment strategy. (By regulation, DIYS funds must have a written strategy, which is a good idea anyway.)

Providing you have the time and skills to build a strong portfolio that will support you in the decades of retirement, DIYS is a perfectly valid option. To set one up I'd suggest you talk to an accountant, but do make sure you understand the fees to establish and run the fund before you proceed. After all, you want your DIYS to support *your* future plans, not your accountant's.

Proposed new minimum income levels

If you earn under $450 a month, your employer can get an exemption and simply pay the compulsory super surcharge *to you in your regular pay cheque*, rather than putting it in a super fund. Some years ago the Government proposed to raise this income limit to $900 a month (or $1,800 over two months if you are less than 18). This proposal was to have been introduced in July 1998 and again in July 1999, but was deferred each time and at the time of writing there is still no word on when this option will become available.

So, assuming this long-mooted change eventually comes to pass, what should you do?

Firstly, it will be *up to you to negotiate with your employer* if you want the extra super money in the hand, rather than it going to a fund. Then if you really need the money to survive, or if you are only working for a short period of time, I'd take the cash. But if you are a permanent part-time worker, I'd seriously think about sticking with super unless you are a good saver. Sure, if you put the extra money into your mortgage each pay day, then I'd do just that. But if the extra money in your pocket will just get spent, then I reckon you're better off building it up for your future in a decent super fund.

High income superannuation surcharge

Now to the bad news. Until August 1996 all contributions made to super with a pre-tax dollar were only liable to pay a 15% contributions tax. The Government has since decided that this was too favourable to high-income earners and has imposed a new surcharge. In 2001/02 for each $1,000 you earn over $85,242 (indexed), this surcharge adds 1% to your super contributions tax until you reach $103,507 (indexed). At this stage the surcharge is 15%, giving someone on this salary or above it a *total super contributions tax of 30%*.

The obvious question here is, 'Should high-income earners give up on superannuation?' and my answer remains, 'No'. Let's not forget that at this level of income you'll be paying personal income tax of 48.5%, including the Medicare levy. Sure, if this is you I'm certain you'll hate paying a 30% contributions tax to super, but paying 48.5% income tax on that money if you take it home is much worse.

From a tax planning strategy viewpoint this may be a good time to consider whether you have any flexibility in managing your income levels. Many Australians in small business will undoubtedly consider lowering their salary, or their partner's (if they are involved in the business) to ensure that this new super surcharge is kept to a minimum.

If you are self-employed and planning big super contributions this year, then get along to your accountant or financial planner to see what flexibility there is with your income to legally minimise the impact of this tax.

Rolling over your benefits

While *rolling over* (where you transfer your money from one concessionally taxed super fund to another) sounds like something your pet dog may do, it does have a number of advantages.
- Lump sum tax is not paid. Therefore, you have more money working for you.

Making Money

- You continue to pay a maximum tax rate of 15% on investment earnings in 'lump sum' rollovers such as approved deposit funds or deferred annuities, and zero tax if you rollover into an annuity or pension.
- If you at least rollover until age 55, your lump sum tax on taking the money drops quite significantly as you can see in the table on page 125.

So far so good, but just what are your rollover options? You actually have quite a few. You can rollover into:
- another super fund
- an approved deposit fund (ADF)
- a deferred annuity (DA)
- an immediate annuity
- a lifetime pension or annuity
- an allocated pension.

A brief description of these will help here, as follows.

Approved deposit funds and deferred annuities

Approved deposit funds and deferred annuities are managed investment funds within the superannuation environment into which you can transfer (rollover) any eligible termination payments you receive when you change jobs or retire. You can remain invested in an ADF or DA until age 65.

There's no real difference between approved deposit funds and deferred annuities except most banks, fund managers and credit unions offer ADFs, while life insurance companies and friendly societies offer DAs.

Inside an ADF or DA you can choose your investment options and alter these as you see fit. You can also rollover from one organisation's ADF or DA to another – but watch the fees! Your investment income will be taxed at the maximum 15% concessional rate while inside an ADF or DA.

Immediate annuities

Typically you would buy one of these from a life insurance company. In exchange for your lump sum investment you get a regular income stream. The amount of income you get depends upon your age, sex and the interest rate at the time you buy.

You can nominate a *lifetime annuity*, but I'd suggest you'd want to be in good health to do this. With a traditional lifetime annuity, if you buy it one day and die the next, all your money is gone.

A *term-certain annuity* is the same as a lifetime annuity except payments are guaranteed for a fixed time. If you bought a 10-year term-certain annuity on Tuesday and died on Wednesday, your estate would receive the annuity payments for 10 years – a much safer bet for your beneficiaries.

Part of your income may be considered tax-free and you may also be able to get a tax rebate.

Lifetime pension or annuity

Also known as 'immediate annuities', these are a retirement income investment where an individual invests their superannuation or other money and receives an income periodically. The capital is not accessible, and there is little income flexibility. The payments are guaranteed for the person's lifetime and the amount of income you get depends on your age, sex and the interest rate prevailing at the time you bought the policy.

Allocated pensions and allocated annuities

You can choose to rollover into an allocated pension or allocated annuity with your ETP benefits. These can be benefits that are not preserved if you are under 55, are 55 or over and retired, or over 65 and not retired.

The big pluses with an allocated pension/annuity are: that you do not pay any capital gains tax on investment earnings within the fund and you will receive a 15% tax rebate on part (or all) of your income, depending on which part is 'deductible' and which part is 'undeductible'.*

---

* If you had contributed undeducted contributions (extra money that you have contributed yourself), you would receive a tax deduction for these based on your life expectancy. For example, let's assume you have $100,000 in an allocated pension. Of this amount, $50,000 comes from post-1983 employer contributions and the remaining $50,000 comes from undeducted contributions. If your life expectancy is 20 years, then you'll receive an annual tax deduction of $2,500 (being the $50,000 undeducted contributions divided by 20 years). This is the 'deductible' amount.

Making Money

Other benefits of allocated pensions include being able to determine the level of income you want (within maximum and minimum levels), and being able to access lump sums at the normal lump sum tax rate. Also from 1 July 2001, franking credits from Australian shares held by the pension fund will be passed on to members.

But do be careful. Unlike a normal lifetime annuity which pays you for your lifetime, with an allocated pension or annuity you can spend all your money taking a higher income stream (or cash withdrawals) than your money earns in income and capital growth.

This should be carefully planned for in your retirement strategy. I don't mind you spending capital, in fact I encourage it, but not so that you run out of money too soon!

⊶ KEY THOUGHT

How you get your money out of superannuation depends on your age and your personal plan. But always ensure you look at all the options and weigh them up before you do anything. A mistake here can be very expensive.

What about insurance?

If you need life insurance, your super fund is likely to be a good place to buy it. Many funds offer automatic cover, other funds allow you to choose what you want. Make sure you know where you stand with your fund.

Do remember that any death benefit you get will count against your RBL. Your fund administrator can help here.

The reason I like to buy my death cover inside my company super fund is that it is done on a group, wholesale basis. That makes it cheaper, and rather than buying it with an after-tax dollar that I get in my pocket, it's paid for with a dollar which has only had the 15% contributions tax taken out, or 30% taken out if you earn $103,507 or more.

Spouse superannuation

This is all about getting a tax rebate of up to $540 p.a. for the super contributions you make. These are the conditions.

- You have a spouse.
- You contribute to your spouse's super fund.
- The contributions are not deductible to you the taxpayer.
- Both you and your spouse are Australian citizens.

For you to get the maximum tax rebate of $540, your spouse must earn no more than $10,800 p.a., and you must make a contribution of $3,000 p.a. to their super fund. If your total annual contribution exceeds $3,000, that portion above $3,000 is non-rebatable, and any annual contribution less than $3,000 is rebatable at 18%.

If your spouse earns more than $10,800, but less than $13,800, you will be eligible for a *part* tax rebate on your annual contributions to their super.

You can make contributions to your spouse's super by instalments throughout the financial year, or by contributing one lump sum by June 30.

Look, if you can cut your tax bill by up to $540 and make an investment for your spouse, it's certainly worth considering.

⌐ KEY THOUGHTS

- Super should be a part of your financial strategy.
- The ideal plan is to build three pools of wealth – home, super and other investments.
- Concentrate on your mortgage first, then build up your personal contributions to super.
- At present super is complex, confusing and the rules change. But if super is made unattractive or the Government 'steals' it with increased taxes, future governments will just have to pay us a pension.
- Super must remain an attractive option, and most new rule changes are making things simpler – not harder.
- Super *is* good. It is tax advantaged, it compounds in value over the years and, more importantly, you can't touch most of it until you retire!

CHAPTER TEN
Tax

Death and taxes – life's only certainties, so the old saying goes. However, since the introduction of The New Tax System in July 2000 there has even been uncertainty about tax. Well, while it's still certain we will have to pay it, for many people a great deal of confusion surrounds the new reporting obligations to the Tax Office and how much tax they will have to pay, and when.

The most significant feature of The New Tax System has been the introduction of a 10% goods and services tax (GST). GST is an indirect tax, meaning it is applied to goods and services rather than being directly levied on income. We have always had indirect taxes, most notably the now abolished wholesale sales tax, and a number of indirect taxes still remain, including stamp duty.

What is different about GST is that it is what the experts call a 'broad-based consumption tax', which in English means it's paid on the consumption or purchase of goods, that it's ultimately paid by consumers, and with few exceptions it applies to all taxpayers. This is no coincidence, since the GST is an attempt by Government to take some of the tax burden away from wage and salary earners, and to collect at least some tax from those involved in the so-called 'black' (cash) economy, who previously managed to pay little or no tax at all.

Now, I am strongly in favour of the principles behind a goods and services tax, and given the income tax cuts, most consumers have in reality felt little pain from the GST. Its implementation, however, has been a disaster at a business level, but the concept of reducing income taxes when we make money and taxing us when we buy things makes absolute sense to me. People should be given encouragement to work and do well, and high taxes on income don't provide it. The other benefit of a GST is that, because you pay tax as you spend, it makes those in the cash economy contribute at least something through the tax system to our schools, hospitals and infrastructure.

Now, whilst the GST, the BAS, PAYG and all the rest of it are very much with us, many of the fundamentals of the tax system remain unchanged. We still have normal income tax to pay, and there's not much likelihood of that being ditched in a hurry.

Of course, you don't have any reason to worry about income tax if you don't have any income. I am always quite amused when people complain to me about how much tax they're paying. No one *enjoys* paying tax but, it seems to me that if someone is paying a small fortune in tax, then they're also making at least twice as much.

Having said this, there's no sense in paying more tax than you have to. And there are a number of perfectly sound and legal ways of reducing your tax bill which you should take advantage of if you can. In other words, you should try to *avoid* tax where possible as distinct from *evading* tax, which is illegal as well as quite unproductive.

So this means that you shouldn't participate in an investment simply because it will reduce your tax bill. You should only ever invest in something if you are well satisfied it will increase your wealth, treating any tax reductions that the investment receives or generates along the way as a bonus. Think about it – no one has ever become rich by taking losses and building up consequent tax write-offs.

⚬— KEY THOUGHT

Try to reduce your tax, certainly, but aim to increase your wealth.

Steps to tax minimisation

Regardless of any tax benefits that may flow to you from participating in certain investments, from the method in which you invest, or from how you structure the way you receive your income, on a day-to-day basis there are a few fundamental and simple tax reducing steps you need to follow.

Step 1. Check permissible tax deductions

The most fundamental step is to make yourself aware of all the permissible tax deductions that relate to your job. I can give a few examples here – though I wouldn't attempt to nominate and detail all the possible tax deductions that relate to all jobs as they are so varied. Some deductions are the cost of toys for nannies, black suits (but not shirts) for funeral directors, calculator batteries for draftsmen, safety boots for doctors, the depreciation of television sets and anti-VDU-glare tinted glasses for advertising executives, and self-education expenses for students studying in the same field they are working in.

Special deductions unique to certain industries apply to the following: airline industry and Australian Defence Force personnel, building industry workers, cleaners, employee lawyers, factory workers, hairdressers, hospitality industry employees, nurses, performing artists, police, real-estate sales employees, shop assistants, teachers and truck drivers. Information on these industry-specific deductions, as well as on general deductions, is readily available from the Australian Taxation Office (ATO). You can also find out what work-related expenses you can claim by talking to an accountant, to a representative of your union or industry association, or to someone in your company's accounting or personnel department.

Step 2. Keep good records

Making sure you record all your expenses properly and having adequate proof of incurring them is fundamental to good tax management. In the likelihood of undergoing a desk audit – where you get to meet very inquisitive representatives from the Tax Office face to face – make sure you can verify whatever work-related expenses you have claimed as deductions in your tax returns. If your records are inadequate and you cannot substantiate your claims, you may have to pay additional tax and a penalty. In more serious cases, you can be prosecuted.

If the total of your claims is $300 or less, you must keep a record of how you worked out each of your claims. If the total of your claims is more than $300, the records you will need are receipts, invoices or similar documentary evidence. Cheque butts are not acceptable.

Whatever you do, make sure you keep your records for five years from the date you lodged your tax return. This is the period stipulated by the Tax Office.

Step 3. Strategies and investments

There are a number of worthwhile tax minimisation strategies and preferentially taxed investments available to everyone, no matter what their occupation is. These include:
- income splitting
- income timing
- negative gearing
- franked dividends
- superannuation and managed investments in retirement
- offset accounts.

Now, let's look at these tax minimisation ideas in some detail.

Income splitting
Income splitting is a highly effective way in which couples can minimise the total amount of tax they pay. The principle is very simple – income is held in the name of the partner on the lower marginal tax rate so that the actual amount of tax paid is minimised. (Your 'marginal rate' is the highest level of income tax you pay.)

Let's say we have a couple, Kevin and Fay. Kevin earns $38,000 p.a. and Fay, who does some part-time work when not looking after the children, earns $3,000 p.a. Fay's income is below the (current) tax-free threshold of $6,000 so she pays no tax. Kevin, a PAYG (Pay As You Go) employee, has $7,780 in tax deducted from his annual pay.

Now, let's assume the couple has $25,000 cash which they wish to put into a term deposit paying interest of 6% p.a. ($1,500). If the term deposit is put in Kevin's name, his annual income will rise to $39,500 ($38,000 + $1,500). At this income level his marginal tax rate will be 30%. Therefore, he would pay $450 in tax on the $1,500 income, retaining only $1,050 ($1,500 x 30% = $450).

It would make much more sense from a tax point of view to put the term deposit in Fay's name. The $1,500 income flowing from it would raise her overall income level to $4,500 – which is still below the $6,000 threshold at which tax kicks in. Therefore Fay would pay no tax on the $1,500 interest income.

Making Money

Timing income

Income is generally taxable only in the year in which it is *received*, not the year in which it is *earned*. So if you did some extra paid work towards the end of one financial year knowing that you were going to do less paid work in the following financial year, it would be a good idea to defer payment for the work until July. This payment would be counted as income for the new year where your lower overall level of income could attract a lower marginal tax rate.

This is especially relevant if you are just about to retire, because you can save yourself thousands of dollars in tax liabilities by retiring in July rather than June. It's also relevant as far as capital gains tax is concerned. If you choose to sell assets that are subject to capital gains tax, you should always try to do so at times when you are receiving the least amount of income. This is because capital gains are added to your income and then taxed at your marginal tax rate.* Adding capital gains to your income when it and your marginal tax rate are lower means paying less tax.

To illustrate, let's say you decided to have six months off work to take an extended overseas holiday, and decided to sell some shares (purchased after 19 September 1985 when capital gains tax was introduced) to help pay for the trip. The best time to sell the shares would be in the tax year where you weren't earning a full year's income. So, for example, if you intended to leave in June you'd end up paying a full year's tax on that financial year's income plus the capital gains tax on the sale of the shares – all of which could raise your marginal tax rate for the year. But, if you delayed your trip by one month to July, the capital gains from the shares would be your only income for the next six months – meaning your total income for that tax year (and thus your marginal tax rate) could be much lower.

You can also maximise your deductions in years of high income by early payment of deductible expenses. For example, you could pay your income protection insurance – which is fully tax deductible – for 12 months in advance. If you're self-employed you could also put extra money into superannuation in the high-income years.

---

* Your marginal tax rate is the rate of tax you pay on any additional income you may earn. It is therefore the *highest* rate of tax you pay.

Negative gearing

An investment is said to be negatively geared when the costs of holding it – including interest charges on the loan used to finance it – exceed the income the investment produces. In other words, the investment is negatively geared if it produces a running loss when all income and costs, including interest, are taken into account. In most cases negative gearing occurs in connection with property investment, though it can arise when borrowing to invest in any income-producing asset, such as shares.

The significance of the running loss is that it is tax deductible against any other assessable income you may have, including your salary or wages. This has the effect of reducing the *real* size of the loss, especially if you are on higher marginal tax rates.

Let's say, for example, you borrowed to buy an investment property that after 12 months generated a loss of $2,000, including interest repayments on the loan. This $2,000 would be tax deductible against your other income.

If your marginal tax rate was 47%, this tax deduction would reduce the *real* cost of holding the property to $1,060.* If your marginal tax rate was 30%, the *real* cost of holding the property would be reduced to $1,400.†

Now, borrowing is a perfectly legitimate way to fund certain investments. But be very aware that when you borrow to invest, you are using money you don't own. If the investment fails, you still owe this money – and that will not make you very happy!

The key thing about borrowing to invest is to make as sure as possible that the underlying investment is sound, meaning that when you realise (sell) the asset you stand a good chance of making a positive return – after all the costs of buying, holding and selling are accounted for. While negative gearing generates tax deductions that minimise the real cost of borrowing to invest, it should never of itself be the reason for investing. For more detail on negative gearing see Chapter Twelve, 'Investing in Property'.

---

* $2,000 × 47% = $940; $2,000 – $940 = $1,060.
† $2,000 × 30% = $600; $2,000 – $600 = $1,400.

☞ KEY THOUGHT

Don't ever participate in an investment simply because it promises good tax deductions. You should only ever invest if you believe the asset will ultimately realise a profit and, if you enjoy tax deductions along the way, treat that as a bonus.

Franked share dividends

Share dividend income is taxable, but if the dividends are 'franked', it means they are distributed to shareholders from after-tax company profits. Now, because tax is paid by the company before you receive these franked dividends, and because you as a shareholder are a co-owner of the company, these dividends are deemed by the Tax Office to be income on which *you* have already paid (some) tax. And depending on your tax rate, it's income on which you may not have to pay any more tax, or may even be owed a refund.

Dividends can be 'fully franked', which is where they have been distributed from profits taxed at the full company tax rate of 30% (34% for the year ended 30 June 2001). They can also be 'partly franked' – where tax has been paid against them at anything up to 30% – and 'unfranked', which is where no tax has been paid against them, making them fully taxable as income in your hands.

If you receive fully franked dividends (pre-taxed at 30%), and your tax rate is also 30%, you will owe no further tax on this dividend income. If your tax rate is higher than the fully franked dividend tax rate, say 47%, you will still owe the Tax Office some tax on these dividends, being the difference between the fully franked rate of 30% and your rate of 47%. In this example you will need to pay tax that is equivalent to 17% of the dividends' value (47% – 30% = 17%).

Conversely, if your tax rate is below the rate at which the dividends have been taxed, you will receive a tax credit equivalent to the value of that difference to reduce your overall tax liability. Since July 2001, once franking credits have been used to reduce any tax to nil, any remaining credits will be refunded. Previously the franking credits could only be used to offset the amount of tax payable, and this new rule is a commendable move by the Government to make shares a more attractive investment for low-income earners.

Again, just as you shouldn't borrow to invest in property just to take advantage of the tax benefits of negative gearing, nor should you buy shares simply because their dividends are fully franked and will give you after-tax money. Only buy shares if you believe that they will show decent and steady growth over time. If their dividends are franked, that's fine, but it should not be the reason for buying the shares. As ever, it's the quality of the underlying asset that really counts. (See Chapter Thirteen, 'Investing in Shares' for more information about franked dividends.)

Superannuation and related managed investments

Superannuation is taxed very preferentially in order to encourage good long-term growth and a high level of public support. In the simplest terms, your contributions to super are generally taxed lightly, your earnings whilst in the fund are also taxed lightly, and the tax on your eventual pay-out is favourable too.

Once in retirement, your superannuation pay-out can be put towards a range of other preferentially taxed managed investments including rollovers, annuities and allocated pensions. The tax provisions applying to these investments are substantial and can be very complicated, particularly in the case of exiting super, and I have already detailed them in Chapter Nine, 'Superannuation'.

So should you just invest in these retirement-related investments simply because they receive good tax treatment? Well, super does generate respectable returns which alone would make it worthy of an investor's attention. At ipac securities our research shows that you can expect real, long-term returns from balanced super funds in the range of 3% to 5%, and for growth super funds in the range of 5% to 8%, all after fees, tax and inflation, and there is nothing wrong with these numbers.

The fundamental answer to the question is that, once again, you should not participate in these investments simply because of their tax treatment. The sometimes stringent conditions that apply to them may not suit your circumstances or wishes and, as ever, the quality of the investment's asset base, earning potential and financial structure should remain the most important considerations. However, that said, the tax treatment of these investments (super especially) is so attractive that you would need some pretty serious doubts about the products' underlying worth or appropriateness not to make them a part of your retirement plans.

Making Money

Interest-offset accounts

If you have a savings account earning interest and the interest is added to the balance of the account, you'll obviously pay tax on it. But, instead of having the interest added to your savings account, you can 'offset' it against a loan account such as your mortgage where it will reduce the size of the debt – *and attract no tax*. Interest earned on one account and offset against debt in another account is tax-free – because you haven't really earned any income.

If you do offset interest against a mortgage account, you can benefit from the double-whammy effect of putting a real hole in your long-term interest costs without any dilution through tax.

Here's how it works. Let's say you have a mortgage of $100,000 with interest charged at 7.5%, and an offset account (a deposit) with a balance of $10,000. Instead of receiving interest on the deposit of $10,000 and paying interest on the full balance of the mortgage, interest of 7.5% is charged only on the *first* $90,000 of the mortgage ($100,000 less $10,000) and no interest is paid on the deposit.

This has significant tax benefits, as you have never received the interest on the offset account, so you pay no tax on it. But it means you are getting the full benefit of the return without losing up to half in tax, and paying off your mortgage sooner.

End-of-year tax schemes

End-of-year tax schemes sit at the other end of the tax minimisation spectrum – the bad end. With depressing regularity, my in-tray overflows with prospectuses for tax-driven investment schemes at the end of each financial year.

My general advice on tax schemes is like the old saying about trading the futures market, that is, 'If you feel like becoming involved, lie down until the feeling goes away.' Sadly, many tax-driven investment schemes offer little more than a tremendous opportunity for shysters to separate you from your money.

Often the investments promise outstanding longer term returns, coupled with short-term, indeed immediate, tax write-offs while the venture is in the establishment phase. These immediate tax write-offs (or, more accurately, 'claimed' immediate tax write-offs – only the Tax Office can rule decisively on this after you've submitted your tax return), can be used to reduce your tax liability in the current financial year – and this is their significant selling point.

Now, there is normally nothing intrinsically wrong with the products at the heart of these investment schemes. They may be flowers, farmed prawns, yabbies, pine plantations, or feature films, which, in the right hands and circumstances, can generate good returns. What is wrong is that many of the schemes are put together by, to put it politely, 'city financiers', whose main interest is in raising money for a fee.

How do the schemes work?

Normally, the investor purchases a share in a venture in the form of one or more monetary units. Each unit may be worth $1,000, $5,000, whatever. There are a finite number of units for sale. The venture is often a start-up operation and the proceeds from the sale of the units are designed to fund its establishment.

Let's take the theoretical example of a cut-flower venture, a protea plantation. Financial projections for the first two or three years will show a loss while the plants are still too young to bear commercial quantities of flowers. During this stage the investor generates ongoing tax losses to be offset against other income. So far so good, if you don't mind making losses, that is.

Projections show that the protea plantation will generate positive cash flows from Year 4 when the plants have reached maturity. From Years 5 through to 15 the money will roll in and the investor will supposedly laugh all the way to the bank.

Odds are, though, this won't happen. What is more likely to happen is that the scheme will fail. Any amount of things can go wrong. The market may be weaker than predicted or harder to crack, the plants may be struck by one or more fatal diseases, a killer frost may strike, some plants may have a commercial life of only five years instead of 15, the operators may be incompetent or even downright crooked. (Most of these problems actually did befall a major flower investment scheme featuring proteas. There have also been a string of badly performing investment schemes based on blueberries, macadamias, avocados, yabbies, pine trees and movies.)

Generally, the highly optimistic projections of tax-driven investment schemes are rarely achieved, and investors invariably end up taking a bath, getting far greater tax losses than they bargained for. And no matter how you dress them up, tax deductible losses are still just that – losses.

Making Money

But the capital losses are not the whole of the story. All too often the tax deductions you claim are ultimately disallowed by the Tax Office. Amongst other things, this happens if the promoters of the scheme do not do what they say they will do in the prospectus, or if the scheme never earns any income. It's worth noting too that where a so-called *product ruling* has been obtained from the Tax Office for the scheme, supposedly guaranteeing the tax deductibility of the scheme, that this 'guarantee' is absolutely conditional, once again, on the promoters following the prospectus and the scheme earning income. If either are not met, the product ruling is made void and the tax deductions are disallowed. And when the tax deductions you have claimed are disallowed, this is money you then owe the Tax Office. What's more, on top of this, you may also be slugged with a tax 'underpayment penalty', which depending on the circumstances can be up to 100% of the unpaid tax.

Be aware too that the odds of picking a tax-driven investment scheme that does deliver the goods are very poor, at best. Investment analysts Van Eyk Capital reviewed 73 of these tax schemes in 2000, but were only able to recommend five. Furthermore, it found that around $800 million was invested in tax schemes in 2000, and that about 80% of that money was lost. It also concluded that about half of the schemes people invested in had no possibility of ever being viable.

Look, the trick is not to get into an end-of-financial-year panic about paying too much tax and then go jumping into a tax minimising investment scheme. If you really have a swag of tax to pay (meaning you have earned an even bigger swag of income), try a short-term tax minimising strategy instead, like borrowing to invest in shares or property (as a long-term investment) and, pre-paying the interest on your borrowings, thereby getting a tax deduction this financial year.

☞ KEY THOUGHT

The correct approach to tax planning is to start on 1 July. Making tax decisions in consultation with a tax accountant and making sensible investment decisions throughout the year will see you much richer in the long term, and much less stressed in the lead up to 30 June.

Should you do your own tax?

There are around ten million Australian taxpayers, about a third of whom it's estimated do their own tax returns. Now, given the relative difficulty and potential pitfalls of completing your own returns, three million-odd do-it-yourselfers may seem to be a surprisingly large number. But if you take care, doing your own tax is a sensible and inexpensive choice – so long as your financial affairs are uncomplicated.

If you are a salaried employee with simple work deductions and no involvement in, say, a family trust or company, there really should be no need to seek the assistance of an accountant or tax agent to handle your return. But just remember you can seriously short-change yourself by not knowing what work-related expenses you are legitimately entitled to claim as tax deductions, and by keeping inadequate records.

Also remember that acceptable work-related expenses vary tremendously from occupation to occupation and advice from friends and colleagues should not be acted upon until its accuracy can be checked. The Tax Office is the right place to get this basic advice.

Do-it-yourself tax returns are the wrong choice, however, if you have complex financial affairs. By 'complex', I mean, for example, being involved in a family trust, partnership or company; receiving income from property which involves depreciation adjustments; receiving franked dividends from shares; and almost any matter involving capital gains. (In other words, the present or future financial affairs of many of the readers of this book!)

It's been my overwhelming experience with clients in these circumstances that employing a competent accountant to do your tax returns (and provide you with tax advice throughout the year) is a move that more than pays for itself. It saves you time and headaches, you'll probably pay less tax or get bigger rebates, you'll be better prepared in the event of an audit, and your accountant's fees are fully tax deductible!

Tax and investment

From July 2000, Australia's tax system underwent a major overhaul, which following something of an uproar, is still being fine-tuned as I write in early 2001. However, the taxes most relevant to anyone

Making Money

involved in investment are personal income tax, Pay As You Go (PAYG) tax (which replaced the Pay As You Earn and provisional tax systems from July 2000), and capital gains tax.

Personal income tax

Income is clearly more than just your salary or wages. It also includes returns from investments such as interest on term deposits or from bonds, rental income or dividend income from shares. This investment income, over and above the income you generate from your paid employment, is fully taxable at your highest rate of tax (your marginal rate) as per the current personal income tax rates.

The income tax rates are subject to change at any time, but in 2000–2001 were as follows.

Taxable income ($)	Tax ($)	% on excess
6,000	Nil	17
20,000	2,380	30
50,000	11,380	42
60,000	15,580	47

To this tax a Medicare levy of 1.5% of your total taxable income should be added. It applies to most residents whose income exceeds a certain level, which in 2001/01 was $13,807.

Let's say your annual taxable salary is $40,000. Based on the scale above, up to $20,000 will be taxed $2,380, and on the remaininag $20,000, you will be taxed at 30% (your 'marginal' tax rate, or the highest rate of tax you pay). The total tax on your salary will therefore be $8,380, which represents an *average* tax rate of 21% of your salary.* To the tax of $8,380 must be added the Medicare levy of $600 ($40,000 × 1.5% = $600) making the total tax payable $8,980.

On top of your salary, if you received $900 in interest income from a term deposit, the $900 would be added to your salary to produce a total income of $40,900. The $900 would, therefore, be taxed at the relevant marginal rate which in this case is 30% (plus the 1.5% Medicare levy).

Also note that a 1% levy on your total taxable income – *in addition* to the 1.5% Medicare levy – applies to individuals earning more than

* $2,380 + ($20,000 × 30%) = $2,380 + $6,000 = $8,380.

$50,000 p.a., or to couples earning over $100,000 *who don't have private health insurance*. If you do have private health insurance, this 1% levy does not apply.

Pay As You Go tax

Before the introduction of The New Tax System in July 2000, investors who earned over $1,000 in 'unearned' income (dividends, interest and other investment returns) were required to pay provisional tax. However, post-July 2000, provisional tax has been scrapped, and now income from investments is covered by the Pay As You Go (PAYG) tax system. As I write in early 2001, changes have recently been made to the reporting requirements for people earning investment income, and by the time you read this, further changes may have been made.

As it currently stands, however, if you receive income from investments and you *are* registered for GST, for example you run a business as a sole trader, you are required to complete a Business Activity Statement (BAS), which is a form for reporting your tax obligations to the Tax Office (for more on the BAS refer to 'Businesses and tax' on pages 154–156). If you are an investor and you are *not* registered for GST, the form you complete to let the Tax Office know your tax payments is an Instalment Activity Statement (IAS).

If you paid tax of less than $250 in the previous year, you are excluded from the PAYG system and only need to lodge an annual tax return, upon which the Tax Office assesses your income.

As a general rule, if you paid provisional tax on your investment income under the old system, you will pay PAYG tax under the current system. If your last tax return showed investment income of over $1,000, it's likely the Tax Office will notify you that you are now required to pay PAYG. They will also tell you what your 'instalment rate' is. This is the rate of tax that you can use to calculate your PAYG tax instalments, and it is based on your 'effective' rate of tax, which is the overall percentage of tax you paid on last year's income.

For people receiving investment income, if you paid *less* than $8,000 tax in the previous year, you can pay your PAYG in just one instalment, and your annual income tax instalment notice will tell you the amount to pay.

If you pay PAYG annually, you need to lodge an annual Instalment

Making Money

Activity Statement (IAS) together with your PAYG payment. This is due in April 2002, but from 2003 the payment date will be moved to 21 October to bring individuals into line with small companies. You still need to lodge an Income Tax return for each year.

If your tax bill in the previous year was *more* than $8,000, instead of paying your PAYG annually, you are required to pay quarterly. You fill out an IAS form each quarter and, as a rule of thumb, you can either:

- pay an instalment the Tax Office calculates for you, or
- work out the instalment yourself, multiplying your investment income for the quarter by your instalment rate.

Whichever method you choose for your first quarterly instalment, you must continue to use it for the remaining instalments of the tax year.

Payments are made for the quarters July to September, October to December, January to March and April to June, with the payment being due in the month following. For example, your PAYG tax is due in October for income earned in July to September.

Remember, these requirements are for people who are *not* registered for GST. If you also face the spectre of calculating and paying GST, you need to complete a BAS. Note also that the IAS and BAS are not the same as your annual tax return, which you still need to complete every year in addition to the IAS or BAS.

For people earning investment income, PAYG looks a lot like the old provisional tax, particularly following changes made in early 2001. One of the complaints levelled at provisional tax was that tax was often paid on investment income before it was even received by the investor. Under the current system, if you are required to pay quarterly PAYG and you pay the sum determined by the Tax Office, you could once again find yourself in this position.

Most importantly for investors, you need to be careful to put aside part of your investment income to meet the demands of the Tax Office.

Capital gains tax

Capital gains tax (CGT) is another tax of relevance to investors. It's enormously complicated and, personally, I leave the calculations to my accountant. Having said that, it's useful to know how CGT is calculated and to understand the principles behind it, particularly since the way the Tax Office calculates capital gains has undergone a major overhaul since September 1999.

Now, the tax office offers an explanation (of sorts) at its web site located at www.ato.gov.au as to how capital gains tax is calculated for shares and other investments, and when capital gains tax needs to be paid on the family home.

If you think you may be liable for capital gains you should read this material – and then ask an accountant to explain it to you! Also, make sure you keep good records for any investment prone to capital gains, such as shares or property, otherwise you'll end up paying too much.

- Capital gains tax is payable on any capital gain made after the disposal of non-exempt assets (the family home is exempt from CGT, for example) acquired after 19 September 1985.
- A 'capital gain' is the difference between the cost of the asset and the amount you receive when you sell it (so long as you get more than you paid for it).
- The 'cost' includes the original purchase price, the incidental expenses of acquisition and disposal, and any capital improvements in between.
- Prior to 21 September 1999, capital gains on assets held for over 12 months were calculated by converting the investment's costs into today's dollars using a calculation based on an inflation index. This had the effect of reducing any tax you might pay, as the gain was worked out according to the real (adjusted-for-inflation) value of the asset, not the nominal (dollar) value.
- A new way of calculating the capital gain has been introduced for assets purchased after 11 a.m. AEST, 21 September 1999. If the asset has been held for over 12 months, a 'discount method' is used, where only 50% of the capital gain is taxable, but the cost base is calculated without the use of indexation.
- For assets purchased before 11 a.m. AEST, on 21 September 1999, you have the choice of using either the 'indexation method' or the 'discount method', and it would certainly be wise to see which method will give you the smaller capital gain to report to the Tax Office (this is perfectly legal!).
- For assets held for less than 12 months, neither indexing nor the discount method can be used. The capital gain is calculated simply by deducting the cost from the sale proceeds.

Making Money

- Capital gains tax can apply whether you acquired the asset by purchase, inheritance, construction or received it as a gift.
- Similarly it will be considered 'sold' (that is, it will have a 'disposal cost') even if you give it away, if it is lost, or if it is destroyed.

The following examples show the two methods of calculating capital gains tax.

Let's say Jim bought an investment property for $150,000. He paid a deposit of $15,000 in June 1995, and the balance at settlement in August 1995. However, because he became liable for the full amount on the exchange of contracts in June 1995, he is deemed (as far as CGT is concerned) to have incurred the full cost of $150,000 in June. As you will see, *timing is significant with CGT if you use the indexation method.*

Jim paid stamp duty of $5,000 in July 1995, and paid his solicitor's fees of $2,000 in August 1995. In April 1997 he spent $3,000 on a pergola, which is a 'capital improvement'. Jim subsequently sold the property in October 1999 for $195,000, incurring costs of $1,500 in solicitor's fees and $1,000 in real-estate agent's fees.

As Jim purchased the property in 1995, and sold it in October 1999, he has a choice as to how he calculates his capital gain. He can choose between either indexing the cost base, or discounting the unindexed gain. Each method will arrive at a different figure and it is essential that Jim calculate the taxable gain using both methods to see which one provides the lesser amount.

Calculating the gain using the 'indexation method'

To calculate Jim's capital gain using the indexation method, you need to arrive at a total base cost which has been indexed for inflation. To do that, each cost in each time period is multiplied by a special 'indexation factor', and then these costs are added together to give a total indexed base cost (a 'real' total cost adjusted for inflation at the time the capital gain is realised, namely when the asset is sold).

$$\text{The indexation factor} = \frac{\text{sale date CPI figure}}{\text{expenditure date CPI figure}}$$

CPI indexation figures used for calculating CGT can be obtained from the Tax Office, but here are the relevant CPI figures for these transactions.

		(CPI)
June 1995	(purchase)	116.2
July 1995	(stamp duty)	117.6
August 1995	(solicitor's fees on purchase)	117.6
April 1997	(build pergola)	120.2
July 1999	(solicitor's fees on sale)	123.4
October 1999	(agent's fees on sale)	123.4

Each cost is multiplied by the indexation factor to give you the indexed cost base in real dollars at the time the capital gain is made. So, in Jim's case ...

Purchase price: $\$150,000 \times \dfrac{123.4}{116.2} = \$159,294$

Stamp duty: $\$5,000 \times \dfrac{123.4}{117.6} = \$5,247$

Solicitor's fees on purchase: $\$2,000 \times \dfrac{123.4}{117.6} = \$2,099$

Pergola: $\$3,000 \times \dfrac{123.4}{120.2} = \$3,080$

Solicitor's fees on sale: $\$1,500 \times \dfrac{123.4}{123.4} = \$1,500$

Agent's fee on sale: $\$1,000 \times \dfrac{123.4}{123.4} = \$1,000$

Total indexed cost base: $\$172,220$

Therefore the real capital gain after inflation is $22,780
($195,000 (sale price) – $172,220 (indexed cost) = $22,780)

So, out of the $45,000 *nominal* capital gain Jim made on the sale ($195,000 – $150,000), he only has to pay capital gains tax on $22,780 (the *real* capital gain for taxation purposes – which,

Making Money

incidentally, in this example, ignores holding costs such as interest – which are normally high).

Since the introduction of the 'discount method' of calculating capital gains from 21 September 1999, the CPI figure has been 'frozen' at September 1999. This means that even if the asset was sold after September 1999, the CPI figure for that quarter (which is 123.4) is used regardless.

Calculating the gain using the 'discount method'

As Jim purchased the property before 21 September 1999, but sold it after this date, he can choose to use the discount method to calculate his capital gain. Once again this involves taking all the costs that comprise the value of the asset into account, but without indexing them for inflation. In Jim's case the calculation goes something like this:

Cost base	
Purchase price	$150,000
Stamp duty	$ 5,000
Solicitor's fees on purchase	$ 2,000
Pergola	$ 3,000
Solicitor's fees	$ 1,500
Agent's fees on sale	$ 1,000
Total cost base	$162,500
Less proceeds	$195,000
Gross capital gain	$ 32,500
Less 50% discount	$ 16,250
Taxable capital gain	$ 16,250

The 50% discount rule significantly lowers the amount of tax Jim will pay on the sale of his property. But the discount method might not always give you the best result, as the benefit of indexing is most pronounced when the purchase was made some time ago, giving you the full effect of inflation.

It is important to note that for those assets purchased after 21 September 1999 and held for more than a year, the 50% discount method is the *only* method of calculating your taxable capital gain – you cannot use the indexation method for assets purchased after this date.

While I repeat my recommendation that anyone facing CGT should leave it all to their accountant, the use of indexing to calculate capital gains certainly throws a revealing light on the capital gain you *appear* to make on an investment versus the capital gain you have actually made, once costs and inflation are taken into account.

Whether you use the indexation method or the 50% discount to calculate your capital gain, it's worth noting that the year in which the capital gain is realised is the year in which you are taxed on it. So it can certainly be worth delaying the sale of an asset to the following tax year if your income for the current tax year is already high, and, conversely, there is merit in bringing forward the sale of an asset into an otherwise low-income year.

The GST (Goods and Services Tax)

Unless you own or operate a business, the introduction of the Goods and Services Tax (GST) in July 2000 has probably had relatively little impact on your life once all the fanfare died down. However, no chapter on tax would be complete if it didn't make mention of how GST works, even though many of the finer points are still being worked out as I write (in early 2001).

Whilst the Tax Office has made the collecting and reporting of GST confusing, the fundamentals behind it are relatively straightforward. Here's how it works.

The Tax Office has set the rate for GST at 10% and it is included in the price of most (but not all) goods and services. When a business buys goods to sell, it can claim a credit for the GST component of the purchase price. This is called an 'input tax credit' because it is an input in running the business, and the business receives a tax credit for it.

When the business then sells these goods, it adds 10% for GST onto the price. The business sends to the Tax Office the total GST it has collected on the goods it has sold, less any GST it paid in buying the stock. Consumers cannot claim a credit for the GST they pay when buying goods or services, so they are the ones who ultimately pay the tax.

Let's say for example, a farm sells a bale of cotton to a cotton mill for $11 (this includes $1 GST). When the farmer completes the BAS, he takes the GST he collected on the sale ($1) and deducts any input credits (let's assume nil), and sends the net amount of $1 to the Tax Office.

The cotton mill processes the raw cotton into fabric and sells it to a linen manufacturer for $33 (includes GST of $3). The mill completes its BAS and takes the GST collected ($3) less any input credits ($1), and sends $2 to the Tax Office.

The linen manufacturer makes the fabric into sheets and sells them to a homewares retailer for $55 (includes $5 GST). The manufacturer completes its BAS and takes the $5 GST collected less any input credit ($3) and sends in $2 to the Tax Office.

The homewares retailer sells the sheets for $99 (including $9 GST). When it fills in its BAS, the retailer takes the $9 GST collected and deducts the input credit of $5, and so sends $4 to the Tax Office.

The Tax Office will have collected a total of $9 GST, being $1 from the farmer, $2 from the mill, $2 from the manufacturer and $4 from the retailer. And although the consumer is the one who actually pays the GST of $9, each business acts as a tax collector along the way.

Glossary of Terms for The New Tax System

Australian Business Number (ABN) This is a single number for businesses to use in their dealings with the Tax Office and other Government departments and agencies. Eventually it will replace Australian Company Numbers. To register for GST, you or your business will need to have an ABN.

Business Activity Statement (BAS) This is the form used by people and businesses registered for GST to report their tax obligations to the Tax Office. Whilst it replaces a range of forms that were required under the old tax system, it is not the same as an income tax return, which still needs to be lodged annually.

Input tax credit This is the amount of GST a business has paid for goods or services used in their business. This amount can be claimed back (offset against the GST collected on sales) when a business makes a PAYG payment.

Input taxed supplies These are supplies used in running a business that have GST charged on them, but for which the business cannot claim an input tax credit. For example, if you earn rent from a residential property, you will pay GST on the supplies you use in letting the property. But you cannot charge the tenant GST on the rent, nor can you claim input tax credits for the GST you have paid, so in effect you absorb the cost of the GST yourself.

Instalment Activity Statement (IAS) This is the form used by people who are not registered for GST, but who receive investment income to report their tax obligations to the Tax Office. As with the BAS you will still need to lodge a separate income tax return.

Pay As You Go tax (PAYG) This is a comprehensive tax that replaces the range of payment and reporting requirements that existed prior to 1 July 2000. The idea is that individuals or businesses have a single set of due dates and forms for payment, and by offsetting amounts payable against amounts that are refundable, the person or business pays only a single instalment. PAYG covers amounts payable for PAYG instalments, PAYG amounts withheld and any GST payable.

PAYG instalments These are the amounts you pay in relation to your own income tax, and they replace provisional tax and company tax instalments.

PAYG withholding These are amounts businesses or individuals withhold from employees and contractors to pay to the Tax Office. This covers the amounts taken out of salaries and wages under the old Pay As You Earn (PAYE) system, and amounts paid to contractors under the old Prescribed Payments System (PPS).

Tax invoice This is a special type of invoice that sets out the supplier's name and ABN, a description of the goods or services supplied and the price charged – including GST. A tax invoice is needed to claim an input tax credit.

Taxable supplies These are items used in running a business on which GST has been paid. The business can claim an input tax credit for the GST paid on these.

Making Money

GST and investors

The Tax Office classifies many forms of investment as 'financial supplies', which are 'input taxed'. In plain English this means there is no GST payable on a number of investments, including for example, shares or units in a unit trust. But some of the costs of buying and selling them *are* subject to GST, for example, GST is payable on brokerage. However, as there is no GST payable on the investment itself, you cannot claim back the GST you pay on the transaction costs. Put simply, it means the investor wears the cost of any GST they pay in buying and selling investments.

Investors face a number of costs that are subject to GST, including advice from financial planners and accountants' fees. Since an investor cannot pass the GST further down the line in the way a business can, he or she has to bear the cost.

Businesses and tax

Before The New Tax System came into effect in July 2000, businesses were required to remit a range of taxes at various times in the year, including tax deducted from employees' wages, various sales taxes, and their own income tax. This latter tax was paid either through the provisional tax system if the business was run in the name of a person or a few partners, or through the company tax system if the business was incorporated.

Under the new system a number of indirect taxes (though not all) were scrapped and a single Goods and Services Tax (GST) was introduced. Provisional tax and the company tax instalment system have been replaced by the Pay As You Go (PAYG) system.

As a result of the introduction of GST, businesses operating in Australia with an annual turnover of more than $50,000 are required to register for Goods and Services Tax (GST). Even if your business doesn't reach $50,000, it is probably a good idea to register anyway as your turnover may well come close to this.

If your business is registered for GST, you will need to complete a Business Activity Statement (BAS) at some time during the year. The BAS is the form that accompanies your tax payments to the Tax Office, and covers GST, PAYG withheld from employee's wages, PAYG payable on the income of the business, and any fringe benefits tax (FBT). All of these amounts are netted off against each other to give a single figure payable, or if you are extraordinarily lucky, a refund due to you. For example, a business may:

■ have collected net GST of $5,000
■ have withheld $2,000 in tax from employee wages
■ owe $3,000 in PAYG tax on its own income for the period.

In this case the business will pay $10,000 for the period (being $5,000 + $2,000 + $3,000).

As I write in early 2001, there have been a number of changes made to the BAS, both in terms of calculating the GST and PAYG instalments and the information that needs to be provided on a quarterly basis. With the BAS and IAS system electorally on the nose, there are bound to be further changes yet to come in this area, but here are the requirements as they currently stand.

As you can see from the table below, most small businesses need to report and pay their tax obligations quarterly, while their larger counterparts do so on a monthly basis, and as part of the new system this is all done via one form: the BAS.

Your tax liabilities	Payment and reporting
Goods and Services Tax	
Annual turnover is below $20 million	Quarterly
Annual turnover is over $20 million	Monthly
PAYG withholding (from salaries and wages)	
Annual tax withheld from salaries and wages is below $25,000	Quarterly
Annual tax withheld from wages and salaries is over $25,000	Monthly
PAYG instalments (on the income of the business)	Quarterly

It's worth stressing that for most businesses each quarterly payment is made up of tax deducted from employee wages, income tax instalments for the business, GST collected (net of GST paid on inputs) and any FBT, all netted off against each other to give one amount payable.

Following the introduction of The New Tax System, many small businesses found it difficult to meet the rigorous reporting schedule.

Making Money

The need to calculate their income as well as their GST obligations each quarter proved particularly onerous, so some relief was introduced for small businesses in the way their quarterly GST and PAYG instalments are calculated. These are set out below and whilst these provisions are current at the time of writing (in March 2001), they will undoubtedly be the subject of further change.

Calculating your PAYG

For people registered for GST in their own name (usually sole traders and business partners), as well as small companies and small super funds (small being an annual turnover of less than $1 million), the Tax Office gives you a choice in how the quarterly PAYG instalments are calculated. You can calculate your own PAYG by taking your income for the quarter multiplied by your instalment rate (this is the rate of tax the Tax Office feels is right for your business based on your prior year tax bill). Or you can let the Tax Office calculate the amount for you. This figure is based on your previous year's income, adjusted (upwards, of course!) for a factor based on the economy's performance.

Calculating your GST

Businesses with a turnover of less than $2 million also make quarterly payments. If their turnover is over $1 million, they need to calculate their own PAYG instalment, based on their quarterly income multiplied by the instalment rate advised by the Tax Office. However, these businesses do have a choice in how their GST payment is calculated (remember GST is just one of the taxes that make up the quarterly payment a business remits to the Tax Office). They can work out their actual GST payable, based on GST paid on purchases and GST collected on sales, or they can choose to pay a GST instalment that has been determined by the Tax Office. This figure is based on the GST the business paid in the previous year, increased by a factor for the economy's performance.

For businesses that choose to let the Tax Office calculate their GST instalments, the quarterly BAS is a simple remittance form with the GST payable pre-printed onto it. A more detailed BAS needs to be completed annually, which will be due when the business lodges its annual income tax return.

If at this point you're completely bamboozled, take heart: the majority of taxpayers are. The main things to bear in mind are that for businesses with a turnover of less than $1 million, you can have your GST and PAYG on your income calculated for you on a quarterly basis. And larger businesses with a turnover of up to $2 million can have the quarterly GST instalment calculated by the Tax Office. All these amounts are paid quarterly on a simple remittance form, which is a toned-down version of the full BAS, which still needs to be completed annually.

For businesses with a turnover below $20 million, GST payments are again made quarterly. If the business has a turnover of more than $2 million, it doesn't have the option of having the Tax Office estimate a GST figure, but instead calculates its own GST using a simple remittance form that sets out sales, GST collected on sales and GST paid on purchases. A more detailed BAS is completed annually and lodged together with the annual income tax return.

Now, may I suggest you pour yourself a very large Scotch (even if you're a teetotaller), as I'm certainly about to. I'm so impressed at how simple and understandable the Tax Office has made the reporting requirements of The New Tax System – not!

Tax Office scrutiny

Australian taxation is based on self-assessment – the Tax Office trusts you to work out your own tax liability (with or without the help of an accountant) and then to submit a tax return that reveals what you owe them or what they owe you.

However, the Tax Office performs both random and targeted checks – known as audits – just to keep everyone honest. And if the tax officer finds there is a mistake in your return (your way, of course), it may cost you a lot of money. You can be fined on any amount found owing – as well as still having to pay the outstanding tax itself.

There are three main types of audit. One is a simple *mail check* where you receive a letter asking for clarification and/or documentary proof of one or more deductions you've claimed.

Another is an *income matching check* where the Tax Office asks your bank to provide it with your financial details on matters such as the amount of interest you've earned.

Then there is the *full audit*. Contrary to popular belief, tax officers don't suddenly leap through your window in the middle of the night or break down the door demanding you show them your receipts – unless you're Al Capone. It's a more civilised process than that, but nonetheless unsettling.

With a full audit you firstly receive a letter or a phone call requesting a meeting. At this and any subsequent meetings you can then expect a thorough examination of your books, records, receipts and deductions. The audit can go back five years, so you must keep all your documentation for at least that long.

If you have an accountant who has been doing your tax returns, you should contact him or her immediately after you are contacted by the Tax Office and discuss the situation. If the Tax Office is doing a full audit, it would be a very good idea to have your accountant present at all meetings with tax officers.

So what are the odds of being audited? Pretty high. In recent years, around 240,000 taxpayers have been audited annually out of a total population of 10 million-plus Australian taxpayers. Of those who undergo bank income matching, around 90% have their tax reassessed, and of those who are targeted for a full audit, between 60% and 70% are reassessed. Also note that 250,000 Australian businesses are audited annually in addition to the 240,000 individuals.

Look, no one enjoys being audited, and it can be a cause of much anxiety. However, if you keep all your receipts, maintain good records and don't fudge on your tax returns, you won't have a thing to worry about!

CHAPTER ELEVEN

Ten Keys to Successful Investing

How often have you had one of those great moments where, when you least expect it, you notice a small detail that helps put the world into greater perspective? I once had such a moment at Warwick Farm Racecourse. And no, unfortunately, I didn't suddenly realise a 100-to-1 outsider was going to win and put all my money on it.

The revealing detail was the nature of the car parks that you walk past on the way into the course. There is a large one for the public – the punters – and another smaller one for the book-makers, and what really struck me was the stark difference in the types of cars in the two parking areas.

One was full of old, clapped-out Valiants, Datsuns and Kings-woods, the other full of gleaming new BMWs, Jaguars, Mercedes Benz and the odd Rolls Royce. There are no prizes for guessing which cars belonged to the bookies, and the extreme contrast between their cars and the punters' spoke volumes about who was (and is) making all the money at the track.

So, why is it that over time the bookies always seem to win? What do they do right that the punters do wrong?

Well, apart from having a better idea than the punters about which horses are good and which are not, what they do is *spread their risks*, while the punters concentrate theirs. And, over time, the racecourse car parks tell you which is the better strategy.

A bookie spreads risks by continually changing the odds in such a way as to encourage punters to back as many different horses as possible in each race – ideally, every horse in the race. If, despite this technique of encouraging a wide spread of bets, one particular horse is very heavily backed, the bookie then minimises exposure by backing it with other bookmakers. This way, no matter which horse wins, the bookie will have a mix of wins and losses. If bookies spread their risks well, wins should outweigh losses.

The punter takes the opposite tack. He doesn't spread risk at all.

He concentrates it all on one or two horses in each race without knowing too much about them and, if he has my luck, they usually run backwards. At the end of the day, pockets empty, he limps home in his battered old Cortina.

What punters do at the track is lay bets against horses that generally have a low chance of winning. They punt, bet or speculate. Call it what you will, they *gamble* – looking for a spectacular, instant gain. They take a chance on something performing well. If it does, they're rewarded handsomely; if it doesn't, they lose the lot. Not only that, the more they do it, the more they increase their chances of losing.

This is not what I call 'investing'. In my book investing means putting your money into something that has a good chance of winning in the short to medium term, and an even better, if not dead certain, chance of winning *in the long term*. The wonderful thing is, there are money-making vehicles that fit this description, and they are the classic assets of quality shares, property, fixed interest securities and cash deposits.

To strengthen your returns from these assets you should, ideally, invest a little in all of them, not a lot in one. Investors call this 'diversification', bookies call it 'hedging their bets'. They both mean the same thing; namely, not putting all your eggs in the one basket.

Let's take a look at my 10 keys to successful investing. Ignore them at your peril because they represent a combination of everything I have learnt – from all the books on investment I've read, from the professional investors I have spoken with over the years, from the real-life experience obtained from my own clients, and from the many people who write to me about their investment experiences.

1. Understand that risk equals return

Etch the words 'risk equals return' into your bathroom mirror so you can see them every morning. Taking excessive risk in looking for a big return is the number one reason why investors lose their money. They get too greedy – and investment salespeople know this.

The only way you can circumvent the classic relationship between risk and return is to obtain information that is not widely known. With shares it is called 'insider trading', and the penalties are high if you get caught. With property, inside knowledge about things like rezoning can be very valuable but, unfortunately, over the years a number of people have abused their position of trust on such matters. For most of us, inside knowledge isn't available and we must invest on the premise that the return we get will be related to the risk we take.

If you see an investment offering a high return, don't say 'Oh good', ask 'Why?'. Examples such as Estate Mortgage and Pyramid Building Society spring to mind. To attract money they offered higher rates of interest than their competitors. To pay this higher rate they lent the money on more risky projects. The result? Investors lost most of their money when it all collapsed.

Now, I'm not saying risk is to be avoided. If you take no risk, you get no return. Everything has some risk, but you must be aware of risk. The real trick is to consider how much risk you can sleep with, and to invest accordingly.

To illustrate this, let me describe my family's investment strategy.

For my young kids, I put around $500 a year into an international managed share fund with a strong focus on emerging markets such as in Asia. Sure, this is risky and Asian markets took a hiding in the late 90s. However, with a 20-year view I think this international strategy will give my kids the highest return over the decades. Look, if the kids make 60% one year and lose 60% the next, it doesn't matter – they don't even know about it! At their age, investment risk is irrelevant to them.

At my age (46), I would not invest all my money in emerging markets shares because of the high risk. However, I have been more than willing to invest some of my super money in this area – because I won't be touching it for many years.

Having paid off my mortgage, my main plan at this stage is to build up my super and a portfolio of other investments, such as Australian shares and perhaps even some investment property.

As I age, my attitude to risk will change. I'll be more concerned with protecting my wealth, not growing it, so I will gradually switch to lower risk investments such as cash, fixed interest and blue chip shares.

⚬━ KEY THOUGHT

Be aware of risk. Ask questions and understand the true nature of risk in any investment before you do anything.

Making Money

The table below gives the type of return you can expect reasonably over the very long term, by which I mean 10 years plus. This is a 'real' return, meaning the return in excess of inflation. It's important to look at long-term returns because short-term returns (under three years) are very unpredictable.

As you can see again, the higher the risk you take, the higher the expected return. Conversely, if you take very low risk and put all your money into the bank, your long-term returns will be very low.

Investment	Risk	Projected real annual long-term returns
Cash in bank	Very low	0% to 1%
Term deposits (1 to 3 years)	Low	0% to 2%
Long-term fixed interest and bonds (3 to 10 years)	Medium	0% to 3%
Residential property	Medium	1% to 3%
Commercial property	Medium–high	3% to 5%
Australian shares	High	5% to 8%
International shares	High	6% to 9%
Emerging markets (e.g. South-East Asia, Latin America)	Extremely high	10% to 25%

The trick to managing risk is to consider how much risk you can tolerate given your personal situation, and then to build a portfolio of assets that suits you.

Put simply, a youngster with $500 may be happy to take a very high risk. This would see a 100% exposure to shares. A middle-aged person may want to be moderately aggressive and invest in a mix of medium- and high-risk investments. A retiree is likely to take a low-risk approach and invest mainly in low-risk assets like cash and fixed interest with a smaller exposure to high-risk investments such as shares.

Speaking of high risk, you may be wondering about the projected long-term returns of 10% to 25% from emerging markets given the savage downturn in these markets in 1997 and 1998. Well, this is nothing terribly new. Despite the dramatic decline, nothing alters the fact that Asia is occupied by millions of people who want to get ahead and are willing to work hard.

When we look back in a decade or two we will certainly see major ups and downs in the market, but over long-term periods investment in a well-diversified emerging markets portfolio will see solid returns.

2. Don't try to time the market

It's pretty obvious that you should buy when things are cheap and sell when they are expensive. It's so delightfully simple, but guess what most investors tend to do? When the news is good and investments are expensive, they buy, and when the news is bad and investments have fallen in value, they sell. It's a recipe for financial ruin.

'Good market timing' is all about buying at the bottom and selling at the top, and being a 'market timer' means trying to do just that. But no market timer I know consistently gets their timing right year after year, as no one has yet worked out how to read the future.

The following tables, from ipac securities, help illustrate the difficulties of trying to consistently pick the right markets to invest in, year in, year out.

The *best* performing markets 1983–2000

Year	Asset class	Annual return %
1983	Australian shares	66.8
1984	International fixed interest	15.2
1985	International shares	70.8
1986	Australian shares	52.2
1987	Australian fixed interest	18.6
1988	Australian shares	17.9
1989	International shares	26.2
1990	Australian fixed interest	19.1
1991	Australian shares	34.2
1992	International fixed interest	10.4
1993	Australian shares	45.4

1994	Cash	5.3
1995	International shares	26.1
1996	Australian shares	14.6
1997	International shares	41.6
1998	International shares	32.3
1999	International shares	17.2
2000	Australian listed property	17.9

Let's say you were genius enough to pick these top performing asset classes every year and you invested in them solely – your average annual return would have been a very healthy 29.5%. Fantastic! But what would have been the likelihood of pulling off such a staggering feat of prognostication? Well, unless you were a cross between Nostradamus, Albert Einstein and King Solomon, I'd say about nil.

At the other end of the performance spectrum, the following table shows the markets you would *not* want to have invested in during this period.

The *worst* performing markets 1983–2000

Year	Asset class	Annual return %
1983	Cash	13.6
1984	Australian shares	−2.3
1985	Australian listed property	5.3
1986	Cash	18.1
1987	Australian shares	−7.9
1988	International shares	4.1
1989	Australian listed property	2.4
1990	Australian shares	−17.5
1991	Cash	11.2
1992	Australian shares	−2.3
1993	Cash	5.4
1994	Australian shares	−8.7
1995	Cash	8.1
1996	International shares	6.2
1997	Cash	5.6
1998	Cash	5.1
1999	Australian listed property	−5.0
2000	International shares	2.2

If you had been incredibly unlucky and managed to invest solely in the worst performing asset classes each year, every year, your average annual return would have been a very sad 2.4% (though note, intriguingly, it's still positive!).

Fortunately, however, your chances of consistently picking the worst investments are the same as consistently picking the best – about zero. So this means most investors would have earned somewhere in the middle of our best average annual return of 29.5% and our worst of 2.4%.

Punting (and it *is* punting) on trying to move in and out of the markets at optimal times is a mug's game. Even the maths is against punters.

A gambler's lament

- Invest $1 and lose 50%. You now have 50 cents.
- Invest 50 cents and earn 50%. You now have 75 cents, 25 cents less than you started with.

Try it the other way around . . .

- Invest $1 and earn 50%. You now have $1.50.
- Invest $1.50 and lose 50%. You're back to 75 cents again, still 25 cents less than what you started with.

As the 'gambler's lament' above shows, two consecutive returns of equal size see you losing money. And, in the context of investment dealing, this is before you pay any commission, stamp duty or brokerage. Pretty obviously, therefore, you need to be right with your investment timing decisions around two-thirds of the time to break even – and that's just too difficult.

I'm not saying you shouldn't use research to guide you to better investment areas. But when it comes down to it, determining how much risk you can live with and then buying investments that suit your risk profile and monitoring these is a better strategy than switching from one investment area to another on a regular basis. The only winner in this is the broker or salesperson who is doing the buying and selling – or the Stamp Duties Office!

Making Money

3. Diversify

In broad terms, I recommend that you have a plan to create three pools of wealth – your home, your superannuation and other investments. This is based on a simple view about diversification. This strategy gives you exposure to property (your home), shares and fixed interest (through your super) and other investments you buy yourself. These might be shares, money in the bank or an investment property.

It also gives you diversification from a tax and legislative perspective. Super is a highly regulated area, and the main reason I would not rely solely on super is another type of risk – the risk of changing legislation.

How you diversify depends upon your age, income, family and so on. The younger you are the less diversification you are likely to have, but as you get older you will diversify more as your wealth grows and you want to reduce the amount of risk you are taking.

As I mentioned, my kids are concentrating their investments on international markets with a high weighting to emerging economies. My retired clients on the other hand have a very diversified portfolio because they are trying to minimise risks.

You can also take diversification into a more narrow context. For example, with a share portfolio you should diversify by choosing different sectors within the market. You might invest in the following areas:
- banking and finance
- building and construction
- media
- health
- resources.

Inside, say, the banking and finance sector you might further diversify by choosing several shares such as Westpac, National Australia Bank and a smaller bank such as St George.

With international shares your level of diversification can become very extensive, as the graph on the next page shows.

> **⚬— KEY THOUGHT**
> No one knows the future. Don't gamble yours by relying on one type of investment only.

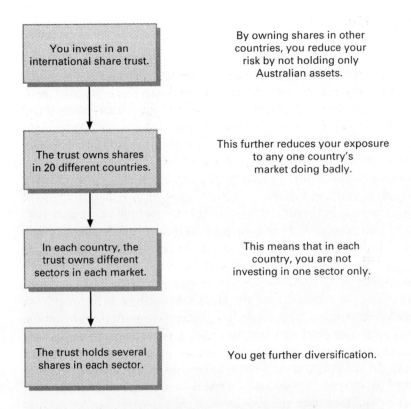

You invest in an international share trust.	By owning shares in other countries, you reduce your risk by not holding only Australian assets.
The trust owns shares in 20 different countries.	This further reduces your exposure to any one country's market doing badly.
In each country, the trust owns different sectors in each market.	This means that in each country, you are not investing in one sector only.
The trust holds several shares in each sector.	You get further diversification.

4. Invest in growth assets for the long term

A growth asset is simply something that grows in capital value as well as producing income. To maintain your standard of living once you stop work, you need your income to grow with inflation. Growth assets such as property and shares will help to do this. Property rentals increase over time, as do share dividends on good companies.

Be careful about being seduced by high (and fully taxable!) income returns on bank deposits or other such investments. Let me try to highlight this with an imaginary investor who has $10,000 to invest for her future. She is 40 years old and wants to stop work at age 55.

If the $10,000 is invested in, say, a term deposit at 5%, it will generate an annual return of $500. Depending on our investor's total income, up to 48.5% (including Medicare levy) of this $500 could be lost to tax. And if whatever's left over gets spent – as is often the case – 15 years down the track our investor will still have the $10,000 (with its value much eroded by inflation) and that's about all.

By investing the $10,000 into growth assets like shares, our investor would probably (though not necessarily) earn less income today than the term deposit investor. However, the share investment would most likely grow in value over the years. Let's say three shares were purchased with the money: BHP, National Australia Bank and Woolworths. (You'll note I've chosen shares from three different sectors and, incidentally, investing in a managed share trust would do the job equally well.)

Now, our share investment would generate income of around 4%. Much of this would be in the form of fully franked dividends with tax already having been paid on them at the company tax rate of 30%, but let's compare apples with apples and assume this income is also spent.

It's realistic to assume that the shares would grow (in price) on average at around 6% p.a. (before inflation) and that inflation would average around 4% for the period. With these assumptions the shares would be worth around $24,000 in 15 years. So at retirement at 55, our investor would have $24,000 worth of shares earning 4% income ($960) and this $960 would have had tax paid on it at 30% (assuming the dividends were fully franked).

Compare this income to that provided by the $10,000 still sitting there in the term deposit (and getting eaten by inflation). It's still only earning 5% ($500) – and this $500 is fully taxable.

If the investor's effective tax rate was 30%, the shares would provide an after-tax income of $960, and the term deposit an after-tax income of $350.

In 15 years' time, would you rather have $500 of fully taxable income or $960 of income after 30% tax has been paid on it?

Sure, growth assets are far more risky in the short term, but over 10 to 15 years, quality growth assets will tend to grow in value, and so will the income they generate for you.

O— KEY THOUGHT

Growth assets increase in value, have tax advantages and, therefore, generate more income as time goes by.

5. Invest internationally

One of the truly historic changes during my time in the money industry has been the fact that, when it comes to investment, the world really is a global village. By this I mean that money flows instantly from country to country via the banks' computer systems. You can buy assets such as shares, fixed interest or even property in practically any country you like.

Okay, you may be thinking that it has nothing to do with you but, for better or worse, it does. Our long-term standard of living depends on how competitive we are as a nation. If we are under-productive and continue to allow our economy to build foreign debt, a fall in our dollar is inevitable. If our dollar falls, imports cost more and, no matter how hard you try, you cannot buy only Australian.

Arun Abey, one of my partners at ipac securities, is fond of making this point by asking people, 'How much more Australian can you get than a steak sandwich?' I must admit, at first, I couldn't quite understand what he was getting at. 'Of course it's Australian,' we all say. 'Australian meat served with Australian salad on Australian bread.'

Then he points out that the cattle the meat comes from are looked after with foreign pharmaceuticals; eat pasture grown with foreign fertiliser; are transported to the abattoirs in an American, Japanese or German truck; are cut up by German equipment; are transported again in a foreign truck; are wrapped in Taiwanese plastic; and then served to you with a plate, knife and fork also made in Taiwan. Even your cash will be put into a cash register that may not be made here! All in all, our $4 steak sandwich could have 40% of its cost determined by 'foreign' value-added items.

What am I getting at? Well, many of you may have had an overseas holiday 10 or 15 years ago. Do you remember that at one stage your Aussie dollar bought you nearly US$1.50, UK£1, 3 Swiss francs and so on?

What does it buy today? At the time of writing in early 2001, around 50 cents American, 36 English pence and just under 1 Swiss franc. Our dollar has fallen in value significantly over the past 20 years. If you had held American, English, Swiss or Japanese investments, you would have been protected from this fall in the value of our currency.

I'm very positive about our country. In fact, I can't think of a better place to live, work and bring up a family, but I do want to protect my standard of living and I can't do that by investing all of my assets in Australia. Sure, the Aussie dollar may hold its value or even rise against other currencies in the next 20 years – but I doubt it. We still have a number of problems such as too much debt, some poor workplace practices, and too great a dependence on welfare for me to be absolutely confident that we will be competitive and productive in comparison to our trading partners. So, for me, having some of my money invested offshore is a matter of commonsense.

While protection against falls in our currency is a negative reason for investing offshore, there is another, very positive one. It allows you to participate in a range of exciting investments. You can buy shares in companies in the huge economies of the world such as the USA and Japan. You can participate in the rebuilding of Eastern Europe, or take a stake in the economies of South-East Asia or Latin America. You can even get a slice of, potentially, the biggest market of all – China.

Don't be surprised I say this despite the major falls and volatility in the Asian markets in the late 1990s. The underlying economies still remain strong and viable when taking a long-term view, particularly one of, say, 20 years, and I am continuing to hold Asian investments.

The graph on the opposite page looks at the performance of various investments over the past 18 calendar years to the end of 2000. As you can see, international shares have performed best. And, interestingly, investment in the major international sharemarkets is actually less risky than investment in the Australian sharemarket. You need to be aware that our market accounts for less than 2% of the world's stockmarkets, and we have a market with a high percentage of resource stocks (companies mining coal, aluminium, gold, copper and so on). Resource prices move rapidly on world markets – and so do resource stocks' values!

I've mentioned before that as part of my portfolio I invest around $500 ($10 a week) for each of my three children into international and 'emerging markets'. This is where I see the fastest economic growth, and my children can benefit from this by owning shares in companies in these economies. I do this by using a managed international and 'emerging markets' share fund. These typically invest in a dozen economies and hold hundreds of different shares in Asia, Latin America, North America and Europe. There is no way I'd try to pick international shares myself – it's all too hard. For an initial investment in one of these funds of between

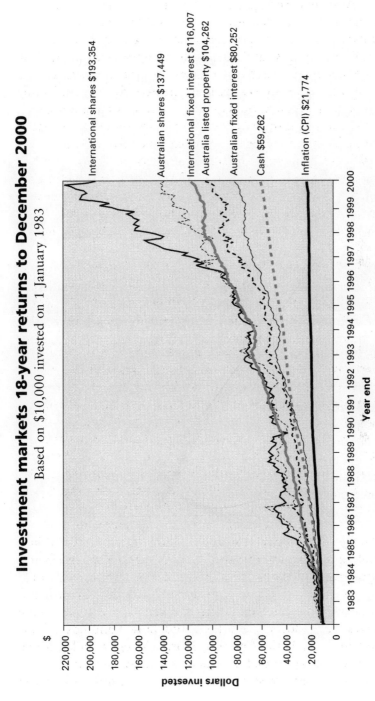

Investment markets 18-year returns to December 2000

Based on $10,000 invested on 1 January 1983

International shares $193,354

Australian shares $137,449

International fixed interest $116,007

Australia listed property $104,262

Australian fixed interest $80,252

Cash $59,262

Inflation (CPI) $21,774

Dollars invested

$

220,000

200,000

180,000

160,000

140,000

120,000

100,000

80,000

60,000

40,000

20,000

0

1983 1984 1985 1986 1987 1988 1989 1990 1991 1992 1993 1994 1995 1996 1997 1998 1999 2000

Year end

(*Source*: ipac securities.)

Making Money

$1,000 and $2,000 you do get an amazing spread of economies and individual shares.

However, don't let the spread trick you into thinking that the risk is therefore low. It's not. The actual economies and companies in them can be risky. A standard salesperson's line might be that the average annual return from emerging markets over 13 years (1988 to 2000) was 19.5%. Now, while this is true, what they don't tell you is that the actual returns year by year for emerging markets were:

1988	19%	1995	−1%
1989	78%	1996	−1%
1990	−9%	1997	8%
1991	63%	1998	−21%
1992	23%	1999	56%
1993	76%	2000	−18%
1994	−19%		

(*Source*: ipac securities; MSCI Emerging Markets Free Index, dividends reinvested.)

See? The average is terrific but year by year things are very risky. Naturally, though, the bigger international markets such as Europe and the USA are less volatile.

Why invest overseas?
- to spread risk
- to protect yourself against a falling Australian dollar
- to invest in the world's major economies
- to participate in the recovery of emerging markets such as Asia
- to protect your long-term standard of living.

○━ KEY THOUGHT

While I want to live in Australia, I want to protect my standard of living in a global context. I invest offshore because it makes sense to me not to have everything in one small economy such as ours. It allows me to participate in the major world economies and dynamic smaller economies.

6. Rebalance your investments regularly

I can't tell you how often I have seen investors get bitten by a failure to rebalance their investments. So, what's 'rebalancing'?

If you have constructed a diversified portfolio of investments, I would hope that you have made a deliberate decision about how your investments are spread – the technical jargon for this is 'asset allocation'.

This means that on Day 1, your investment portfolio may look like this:

Australian shares	30% (in value)
International shares	22%
Australian fixed interest	25%
International fixed interest	15%
Property	8%
Total	**100%**

If the sharemarket then roared ahead and you did nothing, sometime later your portfolio could look something like this:

Australian shares	36% (in value)
International shares	26%
Australian fixed interest	18%
International fixed interest	11%
Property	9%
Total	**100%**

See how your share weighting (the value that shares proportionally comprise of your portfolio) has increased dramatically without you having done anything to it? The sharemarket's upward movement has caused it. The higher share weighting now means that your overall portfolio risk is higher than on Day 1, because shares are the riskiest of the main investment classes.

Unless your attitude to risk has changed, you should rebalance back to your correct portfolio mix at least twice a year. Yes, you may incur switching fees in some cases and pay capital gains tax on profits, but if you don't rebalance, don't be surprised at how much you might lose when markets fall!

Rebalancing also has the added attraction of enforced discipline. It forces you to sell when assets are expensive and buy when they are cheap. How? Well, if you always keep the original 30% value of your portfolio in Australian shares and rebalance if this falls or rises by 2% (for example, at 32% you sell some shares, at 28% you buy some shares), by definition you must *sell when expensive* and *buy when cheap*. It's a simple discipline but, believe me, it works.

7. Watch your gearing

Gearing refers to debt levels, and in particular, most commonly refers to the borrowings you enter into in order to fund your investments. Akin to the way the gears in your car transfer engine speed to road speed, financial gearing accelerates (or decelerates) your returns on investment. Many investors in the late 1980s borrowed money to buy unlisted property trusts, some of which themselves had borrowed money to buy property. This in effect was gearing on gearing, and led to some terrible losses.

I give a lot more detail on this subject in Chapter Twelve, but as one of your central investment rules, please watch carefully any gearing that you use – and any gearing inside investments that you make.

In brief, gearing works as follows:

- Invest $200,000 of your money into a $200,000 property – in other words pay for it outright and borrow nothing. If the property then rises by 10%, you make $20,000 on your $200,000 investment, or (also) 10%.
- Invest $100,000 of your money into a $200,000 property – in other words pay for half of it and borrow the other half. If the property then rises by 10%, you make $20,000 on your $100,000 investment, or 20%.
- Invest $20,000 of your money into a $200,000 property – in other words pay for one-tenth of it and borrow the rest. If the property then rises by 10%, you make $20,000 on your $20,000 investment, or 100%.

In the last case, you double your money if the $200,000 property only increases in value by 10%. This sounds terrific and many investment salespeople use this to great advantage. What they don't mention is the fact that gearing can multiply your returns – *in both directions*.

In our example, if the property falls by 10%, you lose $20,000 – or all of the money that you put in. If the investment falls, by say $40,000, you lose not only your original $20,000, but another $20,000, which you still have to repay.

> ### ☞ KEY THOUGHT
> Only gear your investments if you fully understand the risk you are taking.

Borrowing against your home – beware!

A number of so-called 'advisers' strongly promote borrowing against your own home to buy shares. They may give you a very attractive presentation about how you will get tax deductions and pay off your mortgage more quickly.

This is a great deal for them as they typically make a commission on arranging the finance and on the investments they buy for you. On a $100,000 investment their take could be as high as $6,000.

Now, if the shares go up in value (and in the *long term* they will), their presentations show that you are well in front. What they seem to forget to tell you (except in the fine print) is that if shares fall in value over the short to medium term, you will lose equity in your home and may even jeopardise it.

Yet, if you genuinely understand the risks and are comfortable that the market could easily fall 30% or 40% in the next major downturn, are willing to take a long-term view and have the cash flow to keep up your repayments, I have relaxed my view stated in previous editions of this book that you should never borrow against your home to buy shares.

I accept that our sophistication about investment is growing and for some people this is a sensible strategy, but if you don't fully understand the risks or would panic and sell in a market downturn, my advice remains the same: don't borrow money against your house to buy shares. If you do choose to use this strategy, however, negotiate with the adviser on the entry fees. These days you really should not pay more than 1% or 2% on an investment of a reasonable size.

8. Avoid tax schemes

When it comes to tax and investment, please do be cautious about tax schemes. Prawns, salmon, flowers, horses, helicopters and port – you name it, I've seen it – tax schemes in every colour, shape and size that are usually bought in a desperate panic in June by people with a tax problem.

The typical scheme will arrange finance so that you can borrow the money to get the tax deduction. If, say, you borrowed $10,000 for one of these schemes, a maximum-rate taxpayer would get a reduction in tax of $4,850 (including Medicare levy). Now, that's not to be sneezed at. But if, as inevitably happens, the scheme fails, you might have a $4,850 tax deduction but you have lost another $5,150. That doesn't sound very appealing to me.

My advice is quite simple. Unless you *really* understand the nature of the investment, don't do it. Looking at my own clients, I find that those who have simply concentrated on minimising their tax in the usual ways, paid what they owed and concentrated on a sensible investment strategy end up miles in front. You can read more about it in Chapter Ten, 'Tax'.

9. Try 'dollar cost averaging'

This is a great tip, simply because it works so well. In 'Don't try to time the market' (pages 163–165), I pointed out how hard it is to pick the right investment except with hindsight. Well, *dollar cost averaging* makes things very easy. All you have to do is simply decide how much and how often you are going to invest. You may decide to invest on a monthly, six monthly or yearly basis – it really doesn't matter.

Let's imagine you decide to invest $1,000 twice a year into a particular share. Its price, like all shares, rises and falls over time. This is what could happen.

	Share price	Number of shares you get
1 January 2001	$1.00	1,000
1 July 2001	$1.20	833
1 January 2002	$0.80	1,250
1 July 2002	$1.00	1,000
1 January 2003	$1.40	714
1 July 2003	$1.30	769

Look at when you bought the most shares – in January 2002, when our imaginary share's price was 80 cents. When did you buy the least? In January 2003, when the share price was $1.40.

Human nature tends to lead us to sell when things are cheap (times are bad) and buy when they are expensive (things are good). Dollar cost averaging forces you to buy most shares when they are cheapest, and buy the least when they are the most expensive. This is a discipline worth using.

10. Take advice if necessary

I'm the first to argue that the more you know about your money, the better off you are. But there are some things you don't need to know nor, unless you have a huge amount of spare time, will you be able to know. It's like your health – you don't have the time or training to be able to self-diagnose and treat your own health problems. When necessary you go to see a doctor. With money matters you go to a financial adviser. But if you thought finding a good doctor was hard, finding a good financial adviser is even harder.

The reason is that the whole field of professional financial advice is reasonably new. Commissioned salespeople have been around for years, but it has only been in the last 15 years or so that qualified, professional advisers have started to appear in reasonable numbers. You'll find more about this in Chapter Nineteen, 'Choosing an Adviser'.

Take action!

Anyone can be a successful investor rather than a losing punter by following a pretty simple prescription – spreading risk over a diversified range of assets, and hanging on to these assets for the long term, through the good and the bad times.

And yes, there is something else – taking action. No one ever got rich by doing nothing (unless you're lucky enough to inherit a fortune). You generate wealth by *doing something*. This might seem like a statement of the obvious, but it needs to be said.

All the main investment classes produce reasonable returns over time. And even if you only invest in one or two of the poorer performing ones, this is still far, far better than not having invested at all. Yes, I know I say that diversifying across all the main asset

Making Money

classes is the *best* investment strategy, but let's say you only invest in residential property, well, good, at least you have invested in *one* viable asset class. In fact, in the end it doesn't really make an enormous amount of difference which quality assets you invest in, be they shares, property, cash or fixed interest, just so long as you *do invest*!

Keys to successful investing

1. Understand that risk equals return.
2. Don't try to time the market.
3. Diversify.
4. Invest in growth assets for the long term.
5. Invest internationally.
6. Rebalance your investments regularly.
7. Watch your gearing.
8. Avoid tax schemes.
9. Try 'dollar cost averaging'.
10. Take advice if necessary – and take action!

CHAPTER TWELVE

Investing in Property

When Australians think investment, many think property, particularly residential property. Indeed, of the two million Australian households renting, 73% rent from private landlords (*Source:* ABS, 2000), which is a massive show of support for residential property as an investment.

Like buying a home to live in, buying a property to rent out and, hopefully sell at a profit one day, is an easy concept to grasp. It's a more tangible investment than shares or bonds and I am sure this goes a long way towards explaining its great popularity.

Don't let me give you the impression that residential property investment is straightforward though. It may appear to be, but getting it right can take a lot more than meets the eye. Anyone with the money can go out and buy a property but, if you don't choose carefully, you may find your returns are low or even negative. What you need to ensure is that you do your homework properly and make sure you buy the right property at the right price.

It's fair to say in fact that direct investment in property normally requires greater care, is more complex and has more pitfalls than investment in any of the other main asset classes.

Returns from property

Like all investments, returns from residential property investment depend on which period you look at because all investments have their good and bad years. To get an accurate picture of an investment's performance you need to look at returns that have been calculated over as long a term as possible.

Our research at ipac securities indicates that over the very long term, residential property increases in value at an average rate of 1% to 3% above the rate of inflation.

This is not to say that at *certain times* residential property has not performed much better, and much worse, than these ipac long-term figures, as the Sydney property market since the late

Making Money

1980s shows. In August 1987 the median price of a three-bedroom Sydney house was $115,000. By August 1989 it had risen to a peak of $209,000, a phenomenal increase over two years. However, by March 1991 the median price was down to $171,000, rising in fits and starts to $203,000 by August 1996, still $6,000 below its peak seven years before. It then skyrocketed to $261,000 by December 1997 and has climbed steadily to $305,000 in December 2000. (*Source*: Real Estate Institute of Australia.)

Let's look at some other recent short- and longer term Australian residential property returns, and performance comparisons with other mainstream investments. (The 2, 5 and 10 year columns are annualised returns.)

Residential property and other investments' returns as at 31 December 2000

	1 year %	2 years %	5 years %	10 years %
Residential Property				
Sydney	12.2	12.8	14.0	10.9
Melbourne	5.3	14.9	15.4	10.4
Brisbane	18.4	10.3	9.2	9.5
Adelaide	0.7	9.7	8.5	7.3
Perth	9.5	9.5	9.3	10.4
Total Australian				
Property	10.4	12.5	12.7	10.4
Australian shares	4.8	10.3	11.8	13.8
International shares	3.4	9.8	19.4	16.2
Fixed interest	12.0	5.2	8.8	10.7
Cash	6.3	5.7	5.8	6.4
Gold bullion	11.7	2.1	−1.2	−0.4
Superannuation funds				
(after tax)	6.9	8.3	10.3	10.9
Inflation (CPI)	5.9	3.8	2.1	2.2

(*Source*: ANZ Funds Management Investment Monitor.)

These figures show residential property is a decent and steady performer over time. They also show it's a volatile asset in the shorter term and a varying performer across different markets.

Transaction costs and capital improvements

The ANZ Investment Monitor's residential property returns derived from Real Estate Institute of Australia (REIA) data, are based on the average annual total returns of three-bedroom houses taking into account capital (price) growth, plus rental income, minus outgoings (calculated as 25% of rent).

However, and this is significant, these performance figures *do not* take into account buying and selling (transaction) costs for residential property, which are generally much higher than for shares, cash or fixed interest.

Property transaction costs include stamp duty, conveyancing fees and agent's fees, and normally run into many thousands of dollars, significantly influencing when and if a property investment goes into the black. Transaction costs are certainly not to be sneezed at, and if factored into the above returns would definitely make residential property look less attractive compared with the other investments.

To further cloud the picture presented by these figures, they give no indication of how much of the growth in residential property values is due to *owners injecting their own capital* into their properties through renovations, extensions, landscaping and general upgrading.

To clarify, let's say you bought a three-bedroom house for $250,000 in 2000, then sold it in 2001 for $350,000. These two transactions would go into REIA calculations and could help create the impression that residential property prices were going through the roof. *But, what if you had spent $120,000 renovating the property in the year you owned it?* It might look like you had made a real-estate killing, but the reality is otherwise – you would have taken a bath.

Most median home prices published in the media from time to time – from a variety of sources – do not take into account the capital value added to homes by their owners' own money, as distinct from the more mysterious price-increasing effect of 'market forces'. Remember this when working out just what sort of returns you would like to achieve from a residential property investment, and try to answer this (difficult) question – how much growth in the property's capital value is likely to come from a buoyant market and how much growth is likely to come from your own pocket? If you pick the right property, most of it should come from the market. If you pick the wrong property, then you'll generate most of the 'growth' yourself.

181

Making Money

Micro markets within larger markets

Remember that the just-mentioned REIA/ANZ Investment Monitor returns are based on the average price plus net rentals of three-bedroom houses across all Australian cities. But be very aware that particular areas within a city or township, as well as other types of dwellings, produce both higher and lower returns than these.

To illustrate just how variable the property market can be within one city, let's look at the Melbourne housing market in the year between December 1999 and December 2000. At one extreme, Brighton experienced a 23% increase in median house prices over the year from $542,500 to $668,000. At the other end, the median house prices in Frankston fell by 14.3% from $146,750 to $125,750. Overall, median Melbourne house prices rose 10.2% over the 12 months from $245,000 to $270,000. (*Source:* Real Estate Institute of Victoria.)

In Perth during the year to June 2000, median house prices in Kallaroo rose 18.8% to $221,900, while they fell by 4% to $159,200 in Mundaring and fell by 2% to $104,800 in Kelmscott. Overall, the median house price of established houses in Perth rose by 25.5% from $149,900 to $187,000. (*Source:* Real Estate Institute of Western Australia.)

In Sydney, one of the biggest increases in median house prices in the year to September 2000 came from Woollahra with a rise of 26% to $830,000. On the other hand, Randwick, nearby, experienced a drop of 6.1% to $540,000. Overall, the median house price of established houses in Sydney rose by 2.2% to $305,000. (*Source:* Real Estate Institute of NSW.)

The best performing micro markets

It has been a trend for some years that areas close to the centre of major Australian cities have tended to show stronger price growth than areas further out.

What's happening is that the oldest and closest suburbs to the city are being done up and gentrified, and then attention is turning to nearby, similar suburbs a bit further out. Urban renewal of this type thus tends to spread out in concentric circles from the centre of the city.

It seems that we are increasingly turning our backs on the traditional suburban dream of a house with a back yard in favour of a more cramped, but more convenient and probably more snazzy inner-city lifestyle. This is reflected in the escalating prices of prime inner-city properties in comparison with the generally lower levels of price growth in outer-lying regions.

In general (and I stress *in general* – there are *always* exceptions) try to buy a property that:

- is close to the city centre
- is in an area where gentrification is under way or is likely to be soon
- is aesthetically pleasing or at least has the potential to be
- has a unique or rare positive characteristic. Remember that scarcity adds value to any asset.

Now, if your foresight is good and you buy into an area just before gentrification takes off, your property will show very good capital returns – but be aware of the risks. Some areas take ages before they become popular and in some areas it may not happen at all. These include places where there has been haphazard industrial development, often accompanied by high levels of air and noise pollution. You find such areas in all Australian cities, and I advise you to look elsewhere for investment.

Obviously, everyone wants to live in a place that is as pleasant and as attractive as possible. And being an investor you can't afford to hang on to a property in an unattractive locality for too long waiting for the caffe latte set to move in and tart the place up. The longer a property sits around effectively doing nothing, the less money you are making. And, if you have borrowed to buy, you will actually be losing money while the property stagnates.

⚬━ KEY THOUGHT

One of the basic truths in buying real estate is: position is paramount. Beauty, scarcity and convenience are some of the qualities to look for.

Making Money

Satisfy the baby boomers (the 'empty nesters')

What sort of individual property is likely to produce the best investment returns, both in terms of capital (price) and income (rental) growth? Well, we've seen above how hard it is to answer this question just by looking at short-term property results for specific areas, the sort of information regularly presented to us in the media.

An answer, however, begins to emerge if you look at Australia's changing demographic patterns and use this as the basis for your real-estate decisions. There are two key points to consider. Firstly, Australia's largest demographic grouping, the post-war baby boomers (born between 1945 and the mid 1960s), are now moving into middle and older age. Secondly, due to lower immigration and a reduced birthrate the aging baby boomers will remain the largest demographic grouping for many years. This means the overall Australian population is aging – *and older people have different housing requirements than younger people.*

When the older baby boomers were young parents they mostly wanted as big a house as possible with a backyard for the children – like parents of any era. This invariably meant living in the suburbs but now, as they slowly age and the children move out, they don't need the big family home and garden any more. Increasingly, baby boomers will sell their large suburban houses and move to smaller dwellings, such as townhouses closer to the city or to coastal retirement enclaves. Without a family to feed, these 'empty nesters', as they have become known, will have few or no debts and possibly a superannuation pay-out, and many will be able to afford to move more or less where they please.

Generally, the dwellings they move to will be low-maintenance (little or no gardens), made of good quality materials, will be well appointed and well positioned. They will want as few stairs as possible, good security, ample parking and storage, proximity to all amenities, and preferably a level stroll to shops and transport. They will also prefer localities that are attractive, as well as clean, quiet and safe.

If you want to buy an investment residential property, I recommend you buy something that fits these parameters. The type of housing that will appeal to many of the aging baby boomers will remain in greater demand than the type of housing appealing to other, less robust demographic groups – and hence show greater growth. It should also mean that the general localities best suited to baby boomers' needs should show relatively stronger price and rental growth than other localities.

⚿ KEY THOUGHT

Pick a property and a location that will appeal to aging baby boomers. They've got the numbers, they've got the money. There will be more than 5 million Australians aged 65 or older in the year 2031.

Residential property – problems ahead?

A lot of concern has been expressed by investment commentators about Australia's slowing rate of natural population growth. In 1921 the number of Australian-born residents was increasing at 2.2% per year; by 1997–98 the rate had fallen to 0.4%. In 1970 there were 20.6 births per 1,000 Australian residents; in 2000 the rate had dropped to 13.3 births per 1,000, a fall of 35.4%.

Our declining birthrate was accompanied by a net immigration intake of 1.3 million between 1994 and 1999. (*Source:* ABS.) In 1950 at the high point of the post-war baby boom and following an influx of migrants from overseas, Australia's population was growing at the rate of 3.3%. But by 1999, this rate of growth had slowed to 1.2%. (*Source:* ABS.)

Now, the relevance of all this to residential property is that population growth, accompanied by growing business activity and employment, is the key driver of real (after-inflation) property growth. So, all being equal, if there is a decline in population growth – due either to natural causes or reduced immigration – there should also be a corresponding relative decline in property returns.

It's important to recognise that a residential property is not like a business. Other than renovating the dwelling and upgrading the grounds, or getting the land rezoned, you don't have much influence over its financial performance. To what extent it appreciates is largely beyond your control. You're in the hands of the market – and where population growth is slow, market growth is likely to be slow too.

Now, I don't believe that the rate of our population growth will ever be allowed to get so low as to bring on a sustained decline in property values, but it is quite likely that residential property returns in general will not be as good in the future as they have been. Australia's slowing rate of population growth is partly to blame for this, and so is our changing demographic structure.

Let me explain. The older 45- to 65-year age group is the fastest growing segment of the working population, and it will continue to grow until about the year 2020, when every other age segment will be in decline. Significantly, the younger 25- to 45-year age group will fall sharply as a proportion of the total working population over the same period. And because the 25- to 45-year age group is the one most involved in the formation of new households, its relative decline over the next 20 years is likely to lead to a corresponding relative decline in the demand for new housing. Therefore, I would advise you to look to other areas of the residential market to invest in rather than investing in property primarily designed for new, young families.

Outgoings

You will recall the REIA-derived residential property returns reflect the total investment performance of three-bedroom houses, arrived at by adding both the average price growth and the average rental growth of this type of dwelling, *minus all outgoings*. So, what do we mean by 'outgoings'? Well, they include:

- council and water rates
- insurances
- body corporate fees
- property management fees to real-estate agents
- maintenance
- bookkeeping fees
- accountancy fees
- legal fees (for drawing up leases)
- advertising costs to find tenants
- costs involved in employing people (for example, worker's compensation)
- bank charges
- petrol, phone, postage and stationery.

While ongoing costs vary from property to property, a reasonable rule of thumb is that residential outgoings average 20% of gross rentals. (This is the percentage used by the REIA, based on three-bedroom houses. Net rent is, therefore, around 80% of gross rent.)

Some property costs are unavoidable, like insurance and rates, but it may be possible to save some money by managing your own property, doing your own maintenance or finding your own tenants. These chores might give you a headache, but they will help you achieve a better than average net return (yield) from your investment property.

Buying costs

When you buy a property there is no agent's commission to pay, but you will be up for stamp duty and legal fees and probably some other costs. Stamp duties and legal fees in particular vary across the States, and are calculated on a (normally sliding) scale dependent on the value of the property.

The following is an approximate breakdown of what buying a home for $200,000 (with a mortgage of $150,000) can cost. I stress that all these costs, apart from stamp duties, are open to market forces and negotiation and there may be no need to pay for pest and/or building reports if they have already been provided by the vendor.

Property price: $200,000
Location: Wollongong
Mortgage: $150,000

Stamp duty on property	$5,490
Stamp duty on mortgage	$ 541
Buyer's legal fees	$2,000
Bank loan application fee	$ 600
Survey	$ 325
Pest and building reports	$ 320
Total	$9,276

In this example, buying costs represent 4.6% of the $200,000 purchase price.

Making Money

Selling costs

When you sell your investment property you will be up for some or all of the following costs: agent's commission, advertising, solicitor's fees (to prepare the mortgage and exchange documents), early mortgage pay-out fee, building and pest reports, surveys and possibly cosmetic renovations.

Agent's fees vary from State to State and, in some instances, are simply arrived at through negotiation between the vendor and the agent. As a guide, work on the agent's selling fee being 2% to 2.5% of the value of the property.

Here is approximately what it would cost to sell the same property for $200,000 in Wollongong. (Bear in mind that lenders may not charge an early repayment fee or may charge more than is quoted here. Also, some vendors make no financial contribution towards a property's advertising campaign, while others contribute significantly more than quoted here.)

Solicitor's fees (including contract preparation)	$1,800
Early mortgage pay-out bank fee	$ 500
Agent's fees 2.5% (negotiable)	$5,000
Vendor's contribution costs for advertising	$ 500
Total	$7,800

In this example, selling costs represent 3.9% of the $200,000 selling price.

Recouping costs

You can see how buying and selling costs add up to a very significant proportion of a property's value. In this case – based on real quotes taken – **transaction costs total $17,076 or 8.5% of the property's total value** (assuming that the purchase price and selling price are the same).

A property has to appreciate by this much before you recoup these transaction costs. Remember, too, that these are not the only costs of investing in property. If, like most property investors, you have borrowed to buy, you will have interest payments to make, possibly tax to pay on the rent you receive, and capital gains tax to contend with on selling the property (applying to any investment property bought after 19 September 1985). Of course interest repayments, income tax and capital gains tax can be a feature of any other investment you make and, though not unique to property, you still have to account for them in working out your overall returns.

While all this might sound as though I'm a little down on residential property as an investment, that's not the case. Over time it has proved to be a decent investment, and as long as you *pick the right property in the right location at the right price*, it should continue to be so.

Take a long-term position

As is the case with other mainstream investments taking a long-term position in residential real estate is generally the best policy. The reason is simple. Property prices can go through major swings that can occur with little warning. Consequently, if you buy and sell over a short time frame, you are just as likely to catch a bust as you are a boom and while you can make a lot of money in real estate in two or three years, you can lose your shirt just as quickly.

The thing to be aware of is that growth in property prices does not occur smoothly over time. A relatively common pattern includes a price surge of one to two years' duration followed by a price fall, in turn followed by a period of stagnation and/or modest price growth lasting around four to five years. The solution is to buy and hold property for the long term (meaning at least for seven years). This way you increase the likelihood of catching a price surge and consequently of generating good *average* annual returns. You can also stop worrying about *when* to buy because, over time, this question becomes irrelevant. So, when is the right time to buy? When you're able to!

As we have noted above, too, you need to hold on to property for at least as long as it takes to appreciate to the point of covering the buying and selling costs. Under flat market conditions just meeting this requirement alone could take years.

Making Money

Cash flow

Investing in property is a bit different from other asset classes. With shares and bonds you hand over your money and then sit back and wait for the investment to start producing (all being equal). With property it's a different story. You hand over the money ... and then you hand over some more ... and then you hand over some more ... Just like your home, a property investment is a constant source of expense.

Your rental income should more than cover the ongoing costs of holding a property (approximately 20% of gross rentals). But for most property investors the biggest cost is interest on the loan and, in most cases, in the early years of a property investment net rentals do not cover interest costs. (Of course this is dependent on what proportion of the property's value is borrowed, what the interest rate on the loan is, what the rental income is and what the ongoing costs actually are.)

Because most property investors will be out of pocket for the first years of the investment, a very important question to consider before you start looking for funds is: what other sources of income do you have to make up any shortfalls, and how secure is this other source of income? When thinking about this, bear in mind that there are bound to be times when your property is vacant – indeed, it is common practice to allow for at least two weeks of vacancy per year.

Lenders will clearly want to know how you intend to repay the loan. What you should do for their sake (as well as for your own) is to prepare a cash-flow analysis on the property you are interested in, projected out for as many years as it takes for income to at least equal outgoings. The point of this exercise is to find out how long (if at all) the investment will leave you out of pocket.

This projection should list all anticipated rental income and all anticipated expenses against the property, including interest. Starting at the beginning of Year 1 with a $0 balance, by the end of the first year it will indicate a cash surplus or shortfall for the year. This amount is then carried forward as the starting balance for Year 2, and so on, for every following year. Just make sure that from Year 2 onwards all income and expenses are adjusted for anticipated inflation. In the 18 years to 2000, inflation averaged 4.42% p.a.

When doing a cash-flow analysis, for safety, factor in a higher rather than lower rate of inflation.

At some stage the cash-flow analysis will indicate you have moved into a cash surplus, as rentals, boosted by inflation, finally outstrip expenses (though at this point you will have another expense to contend with – income tax). Depending on how many years the analysis indicates it will take to move into a cash surplus, you will then be able to decide if you have sufficient other income to afford the holding costs of the investment.

If you decide you can fund the initial losses that your property investment is likely to make (*and be aware that these losses are tax deductible against your other income* – see 'Borrowing to invest' pages 195–197), show the projections to your lending institution and demonstrate how you intend to make up the cash shortfall in the first few years. If you do all this credibly, there is little reason why you shouldn't get the loan.

Preparing cash-flow projections involves a fair amount of homework, effort and time – and a personal computer spreadsheet is perfectly suited to the task if you know how to use one. If you don't feel confident about doing this yourself, don't worry, an accountant will gladly do it for you for a reasonable fee – and I suggest it's money well spent given the stakes involved.

On the next page is an example of a property investment cash-flow analysis, prepared by Peter Wills, Senior Lecturer in Property at the University of Western Sydney. It is based on the following assumptions.

Property purchase price	$200,000
Purchase costs	$9,000 (stamp duty, legals, etc.)
Real capital cost	$209,000
Size of loan	$140,000
Type of loan	Interest-only fixed rate
Interest rate	7% p.a. (calculated annually)
Starting rent	$230 per week

Cash flows under three different annual growth rates are calculated on the following pages. These are at a 'most likely' case scenario growth rate of 5%, a 'least likely' case scenario growth rate of 2%, and a 'best' case scenario growth rate of 10%.

Making Money

In each scenario the property's value, the rent and the outgoings are increased annually in line with these growth rates. But do note the following.

- For simplicity, annual changes to some variables are non-compounding. The annual changes used throughout the cash-flow analysis are derived from the change in values from Year 1 to Year 2.
- All amounts are rounded off to the nearest dollar.

Cash flow tables

'Most likely' case scenario with all growth calculated at 5% p.a.

Purchase price $200,000	Year 1	Year 2	Year 3	Year 4	Year 5
	$	$	$	$	$
Weekly rent	230	242	253	265	276
Gross rent (p.a.)	11,960	12,558	13,156	13,754	14,352
Vacancy (allow 2 weeks p.a.)	460	483	506	529	552
Outgoings	2,990	3,140	3,289	3,439	3,558
Net income p.a.	8,510	8,936	9,361	9,787	10,212
Interest only @ 7% p.a.	9,800	9,800	9,800	9,800	9,800
Net return (loss) p.a.	−1,290	−865	−439	−14	+412
per week	−25	−17	−8	0	+8
Property value at end of each period	210,000	220,000	230,000	240,000	250,000

Total capital gain (over the 5-year period)	$50,000
Less: net return (loss) (over 5 years)	$−2,196
Less: purchase costs	$−9,000
Overall capital gain	$38,804

'Least likely' case scenario with growth calculated at 2% p.a.

Purchase price $200,000	Year 1	Year 2	Year 3	Year 4	Year 5
	$	$	$	$	$
Weekly rent	230	235	240	245	250
Gross rent (p.a.)	11,960	12,220	12,480	12,740	13,000
Vacancy	460	470	480	490	500
Outgoings	2,990	3,055	3,120	3,185	3,250
Net income	8,510	8,695	8,880	9,065	9,250
Interest	9,800	9,800	9,800	9,800	9,800
Net return (loss) p.a.	−1,290	−1,105	−920	−735	−550
per week	−25	−21	−18	−14	−11
Property value at end of each period	204,000	208,000	212,000	216,000	220,000

Total capital gain (over 5 years)	$20,000
Less: Net return (loss) (over 5 years)	$−4,600
Less: purchase costs	$−9,000
Overall capital gain	$ 6,400

'Best case' scenario with growth calculated at 10% p.a.

Purchase price $200,000	Year 1	Year 2	Year 3	Year 4	Year 5
	$	$	$	$	$
Weekly rent	230	253	276	299	322
Gross rent (p.a.)	11,960	13,156	14,352	15,548	16,744
Vacancy	460	506	552	598	644
Outgoings	2,990	3,289	3,558	3,887	4,168
Net income	8,510	9,361	10,212	11,063	11,914
Interest	9,800	9,800	9,800	9,800	9,800
Net return (loss) p.a.	−1,290	−439	+412	+1,263	+2,114
per week	−25	−8	+8	+24	+40
Property value at end of each period	220,000	240,000	260,000	280,000	300,000

Total capital gain (over 5 years)	$ 100,000
Less: net return (loss) (over 5 years)	$ 2,060
Less: purchase costs	$−9,000
Overall capital gain	$ 93,060

Making Money

Taking the projections for the property's long-term performance at 5% growth (the 'most likely' rate), you would be out of pocket for $25, $17 and $8 per week for Years 1, 2 and 3 respectively. In Year 4 the property would be fully self-funding, but producing no income, while in Year 5 it would be generating a small weekly net income of $8.

As a matter of comparison, if the property showed only 2% annual growth, you would be dipping into your pocket to fund it until Year 7, with it producing a modest $7 net weekly income by Year 10.

This is of course the point of a cash-flow analysis – it shows you just how much you will be reaching for on a weekly and annual basis, and enables you to rationally answer the question, 'Can I afford this investment?'

Earnings projections

Now, while projecting a long way into the future is a highly conjectural exercise, based on the assumptions given above, the overall returns from the three investment scenarios after *10 years* would be:

'Most likely' case scenario (5% annual growth)

Total gross capital gain		$ 100,000
Net cumulative income	$ 6,248	
Purchase costs	$ −9,000	
Subtotal (less)		$ −2,752
Overall capital gain over 10 years		$ 97,248

'Least likely' scenario (2% annual growth)

Total gross capital gain		$ 40,000
Net cumulative income	$ −4,575	
Purchase costs	$ −9,000	
Subtotal (less)		$−13,575
Overall capital gain over 10 years		$ 26,425

'Best case' scenario (10% annual growth)

Total gross capital gain		$ 200,000
Net cumulative income	$ 25,395	
Purchase costs	$−9,000	
Subtotal (add)		$ 16,395
Overall capital gain over 10 years		$ 216,395

These earnings projections dramatically illustrate how important capital growth is to the viability of a property investment. Note that after 10 years at only 2% annual growth the property has generated a total return of only 38% on your initial $69,000 investment (remember you borrowed the other $140,000 of the $209,000 total purchase price). Compare this with the total return over the 10 years of 314% at 10% annual growth.

⟲ KEY THOUGHT

Successful property investment is absolutely dependent on good rates of capital growth.

Borrowing to invest

Not many people buy an investment property with their own funds. The beauty about borrowing to invest is that it enables you to participate in investments that would otherwise be closed to you by virtue of their sheer cost, whether it's property, shares, bonds or art works.

There is nothing intrinsically wrong with borrowing to invest, or 'gearing', and as far as property investment is concerned it's the time-honoured method. It's just important that you do it sensibly.

The dynamic of borrowing to invest is that it enables you to increase your stake in an asset (over and above what you could afford out of your own savings) which in turn amplifies the size of its return to you – be this a positive (profit) or negative (loss) return. In other words, the more you borrow the more you stand to gain or to lose. The higher your borrowings, therefore, the higher your risk.

It's for this reason when borrowing that you must exercise great caution. You must be as sure as you possibly can be that the asset *will show positive returns*, because if it doesn't you will simply magnify your losses.

I receive many letters on this subject and it seems from this correspondence that many people believe the main attraction of borrowing to invest is the tax advantage derived from *negative gearing*. This is worrying, so let's look at it.

For a start, an investment property is said to be negatively geared when the costs of holding it (including interest costs) exceed the rent received. Because the property is an investment, this loss is tax deductible and this tax deduction can be put towards reducing the tax payable on the investor's other assessable income.

For example, take this property investment:

Home price	$120,000
Deposit	$20,000
Loan	$100,000
Interest rate 7%	$7,000 p.a.
Rent	$120 p.w. or $6,240 p.a.

Ongoing expenses; including rates, water, insurance, maintenance and depreciation	$1,250 p.a.
After-expenses annual income [$6,240 − $1,250]	$4,990
Annual interest	$7,000
Annual profit/**loss** [$4,990 − $7,000]	**−$2,010**

Here, the investor can reduce the tax liability on their other assessable income by applying the investment property's pre-tax loss of $2,010 to it.

If they were on the highest marginal tax rate of 48.5% (including Medicare levy), their *after tax* loss on the property investment would be reduced to $1,035, calculated thus:

$2,010 × 48.5%	$ 975
$2,010 − $975	$1,035
After-tax loss	**$1,035**

A reduction in the property's annual loss from $2,010 to $1,035 due to tax treatment is a major saving.

If our investor were on the *lowest marginal* tax rate of 18.5% (including Medicare levy), the after-tax loss on the investment would be reduced from $2,010 to $1,638, calculated thus:

$2,010 × 18.5%	$ 372
$2,010 − $372	$1,638
Real loss	**$1,638**

A reduction in real loss on the property from $2,010 to $1,638, while not as good as the savings at the highest marginal rate, is not bad all the same! These two calculations clearly demonstrate how *negative gearing benefits those on higher marginal rates more so than those on lower marginal income tax rates.*

While negative gearing can reduce the real size of your annual loss on an investment – which is certainly welcome – it should not be the main attraction of the investment. A loss, albeit a reduced one, *is still a loss*! And no one has ever grown rich out of tax losses! You should only ever invest if you believe the investment will show genuine positive returns over time. If it provides tax deductions in the process, take that as a bonus, but realise that it is not the main game.

Borrowing to invest and negative gearing were particularly popular and successful strategies for accumulating wealth in the 1970s and 1980s. All you had to do was raise a loan, buy a property, sit back and then let the high rate of inflation and the relatively high levels of population growth do the work for you. And if you bought the property before 20 September 1985, there was no capital gains tax to pay on it. It was a property investors' dream! Like hundreds of thousands of other Australians, I bene-fited from borrowing to invest in property. In 1983 I went into hock to buy a modest semi-detached house in Sydney for what then seemed like an exorbitant price, only to find that four years later it had increased in value by 250%! I am the first to admit that there was no great skill on my part in generating this fabu-lous return – it was just the way the market was at the time.

Things are a bit different now. Our current levels of low infla-tion are expected to remain low for a while yet, and in a low inflationary environment residential property growth tends to be low too (though not always). This is significant because, when you borrow to invest in property, you are primarily borrowing for capital gains.

So, with all these words of warning, is borrowing to invest in residential property still a viable proposition? With qualification, my answer is 'yes'. The qualification is this – do your homework well and select your property with great care, ensuring you pay a fair price for it. Good property will continue to produce good returns over time but, whatever you do, when borrowing to invest in prop-erty, make sure that your other sources of income are secure enough to cover any running losses. If you do generate some tax deductions from the losses along the way, good, but don't enter into the invest-ment because of them.

☛ KEY THOUGHT

Only borrow to invest in residential property (or any other asset for that matter) if you are as sure as you possibly can be that the investment will ultimately show a decent positive return, which will generally be realised when you sell it.

Selecting a lender

You've done your homework, you've picked the property, you've done your projections, now, who should you go to for finance? Well, assuming the answer is not 'anyone who's game enough', the type of lender to look for is one whose interest rate is competitive and no higher for property investment loans than it is for owner-occupier loans.

Since the increase in competition brought to the home-lending market by the mushrooming of players in it, getting an investment property loan at the same rate as an owner-occupier loan is easy. Interestingly, when the first edition of this book was written six years ago, most lenders were charging investors a higher rate than owner-occupiers, generally in the order of an extra 1%.

There is a significant difference between the highest and lowest rates on the market, so it will pay you to speak to a number of lenders. Also bear in mind there is more to a competitive loan than just the interest rate. You should also investigate the lender's establishment fees, ongoing charges, fees for switching from a fixed rate to variable rate loan or vice versa, and policies on additional lump sum repayments and/or total early repayment. (These areas are looked at in some detail in Chapter Seven, 'Mortgages'.)

Whichever lenders you speak to, don't be afraid to push for a better deal. There is always room for negotiation. If you're considered a good risk the lender may offer you 'a better than the advertised' rate.

Another area of difference between lenders is the amount they will lend you against the valuation of the property, known as the 'loan to valuation ratio'. Not so long ago, some lenders were inclined to offer loans to investors on a lower loan to value ratio than they were to owner-occupiers. An example of this is a lender offering a loan of up to 85% of the valuation on a particular property to an investor, but offering a loan of up to 95% of valuation on the same property to an owner-occupier. Increasingly, this loan to valuation difference between investment loans and owner-occupier loans is being eroded.

Your loan

As a potential or existing property investor it's likely you already own the home in which you live, outright or partially. It's also likely that when you approach a lender to finance an investment property, the lender will want to take additional security over your home to partly secure the new loan.

If this is the case, try to avoid having the lender bundle up both the mortgage on your home and the loan on the investment property into one big loan covering both properties (unless the new loan is at a lower rate than your home mortgage rate). Generally, it's best to keep the two properties on separate loans, as you can see.

- Interest and the costs associated with an investment property are tax deductible, whereas the interest and costs associated with your own home are not. If they're covered by separate loans, it's easier to keep track of both for taxation purposes.
- Separate loans give you flexibility to, say, have your home on a principal and interest, variable rate loan, and the investment property on an interest-only fixed rate loan (which costs less to service).
- With two loans you can continue to put additional payments towards your home with the aim of making it debt free, both for peace of mind and to allow you to borrow more money against it later for another investment!
- If the interest rate on the investment loan is at a high investment rate, the bundled loan will also be at this high rate.

Of course, having one loan means you only have one set of fees. However, the advantages of having two loans will normally outweigh this.

So, what sort of loan is best for you – variable rate, fixed rate, principal and interest, or interest-only? Well, given that rising interest rates have brought many a property investor undone, a fixed rate loan is generally preferable to a variable rate loan. At least when the interest rate is fixed you know exactly what your interest repayments will be – which is good for controlling your costs, and controlling your costs is essential for successful property investment. The problem with fixed rate loans is that if interest rates drop after you've fixed your rate, you'll find you're paying more interest than you would on a variable rate loan, and refinancing out of a fixed rate loan can be very expensive.

Interest-only loans are useful if your budgeting is tight, because repayments are less than on principal and interest loans. However, interest-only loans are rarely available for more than a five-year term, at the end of which you will still owe the lender all of the principal. At that point you will have the option of either refinancing for another term or selling the property to repay the principal, hopefully realising a capital gain in the process.

Be aware that an interest-only loan will not 'buy' you any equity in a property. You will only acquire equity in a property financed this way through capital appreciation, meaning, through an increase in its market value. You can, therefore, look at the loan repayments as simply the price you must pay for the right to hold the property in your name (which also gives you the right to sell it) while the process of capital appreciation occurs.

Take note that if you start with an interest-only loan, you can refinance into a principal and interest loan when the interest-only term expires. Also be aware that if you do refinance rather than sell, your new loan will almost certainly have a different interest rate which will affect your cash-flow projections.

Investment loan checklist

- Is the income you need to meet interest payments secure?
- Do you clearly understand the risks involved?
- What are the costs involved in holding the investment?
- Can you easily sell the investment if your situation changes, and what is the cost of doing so?
- Are you doing this only for tax reasons or is it a good long-term investment?
- Do you understand the loan documentation?
- Is the rate of interest reasonable, and stable?
- Will you sleep at night if the investment falls in value in the short term?
- If you do take a principal and interest loan, remember that only the interest component is tax deductible.

If you purchase your investment property with a principal and interest loan, every repayment you make marginally increases your equity in the property, but your repayments are higher than with an interest-only loan. For those intending to hold their property investment for the long term, and who are in a position to make additional repayments, a principal and interest loan is probably the best choice.

Rental income

While long-term capital appreciation is definitely the most important aspect of residential property investment, the rental income it can produce may be quite significant, particularly if you hold a property for some years. Indeed, in time, you may be able to live quite comfortably off the rental income from two, three or four good residential properties.

What sort of rental income does a residential property normally produce? Well, it varies tremendously depending on the type of property and where it is located. However, the gross median weekly rentals for three-bedroom, unfurnished houses in the December 2000 quarter were as follows.

Sydney	Melbourne	Brisbane	Adelaide	Perth	Canberra	Hobart	Darwin
$235	$195	$175	$160	$154	$210	$155	$220

Median prices for all types of houses at that time were:

Sydney	Melbourne	Brisbane	Adelaide
$305,000	$270,000	$145,000	$137,000

Perth	Canberra	Hobart	Darwin
$158,000	$187,000	$115,000	$180,000

(*Source*: Real Estate Institute of Australia.)

Based on these figures, the average gross rental yields (calculated by expressing the gross annual rent as a proportion of the market value of the property) in these markets during the December 2000 quarter were:

Sydney	Melbourne	Brisbane	Adelaide	Perth	Canberra	Hobart	Darwin
4.0%	3.8%	6.3%	6.1%	5.1%	5.8%	7.0%	6.4%

Making Money

Managing your investment property

The above yields are calculated on the assumption your property is let for 52 weeks per year (which is unrealistic – you ought to allow for at least two weeks' vacancy per year), and also on the assumption that the relationship between you and your tenants (directly or through a property manager) is a fair and reasonable one. But there are such things as bad landlords and bad tenants and where this situation occurs below average yields are generated. Conversely, good landlords and good tenants tend to produce better than average yields. It's often said in property circles that *landlords get the tenants they deserve*, and vice versa.

A 'good' landlord is one who ensures the property is well maintained and who attends to problems promptly and properly when they occur, charges a fair rent and stays out of the tenant's hair. 'Bad' landlords do the opposite.

'Good' tenants are those who pay the rent on time, take good care of the property, don't generate complaints from the neighbours and don't ask the property manager or landlord to come around and change a light bulb. Again, 'bad' tenants do the opposite.

Clearly if you want optimum long-term returns from your property be prepared to spend the necessary money on it to make it attractive to good tenants. Not only will you have to spend less on the property after they have moved out (compared with having bad tenants), but they will give you far fewer headaches while they are there. And if attracting and keeping good tenants means accepting a slightly lower rent, do it. It's much better to have a good tenant at a moderate rent than a problematic one at a high rent.

How do you select a tenant? Whether you place ads in the newspaper and interview candidates yourself or have a real-estate agency property manager choose a tenant for you, make sure it's done carefully. It's difficult to shift a bad tenant unless they specifically contravene the lease, and then an eviction can take ages, at least eight weeks, during which time you'll probably receive no rent.

If a property manager finds a tenant for you, they will charge a 'leasing fee', which is normally equivalent to one or two weeks' rent. (You do have the right to veto the choice of tenant until the lease is signed.) If you choose to let the real-estate agency manage the property for you on an ongoing basis, the management charge is around 7% to 10% of gross rentals. For this fee the property manager collects the rent (and chases it up if late), organises minor repairs, and represents you in all dealings with the tenant including, if needs be, before the Residential Tenancies Tribunal in the event of a dispute. In other words, you won't have to deal with the tenant at all – which is the way many landlords and tenants prefer it.

Leases – obligations, rights and conditions

When you feel you have found the right tenant for your property, it's best to make sure you get everything clear from the start. This includes: conditions of the lease; when the rent is due, to whom and where it should be paid; and details of the bond.

A tenancy is not formalised until a lease is signed by both the landlord (or their agent) and the tenant. The lease is a legally binding document that lays down the terms of the tenancy, rental and any special conditions that might apply, such as the requirement for the tenant to mow the lawn once a month. The lease is designed to protect your interests and the tenant's, and assigns rights and obligations on both parties. Leases come under the jurisdiction of each State's tenancy Acts, so the rules and regulations vary across Australia to some degree. In most States, the *Tenancy Act* ensures a highly regulated system where a tenancy tribunal exists to mediate disputes between tenants and landlords. Rather than detailing all the differences here, I have chosen to look at the *NSW Tenancy Act*, because it's probably the most rigorous in Australia and most of the other States either have or are moving towards a similar system.

Leases generally fall within two categories: fixed term or continuing tenancy. A tenancy agreement (or lease) is a standard form, which is simply completed by both parties and covers obligations, rights and conditions. These include:

- *Inspections* detailing the condition of the property before your tenants move in and after they move out to determine if any damage is attributable to the tenants, or if it was pre-existing.
- *Rights of entry* to rented premises usually require the consent of the tenants or an order from the State's residential tenancy authority. In New South Wales you are entitled to inspect the property up to four times a year, but you must give seven days notice to the tenants. You are allowed to enter at any time to carry out emergency repairs.

Making Money

- *Rent* increases don't carry any restrictions as long as the required notice is given. In New South Wales, if the tenant considers the rent increase excessive they can take the matter to the Residential Tenancies Tribunal. A ruling can be made in favour of the tenant for a lesser rent to be paid and is valid for a specified time (usually one year).

- *Repairs*, where urgent and essential, are the landlord's responsibility, and you are obliged to attend to things like a burst water pipe or a leaking roof. If the landlord is unavailable or refuses (and this is where a property manager can be such a blessing), the tenant can arrange to carry out the repairs and then apply for reimbursement of their costs. If the landlord refuses to pay, the matter can be taken to the Residential Tenancies Tribunal and payment can be ordered.

- *Eviction* orders can be issued if rent remains unpaid. If the tenant falls behind in rent (normally payable two weeks in advance) you are entitled to issue an eviction notice, giving the client two weeks to vacate the premises. Even if the rent is brought up to date, the notice stands and can be enforced if you wish.

- *Residential tenancy tribunals and authorities* have been set up to hear disputes between landlords and tenants with the judgments being legally binding and penalties applying for noncompliance.

- *The Anti-discrimination Act* makes it illegal for a landlord or agent to advertise for or refuse a letting to potential tenants on the grounds of sex, race, marital status, sexuality, physical and intellectual impairment (with some exceptions) and whether or not they have children. This could mean that you may be legally obliged to offer tenancy to someone you'd otherwise prefer not to.

Bond money

You are within your rights (and you are recommended) to ask for bond money as security against any damage tenants may cause or against any rent they may not pay. Generally the bond is equivalent to four to six weeks' rent, depending on the nature of the premises and the size of the rent.

In New South Wales (other States' procedures are similar), the bond must be lodged with the Rental Bond Board (or equivalent) within seven days of payment to you or the agent by the tenant. The tenant is then sent a receipt from the Board as evidence that the money has been lodged. At the end of the tenancy the tenant fills out a bond refund form which must be countersigned by you or the property manager. Clearly this is only countersigned for a full refund if everything is above board, namely, the property is in the same condition as when the tenancy began (taking into account fair wear and tear), the rent is up-to-date, and adequate notice to vacate was provided.

If everything is not above board and you wish to be paid part or all of the bond as compensation for damage, unpaid rent or inadequate notice to vacate, you must apply directly to the Rental Bond Board. If the tenant has agreed to relinquish a part or all of the bond it will be noted on the refund form. The Rental Bond Board will then deduct this amount from the bond and send it directly to you – the remainder, if any, being returned to the tenant. If you can't reach agreement with the tenant over the bond, send a refund form to the Rental Bond Board anyway without the tenant's signature. This obliges the Board to write to the tenant notifying them that a claim has been made on the bond and advising them they have 14 days to apply to the Residential Tenancies Tribunal if they wish to dispute the claim. If the tenant does not reply in 14 days, the bond is paid out to the landlord. This is what happens in New South Wales, and in other States and Territories similar procedures apply.

Tax on investment property

Land tax

Land tax is an annual tax generally imposed by each State and Territory government (including the ACT, but excluding the Northern Territory) on land of higher value. Land on which the owner's principal place of residence is built and land used for primary production are generally exempt from land tax. It is usually calculated on the unimproved value of land as determined by municipal council rate notices and this means land tax does not take into account the value of buildings or other works on the land.

The taxes vary significantly from State to State, so make sure you discuss it with your accountant before you invest.

Making Money

Building depreciation allowances

As a property investor you are allowed to deduct from your assessable income an amount equivalent to 2.5% p.a. of the original construction cost of a residential building from which you derive income, if its construction was commenced on or after 16 September 1987. This deduction is allowable for a total of 40 years from commencement.

On a residential building commenced between 18 July 1985 and 15 September 1987 from which you derive income, the special write-off is 4% p.a. over a total of 25 years from commencement. These depreciation allowances against assessable income also apply to extensions, alterations and improvements to income-producing residential buildings (which includes strata title properties).

Building depreciation allowances provide a strong incentive for investing in newer rather than older properties, and can make the difference between a good and bad return on residential property investment.

Depreciation of furniture and fittings

If you are the landlord of furnished premises that contain large household items which have a limited life, you can depreciate these and claim them as a deduction against the property's taxable income. The Tax Office allows you to set your own depreciation rates based on the 'useful life' of the items, or you can use the rates set out by the Tax Office. The official depreciation rates for items purchased after 21 September 1999 vary according to the date of purchase, but, as a guide, carpets and heaters are depreciated at 10% a year, and stoves at 5%. You can only depreciate these items for a certain period; that is, until their useful life is over. Smaller items, such as cutlery, glassware and bedding can either be claimed as an expense in the year they are purchased if they cost less than $300, or they can be pooled together to be depreciated if they cost more than $300 but less than $1,000.

What you are doing with depreciation is effectively claiming as a genuine business cost the loss in value, over time, of material goods used in conducting the business. There's no doubt in the case of furnished premises that wear and tear on furniture is a genuine business cost.

Depreciation allowances can make the difference between running a profit or running a loss on your property investment in any given year which, of course, has income-tax implications. A discussion of the accounting procedures for depreciation is not appropriate here, but it can be important for property investors, and I recommend you discuss this with your accountant or the Tax Office.

Goods and Services Tax (GST)

Under The New Tax System, the provision of residential rental property is classed as an 'input taxed' supply. In plain English, this means that as a landlord, when you pay for goods and services used in letting the property, such as stationery or cleaning supplies, you will pay the GST included in their price. But you *cannot* claim an input tax credit on these items and nor can you charge the tenant GST on the rent. In other words, you the landlord wear the extra cost of the GST. (Note this 'input taxed' status only applies to residential property, not to commercial property.)

As a landlord, some of the items on which you can expect to pay GST include agent's letting and management fees, repair and maintenance costs, and purchases of equipment, including appliances.

For a more detailed explanation of how GST works, please refer to Chapter Ten.

Pay As You Go tax

Before the introduction of The New Tax System in July 2000, anyone receiving 'non-salary or wage' income of over $1,000 was subject to provisional tax. This was tax payable on your anticipated income for the following year, based on your current earnings. Since July 2000, provisional tax has come under the umbrella of Pay As You Go (PAYG) tax. As rental income is 'non-salary' earnings, when your property's rentals begin to make a profit, of at least $1,000, you need to be prepared to put aside funds for PAYG tax.

For people with investment income, which includes property rental, if your tax was *less* than $8,000 but more than $250 for the previous year (and you are *not* registered for the GST), you pay only one PAYG instalment annually, together with an Instalment Activity Statement (IAS) detailing your income and expenditure for the period. If your tax was *more* than $8,000 (and you're not registered for the GST), you need to make quarterly tax instalments and submit an IAS.

Regardless of whether you pay your tax in quarterly instalments or annually, I stress again how important it is to set aside sufficient funds to meet your tax obligations. The Tax Office takes a very unsporting view of investors who are unable to pay their tax!

Reducing your regular tax payments

For investors earning a wage or salary, a loss-making negatively geared property can significantly reduce both your taxable income and the amount of tax you regularly need to pay. Instead of waiting for a big tax refund at the *end of the financial year*, brought about by a negatively geared property investment, you can apply to the Tax Office to have the amount of tax that's automatically deducted from your regular weekly, fortnightly or monthly paypacket reduced. If the Tax Office believes you have a valid claim, it will advise your employer of the appropriate, lesser amount of tax to be withheld from your wage or salary payments. Having the extra cash spread throughout the year relieves some of the burden of paying property expenses as they arise, and if you can put the rest of the extra money into the mortgage, you can save a lot in interest.

Capital gains tax

The impact of capital gains tax (CGT) on your overall property investment returns can be significant, so it's vital you understand the effect and operation of CGT before you invest. CGT is complicated and is also looked at more closely in Chapter Ten, 'Tax'.

Briefly, if you hold an asset for more than 12 months, and you bought it after 19 September 1985, you will be liable for CGT when you sell it, if you have made a capital gain on it. A capital gain is regarded by the Tax Office as the difference between the cost of an asset and the amount you receive when you sell it (assuming the selling price is *higher* than the asset's cost), where the cost of the asset includes the original purchase price, the incidental expenses incurred in buying and selling it, and any capital improvements made in between.

Under The New Tax System, only *half* the capital gain is included in your taxable income. To be specific, tax is only charged on half of the 'notional' capital gain, which is the gain that does *not* take into account the effect of inflation. Prior to 21 September 1999, you were taxed on the (full), inflation-adjusted capital gain.

Overall, the factors that determine how much CGT you'll have to pay are: the size of the capital gain itself; your other level of income in the year the asset was sold; and, your marginal income tax rate.

Once again, I stress how important capital gains tax is for property investors, and strongly recommend you discuss this and other taxes that impact on property with your accountant before you invest.

What enhances and diminishes returns

These will *reduce* your property investment returns:
- buying a property in a poor position
- buying a property in an area showing below-average growth
- buying a property in poor structural condition with high maintenance costs
- buying a property with no aesthetic appeal or no potential to have it
- buying at the top of the market
- paying too much
- selling at the bottom of the market
- overcapitalising
- inadequate maintenance
- bad tenants
- excessive vacancy
- being a bad landlord
- inadequate planning for capital gains, land and Pay As You Go tax
- relatively high land value proportional to building value generating relatively high land tax
- rising interest rates
- general economic malaise with low rates of growth
- nearby construction of a major road or factory
- inadequate insurance to cover any property damage such as fire,

or to cover any claims for damages brought by tenants or neighbours for which you may be legally liable (such as an injury caused to your tenant by them falling through your rotting balcony)
- ineligibility for depreciation allowances
- poor record keeping, poor bookkeeping and poor overall control of costs
- not employing an accountant.

These will *increase* your returns:
- buying a property with a good position in a strongly performing area
- buying an aesthetically pleasing property or one with potential to be so
- buying a property which appeals to baby boomers
- buying a property that has a unique, positive feature
- buying a property in good structural order
- buying at the bottom of the market
- paying a fair price
- selling at the top of the market
- a property rezoning in your favour, for example, permission to subdivide a large block of land into two separate blocks, or to convert an old block of flats to strata title units
- low maintenance and other running costs
- relatively low land value proportional to building value for relatively lower land tax
- good tenants on long-term leases
- low vacancy
- being a good landlord
- an appropriate degree of sympathetic renovation
- low interest rates
- a healthy economy with strong rates of growth
- proper maintenance
- adequate insurance cover
- sufficient planning for taxes
- eligibility for depreciation allowances
- good records, good bookkeeping, good accountancy and good overall control of costs.

Commercial property investment

Now, some of you may be wondering why this chapter has dealt solely with residential property. What about commercial property?

Well, okay, this is a major investment sector and has been the source of extraordinary wealth for some people, but it is not a traditional area of direct investment for the average small investor. That's not because it's a second-rate investment – far from it. It's because commercial property is too specialised, too expensive and just too difficult an area of investment for most people. If you thought residential property investment sounded involved, it's nothing compared to commercial.

I would recommend anyone contemplating direct property investment to start at the easiest end of the spectrum – residential. If this works for you – and if you do it properly there is no reason why it shouldn't – after a few years think about a small commercial property investment, such as buying a shop. By this stage you will have developed a feel for property. You'll know all about the value of good tenants, you'll understand leases, you'll understand property management, you'll have discovered how time-consuming and frustrating dealing with councils and Government departments is, you'll know how much time and expense is involved in renovations, and so on. In other words, you won't be so green, which is something you cannot afford to be in commercial property investment. There are so many ways to go wrong in commercial property and being a novice is one of the main ones.

There is another way to invest in commercial property other than directly and this is through becoming a unit holder in a listed or unlisted property trust. I won't go into the details here because you'll find them in Chapter Fifteen, 'Managed Funds' but, briefly, when you invest in a property trust you effectively become a part-owner of the underlying assets held by the trust. These typically include shopping centres, office blocks, industrial properties, residential estates, hotels and apartment buildings.

A minimum investment in a property trust is usually $1,000. It's a lot less money and a lot less risk than a minimum direct investment in commercial property which could easily run into hundreds of thousands of dollars.

CHAPTER THIRTEEN

Investing in Shares

If you start asking people in the street what they think about shares, you'll find plenty fit into the 'I don't think about them at all', 'I don't understand them' or 'they're too risky' camps. Some of the images that spring to some people's minds when you mention shares are of well-fed, top-hatted, cigar-chomping stockbrokers leaping out of office-block windows clutching the latest bad market news, or desperate, sweaty shareholders, ties askew, eyes and veins bulging, screaming down the line, 'Sell! Sell! Sell!'.

Fortunately, these are B-grade movie depictions that bear no resemblance to the sharemarket experience of most shareholders – assuming they are *long-term* shareholders, that is. Like the other main asset classes of property, cash, and fixed interest, over time shares have produced very healthy returns – despite occasional market reversals and even free falls!

Share returns

Many studies have been done on the Australian and overseas share markets which illustrate just how attractive investment shares can be. Briefly, here are some findings:

Average annual returns from Australian shares

- 5% to 8% after inflation over rolling 10-year periods since 1945. (*Source*: ipac securities.)
- 15.7% before inflation over the 18 years 1983 to 2000. Inflation averaged 4.4% during the period. (*Source*: ipac securities.)

Average annual returns from international shares

- 6% to 9% after inflation over rolling 10-year periods. (*Source*: ipac securities.)
- 17.9% before inflation in the calendar years 1983 to 2000. Inflation averaged 4.4% during the period. (*Source*: ipac securities.)

Making Money

Annualised long-term returns for both domestic and international shares like these ought to satisfy most investors. I reckon the returns are impressive, particularly when you realise they take into account the major losses caused by the global share-market crash of October 1987. Look, the only time you might actually feel like jumping out of a window after investing in shares with these sorts of long-term returns is if you take a big-dollar, short-term punt on a speculative stock that goes wrong. But then again, backing the wrong horse at the track for a lot of money – which is basically no different – could lead to the same urge.

The fact is share ownership has become increasingly popular in the last few years with 41% of Australians directly holding shares in 2000, up from 28.5% in 1998. When you add in indirect share investment (investing in shares via superannuation and managed funds), 54% of Australians hold shares, making us the world's number one shareholders, in front of the Canadians on 52% and the Americans on 48%. (*Source*: Australian Stock Exchange [ASX].)

Clearly, much of the recent, surging participation in shares can be attributed to major, governmental privatisations like Qantas, the Commonwealth Bank and the Telstra float. As well as these there have been the large demutualisations of institutions like Colonial, National Mutual and AMP to further swell the ranks of Australian shareholders.

Now, while share investment in general has my hearty support, you need to remember that there are shares and there are shares. The type I recommend and the type your superannuation fund manager would also consider investing in are shares in established, solid, well-managed companies that have good operational track records and good profitability over the years – 'blue chip' companies, in other words – like Brambles, National Australia Bank and Woolworths. However, I should point out that even blue chips can sometimes fall from grace: the most dramatic example in many years being the near collapse during 1997 of one-time island trading company Burns Philp, whose shares fell from $2.18 at the start of the year to 24 cents by the end of it. Telstra II in particular was a shot of reality for investors when its first instalment of $4.50 dropped to under $3 in the year 2000. And Lend Lease shares dropped from over $23 to a low of $14.50 following the sale of their funds management arm, MLC, to the National Australia Bank. Even BHP, once the 'bluest' of blue chip Australian companies, gave its shareholders a rough trip a few years ago when it experienced a fall in share price from $20 in June 1997 to $12.30 after the October 1997 shake-out. In early 2001 it was once again trading at around $19. And illustrating just how unpredictable the share market can be in the short term, even for blue chips, the year 2000 saw News Corporation shares fluctuating wildly, ranging from $18 in April, to $25 in October, and back down to $14 in December. These examples aside, I should note that most blue chip stocks performed admirably during 1999 and 2000, as usual, and are performing particularly strongly as I write.

Shares I don't normally recommend are those in what could only be called 'speculative ventures' – companies that are small and new, and that will need more than their fair share of good luck to be successful. Plenty of mining companies fit this description. They're the ones that will only convert their potential into dollars if they make a decent strike of gold, oil, diamonds, iron, nickel, copper or whatever. Then there are those high-tech companies trying to find or commercialise that miracle scientific breakthrough. Regard them all as you would the outsiders in a horse race. If they hit their target, they'll make a fortune and so will you, but the odds are slim. There's a better chance they'll go nowhere and you'll lose money.

Investment in any sort of shares carries some risk, but if you buy a basket of good quality shares and hang onto them for the long term, the risk is substantially minimised and your returns should be more than satisfactory.

What are shares?

A share is a part-ownership of a company listed on the share market. When you buy shares in a company you become a part-owner of that company. You take equity in it which is why shares are also known as 'equities'. Sometimes shares are also referred to as 'stock' but this is a broader term which can encompass other types of securities.

Companies offer shares to the public to raise funds to finance, say, an expansion of an existing business, a new venture, or a company takeover. When shares in a company are being offered to the public for the first time it is known as a share 'float'. Subsequent share offerings from the same company are generally called share 'issues'.

In the case of smaller floats and share offerings, those who have a sharebroker may be invited to invest first before the wider public is given the chance to buy. In this case the shares being offered for sale by the company may be fully taken up ('fully subscribed') by those invited to buy. Having a sharebroker, therefore, can be very useful in getting you in on the ground floor of some (particularly smaller) share offerings.

With very large floats – such as the Woolworths, Commonwealth Bank, Qantas and Telstra floats – where many millions of shares are being offered, there are usually enough shares for sale for everyone to get at least some. In large-scale floats the opportunity to buy is widely advertised and prospectuses are freely available through all sharebrokers, some banks and from the companies themselves.

To illustrate, let's say you are invited to invest in the float of XYZ Investments Ltd, where the minimum investment is a parcel of 2,000 shares with each share priced at $1.50. This means your minimum investment is $3,000.

Now, these are new shares that are not yet being traded on the open share market. Their price of $1.50 is an issue price set by the company, reflecting its view of its shares' worth. The market, however, may see things differently. This means that when your $1.50 shares actually start open trading on the share market (the day the float closes) the price may move, sometimes immediately, to a higher or lower level than the issue price. Over subsequent weeks, months and years the trading price may move to the point where it bears virtually no resemblance at all to the issue price. The trading price depends on the market's perceptions of the company's past and present performance and, most importantly, its future potential.

How do you make money from shares?

How you make money from shares is twofold. You make it from an income stream (dividends), and also from capital growth, which derives from increases in the share price, from occasional receipt of free bonus shares, and the purchase of discounted 'rights issues' shares.

Let's look at share income first. If the listed company in which you own shares makes a profit, as a part-owner of the company you are entitled to share in those profits. You receive your share of the profits by means of a dividend, normally paid to you every 6 or 12 months.

The size of the dividend depends on how many shares you hold and what proportion of the company's profits the directors choose to distribute to shareholders. As a general rule the typical dividend paid per annum by a company listed on the Australian Stock Exchange is around 5% of the share's trading price.

Dividend imputation

Share dividend income is taxable, but squaring up with the Tax Office over it at the end of the financial year can be a lot less painful than paying tax on other sources of income. In the case of 'fully franked' dividends, the dividends you receive have been distributed from company profits *after they have been taxed at the full company rate of 30%* (34% for the year ended 30 June 2001). Now, because tax is paid by the company *before* you receive the dividends, these dividends are deemed to be *after-tax income to you*. This means if your effective tax rate is 30%, you will need to pay no further tax on these fully franked dividends – because they have already been taxed at 30% by the time you receive them. Indeed, if your tax rate is lower than 30%, you'll actually get a tax credit from these dividends which can lower the tax payable on your other assessable income! And since July 2000, if your franking credits are greater than your tax bill, you are entitled to a refund of the excess credits. This will apply mainly to shareholders on a low marginal tax rate and is a move by the Government to make shares a more attractive investment to people on a lower income.

Dividend imputation is a relatively recent breakthrough. Before 1 July 1987, when the system was changed, your dividends were effectively taxed twice. Firstly, the company distributed its dividends from its profits, after it had already paid tax on these profits. Secondly, the shareholder receiving the dividends paid personal tax on them as these monies were considered to be (untaxed) income by the Tax Office. Under this arrangement the Tax Office was basically getting two bites at the cherry, and the take on the one stream of income could have been as high as a 78% tax rate.

On 1 July 1987 the dividend imputation scheme was introduced, designed to eliminate this double taxation. It works as follows.

- Firstly, the company pays tax on its profits and 'imputes' (credits) this tax to the shareholders of the company. This means that, as far as the Tax Office is concerned, the tax paid by the company in Australia is deemed to have been paid by the shareholders in the company.

- Secondly, the company distributes dividends out of its profits which have already been taxed. These are called 'franked' (exempt from charges) dividends and are tax paid (normally at 30%) in the hands of the investor.

- Thirdly, when the shareholder fills out their taxation return they include details of any dividends received and the amount of company tax that has been paid on them. The shareholder then receives a tax credit for this amount of tax which can be offset against any other assessable income.

To illustrate, let's say an investor receives dividends in her hand over the year worth $7,000. The company advises her that these dividends are fully franked with an imputation tax credit of $3,000, meaning that the company has already paid $3,000 in tax on them on her behalf. The total to be shown as her taxable dividend income is the sum of the money she has actually received ($7,000) and the imputation tax credit ($3,000), namely, $10,000.

Let's say this investor also earns $15,000 from other sources. Adding the taxable dividend income of $10,000 gives her a total taxable income of $25,000. Now, the tax liability on $25,000 is $3,880 but the company providing the dividend has already paid $3,000 in tax on it which, remember, is tax effectively paid in the name of the investor. So, the amount of tax now outstanding on the $25,000 is reduced to $880 ($3,880 − $3,000 = $880). This is almost half the $1,530 tax the shareholder would otherwise have to find to pay at tax time on just the $15,000 alone, assuming she had no other income. And under new tax rules in force since July 2000, if this investor had no income other than the $7,000 dividend, they would be entitled to a refund of the excess franking credits. Once again the taxable income would be $10,000 ($7,000 + $3,000), on which the investor would pay tax of $680. But as they have an imputation credit of $3,000 on the dividend, they are entitled to a refund of $2,320 ($3,000 − $680).

Now, don't let me give you the impression that franked dividends are a way of avoiding tax or paying less tax than you otherwise might. They're simply a form of (pre-taxed) income that saves you having to dig up the money to pay tax (unless you're paying more than 30% tax) at the end of the financial year. In this sense, they're like your after-tax take-home pay – it's money that you shouldn't have to pay much, if any, more tax on at tax time, and that comes as a relief to most people.

Note that company dividends can be 'fully franked' (tax paid at 30%), 'partly franked' (tax paid at anything up to 30%) and 'un-franked' (no tax paid against them). Also note that if your tax rate is higher than the franked rate, you will still have some tax to pay on these dividends. For example, if your rate is 47% and the franked rate is 30%, then you will still owe 17% tax (47% − 30% = 17%).

The following tables show how franked dividends are treated by the Tax Office. They compare receiving a $1,000 fully franked dividend payment with receiving a $1,000 interest payment. You'll note the investor receiving the dividend income has more money in hand after tax than the fixed interest investor. This illustrates the point that, say, a 5% return on (fully franked) National Australia Bank shares is *not* the same as a 5% return on a fixed term deposit. The 5% share return is better because this is 5% to you *after* (30%) tax and may need no further tax paid on it, while the 5% interest payment is *before* tax and therefore is fully taxable.

Share market investor		Fixed interest investor	
Low marginal tax rate investor			
Dividend payment	$1,000.00	Interest payment	$1,000.00
Add franking credit	$428.57		
Taxable income	$1,428.57	Taxable income	$1,000.00
Tax at marginal rate of 30%	$428.57	Tax at marginal rate of 30%	$300.00
Less franking credit	$428.57		
Tax payable	0.00	Tax payable	$300.00
After-tax income	$1,000.00	After-tax income	$700.00
High marginal tax rate investor			
Dividend payment	$1,000.00	Interest payment	$1,000.00
Add franking credit	$ 428.57		
Taxable income	$1,428.57	Taxable income	$1,000.00

Making Money

Tax at marginal rate of 47%	$671.42	Tax at marginal rate of 47%	$470.00
Less franking credit	$428.57		
Tax payable	$242.85	Tax payable	$470.00
After-tax income	$757.15	After-tax income	$530.00

For investors on the lowest marginal rate of 17%, the return from franked dividends is even more attractive as they are entitled to a refund if their franking credits are greater than the amount of tax on their income.

Capital growth

Now, let's look at capital growth. This occurs when the traded price of shares in a given company rises, reflecting the company's positive performance, a favourable economic environment and a good outlook. If you buy a parcel of shares at $2 per share and their traded price rises to $4 per share you have doubled the value of your holding and if the share price falls to $1, you have halved your money. It's that simple.

Some degree of capital growth can also occur through taking up 'rights issues', although this sort of growth involves you investing more money. A 'rights issue' is where a company, in attempting to raise more capital, invites its existing shareholders to buy new shares *at a discount to the current market price*. (If there was no discount, there would be no incentive for existing shareholders to take up the offer.) The amount of new shares the shareholder is invited to buy is proportional to the number of shares already held. As an example, Lang Corporation was making a rights issue at the time of writing in early 2001. It was offering one new share for every eight shares held, at a price of $10. The trading price was $11.45, so the rights issue represented a discount of 12.6%.

When you are a shareholder you participate in the good fortunes of the company you hold shares in. If the company performs well, you benefit from a strong share price and healthy dividends and, if the company and/or the economy falters, you also suffer its misfortunes. But one thing you don't participate in as a shareholder, fortunately, is a company's indebtedness. This means that if a company collapses leaving behind debts, as a shareholder you are not liable. I doubt the modern sharemarket would exist if this were otherwise.

The share market

We now know how shares have performed over time, what a share is, how you buy shares during a float and how you make money from shares. But what about the share market itself? How does it operate and how do you use it? Well, let's start with a little history.

The first Australian stock market, carried on through the pages of the *Sydney Morning Herald*, was established in Sydney in 1837. In 1859 the first regular stock market came into existence in Melbourne and over the next 30 years stock exchanges were established in all State capitals.

In 1987 all six State stock exchanges were amalgamated into the Australian Stock Exchange (ASX). The pre-ASX State stock exchanges still exist in each capital city – it is just that now they are completely interlinked by computer and effectively operate as one marketplace.

Today there are over 1,300 companies listed on the ASX, ranging in size from News Corp valued at the time of writing (early 2001) at around $76 billion to small, speculative mining exploration companies valued at less than $2 million. In the year 2000 the volume of shares traded on the ASX almost doubled to about $169 billion, up from $87 billion the previous year. Just over $361 billion was turned over on the ASX, a 28% increase on the 1999 turnover of $282 billion.

All companies in Australia have to be registered with the Australian Securities and Investment Commission but they don't have to be listed on the stock exchange, and indeed the vast majority of them aren't. Rather, companies have to apply to be listed on the stock exchange and, at a certain point in their development, some take this route. The reason they want to be listed is that it enables them to raise funds through the sale of shares and other financial instruments.

In order to be listed on the ASX, a company has to be of a certain size (net tangible assets worth at least $2 million) or a certain profitability (at least $1 million pre-tax profits over the last three years); its shares have to be freely available for trading; and the company has to agree to meet ASX requirements for financial reporting and disclosure of key information. (All this is designed to help keep shonky operators out of the share market.)

What the ASX deals in

What is traded through the ASX? Well, it handles a range of financial instruments, not just shares. The ASX also deals in fixed interest securities such as bonds, debentures and convertible notes. All of these can be lumped under the general term of 'stock' (which is why I prefer to call shares 'shares' – it's more specific).

The ASX also handles 'derivatives' (options and warrants) which are derived from the standard products above.

Now, let's take a closer look at these 'financial instruments'.

Ordinary shares

Ordinary shares are the most common type of shares traded on the ASX. They entitle you to any dividends that may be paid and to participate in rights and bonus issues. As an ordinary shareholder you are also entitled to vote at any company meetings (not that the average individual shareholder wields much influence).

Technically, a share is a unit of a company's capital which has a 'par' value, also known as the share's 'face' or 'nominal' value. Common par values are 50 cents and $1. The par value is unrelated to and normally different from the share's market value (the price at which it is trading).

As an individual investor in ordinary shares, par values are of little significance. (It's just useful to be familiar with the term as you will encounter it from time to time.) What is significant to you as a share investor is the share's market value, because that's what determines your fortunes.

Preference shares

Preference shares differ from ordinary shares in that they normally pay a fixed rate of return (still called a 'dividend'). This fixed dividend rate is expressed as a percentage of the par value of the share.

Preference shares have certain privileges – for example, dividends are payable against them before being payable against ordinary shares and, in the event of the company folding, any capital left over from other claimants is distributed among preference shareholders before ordinary shareholders.

Although preference shares may seem to be more attractive than ordinary shares because of these privileges, this is not necessarily the case. They can be restrictive. Having a fixed dividend, for example, can be an enormous disadvantage if a company is performing well because the dividends paid on ordinary shares would be higher. On the other hand, a fixed dividend is advantageous to the investor when the company is performing poorly and may be paying little or no dividends on its ordinary shares.

There are various types of preference shares which include 'converting', 'cumulative', 'participating' and 'redeemable' preference shares – your sharebroker can explain the details of these to you.

Company options

A company option is an option to take up a new, ordinary share from the company by a nominated future date at a fixed price or 'exercise price'. You don't have to take up the new share by the given date, but, if you don't, your option lapses and becomes worthless. (This is a method of raising capital often used by mining companies.)

Listed company options are traded on the ASX in the same way as ordinary shares. The option's price is less than the company's ordinary share price, and the theoretical difference between the option price and share price is the same as the exercise price.

Contributing shares

Contributing shares are ones on which you have paid only a part or a proportion of their par value, the remainder being due when the company requires it in the future. Contributing shares are also known as 'partly paid' shares and are relatively rare.

Fixed interest securities

Debentures
Debentures are a way that industrial and finance companies borrow money. A debenture is effectively a loan from you to a company for a fixed term. You are paid interest on this loan at specified times at

a fixed interest rate. At the end of the term the debenture matures and the original amount of the loan is repaid to the holder in full. Typically, debenture terms range from three months to five years with a minimum investment normally being $5,000.

Debentures are issued like shares during a share float – through a prospectus – and you buy them by filling in the application form and sending it directly to the company. Should you wish to sell your debentures before the maturity date (or buy others) you do so through a stockbroker at the going market rate. The market rate will reflect the interest rate for new debentures being issued at the time you wish to sell (or buy) – if new debentures are paying a higher interest rate you will be offered less for yours, if new debentures are paying a lower interest rate you will be offered more.

It may be easier to find a buyer for the debentures of some companies than it is for others and should a company be wound up, the remaining capital will be distributed to debenture holders before shareholders.

Remember, the security of your capital depends upon the company issuing the debenture, so make sure the company is sound before you invest.

Bonds

Bonds are basically the same as debentures, except they are not issued by private companies but rather by Government and semi-government authorities. They also come with Government guarantees of repayment. Consequently, bonds are safer than other fixed interest securities and, therefore, generally provide lower returns.

Some private companies issue what they call 'bonds' but this is a misnomer – what they should really be called is 'debentures'.

Unsecured notes

Unsecured notes are similar to debentures in that they are loans from you to a company for a specific period at a specific interest rate, but without the same degree of security as debentures. Holders of unsecured notes are on a lower pecking order in the event the company collapses and there is any capital left over to distribute. Staff, the Tax Office and debenture holders will be amongst those paid before unsecured note holders – but unsecured note holders will be paid before shareholders.

The reason these instruments are called 'unsecured notes' is because they have no guaranteed security over the company's assets, which may make you wonder why anyone would want to bother with them. Well, firstly, bear in mind that shareholders have an even less secure stake in a company and, secondly, unsecured notes normally offer a higher interest rate than debentures and many other fixed interest securities. Also, the types of companies that issue unsecured notes are generally big and secure themselves. Obviously, for there to be any market for unsecured notes, the companies issuing them have to be seen to be safe, but it is fair to say that unsecured notes are not common.

Convertible notes

A convertible note is an unsecured note that can be converted at a specified date into shares in the company issuing it. It is really a mixture of a fixed interest security and a share, in that for the first few years the holder of the note receives a regular interest payment from the issuer and then, at a certain time, the holder has the choice to convert the note into shares in the company at a predetermined price. The date at which the note can be converted into shares is spelt out at the time it's issued. If the holder does not want to convert the note to shares prior to its maturity date, the issuing company will repay the value of the convertible note (the value of the original loan) to the holder at maturity.

Issuing convertible notes allows a company to raise money yet to defer the payment of dividends. It is therefore seen as a relatively cheap way of raising funds. Convertible notes can be traded before maturity through stockbrokers at the current market rate, in the same way as debentures and unsecured notes.

Buying and selling shares

There are two main ways of buying shares directly, as distinct from buying them indirectly through a managed fund or through superannuation.

One is from the issuing company via a prospectus. This happens when a company 'floats' or 'goes public', meaning it is offering new shares to the public at a set price per share in specific share parcel sizes. To buy the shares on offer you simply fill in the application form in the prospectus and send it with your cheque, either to the company direct or to a stockbroker.

When a company you have shares in has a rights or bonus issue, the same process applies – you fill out an application form for the number of shares you are entitled to and send it back to the company or a stockbroker with a cheque. It's all very straight-forward.

Buying shares direct from the issuing company is known as buying on the primary market. The secondary market is the trading of existing shares between shareholders. When you want to buy shares that have already been issued and are trading on the share market, the normal way of doing it is through a stockbroker. It is the normal way of selling too. However, you can trade shares directly with other individuals – trading 'off-market', as it's known, and bypassing a stockbroker – though this is pretty rare. You're bound to find most, if not all, your trades will be through a stockbroker.

Finding a stockbroker

Finding yourself a stockbroker isn't hard. In the absence of any that are recommended to you, just phone the ASX. They will give you the names of three brokers to talk to. Alternatively, look in the *Yellow Pages* under 'Stock and Share Brokers'.

It's a good idea to have a chat with a few stockbrokers at different firms before you decide where to open an account or accounts. Brokers have very different personalities and views on investment and it's important to deal with people with whom you feel comfortable. Also, some brokers aren't interested in small investors, others are.

You can have more than one stockbroker if you wish. In fact, some argue it can be beneficial to be a client of two or three firms (including a larger one) to give you more access to new share issues. Some companies only distribute their prospectuses through a small number of stockbrokers, and many floats are only accessible through one stockbroker. So the more stockbrokers you deal with, the more prospectuses you'll receive – providing, of course, you are a regular investor with each of these brokers.

Once you've picked one or more brokers you'll probably have to make your first transaction in person. After that you can place orders over the phone. You'll probably be asked to pay for the first buy order in full (or at least pay a deposit) at the time you make the order.

In keeping with growing competition in other areas of the financial world, *discount stockbrokers* have emerged in recent years. Unlike traditional stockbrokers, discount brokers do not carry out investment research and offer clients no investment advice. The payoff is they're cheap and ideal for investors who know what they want and who simply want to place a buy or sell order. Two discount brokers are Sanford Securities and TD Waterhouse, the latter charging between $53 and $86 for buy or sell orders over the phone worth up to $80,000, or between $16 and $48 for trades worth up to $75,000 over the Internet (at February 2001). On top of all brokerage fees, State Government stamp duties also apply at the rate of 15 cents per $100 transaction value.

Placing a share order

When you instruct your stockbroker to buy or sell shares on your behalf, you can get the broker to act in one of two ways. One is where you nominate your price levels. This means you set the highest price you are prepared to buy at and the lowest price you are prepared to sell at. Under these instructions your broker will only act within your limits.

Alternatively you can tell your broker to buy or sell 'at best' or 'at market' which means they will get you the best price they can under the prevailing market conditions.

Once you have given your buying or selling instructions to your broker, they enter your order into a computer terminal. This is linked to the ASX's centralised computer transaction system and your broker can generally give you an immediate confirmation that the order has been carried out. (There can be delays if there is a rush on particular shares or a lack of interest in others, but generally there will be ready buyers and sellers for most shares.)

After the transaction has taken place, a contract note is sent to you confirming the trade. If you were buying shares, payment would then be due. When the stockbroker gets your cheque, details of the transaction are sent to the company's share register to finalise the share transfer.

If you were selling shares you would need to send your share certificate or 'scrip' (assuming you were issued scrip in the first place) to the stockbroker after you received the contract note. The broker then sends you payment for the shares minus brokerage fees.

Making Money

Computerised trading at the ASX

Buying and selling shares wasn't always done by a few keystrokes on a computer keyboard. Up until 1990 the six State stock exchanges each had brokers exchanging shares on their trading floors, back-up staff recording the orders and doing the paperwork, and young men called 'chalkies' running up and down in front of enormous blackboards marked with all the locally listed companies, chalking in the latest share prices.

In 1990 the ASX swapped floor trading for its new computer trading system known as SEATS (Stock Exchange Automated Trading System). With SEATS, an order for the buying or selling of shares is entered into a computer terminal at any sharebroking office in Australia. The buy or sell order joins a queue in the central computer system which is arranged in order of price and time of lodging.

As soon as a buying bid matches a selling order SEATS executes a trade automatically. Trades at any given price are executed in the sequential order that bids or selling orders have been lodged in the system, whether placed by a large institutional fund or a small private investor. This is designed to give players of all sizes equal access to the market.

In 2000, SEATS handled on average more than 53,000 trades a day, more than doubling the 1998 trading volume, and up from 7,500 per day when the system was first installed.

Other important innovations at the ASX were the introduction in 1989 of the FAST (Flexible Accelerated Securities Transfer) computer system, followed by the 1994 introduction of CHESS (Clearing House Electronic Sub-register System). Both of these computerised systems are designed to process and speed up the transfer and settlement of stocks traded on the ASX.

Previously, when you bought shares in a company you received a share certificate (known as 'scrip') from the company as proof of share ownership. (Some companies still issue scrip, but it is becoming rare.) You kept your scrip in a safe place and when you wanted to sell, you gave it to your broker. This certificate was then forwarded to the company in which you had been a shareholder, so that your sale could be entered into its share register. This paper processing could drag on and, until it was finalised, you were not paid.

The introduction of computerised share transfer and registration processes has done away with the need to physically send share certificates from one broker to another in order to effect an exchange of ownership. Now shareholders have their ownership of shares electronically stored in the ASX's computer system and evidenced by a monthly holding statement, similar to a bank statement. Computerisation has also done away with the need for shareholders to physically sign share transfer forms – which could be very time consuming – by permitting stockbrokers to sign transfers on their behalf. The result is a largely paperless system where share transfers are similar to electronic funds transfers.

These innovations have recently enabled the introduction of a fixed settlement or payment day three days after a trade is made. And to put this in perspective, prior to the computerisation of the ASX, settlement could take as long as six weeks after trade!

Understanding the daily share tables

The daily trading on the ASX is reported in the business section of most Australian metropolitan newspapers. These published share trading tables contain a wealth of information, most of which is relevant to building your share portfolio. But how do you interpret it all?

Let's look on the following page at the share market trading tables as they appeared, for example, in the *Australian Financial Review* on 17 February 2000.

For the shares in any listed company you can discover the following:

Company name: the company names are sometimes abbreviated.

ASX code: the code given by the ASX to every type of share on issue.

Last sale: the price at which the company's shares traded on the last sale of the previous business day. This is the figure used to most accurately measure the value of the company's shares when calculating the value of a share portfolio.

+ or – : the difference (in cents) in the share's last sale price over the last sale price the day before. This shows, on a daily basis, if the share has risen or fallen in price.

Quote (buy): the highest price at which a buyer is prepared to buy shares in the listed company. It is also known as the 'bid' or 'buying price'. Shares may not always have been transacted at this price.

Quote (sell): the lowest price at which a seller is prepared to sell

Company Name	ASX Code	Last Sale	+ or -	Quote Buy	Quote Sell	Volume 100's	Day High	Day Low	52-week High	52-week Low	Dividend ¢ per share	Times cov'd	Net tang assets	Div yield %	Earn share ¢	P/E ratio	Week % move
AGL	AGL	11.32	+7	11.32	11.33	5476	11.35	11.27	13.02	7.63	51.00p	2.62	1.83	4.51	133.80	8.5	+1.16
AJ Group stapled	AJP	1.11	-1	1.10	1.11	4665	1.13	1.11	1.22	1.04	10.50		1.11	9.46			-.89
Amcor	AMC	5.72	+5	5.72	5.73	10841	5.79	5.67	6.10	4.354	38.00p	.86	2.52	6.64	32.70	17.5	-4.03
AMP	AMP	19.19	+3	19.17	19.20	8444	19.23	19.10	20.58	13.58	44.00	1.04	7.15	2.29	45.80	41.9	
AMP Divers unit	ADP	2.37	-3	2.37	2.38	4381	2.41	2.37	2.49	2.17	18.90	1.05	2.31	7.97	19.83	12.0	-1.25
AMP Shop ord unit	ART	1.27	-1	1.27	1.28	11338	1.29	1.27	1.45	1.27	10.50	.82	1.31	8.27	8.57	14.8	-.78
ANZ Bank	ANZ	14.90	-10	14.89	14.90	18003	15.00	14.90	15.41	9.73	64.00 f	1.67	5.49	4.30	106.80	14.0	+1.02
APN N&M	APN	3.88	+6	3.88	3.90	3123	3.89	3.86	5.30	3.45	13.90 f	1.40	1.19	3.58	19.50	19.9	+3.19
Argo	ARG	3.41	+2	3.39	3.41	697	3.41	3.39	3.57	3.00	15.00 f	1.12	3.95	4.40	16.80	20.3	+1.49
Aristocrat	ALL	5.54	-11	5.50	5.54	5140	5.70	5.48	6.75	3.25	7.50 f	1.09	.34	1.35	8.17	67.8	-3.32
ASX	ASX	13.11	+6	13.11	13.14	1136	13.20	13.06	15.491	9.66	56.20 f	.94	1.39	4.29	53.07	24.7	+2.34
Aus.Found.	AFI	2.56	+1	2.56	2.57	2426	2.60	2.55	2.91	2.31	12.25 f	1.29	3.04	4.79	15.76	16.2	-2.66
AXA Asia	AXA	2.64	-1	2.64	2.68	10774	2.66	2.63	3.16	2.28	9.50p	2.23	1.78	3.60	21.22	12.4	-.75
AXA Prop unit	AXP	1.10	-2	1.10	1.11	7120	1.12	1.10	1.25	1.07	8.69	1.00	1.16	7.90	8.72	12.6	-.90
Bankwest	BWA	3.842	-8	3.81	3.84	12272	3.86	3.81	4.35	3.40	18.00 f	1.48	1.73	4.69	26.60	14.4	+1.64
BAT Austra	BAM	17.83	+1.4	17.83	17.90	1122	17.83	17.82	18.00	9.30	75.00p	1.00	1.79	4.21	75.10	23.7	+.24
BHP	BHP	19.65	+29	19.63	19.65	58140	19.66	19.50	20.374	15.042	50.07	1.77	5.53	2.55	88.69	22.2	+5.08
Billabong	BBG	4.53	+9	4.52	4.53	1583	4.57	4.46	4.94	3.01		1.69	2.86	8.04	30.40	7.4	+3.90
Boral Ltd	BLD	2.24	+.8	2.24	2.25	10255	2.27	2.21	2.45	1.80	18.00p	2.00	6.53	1.69	162.00	29.6	+2.75
Brambles	BIL	48.009	+30.9	48.00	48.03	8204	48.10	47.20	53.70	27.418	81.00p	2.28	1.90	1.90	37.70	23.0	-1.08
BRL Hardy	BRL	8.67		8.67	8.69	1424	8.68	8.60	8.90	6.20	16.50 f	1.19	1.48	7.34	12.40	11.5	-.91
BT Office unit	BTO	1.42	-2	1.42	1.43	27723	1.44	1.42	1.56	1.30	10.42		1.33		7.50	50.4	-.70
C&W Optus	CWO	3.78	-6	3.77	3.78	128934	3.87	3.77	7.80	3.31			4.26	2.47	7.50	50.4	-6.44
CC Amatil	CCL	4.849	+6.9	4.85	4.86	4311	4.86	4.80	5.45	3.06	12.00p	1.64	2.48	8.81	19.70	24.6	-1.04
Centro unit	CEP	2.77	-3	2.77	2.78	5599	2.85	2.77	3.09	2.59	24.40	1.02	1.40	1.72	24.80	11.2	-2.81
Chall.Int.	CLI	3.95	-1	3.95	3.96	1561	4.01	3.94	4.65	2.636	6.81	5.80			39.53	10.0	-1.00
Coal & Al.	CNA	19.00	-60	18.55	19.00	80	19.00	19.00	20.50	14.00			.77	.91	142.70	13.3	-5.00
Cochlear	COH	38.30	+24	38.30	38.60	545	38.57	38.00	38.60	20.53	35.00 f	1.43	2.01	8.98	50.10	76.4	+3.15
Col Trust stapled	CFT	2.01	-5	2.00	2.02	4223	2.06	2.01	2.20	1.93	18.05	1.00	2.26	4.26	18.00	11.2	-2.90
Coles.Myer	CML	6.34	+.1	6.33	6.34	15186	6.35	6.32	7.92	5.99	27.00 f	.96	.12	.13	25.90	24.5	+1.60
Cshare	CPU	7.47	+1	7.47	7.49	10132	7.56	7.39	9.90	5.20	1.00 f	7.50	5.32	.66	7.50	99.6	-4.23
CSL	CSL	34.65	+15	34.60	34.65	886	34.744	34.20	40.10	19.30	23.00 f	1.77	5.32		40.80	84.9	-1.00

(*Source: Australian Financial Review.*)

shares, also known as the 'offer price' or 'selling price'. Shares may not always have been transacted at this price.

Volume 100's: the total volume of shares (in hundreds) traded in the company on the previous trading day. This indicates the level of market interest in a particular share.

Day's high and low: the range of prices the share traded between on the latest ASX business (trading) day.

52-week high and low: the highest and the lowest price the share has traded between on the ASX in the year to date.

Dividend ¢ per share: the size of the latest annual dividend distributed by the company per share (in cents and fractions of cents). The 'f' that follows some entries indicates the dividend was fully franked, whilst a 'p' denotes a partly franked dividend.

Dividend times cov'd: stands for 'dividend times covered' which is the number of times the dividend per share (DPS) is covered by the earnings per share (EPS). Dividend times cover is calculated by dividing the EPS figure by the DPS figure. The relevance of the dividend times cover is to show what proportion of the company's net earnings are distributed as dividends.

Net tang. assets: stands for 'net tangible asset backing (per share)' which is designed to give you an idea of what each share would be worth (in dollars and cents) if all assets were liquidated and all debts paid, with the residual then being distributed among all ordinary shareholders on a per share basis.

This figure is arrived at by dividing the value of shareholders' funds as reported in the company's balance sheet by the number of issued shares. Now, if you aren't familiar with company accounting principles (and very few people are) the net asset backing figure will not tell you much. Don't worry, you can easily get by without it.

Div. yield %: the dividend return to the shareholder in relation to the last quoted sale price. It is calculated by dividing dividends per share by the last sale price, expressed as a percentage. This method of calculation means the yield changes as the sale price changes. Indeed, if the share price crashed, the yield would soar – until the next (invariably lower) dividend was declared.

Like net tangible asset backing, the dividend yield is an interesting figure, but due to the vagaries of share prices and accounting practices, it isn't enormously revealing. It is also a measure of past performance and says nothing about the future. As a general rule of thumb, the higher the dividend yield, the healthier the company is perceived to be and the happier its shareholders are likely to be.

Earn share ¢: stands for earnings per share (EPS) expressed in cents. It shows the amount of profit earned for every ordinary issued share. EPS is calculated by dividing the company's net profit by the total number of ordinary issued shares.

P/E ratio: stands for price earnings ratio. It is calculated by dividing the last sale price by the earnings per share. The P/E ratio therefore measures the share price in relation to (as a multiple of) the company's profits.

This ratio provides a means of measuring investors' expectations of the company's performance. If a company has a low P/E compared with other companies *working in the same or similar industries*, this indicates the market anticipates a poor profit performance from the company in the future. A relatively high P/E, on the other hand, indicates the opposite view. A high P/E ratio could also indicate a company is being valued for its asset backing and not for its earnings potential.

Week % move: This shows by what percentage the share price has moved, and in what direction, in one week.

The interpretive ratios above are all very well but, because they are based on historical data, and because this data is so open to mathematical and accounting manipulation, the insights they bring to present and likely *future* performances have to be viewed with some caution. This warning particularly applies to the P/E ratio, to which many investment commentators give far more significance than it deserves.

Studying and understanding share-market performance ratios is certainly useful, but it will not magically reveal which shares you should buy and which you should avoid. These ratios simply provide a way of comparing one share's historical performance with that of another. By all means use them as a guide, but don't rely on them when selecting your shares.

Share indices

When reading or talking about the share market you will come across the term 'All Ordinaries Index' or 'All Ordinaries Accumulation Index'. But what are these indices, and what is their purpose?

Well, stock exchanges all around the world develop indices as a quick way of keeping an eye on what's happening in particular markets. An index reflects a change in the value of a sample selection of shares in a single market or in a sample selection of markets. An index may measure changes in the market's capital value based on share prices alone, or it may also take into account the value of dividends paid (and assumed to be reinvested). The shares and markets chosen for inclusion in the sample are those of the greatest interest and relevance to investors.

When an index is created, a particular day is given a base value (say 1,000) and then changes in market direction are measured in relation to that value. Let's say market activity was strong over a period and this example index rose to 1,024. This would mean the value of the market (or, more accurately, the value of the sampled shares in this market) had risen by 2.4%.

Each stock exchange has a main index that represents the market as a whole and the ones most commonly quoted in the media are: Australia's All Ordinaries (Industrial) Index; New York's Dow Jones Industrial Average; London's FTSE 100 Index; Tokyo's Nikkei Index; and Hong Kong's Hang Seng Index.

In addition to these overall market indices, there are also specific market sector indices such as the Australian All Mining Index, Transport Index, Media Index or the S&P/ASX 100 Index which measures the movement of the largest 100 listed companies. You will find all these listed in the share pages of the major dailies. Let's look at some of the more important ones.

- The All Ordinaries Index is the one most frequently quoted in the Australian media and is the chief index for describing how the market has moved. The All Ords covers the largest 500 companies actively traded on the ASX. The companies are selected according to their market value and between them they represent approximately 98% of the ASX's total value.
- Since April 2000, a number of new indices have been compiled by ratings agency Standard and Poor's (S&P). Designed mainly for specialist fund managers, these indices range from the S&P/ASX 20 index, tracking the value of the 20 largest listed companies (in terms of market capitalisation), to the S&P/ASX 300 listing the 300 largest companies and covering about 90% of the market value of companies listed on the ASX.
- The S&P/ASX 300 Accumulation Index is basically the same as the S&P/ASX 300 Index except it assumes a 100% reinvestment

of all dividends paid by the sample companies. It therefore presents a more complete picture of the market's performance. There are accumulation indices to complement most price-only indices.

- New York's Dow Jones Industrial Average is the oldest and most widely quoted indicator of share market change. It is not really an index (which is a value relative to an earlier established value), but rather indicates the average share price of a group of 30 major companies actively traded on the New York Stock Exchange (and the NYSE is the largest in the world). The 30 stocks represent about a fifth of the $8 trillion plus market value of all US stocks, and about a quarter of the value of stocks listed on the NYSE. Companies comprising the Dow Jones include Exxon, IBM, General Motors and Coca Cola. Like other indices, the Dow Jones is quoted in points not dollars.

- London's FTSE 100 is the UK equivalent of our All Ordinaries or New York's Dow Jones. It's commonly called the 'footsie' and it stands for the Financial Times Stock Exchange (Index). The index is based on the weighted average share price of 100 leading UK listed companies.

- Standard and Poor's 500 (S&P 500) is based on US shares mostly listed on the New York Stock Exchange. It tends to be used by professional investors more than the Dow Jones which is used more in the media. The S&P 500 is a weighted share price index of 400 industrial, 40 financial, 40 public utility and 20 transportation companies. This index accounts for over 80% of the value of the shares listed on the NYSE.

- The Nikkei 300 is the market index for the Tokyo Stock Exchange. It reflects the value of 300 of Japan's leading listed companies.

- The Morgan Stanley Capital International World Index (MSCI World Index) indicates the average change in share prices in a sample of international sharemarkets. The share prices of over 1,500 companies in around 20 different countries comprise the sample, accounting for around 60% of the value of the world's shares. There is also an MSCI World Accumulation Index which takes into account the value of reinvested dividends as well as price.

There are countless other indices in existence and more being developed all the time. So long as you know what they are measuring they are a very useful tool for indicating at a glance the direction in which a market or market sector is travelling and how it has performed over a given time. And when you come across an index you're not familiar with, ring your stockbroker, your funds manager, or the ASX who should have no trouble telling you how the index is constructed, what it measures, and what it can mean to you.

Selecting the right shares

Unless you are very enthusiastic about researching companies, I suggest that you let your broker make some recommendations. Having said that, if you are making your first share investment, I'd go for a major blue chip company such as BHP, Coles Myer or a bank such as National Australia Bank or Commonwealth Bank. Also note that in our rapidly changing world, many so-called blue chip stocks will fall or do poorly. Burns Philp is a dramatic example of this, and even BHP took a battering a few years ago. So make sure you own shares in companies that have a future in the new century.

I'm a strong believer in the Information Age, despite the so-called 'tech-wreck' of 2000, which indicated how silly the valuations of many Internet-based companies were. At the end of the day any companies you invest in have to make profits, not losses, and not in twenty years' time. You need to look for companies that can demonstrate exactly how they will generate profits in the near future. If all they can show is ever-increasing numbers of customers and ever-increasing losses without a powerful strategy as to how this can be turned around, then sooner or later, as we saw in 2000, reality catches up with both them and their shareholders.

Ideally you should end up with a number of shares in different sectors. By 'sectors' I mean mining, banking, media, retail, building and so on. This spreads your risk. If you think this all sounds a bit hard, a managed share fund will take care of diversification for you – and I deal with these in Chapter Fifteen.

When is the right time to buy?

The answer to this question is very simple – when you have the money. If you wait for the market or a particular share to bottom (the optimum time to buy), you could be waiting forever because there is no way of knowing when a share or the market has bottomed!

Making Money

There is no doubt you can make tons of money by good market timing, but, there is also no doubt that good market timing involves a lot of skill and probably an even greater amount of luck.

When is the right time to sell?

The answer to this question is also very simple – when you need the money. If you don't need the money, don't sell. It's not a good strategy to turn your shares over too often. If you do, you will only stack up unnecessarily high brokerage fees, you may miss out on the payment of dividends and you may be out of the market during the 'hot' periods.

Trying to pick the optimum times to buy and sell shares is no different to trying to pick winners at the races. It makes you a punter and we all know how most punters fare – poorly.

Trying to pick market timing

Many financial commentators and investors place great emphasis on making sure you time your entry into and out of the markets correctly. 'Correct' timing means buying when the market or a particular share is at its lowest point and selling when the market or a particular share is at its highest point.

You don't have to be Einstein to see why people urge you to get your market timing right – anyone who can *consistently* pick share movements will end up very rich, in just the same way as anyone who can consistently pick the winning horse or the right number at roulette will do very well. But, like picking the winning horse, getting your timing right with share markets is much easier said than done.

One of the most thorough and sobering studies on 'active trading' (moving in and out of the markets at the supposed 'right' time) was conducted in 1972 by Professor William Sharpe of Stanford University. This study assumed an investor would shift assets between shares and cash on an annual basis depending on his perceptions of the state of the market.

His findings were startling – namely, that an active trader would have to be right over 70% of the time before increasing the value of his portfolio. These findings still hold, so let's look at the logic behind Professor Sharpe's study.

Suppose you make two predictions: firstly, that the share market will go up; and secondly, that it will stay up. So you invest $100.

Say you're right about the market going up, and the rise is by 50%. Your shares are now worth $150.

But then the market falls, again by 50%. Now your shares are only worth $75. A 50% gain followed by a 50% loss has not returned you to your original level; you are in fact down by 25% on your starting point.

This illustrates how the penalty for getting it wrong with market timing is greater than the reward for getting it right. The penalty is the risk of permanent capital loss and the reward is magnified returns. However, the potentially greater rewards are not in proportion to the risks.

If you trade actively, you will theoretically need to get your timing right about 66% of the time to break even – before costs. When you add brokerage fees, and other expenses like phone and fax, you can see why your timing must be right over 70% of the time just to break even.

The price of investments can be affected by a huge array of factors including economic, political and social influences, and markets have an unnerving habit of moving in sudden jolts in reaction to unpredictable causes. This makes it impossible to forecast price movements accurately over short periods of time. Therefore, the prospective gain from correctly timing your entry into or out of a market should be balanced against the risk of either being out of the market completely during a rally, or in the market too long during a sudden downturn.

Consider this: between 1979 and 2000 returns from the US share market for a full-time investor averaged 13% p.a. But look at the graph on the following page which shows the average annual returns an investor would have received if they missed out on just the 10, 20, 30 and 40 biggest days of the period, being respectively: 10.2%, 8.5%, 6.7% and 5.3%.

There are no prizes for guessing which share investment strategy I recommend. Clearly, you should avoid trying to time your entry into and exit out of the share market in the hope of gaining that elusive short-term win. The way to win with shares (or any other mainstream investment) is to hang on for the long term.

Look, there's no denying the share market has its bad days, weeks and years, and that anyone who has invested just as it goes into a tailspin can really hurt at the time. Some reversals have been terrible – the last great stinker occurred on 20 October 1987

Making Money

Time *not* timing – annual returns on the US share market 1979 to 2000

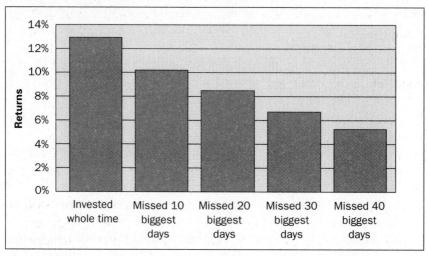

(*Source*: ipac securities.)

Long-term investment *vs* short-term investment (Australian shares)

	Worst 1 year performance	Average annualised performance over the 20 years
1921–1940	−21.3%	11.1%
1941–1960	−27.3%	12.1%
1961–1980	−24.2%	11.8%
1981–2000	−17.5%	12.3%

(*Source*: ipac securities.)

when the market crashed 25% in one day! And within eight weeks a further 25% of market value was wiped. Yet, the Australian share market grew in value by 45.4% in 1993 (then fell by 8.7% in 1994 ... and rose by 16.1% in 1999).

So, if your initial timing isn't good, don't despair. Try to hang in there because, in time, the market is bound to recover and even go on to new heights. Indeed, since 1875 the Australian share market has never failed, following a fall, to rise above the previous high point and there is no reason to believe this pattern will change in the foreseeable future. If you are still not convinced look at the table on the previous page. I think it presents a pretty compelling argument for long-term market involvement and a rejection of short-term market plays.

'Dollar cost averaging'

I mentioned 'dollar cost averaging' in my investment tips, but it's worth thinking about again. Dollar cost averaging is a buying strategy that stands in complete opposition to the active trading strategy of entering and exiting the market in an effort to catch its highs and lows.

It involves investing a fixed amount in the share market (or other investment markets) at regular, fixed intervals. An example would be investing, say, $2,000 in the share market on the first business day of every fourth month.

The logic behind this strategy is simple and compelling. Firstly, it is a disciplined investment regimen. Secondly, it acts to average out the cost of the shares you buy even though the value of the underlying assets and hence the share price have fluctuated. This process frees you up from having to worry about getting your market timing right.

How does it do this? Well, when the market is declining your money buys you more shares than under normal trading conditions, and when the market is climbing it buys you less. You just keep on buying regardless of the state of the market and effectively building your share portfolio at an average market price. This averaging process ultimately means you might not get any bargains, but you should not pay too much for your shares either. You simply keep adding to your share portfolio come rain, hail or shine.

The easiest way and most affordable way of putting this 'get rich slow' technique into effect is by contributing regularly towards a professionally managed share fund (or some other type of managed fund). Not only are the minimum ongoing investment sizes (around $100 to $500) small enough for most investors to be able to handle, but a managed fund takes the effort out of trying to decide which shares to buy.

Making Money

International shares

So far we've concentrated on Australian shares and the Australian share market, but there's a whole world of shares out there trading on share markets from Buenos Aires to Paris to New York to Tokyo. Indeed, the range of share investment opportunities laid out before you is staggering when you start thinking globally.

The Australian share market accounts for less than 1.5% of the volume of the world's share markets. So if you only invest in companies listed on the local share market you restrict your opportunity to participate in the high growth of regions such as China, South-East Asia and Latin America, and miss out altogether on the opportunity to invest in some of the world's best-known companies, such as Boeing, Michelin, Thorn-EMI and Minolta, which are not represented on the ASX.

The table below shows the Australian share market as a percentage of the world's total share markets as at December 2000:

Australia	**1.3%**
Singapore and Hong Kong	1.5%
United Kingdom	10.0%
Other Europe	23.6%
Japan	10.7%
USA	50.5%
Other	2.4%
Total	**100.0%**

(*Source*: ipac securities, MSCI World Index.)

In the 18 years to 31 December 2000, Australian shares returned an average of 15.7% p.a. based on the All Ordinaries Accumulation Index and S&P/ASX300 Accumulation Index. Over the same period, international shares, as measured by the MSCI World Accumulation Index, returned an average of 17.9% p.a.

Now, not all share markets perform similarly at the same time. Some may record losses and others record gains in the same year. In 1984, for instance, the Australian share market lost 2.3% and the Japanese market grew by 27.6%. In 1988, the Australian share market grew by 17.9% and the British market lost 10.4%.

So, given that the world's share markets do not all perform in the same way at the same time, international share investment therefore presents a very good avenue of diversification – which is a foundation stone of effective personal investment. Diversification is all about reducing portfolio risk while at the same time maintaining an acceptable level of return.

The commonly held wisdom is that investing in overseas share markets is riskier than investing in the Australian share market. This is not necessarily the case. The level of risk entailed in international investment depends on *which* overseas share markets you invest in. Some are more risky (more volatile and more variable) than ours, others aren't.

In general, the share markets of the developing world, the so-called 'emerging markets',* are the most risky. They have the potential for the wildest swings which means they may be more prone to plunging, as well as tending to generate the highest levels of growth of any markets. Between 1988 and 2000, for example, average annual returns from the share markets of emerging economies was 14.7%. The world share market averaged 12.8% p.a. during the same period. Also, despite the major downturn in Asian markets in 1997 and 1998 and a shaky outlook in 2001, these economies continue to present exciting long-term investment opportunities. (*Source*: ipac securities.)

The 'mainstream' markets of Western Europe, North America and Japan tend to have lower rates of growth, but also less likelihood of dramatic downturns than emerging markets. And, importantly, investing in mainstream markets is really no riskier than investing in ours. Indeed, investing in certain overseas markets can be less risky than investing in the ASX.

Look at the graph on the following page comparing the returns from Australian shares to the returns from international shares between 1988 and 2000.

Note how the incidence of negative returns is less frequent, as well as being less pronounced, for international shares than for Australian shares. Over this period the returns from the international share markets were less volatile and less risky than the returns from the Australian share market – while at the same time producing a higher average annual return! (International shares over the period

---

* 'Emerging markets' include: in Latin America – Argentina, Brazil, Chile, Columbia, Mexico, Venezuela; in Asia – China, India, Indonesia, Korea, Malaysia, Philippines, Thailand, Taiwan; and in Europe – Greece, Portugal, Turkey.

Comparison of the annual returns of Australian and international shares, 1988–2000

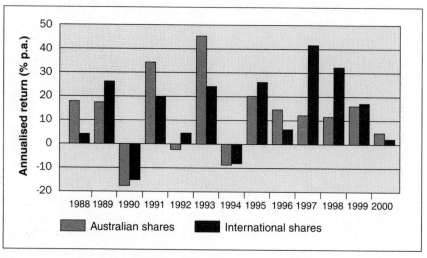

(*Source*: ipac securities, MSCI World Index.)

returned 12.8% p.a.; Australian shares over the period returned 11.6% p.a.) This goes against the normally accepted principle that the higher the return, the higher the risk.

The relationship that existed between risk and return for local and international shares in the five years to December 2000 is plotted in the graph on the opposite page.

At any given point on the curve you can see what the levels of risk (as determined by the 'standard deviation' – don't ask!) and return were during this period for any combination of Australian and international shares. For instance, if you had invested 25% in Australian and 75% in international shares, your annualised return would have been just over 17% with your risk level being less than if you had held 100% Australian shares.

The apex or turning point of the curve – giving the optimum combination of risk and return – occurred at a mix of around 60% Australian and 40% international shares. This illustrates why professional managers hold a mix of local and international assets. It can simultaneously achieve the normally incompatible goals of improving returns *as well as* lowering risk.

The relationship between risk and return for Australian and international shares in the 5 years to December 2000

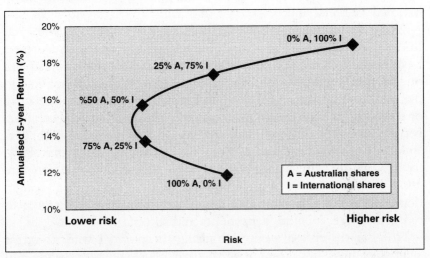

(*Source*: ipac securities.)

Don't lose sight of the fact that we have been looking here at historical figures over a single (five-year) period. However, ipac research has shown that in most 10-year periods international shares slightly outperform Australian shares with a slightly lower degree of risk. So, assuming the pattern is replicated in the future – and there is no reason to think otherwise – diversification into certain international markets makes a lot of sense.

Share returns and risks

Investment	Long-term historic after-inflation return % p.a.	Risk of a negative return (loss)*				
		1 year	3 years	5 years	10 years	20 years
Shares (Aust.)	5–8%	26%	13%	8%	2%	0%
Shares (Int'l)	6–9%	26%	14%	8%	2%	0%

* These numbers are based on ipac's expected return and risk outcomes for the next 3 to 5 years.

Which overseas markets?

By now I suspect you are wondering *which* overseas markets to invest in, *what proportion* of your share portfolio to place into international markets, and *how* to go about it.

As far as international markets selection is concerned, you need to consider their risk and return characteristics. For convenience we have already classified the world's share markets into mainstream or established markets, and emerging markets. We know that emerging markets are more volatile than mainstream markets. The ratio of emerging to mainstream markets that you should hold, therefore, becomes a factor of how much risk you feel comfortable with. Personally, I believe a ratio of 20% to 30% emerging markets to 80% to 70% mainstream markets is a sensible mix that should generate good growth with an acceptable level of risk. Remember though, that investment risk depends entirely on your general attitude to risks, your age, income, dependants and so on.

Now, at the risk of really labouring the point, I want to stress again just how important it is to treat all share investments and especially international emerging market share investments as a long-term proposition. By this I mean holding on to them for at least five years, preferably ten. All share markets have good and bad years and if you are only invested for one, two or three years you may just catch the bad ones.

⌐ KEY THOUGHT

The point not to lose sight of with shares – whether Australian, mainstream international or emerging markets – is that over time they have generated good to very good returns and there is no reason to believe this pattern will change in the foreseeable future.

How many international shares?

To answer the question, 'what proportion of your share portfolio should be allocated to international shares and what should be allocated to Australian shares?', I generally recommend a ratio of around 35% to 40% international to 60% to 65% local. But given that international shares appear to be such strong performers, why not more?

Well, firstly, when you invest in the Australian share market you can invest solely in companies that pay fully franked dividends and this benefit does not apply to international shares. Secondly, when you invest in shares listed on the ASX you are investing to a significant extent in Australia. Companies that operate here (even if foreign owned) provide employment, reinvest in Australia, pay local taxes and generate wealth that benefits all of us. There's room for a bit of nationalism here even if, strictly speaking, it's not a normally accepted personal investment criterion. Thirdly, you can keep track of your Australian shares far more easily than you can your offshore ones. Indeed, knowing what companies to invest in overseas and keeping tabs on these investments is very hard for the average individual investor. Finally, you should keep a reasonable percentage of your assets in the community you live in – unless it's a complete basket case!

How to invest overseas

Direct investment in overseas share markets fits into the 'too hard' basket for most people. You would need to appoint overseas sharebrokers and subscribe to overseas publications to keep track of your investments. You would also need to make a large budget allocation for international phone calls.

The simplest way to go about it is to invest in a managed international share fund. Many are now offered to Australian investors by a wide range of funds managers including AMP, BT, Colonial First State, MLC and Perpetual. You can get information on these direct from the funds managers or from any financial planner.

The details of managed funds are looked at in Chapter Fifteen, but, briefly, managed international share funds can give you access to a large range of investment options. Some funds concentrate on Asian markets, others on the US market, some on a mix of mainstream international markets and others solely on emerging markets. The choice is very wide.

Managed funds have entry, exit and ongoing management fees – which you wouldn't have to contend with as a direct investor – but going through a funds manager is a very easy form of investing. The

Making Money

funds manager selects all the assets to invest in (within the parameters that you choose) and monitors their progress for you. A typical minimum investment would be $1,000, with minimum additions of around $100 to $500.

It's probably fair to say that if you choose to invest in international shares via a managed share fund (and this is the method I recommend), you would indirectly become an investor in literally hundreds of overseas companies. This is because a typical managed fund invests directly in between 50 and 100 companies, which in turn invest in a myriad of other companies, and so on. It follows, therefore, that managed funds provide very good diversification.

Borrowing to buy shares

With the boom of the Australian share market over the last ten years, there has been a dramatic increase in the number of people borrowing to invest in shares, with two of the more popular methods being through *margin loans* and *endowment warrants*.

Margin loans

Generally, margin loans let you borrow 30% to 70% of the market value of your shares, with the shares themselves providing the security for the loan. The lender provides a list of shares you can select from, and also the percentage of each share's value you can borrow against. This percentage usually hovers around 60% if you are borrowing for a diversified parcel of shares. However, if you are borrowing to buy shares in just one company, the percentage of the value you can borrow against plummets to around 30% to 40%. You see, as far as the lender is concerned (and they're right), even the most blue chip share is more volatile on its own than as part of a diverse portfolio of shares.

When you apply for a margin loan the lender will certainly look at your ability to meet the repayments. But because they have already scrutinised the shares you can borrow against, your savings record and borrowing history are not as significant as they would be were you applying for many other types of loan.

When shares are targeted for margin lending, lenders look for two things: A relatively stable share price and more importantly, liquidity, or the ability to easily sell the share to convert it to cash (as measured by its market turnover). This is because at some point in time, you may be asked to pay what is known as a 'margin call'. This is the key point of difference between margin loans and other loans. A margin call is a demand by the lender that you tip cash into the loan if the value of the shares which underpin your loan fall in value below an agreed level. It's the sort of extremely unpleasant thing that can occur during a significant market or company downturn.

And you'll need to act quickly as most lenders only give you 24 hours to come up with the cash. If you can't meet the margin call, the lender usually has the right to sell some or all of the shares to come up with the required cash, and will do so within 48 hours of you failing to meet a margin call. The lender, whether it is a bank or a broker (as a large number of margin lenders are), is able to sell your shares as the CHESS system gives the right to directly sell shares to only two parties – brokers and the 'sponsors' (or margin lenders) of shares. In most cases the lender will only sell enough of your shares to cover the margin call.

The threat of a margin call may sound a bit dire, but bear in mind you can generally only borrow up to around 60% of the value of the shares, and much less if you are buying shares in just one company. So the share value has to fall a fair way before you get the dreaded margin call.

Borrowing to invest can certainly magnify the returns from the share market if times are good. But margin lending also magnifies the risk of investing in shares and is not something I could recommend for first-time investors. It is more suited to investors comfortable with a higher degree of risk, who can pay the interest, and who have the capacity to meet any margin calls, should they occur.

Take note that while margin loans are primarily used to buy shares, they can also be used to buy units in managed funds and fixed interest securities. In addition, the interest you pay on a margin loan is tax deductible, working in much the same way as negative gearing on a rental property (see Chapter Twelve).

Making Money

Endowment warrants

Endowment warrants let you acquire shares at a future date, approximately ten years hence, by paying the issuer of the warrant a deposit based on today's share price.

You pay your initial deposit, anywhere between 30% and 65% of the share's current value, and what's left over is essentially a loan, secured against the shares. This outstanding amount, the difference between what you've paid and what the share was trading at on the day you invested in the endowment warrant, is increased by interest charged against it and reduced by dividends paid into it. The idea is that over time, the dividends will gradually eliminate the debt (the value of the dividends being greater than the interest charged, that is) and that finally you will own the shares outright. So, if all goes well, your initial deposit may be the only payment you ever make.

Now, if after ten years the outstanding amount has not been reduced to zero you can either pay one final instalment to own the shares, or cash out the warrant with the issuer and receive the value of the shares less the outstanding amount (plus costs).

Another option with endowment warrants, if you need the money, is to trade them at any stage on the share market, their value being approximately equivalent to the current share price less the amount outstanding.

Overall, there are a number of factors which impact on the performance of endowment warrants, with dividends and interest rates being the main ones. If the dividends are lower than expected, the value of the warrants will decrease, as lower dividends won't fully fund the amount outstanding. Of course, the opposite is also true, as stronger than expected dividends will pay the outstanding amount out earlier.

And if interest rates rise it will take longer to pay off the outstanding amount. Remember, the outstanding amount is essentially a loan, so if interest rates rise, endowment warrant values will fall, and vice versa.

Finally, the value of endowment warrants move up and down in concert with share price movements. So, if a share does well (or badly), its endowment warrant will too.

There are a number of positives with warrants. Primarily, you get to capture all the benefits of a share's dividends plus all of its capital growth without having to pay the full price for that share. In addition, no capital gains tax is payable until you sell the shares or your endowment warrants. Finally, once you've invested, there's no paperwork, no income tax to worry about and no administrative headaches – you can just put them in a drawer and forget about them for ten years.

The main negative is losing the entire investment through a major share reversal. With any leveraged investment, as this one is, the beneficial effects of upward market movements are magnified, as are the negative effects of any downward movements. Secondly, there are no tax deductions on the interest paid, as there would be if you took out a margin loan to buy some shares.

Shares and tax

The taxes most relevant to anyone investing in shares are capital gains tax (CGT), Pay As You Go (PAYG) and goods and services tax (GST). I won't go into detail here, because these taxes are looked at quite closely in Chapter Ten, but, needless to say, I think it's important to draw your attention to their existence and possible impact.

Capital gains tax

Like many other assets, when you sell shares at a profit (assuming you bought them after 19 September 1985), you are required to pay capital gains tax on the amount of the capital gain.

If you have held onto the shares for *less* than 12 months, the full value of the capital gain is included in your taxable income. If you have owned the shares for *more* than a year, the Tax Office has set out a number of ways of calculating any capital gain or loss, with the method of calculation dependent on when the shares were purchased (see Chapter Ten for details).

Pay As You Go

Before the introduction of The New Tax System in July 2000, shareholders who earned over $1,000 in 'unearned' income (dividends, interest and other investment returns) were required to pay provisional tax. However, since July 2000, provisional tax has come under the umbrella of the new Pay As You Go (PAYG) tax system.

Shareholders receiving dividends will usually need to complete an Instalment Activity Statement (IAS). This form lets the Tax Office know how you arrived at your PAYG tax payment. Whether you pay PAYG annually or quarterly depends on your tax bill in the previous year. As a rule of thumb, if you paid more than $250 but less than $8,000 in tax, you can lodge your IAS and pay PAYG annually, otherwise you need to do so quarterly. For more on this see Chapter Ten.

PAYG is an improvement on the provisional tax system, where in effect you were required to pay tax on the income often before it was received, but you still need to be careful to put aside part of your dividends (or other investment income) to meet the demands of the Tax Office.

Goods and Services Tax

The Tax Office classifies shares as 'financial supplies', which are 'input taxed'. This means you can't claim back any GST you incur in the process of buying the shares (although special rules apply if you trade shares as a business). GST is paid on brokerage, for example, but the shareholder wears this cost. The good news is that brokerage, including GST, is included in the cost of your shares when you calculate capital gains, which has the effect of reducing the capital gain for tax purposes, meaning you pay less capital gains tax.

The world's most successful share investor

In the previous editions of this book I began this section by asking the question, 'Have you ever heard of Warren Buffett?', assuming that many readers outside the investment industry would not have. These days, however, I'm not so sure. In fact I think most people with even a passing interest in making money would have heard about this extraordinary bloke.

His rise to international fame is really not surprising. He is, after all, the world's richest professional investor and America's fourth richest man. According to *Forbes* magazine, in March 2001 he was worth a handy A$54 billion (up from A$16 billion in 1995!).

Buffett built his wealth out of an investment company, Berkshire

Hathaway, that he and some partners set up in 1956 with their own contributions of US$100,000. And if you had invested $5,000 with him at the time, today it would be worth well in excess of $50 million. Incredible but not surprising, I suppose, given that at the time of writing, shares in Berkshire Hathaway were trading on the New York Stock Exchange at US$71,000 each!

Buffett's investment success is an investment morality tale. He shuns the flashy life and conspicuous consumption that typified his high-flying, Gordon Gekko-like contemporaries of the 1980s – most of whom are now either bankrupt, doing time, or on the investment lecture circuit (beware!). Buffett has succeeded when many failed by sticking to his mid-western, frugal instincts, and by eschewing short-term investment gains. He has made billions for himself and for his investors by taking long-term positions in shares in companies often shunned by others.

Buffett likens his search for solid investments to 'bagging rare and fast-moving elephants'. By this he means the secret is not so much picking the so-called 'sunrise industries' as identifying the right opportunities in any industry regardless of its glamour quotient and what the rest of the investment industry thinks.

Buffett says, 'We [Berkshire Hathaway] get excited about shares only when we find businesses that: 1) we understand; 2) have favourable long-term prospects; 3) are operated by honest, competent people; and 4) are priced attractively.'

He says, 'We can usually identify a small number of investments meeting requirements 1, 2 and 3, but meeting 4 often prevents action.'

So, what are some of Buffett's major holdings? Well, he is not big on things like biotechnology outfits and rocket technology shares, much preferring the mainstream. Amongst other stocks, he is a major shareholder in Gillette, Coca Cola and American Express, and says of his Gillette holding that 'It's pleasant to go to bed every night knowing there are 2.5 billion males in the world who have to shave in the morning.'

Buffett's key skill has been his ability to recognise good quality, undervalued stock. Arguably, his perceptions (based on strong analysis) are second to none. Now, I can't tell you exactly how he so consistently picks the right companies (he would keep that a well-guarded trade secret), but I can tell you this much – his methods include the use of 'quality filters' to assess the attractiveness of a share's price. This involves analysing factors like the level of company debt and the strength of cash flow. He also looks for shares that are neglected and, hence, possibly underpriced by the market. (I didn't say it was easy – if it was we would all be billionaires!)

I doubt Buffett would recommend (and I certainly don't) that you try to rival his clairvoyant ability to consistently pick undervalued stock. This is an astoundingly difficult job that even the best-trained investment professionals struggle to get right. So, what are you supposed to do? Well, even if you have a slim chance of emulating his share selection style, one thing you can emulate is his holding style – which is for the very long term.

Once Buffett has bought stock, he hangs on to it. He summarises his company's shareholding philosophy as, 'our favourite holding period is forever'. He also doesn't like too much turnover on his own company's share register. He has told his investors, 'our goal is to attract long-term shareholders who, at the time of purchase, have no time frame or price target for sale but instead plan to stay with us indefinitely'.

Without any doubt this is an uncompromising endorsement for the long term, and while it's perhaps too strong for some, it's a strategy that has proved very beneficial for Buffett and his shareholders.

Buffett also adheres to the view that a diversified portfolio of shares is preferable to a limited range of shares. And, in choosing your shares, Buffett advises you to ignore the sentiments of the crowd as this is likely to lead to some bad investment decisions.

Finally, timing. Against the background of a general recommendation that you don't let your opinion of the market's future overly influence your share buying (because your opinion could well be wrong), Buffett says a bad time to buy shares is when there is a universal mood of investor optimism. This means the share market is bound to be overpriced. Rather, buy when the mood is gloomy and prices are lower. Then, whatever the market does, hang on to your shares for as long as possible.

Warren Buffett's investment strategy

These are the key points that have helped make Buffett the world's richest share investor:

- thrift and prudence, combined with a relatively frugal lifestyle
- thorough analysis and a strict investment criteria leading to the selection of quality, undervalued stock
- a diversified portfolio across all market sectors
- a very long-term approach to share investment, a rejection of market timing strategies and an indifference to popular market sentiment.

CHAPTER FOURTEEN

Interest-bearing Investments

Anyone with a mortgage, a personal loan or a credit card knows all about the rigours of being in debt. It's no fun paying debts off, or paying all that interest into someone else's pocket. So what about putting the boot on the other foot? Why don't *you* be the lender and have someone pay *you* interest for a change? Sounds good? Well, that's what interest-bearing investments (interest-bearing securities or debt investments) are all about.

Whether you put your money in a bank term deposit, invest in Government bonds, or buy finance company debentures, you are basically doing the same thing. You are lending your money to another party on the understanding that interest will be paid to you for the privilege of that money's use. And, as with any loan, at the end of its term, you get your original amount (or 'principal') back.

The beauty of interest-bearing investments is that they are generally safe – they're liquid and they provide a sure return. They are particularly suited to those who need a *regular and dependable income*, such as retirees. They are not as well suited, under normal circumstances, to those looking for long-term capital growth – which is usually the domain of shares and property.

Interest-bearing investments can be broken down into two camps or 'asset classes' which are fixed interest and cash.

Fixed interest

A fixed interest investment is one where you effectively lend a company, a semi-government authority, or the Commonwealth or State Government an amount of money for a fixed period of time at a fixed rate of interest. The interest due on it is paid to you in fixed amounts on a regular, fixed schedule, say, once every month, or every 3, 6 or 12 months, and generally the more frequent the interest payments to the investor, the lower the effective interest rate

254

you receive. (This is because of the higher costs involved in more frequent income distributions.) The original amount is repaid to you in one lump sum at the end of the term, at 'maturity'.

Let me illustrate the way fixed interest investments operate, by looking at the classic example of bonds. If you buy, say, a three-year bond for $10,000 which promises to pay 5% p.a., what you are effectively doing is lending the issuer $10,000 for three years on the understanding that you will be repaid in full at the end of the term and receive regular interest payments in the meantime.

If regular interest payments (known as 'coupons') are due twice yearly on this bond, you will receive a cheque for $250 every six months ($10,000 at 5% p.a. = $500 p.a. = $250 per 6 months). At the end of the third year you would also get your original $10,000 (the 'maturity value' or 'principal amount') back.

In Australia the word 'bond' is usually taken to mean a fixed interest-bearing security issued by the Commonwealth or State governments, however, it can also be applied to fixed interest securities issued by semi-government authorities. And because bonds come with a Government guarantee of repayment, when you hear the word 'bond' you think 'safety and security'.

You can buy Australian bonds for terms ranging typically from one year to ten years, with one- to five-year terms being the more popular. Commonwealth Bonds are available in either three-year or ten-year terms. At the other extreme, you can buy US Government Bonds that mature in 30 years (though individual Australian investors rarely get involved in these because they require a minimum investment of $50,000).

The bonds we are talking about here should not be confused with insurance bonds which are a form of life insurance policy based on managed funds and are distinctly different.

Other fixed interest-bearing investments are described below.

Term deposits

Term deposits with banks, building societies and credit unions are for terms ranging from three months to five years. With these, you deposit a lump sum with the institution on the understanding you don't have access to the money until the end of the agreed term. At that time you get your money back plus interest which is paid to you at set times. To compensate you for tying up your money in this way, term deposits pay a higher rate of interest than normal bank accounts.

Note that your money isn't totally locked away. If an emergency crops up and you need to get your hands on it before the term expires, you can. But you'll probably be charged a penalty fee for breaking the arrangement and have your interest recalculated at a lower rate that's more in line with the normal savings account rate.

Debentures, unsecured notes and convertible notes

Debentures, unsecured notes and convertible notes are dealt with in some detail in Chapter Thirteen, 'Investing in Shares', but briefly:

- Debentures are basically the same as bonds except that they are loans to companies, typically industrial and finance companies, rather than being loans to Government or semi-government bodies. Debentures don't come with Government guarantees, so they are riskier than bonds and consequently normally pay a higher rate of interest.
- Unsecured notes are similar to debentures in that they are a fixed term, fixed rate loan to a company, however, these loans are not secured against the company's assets. This puts them on a higher risk level than debentures but, in compensation, they tend to pay higher returns.
- Like debentures, convertible notes are fixed term, fixed interest loans to companies. Where they differ is that at a set date and at a set price the note can be converted into shares in the issuing company if the note holder so wishes. Up until the time the note is converted into shares the holder receives regular, fixed interest payments from the issuer. If the holder of the note chooses not to convert the note to shares, the issuing company repays the principal value of the note to the investor on the note's maturity.

Cash investments

A 'cash' investment can range from putting your money into a bank account to investing in a cash management trust – which is a managed fund investing in a diversified range of short-term, interest-bearing securities. 'Cash' also covers investments in the short-term money market or in bank bills with terms of usually no more than 180 days.

Interest-bearing Investments

The returns from cash investments are based on short-term market interest rates and, because these rates are variable, you can't be sure exactly what your income will be. This puts cash into direct contrast with fixed interest investments.

Cash is an ideal short-term investment. It's a great place to park funds while you organise a more appropriate long-term use for them. Of course, you can keep your funds in cash forever if you wish, but don't expect high or tax-effective returns.

Performance

Calendar year	Australian fixed interest %	International fixed interest %	Cash %	Inflation (CPI) %
1983	14.3	14.9	13.6	8.6
1984	12.0	15.2	12.4	2.6
1985	8.1	55.8	15.4	8.2
1986	18.9	25.2	18.1	9.8
1987	18.6	13.8	15.3	7.1
1988	9.4	13.4	12.8	7.6
1989	14.4	18.8	18.4	7.8
1990	19.1	13.5	16.2	6.9
1991	24.8	18.1	11.2	1.5
1992	10.4	9.6	7.0	0.3
1993	16.3	14.3	5.4	1.9
1994	−4.7	−3.0	5.3	2.5
1995	18.6	19.9	8.1	5.1
1996	11.9	10.7	7.6	1.5
1997	12.2	10.7	5.6	−0.3
1998	9.5	10.8	5.1	1.6
1999	−1.2	0.3	5.0	1.8
2000	12.1	10.4	6.3	5.8
Annualised return	12.3	14.6	10.4	4.4

(*Source*: ipac securities.)

Research by ipac shows that *over the long term*, traditional *after-inflation* annual returns for cash and fixed interest investments have been:

Making Money

- Australian cash   0% to 1%
- Australian fixed interest   0% to 3%
- International fixed interest   1% to 2%.

In certain periods, however, after-inflation returns have been far better than these, as indicated by the table on the previous page.

Liquidity

Of all the investment classes cash is the most liquid. This means that you can get your hands on the money you have invested immediately in the case of a bank deposit, or within 24 hours in the case of a cash management trust. This liquidity is one of the greatest attributes of cash – the money is there when you need it.

While not quite as liquid as having cash in the bank, fixed interest securities are, nevertheless, liquid enough. This is because they are tradeable, primarily through the stock exchange and, in some cases, by selling them back to the issuer.

Under normal circumstances there should be a buyer for any fixed interest security you wish to sell. The exception to this would be if the security was issued by a company whose financial integrity had come into question, in which case finding a buyer could be very difficult. (In the USA these types of securities are called 'junk bonds'.)

Also, be aware that the price you get for fixed interest securities if sold before maturity will depend on interest rates at the time of sale, which means you may end up getting less than you paid for them.

Risk

Cash is extremely safe. When you deposit it in a bank, or invest in bank bills and Treasury notes via a cash management trust there is no likelihood of losing any of your money except under the most extreme and bizarre circumstances, such as the failure of the bank or the collapse of the entire financial system. And in keeping with the time-honoured relationship between risk and return, the returns from cash are designed to be the lowest of all investments. That's the price you pay for safety. (Of course, cash may not *always* generate the lowest returns – it can do better than a poorly performing share, property, or fixed interest sector, as occurred in 1994.)

Fixed interest investments normally have a higher risk profile than cash investments and, as a result, are designed to generate higher returns under normal market conditions. However, there are some exceptions and provisos to this generalisation. Arguably, nothing is safer than Commonwealth Government bonds with their Government guarantee of repayment. This makes them 'gilt-edged' securities – with the proviso being that you hold them until maturity. If you sell them before maturity, you can lose money, as we'll see in what follows.

Fixed interest securities and variable market value

When you hold bonds, debentures and other fixed interest-bearing investments to maturity you know exactly how much you will receive in interest payments, when you will receive the interest, and you also know you will get your principal back at the end of the term (unless the issuer or the financial system collapses in the meantime). But with many interest-bearing securities it's possible to trade them on the open market before their maturity date. This means they have a 'capital value' or market price, and this capital value fluctuates in line with changing expectations of future interest rates.

The important thing to realise is that the changing capital value of an interest-bearing security is quite separate from its fixed income value, and that the capital value, regardless of whether it rises or falls, is *only realised if and when the security is traded*. So, if you choose to hang on to your interest-bearing investment until maturity, the fact that its capital value fluctuates throughout its term is immaterial.

Bear in mind that the usual reason individual investors buy bonds, debentures and so on is for the regular, dependable income they provide. They are not normally bought by small investors for their capital growth potential. Usually it is only the big players like banks, insurance companies, funds managers and governments who trade in interest-bearing securities with an eye to making a capital gain and, at this level, they are traded in enormous dollar volumes (millions) – well and truly beyond the financial scope of individual investors like you and me.

Making Money

While you might not have any intention of trading your bonds, it's useful to know how their capital value is arrived at. One day you may need the money that's stored up in them or their value could have increased to the point where, by selling them, you'll realise a tidy profit on their purchase price.

Let's say you bought a two-year bond for $1,000 paying (or 'yielding') an annual interest rate of 6% ($60 p.a.). Now, if interest rates were expected to rise to 8% for the next two years, who would then want to pay $1,000 for your bond yielding only a fixed 6% when they could buy brand new bonds for the same price yielding a fixed 8% ($80 p.a.)? The answer isn't 'no one' – people *will* be prepared to buy your relatively lacklustre bond – *but only at a discount*.

So, what's the bond you paid $1,000 for worth now? Well, its new price needs to be set at a value that will give the new buyer a return *equivalent* to an interest rate yield of 8%. In other words, your bond needs to be discounted to the point where it will make no difference to an investor's return whether they buy your old, lower rate bond at a discount or a new, higher rate bond at the full (face) value. And using 'present value' arithmetic the discounted amount works out to be around $966 (I won't explain how this value is calculated – please just trust me!), representing a capital loss on the $1,000 bond of around $34 or 3.4%.

This valuing system works in reverse, too. Let's say interest rates were expected to fall from 8% to 4% for the next two years. People would now have to pay a premium for your 8% bond because it would be returning more than newly issued bonds rated at only 4%. The new price would be around $1,073 and, at that level, it would give the buyer a return equivalent to 4%. It would also give you a capital gain of about 7.3% on the bond you paid $1,000 for.

Added to this is a further factor, namely, the longer the security has to maturity the more pronounced the change in value as interest rate expectations change. For example, if interest rates were expected to rise, the value of a bond with 10 years to maturity would fall further than one with two years to maturity, and vice versa.

When expected interest rates rose from 6% to 8%, in the example above, the bond with two years to maturity fell in value by 3.4%. However, a bond with 10 years to maturity under the same set of circumstances would fall in value by 10.6%. Again, I won't go into the mathematics involved in calculating the size of this fall because it is based on 'present value' calculations and is quite involved. Let a broker do it for you. I am simply illustrating the higher volatility or risk of longer term fixed interest securities compared with shorter term ones.

The process of fixed interest valuing

We can sum up fixed interest valuing like this:

- As expected interest rates rise, the capital value (the market price) of a fixed interest security falls; and as expected interest rates fall, the value of a fixed interest security rises.
- The longer the term to maturity the greater the rise (or fall) in the value of the security as expected interest rates rise (or fall). (This means securities with longer terms to maturity are more volatile or more risky than those with shorter terms to maturity.)

Now you may be able to better understand why bond markets everywhere suffered big capital losses in 1994. The world was emerging from the early 1990s recession and, with growing prosperity, the (utterly inaccurate, as it turned out) expectations about future interest rate levels also rose, and quite sharply. Consequently, bond values tumbled, particularly longer term bonds, and many investors and financial institutions were caught holding too many of them. This is why so-called 'capital stable' managed funds had such a bad year in 1994 – capital stable funds normally hold around 50% of their assets in fixed interest securities.

Let me just add to this my usual remark – the short-term performance of any asset class can be bad, but *over time*, all the mainstream asset classes have performed well. And, interestingly, the bond crash of 1994 was preceded by five years of fabulous returns from the fixed interest sector.

Unfortunately, guess when most smaller investors raced into bonds? Yes, you guessed it, at the end of the five-year bond 'boom' to see losses on their investments. Many then rushed out of this investment to miss out on the fabulous recovery in 1995! This is typical human behaviour, and a lesson worth remembering. (Australian fixed interest returned 18.6% in 1995 and international fixed interest returned 19.9%, which are great results.)

Making Money

Buying and selling fixed interest securities

Buying fixed interest securities is pretty straightforward. There are two basic ways to do it. Firstly, you can buy securities direct from the issuer through an application form found in the prospectus, or you can buy already existing securities from another investor via a stockbroker.

Selling is not quite as straightforward. You can sell some fixed interest securities that have not yet matured to another investor on the open market via a stockbroker, some you can sell back to the issuer, some you cannot sell back to the issuer, and some you may have trouble finding any buyer for at all, obliging you to hang on to them until maturity. It's important, therefore, that you understand how tradeable any particular fixed interest security might be before you buy it and this is specific information you can get from a security's issuer, a broker or a financial adviser. In general, however, Government bonds are more easily tradeable than debentures and, indeed, debentures may not be tradeable at all if the issuing company gets into financial strife.

Note that you will be charged brokerage should you buy or sell securities through a stockbroker. Again, you could simply invest via a fixed interest fund run by a professional manager and you will find more on this in Chapter Fifteen, 'Managed Funds'.

Nominal and effective interest rates and yields

When you see bonds and debentures advertised in the newspapers you will often see the terms 'nominal' and 'effective' interest rates and yields. The nominal interest rate is the simple annual interest rate. It's the amount you would earn if you were paid interest in one lump sum at the end of the year. For example, let's say you invested $20,000 for 12 months at a nominal interest rate of 5%. At the end of the year your nominal return or yield would be $1,000 ($20,000 × 5% = $1,000).

Now, if the interest was paid monthly, and this was then added to the principal for reinvestment, and this process went on for 12 months, at the end of the year you would have earned $1,024 in interest, representing an effective return of 5.12% (The effective return of 5.12% is generated in this case through the compounding of interest, which is where interest is paid upon interest.)

The difference between the effective and nominal returns might seem pretty insignificant here, but with larger sums and more time it can really add up. Just make sure when you invest in a fixed interest product that you clarify which type of return you're getting.

Tax

While tax relief can be found in shares through dividend imputation and in property through a wide range of tax-deductible costs and depreciation allowances, there is no income tax relief to be had with cash or fixed interest investments. All interest payments you receive are classified as income and are taxed at your highest marginal rate.

On the other hand, interest income from fixed interest and cash investments is not subject to capital gains tax, which does apply to share and property investments.

Income investments *vs* growth investments

With long-term investment studies usually (but not always) ranking the gross returns from cash and fixed interest last and second last, you might ask why invest in fixed interest and cash at all?

Well, remember that they do have their place, which is providing relative safety, liquidity, and a *dependable source of income*. Cash and fixed interest also provide good diversification benefits as the asset performance table on pages 163–164 shows. In this period (1983 to 2000), interest-bearing deposits were the best performers out of all the main asset classes in five of the 18 years.

However, you need to shift your portfolio's mix of assets away from interest-bearing income investments and more towards growth investments of shares and property, both Australian and international, if:

- liquidity and regular, dependable income are not high priorities
- you are prepared to take a bit more risk than that involved in cash and fixed interest investment
- you're a taxpayer
- your focus is more towards longer term capital growth.

In the graph over the page look at the end December 2000 value of an initial $10,000 investment made in each of the following four asset classes at the end of 1975. This dramatically shows how growth-producing investments outperform income-producing investments over the long term.

Investment values of four $10,000 investments held over 25 years, 1975–2000

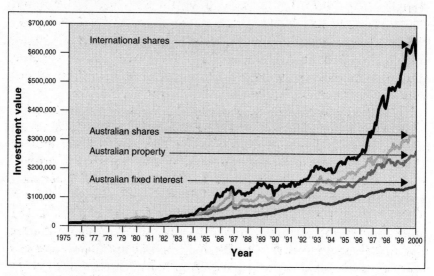

(*Source*: Macquarie Investment Management.)

Now, let's compare the performance of bonds and Australian shares over the 29-year period, from 1971 to 2000:

- over any one-year period shares outperformed bonds 53% of the time
- over any five-year period shares outperformed bonds 65% of the time
- over any 10-year period shares outperformed bonds 62% of the time
- over any 20-year period shares outperformed bonds 94% of the time.

Finally, while income from a fixed interest term deposit is definitely more reliable on a short-term basis than the dividend income from a share-market investment (and is higher in some years), over the longer term the share investment is almost certain to produce greater income. Why? Well, the capital value of a term deposit does not change over time, whereas the capital value of a portfolio of quality shares can increase (and indeed ought to). And, as the capital value of your shareholdings increases, so does the amount of income it generates.

To illustrate, let's say you made a $100,000 investment in the Australian share market at end 1979. Assuming you just let it sit there, by end 2000 this investment would have grown in capital value to around $817,000. Let's say you also made a term deposit of $100,000 at end 1979, and rolled it over every 12 months thereafter. By end 2000 its capital value would have remained unchanged at only $100,000. *Compare the two end values!* (These figures assume *no* interest or dividend income was reinvested.)

Now, the dividend income produced by this share-market investment in the year 2000 would have been around $25,300 and partly tax-paid due to dividend imputation, whereas the interest income from the fixed term investment would have been only around $5,750 and fully taxable. It's a huge difference. (*Source*: Macquarie Investment Management.)

This all looks like a fairly big put down of 'income assets' at the expense of 'growth assets', particularly shares. Let me make it clear that this is not my intention. What I am trying to show are the strengths and weaknesses of the two broad groupings and where one is more appropriate than the other, depending on your circumstances and goals. Generally speaking, shares and property better serve your need for longer term, tax-effective capital growth leading to a strong future income. Cash and fixed interest, on the other hand, better serve your need for security, liquidity, and a reliable source of income right now. There is probably a valid place in most investors' portfolios for both.

⚬⌐ KEY THOUGHTS

The following list sums up the characteristics of cash and fixed interest securities.

Cash

- low risk, low return
- income returns fluctuate in line with current market interest rates
- very low likelihood of capital loss
- high liquidity
- open to erosion through inflation
- suitable for short-term investing
- inappropriate for long-term growth
- returns fully taxed.

Fixed interest

- a suitable investment over a wide range of periods, from relatively short term to long term
- predictable income – returns are fixed until the investment or security matures
- potential for capital gains or losses due to changes in market interest rates if the security is sold before maturity
- less liquid than cash
- generally higher returns than cash
- varying risk profiles, from the safest available investment through to riskier than cash (but less risky than property or shares)
- not suited to long-term growth
- returns fully taxed.

CHAPTER FIFTEEN
Managed Funds

Having read through the preceding sections on property, shares and fixed interest, you'll know that each of these asset classes satisfy certain investment objectives, and that your short-, medium- and long-term needs and goals ought to determine what proportion of each you hold in your portfolio.

If long-term capital growth is your goal, you should bias or 'weight' your portfolio towards shares and property. If you need regular income and security, you should weight your portfolio towards cash and fixed interest. If you want both growth and income, then you should have an even spread of investments across all these assets.

So far, so good, but how are you going to do all this? How do you know what proportion of each class you should hold and how will you know which specific investments to select within each class? What about monitoring your investments' progress? Do you have access to all the raw information you'll need to keep up-to-date with the markets and will you be able to make sense of it when you get it anyway? And what about the time involved – how much have you got to spare?

If it all sounds like too much hard work, don't worry. There is an easy way around the difficulties, namely, investing in professionally managed investment funds.

The idea behind managed funds is very simple. You let investment professionals do some or all of the work involved in creating and managing an investment portfolio for you. They charge a fee for this service but, in return, they save you the time and effort involved in selecting stock and monitoring its performance. Theoretically, they should also be able to achieve better returns than you or the average man or woman on the street because they're the professionals with their fingers on the market pulse. (The theory's good – but it doesn't always hold up in practice.)

Whether managed investments are right for you depends on:
- to what extent you want to control the investment selection process yourself

- how much you want to be involved in your portfolio's ongoing management.

If you have the confidence and the time to manage your own investments and are reluctant to delegate this responsibility to someone else, that's fine – it's a perfectly acceptable way of managing your affairs and one I recommend to many investors, particularly those with some market experience. But for those of you with limited time, limited investment experience, and limited confidence in your ability to pick the right assets, investing through managed funds is a sensible way to go.

Other people would seem to think so too. Managed funds are a very popular investment in many parts of the world and Australians have around $612 billion invested in them, which includes around $288 billion invested in superannuation funds. (*Source*: ABS, December quarter 2000.)

What are managed funds?

The term 'managed (investment) fund' is a generic one covering a range of related investment products including balanced funds, listed or unlisted property trusts, pooled superannuation trusts, insurance company savings bonds and some annuities. Although all are structured differently and may have varying taxation treatments, they share basic similarities. Sometimes managed funds are also referred to as 'managed trusts', 'pooled funds', 'investment trusts' or 'unit trusts'.

A managed fund is an investment vehicle where the money put into it by a large number of smaller investors is pooled together and managed as one large investment portfolio by a professional investment manager. Managed funds can invest in either shares, cash, property or fixed interest securities, or can invest in some or all of them. They can also invest in these assets directly, or indirectly by investing in them through other managed funds.

Managed funds can specialise in all sorts of assets – whether Australian, international, Asian or from any other region or mix of regions. They can also invest in fish farms, pine plantations and feature films. In fact, the mix and type of assets and ventures you can invest in through a managed fund is limited only by the imagination of those offering them.

Investors in a managed fund are effectively part-owners of the assets held by the fund. Earnings generated by the fund's assets can be distributed as income to investors on a regular basis (monthly, quarterly or six monthly) or, alternatively, its earnings can go towards increasing the capital value of the investors' units. This capital appreciation (designated by an increase in unit price) is realised when the units are sold by the investor.

Most managed funds stipulate minimum initial investments in the fund, minimum additional deposits and minimum balances. As a general guide, an average minimum investment would be around $1,000, a minimum additional investment would be $100, and a minimum balance would be around $500.

Fund managers

A fund's investment manager is usually an experienced and reputable investment organisation such as AMP, Macquarie or Rothschild. (You need to select well, but more on this later.)

Working within defined investment parameters for the fund, the fund manager's job is to invest the pooled money in a range of assets. The manager has the right and the responsibility to shift the fund's money in and out of assets as they see fit and as changing market conditions dictate. The manager's objective is to achieve as high a sustainable return on the investors' pooled money as possible within certain (usually conservative) risk limits.

All managed funds are run by a 'single responsible entity'. This replaces the two-tier system that operated in the past: where the fund manager invested and managed your money, and a separate trustee represented the rights of the investors. These days the responsible entity combines these roles, and is required to set up precise systems to protect investors and help prevent breaches of the law.

The Australian Securities and Investment Commission (ASIC) is the statutory authority responsible for regulating the activities of managed funds. ASIC was involved in the establishment of an external complaints resolution scheme to protect the rights of investors, and all fund managers are required by ASIC to register for the scheme as part of their licensing process. Should you have any problems or complaints regarding a managed fund, the number to contact ASIC on is 1300 300 630.

Making Money

Units

Managed funds are divided up into 'units' of equal value. Like an ordinary share, they give you a part-ownership of assets. Although shares and units are technically quite different, the concept is the same and some units – those of 'listed trusts' – are traded on the Australian Stock Exchange.

The number of units issued for sale in some funds is fixed, whereas in other funds new units are always available to anyone who wants to buy them. In general, listed unit trusts are 'closed', meaning the fund has a fixed number of issued units. This number of units can only be increased by a separate offering of new units at a later date.

Unlisted trusts (those not listed on the Australian Stock Exchange) can be either 'open' or 'closed'. An 'open' unlisted unit trust that wants to continue issuing units to the public simply does so by updating its prospectus every six months or so. Managed funds such as superannuation and insurance or friendly society bonds are nearly always open – you can increase your stakeholding in them by as much as you like at any time.

Valuing units

With the exception of listed trusts' units, which are valued (priced) on the share market, other managed funds value their units (put a price on them) daily or, at least, weekly. The method of valuation must be done strictly in accordance with the rules laid out in the Trust Deed (where one exists). Actually, two values per unit are calculated – a value for buying units and another for selling them.

The buying price of a unit is determined by taking the current valuation of the fund's total assets, adding a loading to cover purchase costs like stamp duties and brokerage, and then dividing this amount by the number of issued units. The selling price is calculated similarly – by taking the current valuation of the fund's total assets, adding a loading to cover selling costs, and then dividing this amount by the number of units on issue. The difference between the two prices can be as high as 6%, which reflects these costs as well as commissions payable to a licensed adviser.

Let's look at a very simple illustration of how changes in a unit's value affect you. You invest $10,000 in an unlisted managed trust with units selling for $1; this buys you 10,000 units.

Now, remembering that the value of units fluctuates in line with the value of the fund's underlying assets, if you later wished to redeem 2,000 of these units and the unit price had risen to $1.10 (because the value of the fund's assets had risen), you'd get back $2,200, representing a profit of 10%.

Liquidity

Managed fund units vary significantly in their liquidity. You can get your money out of cash management funds more or less immediately. Converting your units in an insurance bond to cash may take a few days, and redeeming share trust units may take up to two weeks – which is about the maximum it should take under normal circumstances to cash any type of unit. Having said this, real problems with liquidity have occurred with property trusts in the past, due to the relative lack of liquidity of their underlying property assets in tough market times.

There are potentially two main ways of buying units and two main ways of redeeming them. When a managed fund is listed its units can be bought and sold through a stockbroker at a price set by the market, just like shares. The mood of the market will determine just how quickly a buyer or seller is found for a particular fund's units but, under normal circumstances, a transaction should take place almost instantly.

If the managed fund is unlisted, you can normally only buy and redeem units directly from the fund manager. There is no other simple method of trading units in an unlisted fund and, more to the point, there is no other simple method of cashing them. This is why you need to ensure the fund manager or managers you invest with are reputable and competent and therefore likely to keep their doors open.

Note that like other securities you can trade units directly between individuals, bypassing stockbrokers and fund managers, though this type of trading is uncommon.

Safety

Let me make this clear – the vast majority of mainstream managed funds are managed by competent investment professionals who take their jobs seriously and act in good faith. They are aware of their enormous responsibilities and manage accordingly – in a conservative manner. Fund managers are not cowboys by nature or by training.

A disaster like the collapse of the Estate Mortgage unlisted mortgage trust in 1990 was a rarity. The investors in Estate Mortgage were very unlucky – the probability of everything going off the rails in a mainstream managed fund at the same time is very low. Collapses of this kind can happen, but they should remain freak events. However, remember, if everything being said about a particular fund sounds too good to be true, it usually is.

There are thousands of managed funds in which Australians have invested and can invest. The proportion that fail is far less than the proportion of listed companies on the ASX that fizzle out taking their shareholders' funds with them. And the number of those who have lost money in managed funds would certainly be nowhere near as great as the number of direct property investors who have been burnt by buying the wrong property; paying too much; overcapitalising; buying on a market downturn; losing control of costs; poor rentals; bad tenants or interminable delays with the approval of development plans, and so on.

Having said this, different managed funds have different risk profiles. The ones with the lowest risk of management failure are those mainstream ones managed by established organisations like banks, major insurance companies and reputable financial houses. The funds with the lowest risk of major asset devaluation are those investing in (in increasing order of risk):

- cash
- fixed interest
- property and shares.

Following these come more speculative managed investments in areas like feature films, horticultural plantations and even racehorses. Usually these are ventures being established from scratch, where the sale of investment units is the way the promoter raises the necessary capital to get the scheme off the ground.

The failure rate of non-mainstream managed investments like these is high and I generally advise you against them. They are unacceptably risky because:

- *all* new ventures are riskier than established ones

- the fund manager is often the operator of the business venture and may lack the requisite managerial and operational skill and experience
- the underlying area of investment is often very risky by nature, where even having the best managerial and operational team in the world is no guarantee of financial success (for example, movie making).

What to look for in managed funds

From a safety – and performance – point of view you should look for a managed fund with these characteristics:

- investments in diversified, mainstream asset classes
- management by an established and reputable financial organisation, preferably recommended to you by a credible third party
- a track record of sustained investment performance
- a high level of security
- a clear, comprehensive and easily understood prospectus detailing all authorised investments of the fund.

If you don't feel confident about judging these things for yourself, don't hesitate to seek the assistance of an accountant or a financial adviser. Another option is to contact the Investment Funds Association of Australia on (02) 9262 3599.

The pros of managed funds

- Managed funds take the hard work out of selecting which assets to invest in and having to monitor their performance. They are, therefore, a very easy and time-effective means of investing.
- When you invest in a managed fund you effectively employ a team of investment professionals whose combined experience, knowledge of the markets, investment research capability and exposure to the latest information would be hard to match as an independent investor.
- Investing in managed funds provides a level of diversification well beyond the reach of most independent investors. A single investment, for instance, in a share fund ('share trust' or 'equity trust')

could make you an indirect shareholder in hundreds of companies in which the fund has invested.

- Some investments can only be purchased as expensive single items (like city buildings) or in minimum-sized parcels with high ticket prices beyond the reach of small, independent investors. However, these investments are not beyond the reach of many managed funds with their large, pooled financial resources.

- Managed funds can be an effective and relatively painless savings vehicle. Many have a direct debit facility where, say, $300 per month or quarter can be automatically transferred into the fund direct from your cheque or savings account.

- Managed funds can be a regular source of income. Certain funds provide a monthly, quarterly or half-yearly income distribution to unit-holders that reflects the level of income earned by the fund's investments. Unit-holders can take the regular distributions in cash or have them reinvested as additional units in the fund.

The cons of managed funds

- Managed funds charge fees. Normally there are entry, exit and ongoing management fees. Some funds charge no entry fee but have a higher than average exit fee, or vice versa. Some funds only charge an exit fee if you leave the fund within a certain time of first investing. Some funds have no entry and/or exit fees so long as you maintain your investment for a minimum number of years. It varies tremendously and the level of fees is an area of real competition between the funds.

  As a guide, entry fees range from 0% to 5% of the value of your deposit. Ongoing annual fees, primarily going to the fund manager and trustee (often referred to as the Management Expense Ratio or MER) range from 0.5% to 3% of the value of your balance, and exit fees usually range from 0% to 2% of the value of your withdrawal.

- Managed funds dilute the degree of control you have over your asset selection. For instance, when you invest in, say, a share fund, you invest in the shares of companies that the manager, not you, selects.

- Of course, managed funds (like any other investment) can generate losses. In this case, the capital value of your investment declines.

■ Should the fund experience a major devaluation of its underlying assets, or the manager is thought to be or found to be dishonest, a 'run' may be made on it. This is where a number of investors try to bail out and cash their units at the same time. If the fund does not have ample liquid reserves to cope with this rush of redemptions it could be faced with the prospect of a major asset fire-sale in order to raise the necessary cash. This would probably trigger the trustee to step in and 'freeze' the fund, temporarily preventing any further redemptions until the fund could be put in order.

Let me illustrate what can happen. During the 1980s when property prices were booming, unlisted property trusts had no difficulty meeting unit redemptions – the coffers were full of cash because the inflow of investor capital far outweighed the demand for redemptions. This also meant the trusts could offer short redemption times. However, by 1990, when the commercial property market had collapsed and we were having 'the recession we had to have', the demand for unit redemptions increased as investors bailed out of what were, then, very poorly performing investments. The result was that some (unlisted) property trusts found they didn't have enough cash to meet the redemption demand.

To prevent fire-sales of property into a depressed market (in an attempt to raise the necessary cash to meet the level of redemptions) many property trusts indefinitely suspended redemptions altogether or substantially increased the redemption period to 12 months or more.

If fire-sales had been conducted to meet redemption demand, the value of the trusts' units would have been decimated, severely hurting those who were prepared to hang on to their units and ride the recession. It also would have caused the overall property market to decline even further and there would have been enormous realised losses all round.

The approval to extend unit redemption times, or suspend redemptions altogether, would normally be granted to the trustee by investors at an extraordinary general meeting. However, the trustee generally has the right to impose changes to redemption policy in order to protect the assets of the fund. Under severe circumstances of mismanagement and/or lack of integrity the fund manager and/or trustee can be sacked and replaced.

For the record, I should point out that institutions as safe as banks can, like managed funds, also experience mass investor desertion and a consequent run on funds – however, such events are very rare.

Types of managed funds

Let's take a look at some of the forms that managed investment funds can take.

Share or 'equity' trusts

You can select from a range of unit share trusts. Some, for instance, invest solely in:
- shares on the Australian stockmarket
- shares on major international stockmarkets
- shares in companies in 'emerging' or developing world markets
- shares in gold, mining or energy companies
- shares in companies operating in 'ethical' businesses.

You can also buy into share trusts that invest in a mix of these areas, or that, say, only invest in fully franked Australian shares for particularly tax-effective returns. There is probably a share trust for almost every conceivable market and sector mix, each with its own different risk and return profile.

Property trusts

Assets owned by property trusts can include major city office blocks, suburban shopping centres, industrial properties, hotels and residential holdings and can be unlisted or listed on the Australian Stock Exchange.

Many property trusts offer investors a choice between income units and growth units. Holders of income units receive most of the rentals from the properties invested in by the fund, and growth unit holders are allocated most of the capital growth generated by the fund's properties. You can also invest in split property trusts where you hold some income units and some growth units in a ratio that best suits your needs.

Income derived from property trusts may be tax-free or tax-reduced in the hands of investors due to the passed-on benefits of property depreciation and investment allowances.

Fixed interest or bond funds

Bond funds invest – not surprisingly – in bonds. Most bond funds hold a mix of Commonwealth Government bonds, State Government bonds and semi-government bonds. They may also hold some cash and bank bills.

You can invest in funds that only hold international bonds, or invest in funds holding a mix of Australian and overseas bonds for greater diversity. Investing in bonds through a pooled bond fund also gives you access to the big ticket bonds which are beyond the financial reach of most independent investors.

Cash management trusts

Cash management trusts invest in bank bills, treasury notes, cash, and other money market instruments guaranteed or supported by governments, banks or companies. Cash management trusts (or cash management 'funds' – they're the same thing) are very safe and very liquid and some may even have cheque-book facilities. These trusts normally earn more interest than bank deposits and a minimum balance generally needs to be maintained.

Diversified funds

The vast majority of managed funds are diversified to the extent that the vast majority hold more than one asset. A share trust, for instance, may invest in the shares of literally hundreds of companies.

You can invest in managed funds that don't just hold a diversity of assets in *one* asset class (such as all international shares or all Australian fixed interest) but, rather, hold a diversity of assets across *a number* of asset classes. These funds are commonly known as 'diversified funds'.

Diversified funds can be broken down into three broad categories generally known as 'capital stable', 'balanced' and 'growth' funds. Exactly how these three terms are defined is open to wide interpretation within the managed funds industry, but basically:

- *Capital stable funds* invest primarily in a range of cash and fixed interest securities, with a small percentage of share and property assets usually thrown in too. They're designed for investors looking for a regular and reasonably secure source of income over a relatively short term, say one to three years minimum. These funds are characterised by: low risk; low capital growth; strong income; short-term horizon; and few, if any, tax breaks.

- *Balanced funds* are for investors looking for medium to longer term capital growth accompanied by some regular income during the term of the investment. An appropriate investment in a balanced fund would be three to five years minimum. These funds should have a ratio in the vicinity of 75% growth assets (shares and property) to 25% income assets (cash and fixed interest). Balanced funds can be characterised by: low to moderate risk; moderate to good capital growth; low income; medium-term horizon; and reasonable tax breaks (due to share dividend imputation and property allowances or depreciation).
- *Growth funds* have a higher proportion of growth assets and a lower proportion of income assets than balanced funds. They are characterised by: moderate to higher risk; strong capital growth; low income; long-term horizon (five years minimum); and better tax breaks than balanced funds.

To give you a better idea of how capital stable, balanced and growth funds can be structured, look at the graphs opposite. (These show the actual 'asset allocation' – the proportion of the whole fund that each asset class comprises – of ipac's Strategic Investment Service's diversified funds in early 2001.)

The asset allocation in each of these funds is designed to produce the highest probability of achieving the long-term risk and return objectives considered appropriate (by ipac) for each fund. These asset allocations can be adjusted at any time as varying market conditions dictate.

Capital stable fund (Target return: inflation plus 2%)

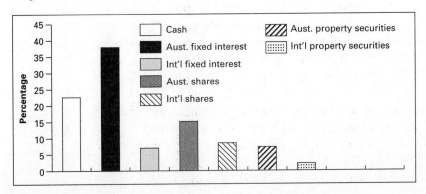

Balanced fund (Target return: inflation plus 4%)

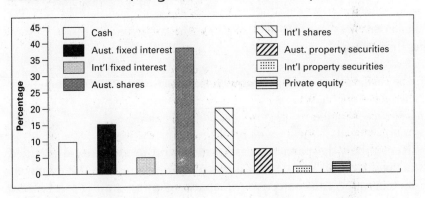

Growth fund (Target return: inflation plus 6%)

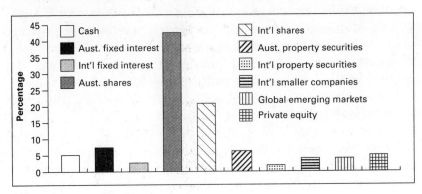

(*Source*: ipac securities.)

Making Money

The following table shows the risk and return relationship for the three diversified funds shown on the previous page.*

	Capital stable	Balanced	Growth
Minimum recommended term	3 years	4 years	5 years
Ratio of income to growth assets	68/32%	30/70%	15/85%
Range of expected annual returns over –			
1 year	−5% to 16%	−11% to 26%	−13% to 31%
3 years (p.a.)	0% to 12%	−3% to 19%	−4% to 22%
Likelihood of a negative return	14%	20%	21%

* The numbers in this table are based on ipac's anticipated risk and return outcomes over the medium term.
(*Source*: ipac securities.)

Remember, the particular asset allocation used in any diversified fund will depend on the risk and return objectives of the manager. For example, the objective of ipac's capital stable fund is to provide average annual returns of 1% to 3% in excess of the current rate of inflation.

The objectives other managers have for their capital stable funds (or any other managed fund for that matter) may be quite different to ipac's and this will be reflected in them having different asset allocations. Just make sure you find out before you invest what the objectives of the fund are, and that these objectives match yours.

Mortgage funds

Mortgage funds invest primarily in residential, industrial and commercial property mortgages. For added security and liquidity they may also have large holdings in cash and fixed interest investments.

Mortgage funds are designed to provide the investor with a dependable income flow that will fluctuate in line with interest rate movements. The security of an investment in mortgage funds is largely underpinned by property values.

It's worth noting that investors should take care with mortgage trusts offering unusually high returns, which invariably means that the quality of the mortgages is not that good. Thousands of Australian investors lost some or all of their money with the collapse of Estate Mortgage in 1990, a trust offering high returns on – as it was revealed – 'high-risk' property. Equally, be just as careful with investing in solicitor-arranged mortgages. In the final analysis, your security is only as good as the property underpinning the mortgage.

Insurance bonds

Insurance bonds are managed investment products offered by life insurance companies and are nothing like the fixed interest securities offered by governments and semi-government authorities. (In fact, labelling these investments 'bonds' is really a misnomer.)

Another source of confusion arises from insurance bonds being officially classified as 'life insurance policies'. They bear no resemblance to classic term or whole-of-life insurance policies at all, or any other form of insurance for that matter. The only conceivable life insurance component in these investments is simply that if the investor, referred to as the 'life insured', dies before the 'bond' matures, the investment is closed, valued (based on the total of all contributions and investment earnings to that point), and then paid out to a beneficiary. There is no typical insurance component in the sense that if you die while insured your beneficiaries will be paid a set amount determined by a premium.

So, insurance bonds are managed funds that may be balanced, may invest primarily in growth assets, may invest primarily in industrial shares, may invest primarily in fixed interest securities or may be 'capital guaranteed' (where the unit value is guaranteed never to fall in value). The choice of underlying assets is wide and, as with all managed funds, the higher the ratio of growth to income assets in the fund, the greater the potential long-term returns – but the higher the risk of an occasional loss.

With insurance bonds, the earnings generated by the fund are accumulated or reinvested back into the fund – there are no regular earnings distributions – causing the capital value of the fund's units to grow over time. These investments are designed to be held for 10 years (at least) at which point they 'mature' and your (hopefully much more valuable) units are paid out in cash. The important thing about these 'bonds' is their treatment of tax. Tax on an insurance bond's investment earnings is paid by the manager each year and after 10 years all the bond's earnings are tax-free in your hands, regardless of your marginal tax rate.

Now, if you wish to close the investment and get your hands on the cash before the 10 years have expired, you can. Your investment earnings, however, will be taxed at your highest marginal rate, but you are entitled to a 34% (proposed to fall to 30% from 1 July 2001) tax rebate against these (taxed) earnings. This applies at any time throughout the 10 years, but this doesn't mean a short-term investment in these funds is a good idea. It means that if your marginal tax rate is less than 34%, you will get all the tax back that's been paid on these earnings. Indeed, if your tax rate is less than 34%, the rebate will actually generate a tax credit (being the difference between your tax rate and the 34% tax rate) which can help reduce the amount of tax you are obliged to pay on your other assessable income.

At the time of writing, tax changes have been proposed for insurance bonds, to apply from July 2001. Should these take effect, it will mean that if you purchase a bond on or after this date, you will have to include your share of the bond's annual earnings in your taxable income, even if you don't physically receive the earnings in that year. But like franking credits on shares, credit will be given for tax already paid on these earnings by the insurance bond manager.

Friendly society bonds

These are basically the same as insurance company bonds in that they are managed funds designed to be held for 10 years, at which point they mature tax-free in your hands. They simply happen to be offered by friendly societies rather than insurance companies.

If you cash a friendly society bond before it matures you will be taxed at your marginal rate on its earnings, however, like insurance bonds, you also get a tax rebate which could actually mean you get all the paid tax back. You may even end up with a tax credit to be offset against other assessable income.

The size of this tax rebate is effectively equivalent to the rate of tax that has already been paid on your investment by the friendly society. During much of the 1980s this rate was 20%. On 1 July 1988 it rose to 30%, then rose to 33% on 1 July 1994.

Friendly society bonds, like insurance bonds, are the subject of tax changes proposed to take effect from July 2001. Under these proposals, the friendly society will pay tax of 30% on the earnings of the bond, with the earnings to be included in investors' income for the year, even if they aren't physically distributed. A tax credit will apply however, similar to franking credits received on dividends.

Performance of managed funds

The managed funds industry is mushrooming. In 1994 there were 1,300 managed funds for Australian investors to choose from; by 2001 there were more than 2,500. With so many funds, and with none of them holding exactly the same mix of assets, it's inevitable that a large range of returns will be generated – far too varied to be detailed here.

In general, managed funds comprised primarily of one asset class, such as all shares, all property or all bonds, perform similarly to the main market indices for those asset classes. Real, after-inflation, long-term average performance figures for the main asset classes are looked at quite closely in Chapter Eleven, but to recap, they have traditionally been as follows.

Australian cash	0% to 1% p.a.
Australian fixed interest	0% to 3% p.a.
International fixed interest	1% to 2% p.a.
Residential property	1% to 3% p.a.
Australian property securities	3% to 5% p.a.
International property securities	3% to 7% p.a.
Australian shares	5% to 8% p.a.
International shares	6% to 9% p.a.

Hopefully, the single sector fund you've invested in will do better than the average market returns for that asset class, though there is no guarantee of this. Indeed, it is a great and understandable source of consternation when, say, your fund investing primarily in

Making Money

Australian industrial shares underperforms the All Ordinaries Index. It raises the obvious, ugly question of why are you paying a team of investment professionals if they can't do better than the market average or, worse still, if they can't do as well? My answer to this is as follows:

- Make sure you clearly understand what the fund manager's risk and return objectives are (they may take a very conservative or a very high-risk line).
- Determine whether these objectives suit yours or not – ideally you should make this decision *before* you invest.
- If these objectives don't really suit you, consider leaving the fund (but be aware of the costs involved in doing so, such as exit fees, the loss of benefits, potential capital gains tax, and the cost of entering into other managed funds or other investments).
- If you are satisfied with the fund's objectives but it fails to achieve them over the longer term, I suggest you take your business elsewhere, despite the costs.

Now, let's say your money was not in single sector funds but in diversified funds. Because of the sheer variety of domestic and international assets they can invest in, in whatever proportion they wish, and at whatever risk level they wish, diversified funds generate a very wide range of returns. That said, in the five years to the end of 2000, *average* annual returns for diversified capital stable funds were in the order of 5.4% to 9.4% after tax and fees; balanced funds averaged in the order of 7.8% to 14.1% after tax and fees; growth funds were in the order of 8.9% to 13.5% after tax and fees. (*Source*: Morningstar.)

Over the long term you could expect real average annual returns of 1% to 3% for diversified capital stable funds, 3% to 5% for balanced funds and 5% to 7% for growth funds. These returns are after fees, tax and inflation.

The spectre of 1994

Any discussion about fund performance is bound to raise the year 1994. Sure, the year 2000 was pretty ordinary for investors (and 2001 isn't looking any better), but in 2000 at least money was made in some areas, such as listed property trusts. But as those of you who held managed fund investments in 1994 will remember (and this includes anyone with superannuation), it was a shocker. It was a year in which most asset classes generated a loss. Indeed, in 1994 only direct property and cash produced positive returns (9.2% and 5.36% respectively).

In 1994 ten-year bonds took an absolute pounding as interest rates rose, the sharemarket drifted relentlessly downwards, and property securities languished below the waterline. It really was unusual for so many asset classes to generate losses in the one year, and it was this very range of losses that caused diversified funds (in particular) to turn in such poor results. They averaged (after fees):

- −4% to −6% for capital stable funds
- −6% to −8% for balanced funds
- −10% to −11% for growth funds.

Ipac's research has concluded that a year like 1994, where almost every sector goes wrong, has a probability of occurring only once every 25 years. Also take note that the following year, 1995, was a vintage year for investors, with Australian shares returning 20.2%, international shares returning 26.5%, Australian fixed interest returning 18.3% and international fixed interest returning 29.5%. Anyone who panicked and abandoned ship during the storms of 1994, thereby making their paper losses real, would be feeling doubly disappointed in light of the consequent (and inevitable) rebound of the markets.

A fascinating study throwing a very revealing light on this area was conducted by US research firm Morningstar. It looked at the five-year (to May 1994) performance of 200 American managed growth funds investing mainly in shares and property securities. While the study showed the pre-inflation return from the funds was an average 12.5% per annum, it also found the average return to investors in those funds during the period was a loss of 2.5%!

How come? Well, while the funds produced an *average* growth of 12.5% p.a. over the five years, the growth was by no means steady on a weekly, monthly or even annual basis. The markets rose then fell, rose then fell again, and so on, for the whole period. In other words, they behaved perfectly normally.

What was happening was a rush of investment into the funds when the markets were at or near their peaks, and an exodus out of them when they were at or near their troughs. People were buying high and selling low and hence losing money. But this was not an accurate reflection of long-term fund performance – which was good. It was a reflection of inappropriate investor reaction to short-term market (and fund value) fluctuations.

The moral is clear – the most effective investment strategy is to be invested at all times. While this way you might experience both good and bad years, overall you'll come out on top.

Buying into retail and wholesale funds

There are two kinds of managed funds you can invest in – retail and wholesale. In essence, retail funds are those you effectively buy into direct 'off the shelf' or, in the case of listed trusts, through the stock-market. Wholesale funds are those you can only invest in indirectly through another managed fund.

Retail funds are the ones you see advertised in the press and on television. You can buy into them for a minimum of, say, $1,000, by approaching the fund manager direct or by going through a financial adviser, securities dealer or stockbroker.

On listed units purchased through the ASX you pay brokerage on top of the units' trading price as you would for shares, and at the same brokerage rates as for shares. With unlisted products you will pay the same entry fee (anything from 0% to 5%) regardless of whom you buy through, be it the fund manager or a financial adviser. However, if you deal through a financial adviser who charges on an hourly fee-for-service basis you'll probably find they'll rebate some, if not all, of the entry commission fee to you. Also, so-called 'discount brokers' will rebate up to 95% of the entry commission fee; however, they provide no investment advice as the trade-off.

Discount brokers advertise regularly in the business section of the main newspapers and are an inexpensive way to buy into a managed fund if you know exactly what you want and what you're doing. If you don't, I recommend you deal through (an advice-giving) financial adviser. I also recommend you shop around for a financial adviser who does rebate managed fund entry commission fees.

Wholesale managed funds have lower fees attached to them, but are effectively unavailable to the average independent investor for direct investment. The reason is simply the minimum investment parcel may be as high as $50,000, $100,000 or more. Specialty funds (such as emerging markets funds) are often structured this way.

You can only access wholesale funds indirectly by investing in a retail managed fund which in turn invests in them (many managed funds invest very heavily in other managed funds), or through a 'mastertrust'.

Mastertrusts

A mastertrust (or 'masterfund') is an investment fund that invests in *other* investment funds (but may also invest directly in assets such as shares, cash and bonds). When you invest through a mastertrust your money goes into a selection of its own funds which, in turn, invest primarily in other managed funds – many of which are wholesale funds beyond the financial reach of most independent investors. It sounds confusing, but really it's not.

There are two types of mastertrusts: 'fund-of-funds' and 'discretionary'. The major difference between the two is the amount of choice you have in selecting which assets the mastertrust invests in.

With a fund-of-funds mastertrust you (together with an adviser) select the appropriate broad asset area or areas to invest in (in terms of risk versus return, income versus growth). You might decide, for instance, to invest in the mastertrust's Australian bond fund (for income) as well as its international shares fund (for long-term capital growth). These two funds will, in turn, invest in a wide range of assets appropriate to their investment parameters.

Now, while you have been free to select the mastertrust's funds that invest in certain *broad* asset areas, you are *not* free to select the *specific* assets (mostly other wholesale managed funds) that these funds invest in. The choice of specific assets is left to the mastertrust's manager who over time may increase the funds' exposure to some investments and withdraw from others as changing market conditions and performances dictate.

In a discretionary mastertrust you *can* select the managed funds from a menu. Discretionary mastertrusts are targeted at those investors who prefer a greater degree of control over their own asset selection.

The cost of investing in managed funds through a mastertrust structure is around the same as investing at a direct level through a retail fund manager. So why deal through a mastertrust? Well, firstly, you normally get a wider choice of managed funds to invest in than through a single retail fund manager. Secondly, mastertrusts claim to provide a generally higher level of client service than that provided by most retail managed funds. This service takes the form of periodic meetings with an adviser to monitor your investments and adjust them if necessary (most mastertrusts allow you to switch between their own funds at no charge). More importantly perhaps, this service may also include regular reports detailing where your money has been placed, how your investments have performed, what tax (if any) has been paid on them, and a tax statement, all being very useful and convenient documents.

Wrap accounts

Wrap accounts, similar to mastertrusts, are an administrative service designed to streamline the management of your portfolio by 'wrapping' your investments into a single account. Primarily, a wrap account focuses on making the management of your portfolio tidier and easier, which in turn can lead to generating better returns by keeping the investor well informed and able to make timely investment decisions based on current information.

At the centre of the wrap, a cash account provides a pool of funds that can be used to buy investments, and pay any fees. It's also the place where sale proceeds, dividends and any other income can be deposited. The remainder of the portfolio consists of managed investments and directly held shares. For reporting purposes only, other investments, for example rental properties, can also be included in the wrap account. The investor still has control and ownership of the portfolio, giving their financial adviser instructions on which investments to buy or sell, and when to do so.

The centralised structure of a wrap account offers a range of advantages. Using relatively new (and still expensive) information technology, financial advisers can determine the value of an entire portfolio and make investment transactions on your behalf under your instructions, almost on the spot.

Wrap accounts also provide streamlined reporting, which is particularly useful at tax time. Gathering your investments into one 'account' overcomes the problem many investors face of several managers sending information in varying formats at different times in the year.

Like mastertrusts, wrap accounts provide investors with access to wholesale (not retail) funds, which charge lower fees. In addition, investors can still hold and trade shares directly through a wrap structure. This enables investors to maintain their shareholder benefits, including shareholder discount cards. It also means existing shareholdings (held pre-wrap) can be transferred easily into the wrap without incurring any capital gains tax liabilities.

Of course, the convenience offered by a wrap account comes at a cost. The relatively high fees charged for wraps have been a source of criticism, and effectively make them uneconomic for smaller investors. But, if your portfolio is substantial (generally over $100,000), or has a diverse range of investments, the more streamlined management and reporting of your portfolio that a wrap account provides may well be worth the price.

Managed funds are convenient

Managed funds are a modern way of achieving your investment goals. I do own some direct property and direct shares, but I use managed funds for the majority of my Australian investments, all of my international investments and specialised Australian investments, such as in small companies.

It really is an issue of attitude and personality. For me, they are the way to go. I'm busy and I know that most of my investment returns will come from the asset mix that I select. In other words, it is more important to me whether I have 30% or 50% of my investment portfolio in shares rather than whether I buy BHP or Coles Myer.

⊶ KEY THOUGHT

Work out your risk tolerance first. Then plan your investment mix. Finally choose between direct investment (buying your own investments) or indirect investment (using managed funds).

Unless you have the time and the knowledge, I think managed funds will work the best for you.

CHAPTER SIXTEEN
Your Own Business

You may be wondering why I've put this chapter at the end of the investment chapters. Well, it's done quite deliberately, because there is another question we need to consider: is owning a business the best way to make money?

This was definitely a belief that I held in my early twenties – that if you wanted to be wealthy you had to own a successful business. I'm not sure if I was influenced by my family, friends or things I read, but I always wanted to start a business of my own.

Now I know I was wrong about this. Wealth can be created by anyone who consistently spends less than they earn and who invests their savings on a regular basis. In fact, the more I look at business failure statistics, the more I wonder about the wisdom of starting any business, despite certainly understanding why people want to.

Once again, we get back to risk and return. Starting or buying a business is risky, but if the business goes well the rewards are high. The business in which I am a shareholder was started by myself and four partners in 1983. We put in $20,000 each and rented a very small, serviced office. Today, we employ well over 280 staff in our Australian offices and South African joint venture and, by any measure, ipac securities has been a great success.

Funnily enough, the 'academic' theory about starting a business is correct. You do need a vision of what you want your business to be and a well-formulated business plan. You must control your cash flow and, in the good years, you must leave money in the company to build up its strength. I feel fortunate that we took the risk in 1983 to quit our quite well-paid jobs, because today business ownership makes me proud, gives me an unbeatable sense of job security and the benefits of controlling my own destiny.

How quickly, though, we forget the reality of starting a business from scratch. In my case, this meant earning next to nothing for five years, working outrageous hours – my partners and I used to laugh about our 35 hours of work. Thirty-five hours on Monday, Tuesday and part of Wednesday; another 35 hours on the other part of

Wednesday, Thursday and Friday; and just to top things up, working on Saturday as well. Sometimes we didn't work on Sunday, holidays were a few days off at Christmas and, as for sick leave, well, we just couldn't afford to get sick!

If you do want to create significant wealth, building a successful business is certainly one way to get there. Look at people in the '500 most wealthy' lists. Some inherit the money, but most create it by building a business.

Few small businesses will ever grow into a News Corporation or a Lend Lease and not too many will ever be worth a lot of money, but running a business has benefits beyond the purely financial side. This really struck me when I was sitting on Avoca Beach (about one hour north of Sydney). While my kids and some friends were paddling around on a hired aqua bike, I started chatting to the owner of the aqua bike business who was originally from Sydney. He explained that the business was no world beater but it was pretty good and, living on a beautiful lagoon, next to a beach, hiring boats to generally pleasant tourists was somewhat better than working in a factory in Sydney's industrial suburbs. He has a point. For him, his business provides lifestyle and a reasonable cash flow. He may have earned more working in Sydney, but tinkering with boats on Avoca lagoon seems much better.

For every success story like this, though, I know of dozens of failures. Buying or setting up a business for lifestyle is a dangerous thing – you may act on emotion, not logic. If you do plan to start up or buy a business for whatever reason, please be careful.

Look, there's no denying owning a business sounds good and, assuming it works, it is. However, as I found, you'll probably end up working an awful lot harder for a lot longer than in the job you leave and, for the short term at least, not earning as much.

You'll also miss out on the benefits that full-time employees are entitled to and often take for granted, such as: employer-funded super; worker's compensation cover; paid sick leave; four weeks' paid annual leave; holiday loadings; long service leave; and maternity (or paternity) leave. You may also have to forgo other goodies which include: discounted goods and services; the full use of a company car; an expense account; paid telephone expenses; low interest loans; employer-funded further education; study leave; holiday expenses; annual bonuses; share options; and the support of a union or industry association. In other words, when you work for yourself there's no safety net – you're on your own.

Don't let me scare the wits out of you, however. While self-employment is not all beer and skittles, the great thing about it is the freedom it gives you to run your own race, which I believe outweighs the negatives.

Clearly, I'm not the only one who feels this. Many people are already involved in, or are moving to self-employment, indeed, between 1994/1995 and 1998/1999, the number of self-employed Australians grew by around 16% to 957,800 persons. This represented about 11% of the entire Australian workforce, and 28% of the small business sector (a 'small business' is statistically defined as having 20 employees or less, or 100 employees or less if in manufacturing). (*Source*: ABS, Small Business in Australia 1998/9, Cat.1321.0.)

Business hazards

Now, while the overall number of self-employed is growing, many fall by the wayside in their attempts to run their own businesses. Estimates of business failure vary tremendously, but include:

- a 1986 study which found that of small firms that became bankrupt, 50% failed in the first two years, and 85.6% failed within five years; only 3.9% survived 10 years
- a 1987 study which found that of small enterprise starts and closures, an average of 35.4% fail in the first year, and an average of 47.4% fail within three years
- a 1992 US study which found that 54% of small businesses survive eight years or more, and that four out of 10 of these change ownership within eight years.
  (*Source*: *Small Business Data Sheet*, NSW Department of State and Regional Development.)

Of the 990,100 small businesses operating in Australia in 1999:
- 11% had been in operation for less than one year
- 34% had been in operation for one year but less than five years
- 22% had been in operation for five years but less than 10 years
- 33% had been in operation for 10 or more years.
(*Source*: ABS, Characteristics of Small Business, Australia, Cat. 8127.0, 1999.)

There are countless factors that can bring a business undone, though the general consensus among small business researchers is that the main one is 'management inadequacy', associated with around 90% of business failures. Other major contributors to failure are poor accounting records, deficient accounting knowledge and lack of management advice. (*Source*: *Small Business Data Sheet*, NSW Department of State and Regional Development.) These business hazards are joined by many more including: inadequate financing; excessive debt; low sales; high costs; high interest rates; market collapse; lack of market knowledge; overwhelming competition; poor product, service or quality; economic downturn; excessive optimism; production inefficiencies; poor planning; poor forecasting and sheer bad luck.

Think the proposed business through

By doing your homework very thoroughly, however, which involves seeking considerable professional advice and preparing a proper business plan, you will address and resolve many of these hazards before you even pass 'Go'.

You may even discover during the research phase that your proposed venture is unlikely to work. As disappointing as this may be, it is infinitely preferable to go back to the drawing board at this point rather than be forced to bail out one or two years into the business. You'd be amazed how many businesses have been set up simply off the back of an idea without any dispassionate research being done. Of course this ad hoc approach can work, sometimes spectacularly, but mostly it doesn't.

> **O── KEY THOUGHT**
> A great sounding business idea does not necessarily translate into a viable business.

Consider the following points because they will help you focus on the issues critical to business success (and note, this list is far from complete).

- What is the main reason why you want to become self-employed – either by buying an existing business or by setting one up from scratch? If it is basically to 'buy' yourself a job, think again. Working for someone else who is established is generally more secure, easier, and initially better paid than working for yourself. (It is also less exciting!)

- Do you have experience or training in the type of business you wish to establish or buy? If you don't, I strongly recommend you spend some time in paid employment in the area you want to enter in order to discover more about the industry's dynamics and performance, and whether it is really for you. This experience will also help reveal how much sheer physical energy and drive you will need to succeed in the industry.

- What are your people skills like? Success in this vital area calls for integrity, wisdom, leadership, authority, humour, patience, intelligence, tact, empathy, fairness, and an ability to listen just as much as an ability to get your message across clearly. Do you believe you can judge people well, and could you recognise merit in a potential employee? How would you motivate staff, win their respect and trust, get the best performance from them, and retain them?

- What about the people closest and most important to you – your family? Their support is vital and can't be taken for granted. You must give first priority to this relationship and be sure that it is sound before you embark on self-employment, because there are times it will be strained by the demands of the business.

- Do you have the financial know-how to run a business? Do you know what the costs of setting up your proposed business would be? Could you construct a cash-flow analysis and predict when the business would generate profits? Having adequate capital to tide you over the early lean times is critical. Where will the money come from? From personal savings, from an equity partnership, or from a bank loan? If a loan, how and when do you intend to pay it back?

- Do you understand marketing? Do you know what competition you will be up against? Can your product or service evolve to meet changing market conditions?

Resolving lack of business experience

At this point you may be thinking self-employment sounds nigh on impossible. You may be wondering how anyone who had never been in business for themselves could possibly know half these things before taking the plunge. Well, the answer to that is many newcomers to self-employment actually don't know much about these things. That's why so many do just jump in – they don't know what they don't know, and if they did they mightn't do it!

Those newcomers to business who do succeed have to climb a very steep learning curve and invariably need and seek plenty of assistance from outside specialists in key areas like finance, sales, marketing and production. This is an eminently sensible and re-commended way of dealing with a lack of business knowledge and experience.

Having said that, if you're contemplating self-employment, I rec-ommend you seek as much information as possible about it your-self before making any commitments. Seriously consider doing a general business course or a specialist course covering the area you wish to work in. At the very least, read extensively on the general principles of running a business, read about your target business or industry, talk to any people running their own businesses, especially in the area you are interested in. At a later point, if you proceed with the business, join the trade association covering your industry to meet other people in it and to keep yourself informed of industry trends and developments.

Both the Commonwealth and State governments have depart-ments that provide excellent support services for those wishing to establish and for those already in their own business. Between them they publish numerous pamphlets and booklets on business basics and specific businesses, provide advice, run courses, and help in the preparation of business plans. Much of this is free or very inexpensive and I strongly recommend you take full advan-tage of it.

Organisations to contact

- *Small Business Advisory Services* operate in all State and Territory capitals, and offer great help to anyone entering self-employment/small business. They should be consulted during the planning and establishment phases of any small business venture. (They are also very helpful for people already in small business.)

Making Money

The Canberra Business Advisory Service
Mungga-iri House
Suite 6
18 Napier Close
Deakin 2600
(02) 6260 5000

Department of State Development
Level 21, 111 George St
Brisbane 4000
(07) 3224 8568
Qld country callers: 13 26 50

Business Tasmania
Department of State Development
3 Terry St
Glenorchy 7010
(03) 6233 5712

Small Business Services at The Business Centre
145 South Terrace
Adelaide 5000
(08) 8233 4600

Small Business Victoria
Level 5, 55 Collins St
Melbourne 3000
(03) 9651 9888
Vic. country callers: 1800 136 034

Sydney Business Enterprise Centre
Level 11, 418A Elizabeth St
Surry Hills 2010
(02) 9282 6977
NSW country callers: 13 11 45

Territory Business Centre
Department of Industries and Business
Ground Floor, Development House
76 The Esplanade
Darwin 0800
(08) 8924 4280
NT country callers: 1800 193 111

WA Small Business Development Corporation
533 Hay St
Perth 6000
(08) 9220 0222

- *The Australian Bureau of Statistics* is a mine of information for anyone in business, with facts and figures on a mind-boggling array of relevant topics.

  The ABS also provides a very useful survey called a '4-Site Report' which is a detailed demographic profile of any specified area within Australia. Costing $210, the reports provide information on the people who live in a specified area, including what they do, what they earn and what language they speak. These reports also provide information on existing businesses and local industry, including the number and type of business in the specified area. This is a very useful marketing tool for targeting the right location for your business – which can be a critical factor in success. The ABS has offices in every capital city.
- *The Australian Chamber of Manufacturers* and local Chambers of Commerce and Industry also provide useful information and assistance to those in business.
- *The Financial Management Research Centre*, at the University of New England, publishes a range of materials to assist small businesses. These can be reviewed at the web site located at www.fmrcbenchmarking.com.au or by phoning the FMRC on (02) 6772 5199.

KEY THOUGHT

It's impossible to be an expert in every area of business – no one is. Successful business people are those who have a good overall understanding of the business and know what's needed to make it work. They have no hesitation using specialists to take care of those areas that they can't attend to themselves. They are also willing to broaden their own business education.

The business plan

Preparing a business plan is an enormously important exercise in getting set for self-employment or for expanding or diversifying your existing business.

What is a business plan? Well, it is a written statement of all the research and thinking you have done in developing your business idea. It is a blueprint for your business, or, if you prefer, a road map. It is also the vital document you'll need to raise capital for the business, be it a loan or equity partnership.

Of course, like many plans or maps you may find a better method or route once you get under way. However, you do need to be pointed in the right direction to start with. And this is where the business plan, or, more to the point, the act of preparing the business plan, is invaluable.

Preparing a business plan will oblige you to address all the factors necessary for running a viable business. This involves finding answers to questions that include (but are not limited to) the following:

- What business and what industry are you in?
- What is your product and who is your market?
- How big is that market?
- Is the market growing?
- What share of the market are you aiming for?
- What will the market look like in five years?
- How will you capture that market?
- Where does your business fit into the industry in which you will be operating?
- Who are your competitors?
- What are their strengths and weaknesses? How will you deal with these?

- What will set your business apart from the competitors?
- What is your 'competitive advantage', that is, what advantage does your business have over the competition?
- How will you overcome any perceived weaknesses your business may have and what are the major threats to it and to the industry? How will you overcome these?
- How will you capitalise on the perceived strengths and opportunities your business and industry has?
- What level of sales do you expect to generate?
- What level of sales do you need to break even?
- What will your establishment costs be?
- What will your ongoing costs be?
- When do you expect to go into profit, and what size will the profit be?
- How will the business be funded, and how much capital is needed?
- How and when will any debt be repaid?
- What production techniques will you use?
- Is production obsolescence a likelihood?
- What staff will you need?
- How will you train them?
- What will be the structure of the business (that is, sole trader, partnership, company or discretionary trust)?
- What will happen to the business if you become sick or leave?
- How much of the business will you own?
- What will be the return for any investors in the business?
- How and when will they receive their return?
- How, if and when, do you intend to exit the business?

If you have got this far and the business still looks viable, then there's a very good chance it will be! But, if in the process of putting the plan together you discover a fatal flaw in the business idea, you can thank your lucky stars the discovery happened at this point rather than after opening your doors. And just bear in mind that successful entrepreneurs (a word badly tarnished in the 1980s and one that deserves to have its positive associations restored) have normally discarded numerous business ideas before hitting on one that stands up to the rigorous analysis that producing a business plan entails.

Putting together a business plan takes a lot of effort and you will very likely need assistance in doing it, particularly in the financial section, which calls for cash flow and profit projections. An accountant can help you with these. However, try to do as much of the work yourself as possible. This will help you understand what running a business involves in general, and in particular what *your* business will need to succeed.

Buying or establishing a business

So, let's assume you decide your business idea is viable and you are determined to forge ahead with it. Let's also assume your idea is fairly straightforward and that it could be realised either by establishing a new venture from scratch or by buying a similar existing business and adapting it to your particular vision. Now, because both routes have pros and cons, trying to decide whether to buy or establish a business can be a very difficult decision indeed.

Buying a business

Buying a business addresses the problems associated with establishing a business from scratch, namely, tight cash flows and low income during the business's formative period, inordinately long hours, and a high probability of ultimate failure. However, buying a business is no Sunday picnic. It's a serious exercise that requires time, effort, money and great care. Don't lose sight of the fact that there are plenty of sharks out there hawking a swag of awful, fundamentally flawed businesses to budding, bright-eyed entrepreneurs ready to be ripped-off.

Regardless of how appealing a business may look and how keen you may be to get your hands on it, don't rush into it. Take plenty of time to confirm the details you are given and look for those details which may have been withheld. It is better to miss the opportunity than to act without adequate research.

The specific areas of any business you (and your accountant) must investigate before deciding whether it's worth buying or not are:

- *Sales.* Is the sales level seasonal or related to a business cycle? Are sales increasing, decreasing or static? Will the business still be able to buy from existing suppliers? Does a new product or new competitor exist – or is one imminent – that will pose a threat to the business? Is the level of stock adequate and up-to-date? Also check

---

The three golden rules to follow when buying a business

- Never decide on the purchase without seeking the advice of someone you trust who has relevant business experience.
- Never commit to the purchase until the figures have been examined by an accountant.
- Never sign the contract until a solicitor has advised you.

If pressure is applied to you to bypass any of these measures, walk away from the deal.

---

if a high proportion of sales are dependent on one or two big customers – vulnerability exists where this is the case.

- *Costs.* Are all costs shown in the records? Will you have the same level of expenses? What effect will increased or decreased sales have on your costs? And take into account the extra cost of interest on the borrowings used to buy the business.
- *Profits.* Check that records – balance sheets, profit and loss statements, purchases and sales records – have been accurately kept, and go back for as many years as possible to determine the profit trend. Determine if gross profit levels are in keeping with industry norms, and consider the likely effect on profits from a rising or decreasing level of sales. At this point you can determine whether the existing and likely future profit levels warrant the risk of investment in the business.
- *Assets.* Make sure you know exactly what it is you are buying. Get a list of all equipment, fixtures, fittings and check them off, and also check the depreciation schedule on these items. Is the equipment in good order, and current? Have a licensed valuer check the equipment for you if you are in doubt.
- *The seller.* Determine why the seller is selling. If they are not being fully cooperative, be wary. Ask to be given a trial period in the business for a few weeks to verify its operations and takings etc.

If everything about the business is still looking positive, then ask yourself this key question – is it really you? Can you see yourself doing the work and serving the customers the business has? Does the business fit your temperament, interests and personality, and is it really an appropriate vehicle for your business concept?

Making Money

You will also need to consider whether you could build the business up into something bigger and better than at present; whether the business's clientele and staff will remain loyal to the business under your ownership; whether the asking price of the business and particularly the price put on its 'goodwill' is fair, realistic and good value; and, whether you can really afford to buy it.

Assuming that, after dealing with all these issues, you still wish to proceed with the purchase, when drafting the purchase agreement ensure all assets and liabilities are specified, and include escape clauses should the performance of the business during the trial period not be as claimed. You will definitely need to engage the services of a solicitor at this point.

> **⊙━ KEY THOUGHT**
>
> Buying a business is a major move requiring great care and consideration. You will need to cover many angles and seek much advice before choosing that path to self-employment.

Establishing a business

Choosing to establish your own business from scratch will save you the hazards of buying a business that could prove unsatisfactory, unworkable, inappropriate, intolerable or a rip-off. It will also save you what could be a very large purchase price. But establishing your own business will present you with a different set of challenges including summoning up and sustaining the sheer drive and energy required to establish a business; having enough capital to fund the establishment costs of the business and supplement the lean cash flows of the early months (or years); finding the right location; developing the right product for the market; getting your pricing right and your promotion right; finding the right staff; and building up a loyal clientele.

As a general rule, the more innovative your business concept, the more appropriate it is to set the business up from scratch. There is little point buying an existing business that needs major adaptation to your idea. But, if you can buy a going, viable business at a fair price that suits your business concept closely, well, it does seem a sensible approach to self-employment.

Franchising

Franchising is another option for anyone seeking self-employment, and is probably more suited to those with limited or no business experience who feel uncomfortable going out into business entirely on their own. Being a franchisee means forgoing some of the freedom of traditional self-employment – that is, the ability to completely call your own shots – in that a franchisee must operate within a strict framework laid down by the franchisor. But, in return, the franchisee has the support of a 'big brother' providing a (*supposedly*) proven business formula.

The most visible franchises include McDonald's, Pizza Hut and KFC, but many other successful franchises exist in areas as diverse as carpet cleaning, building maintenance, hardware, automotive products and services, lawn-mowing, restaurants, greeting cards and real estate.

The main advantages of franchising for a franchisee are the recourse to assistance and expertise provided by the franchisor, cooperative marketing, bulk buying, and the use of an established concept, name and image. Capable franchisors may also save a failing franchisee by arranging a sale, or by purchasing it themselves, thereby avoiding a major loss by the franchisee and damage to the system's public image.

The purchase price of franchises varies dramatically, from a low of around $20,000 to in excess of $1 million. Clearly, the higher the profile of the franchise and the greater its commercial success, the higher the price. However, obtaining bank finance to buy into an established franchise network is generally easier than getting finance to set up a business.

A major cost in running a franchise is the ongoing payment of royalties and service fees to the franchisor, which need to be clearly understood at the outset by a potential franchisee. Other costs and problems can arise with tied supplies and restricted product ranges, or if the ability or integrity of the franchisor is brought into question.

When assessing a potential franchise, you will need to consider the following:

■ The franchise's track record and plans for the future.
■ The managerial ability and background of key franchise personnel.
■ The reasons why the franchisor is seeking expansion.

Making Money

- Is the franchise operating in a growth industry?
- How cooperative and 'open' are key franchise personnel, particularly in relation to financial records?
- Scrutinise the projected figures of the territory you are being offered. Are they realistic, and do the returns justify your effort and risk?
- What is the demand in the marketplace for the franchised product?
- How are other franchisees in the network faring? (Get feedback direct from them, not via the franchisor.)
- Do you fully understand the up-front and/or ongoing fees involved?
- What sort of training is provided for franchisees, and how thorough and binding is the franchise operations manual?
- How long does the franchise agreement last for, and where do you stand at the end of it?

Whatever you do, don't sign any franchise agreement before you have your solicitor and your accountant check it closely. For more information on franchising, I recommend you contact your State or Territory's Small Business Advisory Service (see pp. 296–297).

Working from home

Many people who go into business for themselves choose to work from home, at least to start with. The advantages of doing so include: no commuting; working in a pleasant, familiar environment; no travelling costs; being close to family; no need to wear a suit or tie; no need to pay rent on an office or shop; flexible hours; and the ability to claim a proportion of household costs such as mortgage, rent, home insurance, electricity, rates and maintenance as tax deductions – because a part of your home is now your 'place of business'.

Against this you have to consider the disadvantages which include: a feeling of isolation from the 'real' world of business; limitations placed on running the business by local council ordinances; the need to exercise self discipline in starting and stopping work at sensible times; household distractions such as the needs of a crying baby; limited space; the vaguely unprofessional image of a home-based business; and the potential application of capital gains tax where your home has been used to gain assessable income.

Where it is possible to conduct your business from home, in most circumstances it would make sense to at least start there. It's certainly cheaper than setting up an office or shop somewhere else and, so long as you are not too distracted by other things going on in the house, it can be a lot of fun.

I would recommend that anyone contemplating setting up a business at home talk to as many people as possible who have already done so and get hold of a copy of *Home-based Business – Guidelines for Setting Up a Small Business at Home*, published by the Australian Government Publishing Service and costing $5.35. It's available from Government Info Shops and from Small Business Advisory Services.

Business structure

Once you have decided to go into business for yourself one of the more important matters you will have to address is choosing the right business structure.

The most appropriate selection is likely to be one of the three most common small business structures, which are:
- sole trader
- partnership
- proprietary limited company.

Different taxation treatments, different personal financial liabilities, and different establishment and ongoing compliance costs apply to each. These differences are important, however, their significance, couched in legalistic and accounting concepts and terminology, may not be all that apparent, particularly to business newcomers. Therefore, I strongly recommend you seek professional advice from an accountant and/or a solicitor in making this choice.

That said, the most important characteristics of each structure are as follows.

Sole trader

You are classified as a sole trader if you conduct a business alone, without a partner. This definition applies even if you have employees.

The advantages of operating as a sole trader are:
- you are entirely your own boss

Making Money

- all business profits are yours
- any business losses can be offset against any other present and future income you may have
- it's the cheapest and simplest business structure to establish and maintain
- statutory reporting requirements are less than for other structures.

The disadvantages of operating as a sole trader are:
- you are fully liable for your business's debts – this means your other assets, including your home, can be put at risk
- you pay tax on profits at your marginal tax rate – which may be higher than the company tax rate
- you may be required to register for GST and complete a quarterly or annual Business Activity Statement (BAS)
- you are solely responsible for the business, which can make it hard to get away from.

Partnership

A partnership exists where two or more persons share ownership of a business. Partnerships have the following benefits:
- the responsibility for running the business is shared
- there is a greater potential input of time, talent and money into the business than under sole trading
- taxation benefits may arise if business partners are members of the same family
- partners may be able to take time off from the business without causing undue disruption to it.

Partnerships have the following disadvantages:
- you may be stuck with a bad choice of partners and/or an inadequate partnership agreement
- the retirement or the death of a partner can cause severe capital problems
- liability is unlimited, and it is shared jointly between all partners, even where the liability has arisen from the actions of only one partner (under certain conditions, however, limited liability partnerships can be structured)
- each partner may be required to register for GST and complete a quarterly or annual Business Activity Statement.

Proprietary limited company

This is a structure better suited to a more developed business than the average self-employing, start-up venture.

As of December 1995 a proprietary company need have only one director and one shareholder (though it can have more of each). Ownership of the company rests in the hands of the shareholder/s.

The advantages of a company structure are:

- the liabilities of a company's shareholders are limited. Shareholders' personal assets cannot be seized to pay company debts
- a company pays tax on profits at the company tax rate (34% for 2000/01 and 30% for 2001/02 and later years), which may be lower than its shareholders' marginal personal tax rates
- shareholders receiving company dividends may obtain tax credits through the company imputation tax system (see 'Dividend imputation' in Chapter Thirteen, pages 217–220).

The disadvantages of a company structure are:

- establishment costs are relatively high, normally being between $1,000 and $1,500
- annual fees for preparing accounts and reports are also relatively high, normally being around $1,000
- company losses cannot be offset against shareholders' other income
- greater reporting obligations – to the Tax Office (and to the Australian Securities and Investment Commission) – apply to companies than to other business structures
- company directors have strict obligations under company law.

Please be aware that this list of advantages and disadvantages is far from complete and also note that other business structures exist, such as discretionary trusts and cooperatives. I therefore repeat my recommendation that you must seek professional advice – from your solicitor, accountant or Small Business Advisory Service – in making the involved and important choice of most suitable business structure.

And to all of you who do make the leap into self-employment – work hard and good luck!

CHAPTER SEVENTEEN

Retirement

In the early 1980s, I started doing the occasional talkback radio segment on Sydney radio station 2BL. Retirement was something many callers wanted to discuss. It seems to me that at that time, people planned to retire at 65. Most financial planning was fairly haphazard and tended to take place after the date of retirement.

Today, almost two decades later, we have changed. People plan to retire much earlier and better health means we are living much longer. It has now got to the point where some Australians will spend more time in retirement than in the work force.

This makes retirement a serious business. A 55-year-old male will now live for another 23.8 years, on average, and a 55-year-old female 28.2 years. (*Source*: ABS, 1996.) On top of this, our expectations for retirement have changed. We do not expect to stay at home all day minding the grandchildren. We hope to be healthy, active and doing those things that we did not have time to do in our working lives, such as travel – and in my case, play more golf!

Now, the bad news here is that an active lifestyle tends to cost more. Travel can be done cost effectively, but it still requires money. You will want to run a car, be able to eat out occasionally, and not have to worry about the cost of a meal with friends.

Don't get me wrong. You don't need a fortune to live well. In fact, most Australians don't have a fortune to retire on and, today, around 74% of 65- to 69-year-olds are on an age pension. (*Source*: ABS, 1999.)

A retired couple I know live on a public service pension, plus an investment portfolio of around $150,000. They own a modest but comfortable home. Sure, they are well set up, but not dissimilar to many other retired Australians. Between the income from their portfolio and the pension, their annual income is around $25,000. Due to a few of the simple tax strategies like income splitting and franked dividends that I talk about in Chapter Ten, they pay very little tax – which helps a lot.

What fascinates me about this couple is that they lead a truly global lifestyle. In retirement they decided they wanted to learn the languages and culture of other countries, so they live four months a year in Australia, four months a year in Italy and the other four months in France – all on $25,000 a year. Sounds ridiculous doesn't it? But they are able to do it, and this is how:

- They rent their home for at least six of the eight months they are away. Yes, this is a hassle because they have to store all their personal possessions with their family, but they rent it out fully furnished for a bit below market rent and do very careful reference checks on the people moving in.
- The eight months they are away each year, in France and Italy, they take a small apartment well away from the tourist haunts and they find that they can live more cheaply than in Australia. Remember, they can now speak both languages fluently so they mix and eat with the locals at local, not tourist, prices.
- They book and pay for their airfares well in advance to get the best deals.

Even if the last thing you want to do is live overseas, my point is that your retirement should be, and can be, a time when you reap the rewards of your working life.

Okay, so these days you need to start planning your retirement early. If you are young or middle-aged, just follow my 10 key steps in the opening chapter. If you are getting close to retirement, you need to start thinking about a number of other things as well:

- What are your plans for your retirement? What do you want to do and what will it cost?
- Will your assets provide the income you need to live comfortably? Can you top this up with a pension?
- Where will you live? How will this impact on your lifestyle and your family?
- What are your views on estate planning? Does your will reflect your wishes?
- Investment will become very important. Do you need an adviser, and if so how do you choose one?
- What plan do you have to ensure your retirement is a stimulating time in your life?

My best tip on retirement is, of course, to plan early. For younger readers of this book, or those of you who can influence younger readers, please do think about it and encourage people to plan for retirement from the day they start work. An 18-year-old only needs to put aside about 12% of her salary into super and she can retire on 75% of her final salary, linked to inflation. This would provide quite a decent standard of living. At 35 years of age the requisite contribution increases to around 30%, at 45 around 49% and at 55 you'd need to save 108% of your salary to retire on 75% of your final salary. Now I know some good savers, but putting aside 108% of your salary would not be easy!

Please don't feel depressed if you are retired or close to retirement and have saved very little. After all, the importance of saving has only been made clear in the last few years. Fortunately, we do have a reasonable age pension system. I know it isn't generous, but it does provide a minimum standard of living and is certainly better than nothing.

Entitlement to the age pension

The most basic condition of eligibility for the age pension is that you are aged 65 years or over, regardless of whether you are male or female. It wasn't always like this. Prior to 1 July 1995 the age at which women became eligible for the pension was 60, but in these egalitarian times that's all been swept aside. (Raising the female eligibility age will also save the Government a lot of money!)

For those women presently nearing the eligibility age, the rise from 60 to 65 is being gradually phased in, as the table below illustrates.

Women born between	Eligible for age pension at age
1/7/35 and 31/12/36	60.5
1/1/37 and 30/6/38	61
1/7/38 and 31/12/39	61.5
1/1/40 and 30/6/41	62
1/7/41 and 31/12/42	62.5
1/1/43 and 30/6/44	63
1/7/44 and 31/12/45	63.5
1/1/46 and 30/6/47	64
1/7/47 and 31/12/48	64.5
1/1/49 and later	65

In addition to having to be 65 (except for women as specified in the table above), to satisfy the basic eligibility criteria for the age pension you must also have been an Australian resident for at least 10 years, with at least five of these years comprising one period of residency. You must be resident in Australia on the day the claim is lodged and on the day it becomes payable. Also, being retired is *not* an official prerequisite for age pension eligibility.

Your application for the age pension is subject to an annual means test comprising an appraisal of your assets and income. More on this below but, for now, let's look at what the age pension actually provides.

Age pension benefits

(Note that all the figures below were accurate in March 2001 and that they are revised half yearly in line with changes to the Consumer Price Index.)

If you are on the full age pension (and it is possible to be on a part age pension, dependent on the income and assets test), you are entitled to:

- $402 per fortnight for a single person
- $671 per fortnight for a (married or de facto) couple ($335.50 each).

Age pensioners renting a private home to live in may also be entitled to receive rent assistance in addition to the age pension, to a maximum of:

- $82.80 per fortnight for a couple (combined)
- $88 per fortnight for a single person.

A pharmaceutical benefit of either $5.80 or $2.90 per fortnight is available to most pensioners. In addition to these monies, as an age pensioner you receive a Pensioner Concession Card which entitles you to a wide range of other benefits. These include either free or concessional access to dental care, eye care, hearing services, pharmaceutical prescriptions, council and water rates, gas and electricity charges, driver's licences, car registration, insurance premiums, adult education courses, entertainment, public transport and interstate rail fares.

All age pensioners are entitled to these benefits, regardless of the size of their pension. Even someone on a part age pension of only $1 will qualify. Additionally, a lump-sum advance payment of up to $500 may be available.

Making Money

Means testing

As I've noted on the previous page, any entitlement to the age pension is also subject to means testing, and this is done by separate valuations of both your assets and your income. The size of the age pension you will be entitled to is based on whichever of the two valuations produces the lower rate of benefits.

The assets test

As at March 2001 the total value of the assets you were permitted to hold under the assets test in order to qualify for the age pension was:

Family situation	For full pension*	For part pension#
For home-owners		
Single	up to $133,250	less than $269,250
Couple (combined)	up to $189,500	less than $415,500
For non-home-owners		
Single	up to $228,750	less than $364,750
Couple (combined)	up to $285,000	less than $511,000

* For every $1,000 worth of assets above these amounts the pension reduces by $3 per fortnight.

Limits are increased if rent assistance is received.

The income test

In March 2001 you were permitted to earn the amounts listed below, per fortnight, in order to qualify for the age pension under the income test.

Family situation^	Fortnightly income to receive full pension*	Fortnightly income to receive part pension+#
Single	Up to $106	Less than $1,125.50
Couple (combined)	Up to $188	Less than $1,880.00

^ Limits are more generous if dependent children are involved.

* For every dollar of income per fortnight over these limits the pension reduces by 40 cents for singles and by 20 cents for couples.

+ Pharmaceutical allowance included.

These limits may be higher if rent assistance is paid with the pension.

Now, your assets and income are valued by Centrelink (previously the Department of Social Security) in an idiosyncratic way. They are not valued the same way as they are by the Australian Tax Office for tax purposes.

The income test and 'deeming'

Under the income test, 'income' includes normal things such as salaries and wages, rent, interest and dividends. But there's more. There's also the income that's 'deemed' to be have been earned from a wide range of financial investments including shares, managed funds, insurance bonds, bank deposits and fixed interest securities.

The concept of deeming was introduced in March 1991 in response to pensioners putting large sums of money into low or zero-interest savings accounts. They were doing this to keep their incomes low in order to qualify for the full pension. To discourage this the Government decreed that these low-return investments were 'earning' more interest than they actually were, based on a prescribed interest rate known as the 'deeming rate'. The key point about these deemed, theoretical investment 'earnings' is that they counted as 'income' for the purposes of the income test, whether or not the investments actually produced any real or comparable income at all.

The idea behind deeming was, firstly, to cajole pensioners into putting their money into higher yielding investments than, say, bank savings accounts – after all, if you are going to be deemed to be earning higher theoretical returns and having your pension entitlement reduced as a result of it, you may as well try to earn those higher returns in reality. Secondly, deeming was designed to reduce the drain on the public purse – through overall pensioner income levels rising and overall eligibility for the age pension consequently falling.

On its introduction, the deeming rate was 10%, dropping to 8% in June 1991. In 1994 it was 4%, moving to 5% on 1 July 1995. (The deeming rate was and is supposed to reflect current interest rates and realistic market returns.)

Now, the deeming concept wasn't only applied to low interest savings accounts. A variation of it was and is used to determine the income produced from a wide range of other financial investments including unit trusts, insurance bonds and deferred annuities.

Making Money

The overall return that these financial investments were deemed to be generating was calculated from the pensioner's applicable investments' performance over the 12 months prior to the annual pension assessment. But the calculated rate of return on the investment portfolio may have no longer been a true reflection of the actual current performance of the portfolio (which could have fallen), or of the composition of the pensioner's current portfolio (which could have changed) at the time of assessment.

Most importantly, the assessment ignored the fact that the return on the pensioner's portfolio over the previous year may have been entirely attributable to capital growth and not to income. Yet, for the purposes of the income test this capital growth or gain was deemed to be *income* – even where the capital gain was unrealised!

Clearly, this method of assessment made life unreasonably hard for many pensioners who took a reduction in their age pension entitlement without receiving any actual increase in real income to compensate for it.

By 1995 the deeming system had all become horribly convoluted (much more so than outlined here!) and, particularly in the case of shares and managed growth investments, horribly unfair. This was partly addressed in the May 1995 Federal Budget. The system was overhauled in July 1996 and, while now being far from perfect, is fairer and much simpler with the new rules known as 'extended deeming'.

Under extended deeming, a uniform deeming rate is applied to most types of financial investments including managed funds, shares, friendly society and insurance bonds, bank accounts and fixed interest securities. Also, unrealised capital gains on these investments are no longer treated as income in determining pension eligibility.

With the present rules, Centrelink applies a deeming rate to the total value of the pensioner's financial investments to work out assessable income for the pension. As at early 2001, a deeming rate of 3.5% of income earnings is applied to the first $31,600 worth of (most) financial investments for single pensioners and for the first $52,600 worth of (most) financial investments for couples. Above these thresholds, the deeming rate is 5.5%. Actual performance of the investments is not taken into account, whether higher or lower.

To illustrate this, a single pensioner with $100,000 worth of managed share funds is deemed to be generating $4,868 annual income for the purposes of the income test, calculated thus.

$31,600 \times 3.5\% = \quad \$1,106$
$68,400 \times 5.5\% = \quad \$3,762$

Total deemed income $4,868   ($187.23 per fortnight)

When deeming income has been worked out it is added to any other income sources you may have such as wages, rents or interest payments. The income test is then applied to your total income, including the deemed income. Note that personal assets like the family home, car, furniture, stamp collections, life insurance policies and investment properties are exempt from the deeming rules. Also note that the deeming rate, set by the Government, can be changed at any time.

The assets test and 'deprivation'

Under the assets test, if you own the home in which you live it is excluded from the calculations – until it is actually paid out. Things that aren't excluded include shares, bonds, investment property, managed funds and the present surrender value of any life insurance policies.

All assessable assets, also including items like cars and furniture, are valued at their present market value, not the price you paid for them. Additionally, if there is a loan outstanding against an asset, its value is taken to be its present market value less the amount of the debt.

Now, if the thought crosses your mind of giving away some of your assets ('depriving' yourself of them) to, say, your family or a charity in order to qualify for the age pension under the assets test, think again. This is because Centrelink may treat these gifted assets as still being in your possession and earning income.

Like the rules applying to the income deemed to be earned on certain financial investments, the rules applying to 'deprivation' or 'gifting' also changed on 1 July 1996. Therefore, for reasons of brevity we will only consider these new rules.

Currently, you can give away assets up to the value of $10,000 in any 12-month period without affecting your entitlement to the age pension under the assets test.

However, if you give away assets worth more than $10,000 in any 12-month period, the value of the gifted assets in excess of

Making Money

$10,000 will be added on to the value of your other financial invest-
ments and be subject to evaluation under the deeming regulations.

For example, if you gave away assets worth $100,000 in one year,
$90,000 of this would be treated as still being in your possession.
This $90,000 would then be deemed to be earning annual income
at the rate of 3.5% on the first $31,600 (on the first $52,600 for
couples) and at 5.5% p.a. on the remainder.

In other words, by gifting your assets you can reduce or eliminate
your entitlement to the age pension by falling foul of the income
test under its deeming provisions. Any gifted assets subject to this
treatment will be considered to be in your possession for five years
and will be accounted for in every annual means test reassessment
for five years following the gifting.

Applying for the age pension

Unlike the process for determining your entitlement for the age
pension, applying for it is reasonably straightforward. Simply phone
or visit the nearest Centrelink office to obtain the appropriate forms.
These are quite detailed and require a description of your asset and
income position, and may need to be accompanied by supporting
documentation.

Centrelink has a Financial Information Service (phone 13 63 57),
and an FIS officer will help you with your application if required.
Alternatively, your accountant can assist you. Centrelink's Financial
Information Service will also help you with any inquiries about your
eligibility for the age pension and how your assets, income and
investments affect it. This service is free and I recommend you make
full use of it.

Okay, so that's broadly how the age pension works. The thing that
most surprises many people I know is that you can still get a part
pension if you are a home-owning couple earning up to $48,880
and have up to $415,000 in assets apart from your home (or up to
$511,000 in assets if you don't own a home). (Indexed limits as at
March 2001.) So, if you qualify, you should apply for the age
pension. You theoretically paid for your pension with your taxes (if
past governments didn't save to pay for the pension they promised
you, then it's not really your problem) and, in retirement, every
dollar helps. The fringe benefits, too, are valuable.

Retirement villages

Another big issue to consider is the most suitable place to live in retirement. What do you do when everyday activities – simple things like cooking, cleaning, gardening or climbing stairs – become too much like hard work? What if your health is not 100% and you need easy access to good medical attention? What if you have lost a lifelong partner and are feeling lonely and even a little unsafe?

Well, a growing number of elderly people are hoping the answers to these questions will be found by moving into a retirement village. If you pick a good one and you're of a suitable temperament, moving into a village may well be the right thing to do. However, as demonstrated below, from an investment point of view it's likely not to be.

So what is a retirement village? Well, for starters, it's *not* a nursing home (which is for the elderly who need regular medical care and who can't properly look after themselves), *nor* is it one of those Dickensian horrors that were once called 'old men's' or 'old women's' homes – bleak institutions full of old people just waiting to drop off the twig.

A retirement village is a self-contained community for people aged 55 and over. A typical village has a combination of residences or styles of accommodation for both singles and couples, ranging from independent units with all mod cons and kitchens, to serviced units, to those with a nursing home facility and/or special accommodation for the infirm on site or nearby. Retirement villages provide communal areas for socialising, and may also provide communal dining for those who don't wish to cook or who don't have the facilities to do so.

Typically, retirement villages range from around 20 units to more than 500. They can be very pleasantly set out amidst attractive grounds which might feature bowling greens or tennis courts and the swankiest of them can resemble holiday resorts.

A single person or a couple moving into a retirement village can expect to receive at least as much care and support as they would if they were living in their own homes or possibly even with their families. Much of this support comes from being part of a community of people at a similar stage in life with similar outlooks and interests.

Making Money

Of course the very idea of living in a retirement village fills some people with horror. Many elderly people enjoy the diversity of the larger community – with different age groups and types – and couldn't be dragged off kicking and screaming to a retirement village, no matter how good they may be.

> **⊶ KEY THOUGHT**
> Retirement village living must suit your temperament. To fit in happily you need to be quite social and content in a very homogeneous environment.

Villages are generally poor investments

In most cases buying into a retirement village is a poor investment decision – in one form or another it could be a drain on your funds and/or on the size of your estate. (This won't bother those who are able to afford the costs or who are not interested in leaving behind a large estate.)

Now, whether moving into a retirement village will cost you (or your estate) a lot in real terms, or whether you end up making a small capital gain on the sale of your unit when you move out – to a hostel, nursing home, or coffin – depends to a large extent on the type of tenure or 'occupancy right' you have. You may have strata title ownership, you may own it under company title, or under a licence or leasehold.

What profit or loss you or your estate finally makes from your 'investment' in a retirement village also depends on any special provisions or restrictions the village owners or operators place on your occupancy rights, and these will be stipulated in the contract you sign before taking possession. Make sure you understand these special provisions or restrictions – and for this you will definitely need the help of a solicitor – because retirement village contracts are very complex and very lengthy, commonly running to around 100 pages. Don't even think of signing before you have sought professional legal advice on the contract's meaning and implications.

Your tenure

Let's look at the four main occupancy rights under which retirement villages operate, and which are so important in determining the price you pay on entering and the amount you or your estate receives on exiting.

Strata title

When you buy an ordinary property under strata title you are entitled to sell the property to whomever you like, for whatever price, whenever you like. This may not be the case with the strata title of a retirement village unit – they can come with restrictive clauses attached.

For example, you may only be able to sell the unit to someone 55 or over who is going to live in it, and you will probably be required to sell it if you want to leave the village. In some retirement village strata title contracts it is stipulated that the unit must be sold back to the village if the owner moves out or dies, at a price determined by a formula specified in the contract. Alternatively, the owner may be entitled to sell the unit on the open market, but they will have to pay the developer a 'deferred management fee' (more on this below) and/or a share of the capital gain on the sale.

Believe it or not, strata title is considered the least restrictive of the available forms of retirement village tenure and, consequently, strata village units cost more than any other type.

Leasehold

An increasingly common form of occupancy right is leasehold, generally being a 99- or 199-year transferable lease. Under this arrangement you have no ownership rights over the unit – that remains with the village developer. Your lease simply allows you to occupy your unit and to use the village facilities.

When you enter into a lease you pay the developer a 'lease price' which covers the cost of the unit and a proportion of the communal facilities. When you leave, the developer pays you back the original lease price minus a specified percentage, plus a proportion of the unit's capital appreciation (if any).

Leasehold is cheaper than strata title because it is less secure and more restrictive. Your lease, for instance, may not permit you to sub-let your unit to someone else if you intend to vacate it for some time – to take an overseas trip, for example.

Licence

Another form of tenure (similar to leasehold) is a licence agreement under which you usually pay a fairly large, non-returnable entrance fee – possibly up to 25% of the unit's value – as well as making a compulsory interest-free 'loan' to the village owner for an indefinite period. In return for this you are entitled to live in the village and use its facilities.

When you leave a village under this form of tenure the 'loan' is repaid (minus any deferred management fee) with any capital appreciation on the unit going to the village owner.

The advantage of licence agreements is that they tend to offer you cheaper access to village life than under, say, strata title. But there are trade-offs, particularly in the area of security. For example, under a licence agreement you can be evicted (subject to compliance with the relevant *Residential Tenancy Acts* and *Retirement Village Acts*) and, in the event of the owners selling the village or going into liquidation, you have no guaranteed tenancy rights. This is because the licence is with the original owners only.

Under licence tenure there is also no provision for the residents to have any say in the running of the village – which can lead to serious discontent. Licence arrangements are fairly common in (but not isolated to) villages run by non-profit organisations such as churches and charity groups.

Company title

If you purchase a unit under a company title, you effectively buy shares in the company that owns the village and this entitles you to live there. Company title is a fairly uncommon and unpopular form of tenure due to its perceived disadvantages. The main disadvantage is that you usually can't sell your unit to whomever you like – instead you are obliged to sell your 'shares' (meaning your unit) back to the company – and it controls the sale.

The company's board of directors make the main decisions relating to the village and also appoint the village managers. If the residents have any problems with the board they have to deal with them as any shareholders would – via a general meeting. The shareholders should have a representative director on the board, but they could be out-voted by directors representing the interests of the village developers, its management company, investors, and so on.

Because of the restrictions placed on the sale of units and the potential for difficulty in resolving problems that can arise between residents and the board, company title units are normally cheaper than comparable strata title units.

Fees and charges

The cost of buying into a retirement village can vary tremendously depending on the calibre of the village, the type of accommodation and the occupancy rights. You generally pay a lump sum to buy into a village and then you're up for a range of regular fees which pay for the services and facilities on offer.

On top of the buy-in price you will have a weekly, fortnightly or monthly service or maintenance fee. This is designed to cover regular village expenses like staff salaries, cleaning, grounds maintenance and so on. The service fee varies depending on the size of your unit and how independent you are. For instance, if you are looking after yourself in a small self-care unit the service fee can be as low as $50 to $60 per week. If you are in a large serviced unit, it can be as high as $250 per week plus.

If your tenure is under strata title, you will also have body corporate levies as well as the usual overheads of council rates, water and electricity. It's also wise to check out the village sinking fund requirements. This is an annual fee paid by each resident towards the long-term maintenance of the village.

In addition to these fees some villages also charge a *deferred management fee*. This is a charge that builds up over the term of your tenure, due when you quit the village. It is invariably deducted from the sale price and can be very hefty indeed, usually calculated as a percentage of either the selling price or the purchase price multiplied by the number of years you have lived in the unit. The practice of charging deferred management fees has been widely criticised and is gradually being phased out.

Selling

Wanting to sell your unit can lead to the greatest friction between you and the village owners or operators. Not only could you be

Making Money

presented with the deferred management fee on selling, but you are likely to find the village will retain all or part of the capital gain that your unit has accrued.

You may also find that there are restrictions on the method of selling your unit. In many cases only the village is entitled to handle the sale and this includes setting the price. Now, if the village will only accept top dollar for the unit, this can effectively condemn it to staying on the open market for ages. In the meantime, however, you are still being levied service fees and other charges even if you have already moved out. (If you have died, your estate will be paying these fees.) It can all get very ugly indeed. My recommendation is not to move into a village where this method of selling is practised.

Do your homework well

All these restrictions and charges can make the idea of moving into a retirement village sound quite frightening, but it isn't my intention to put you off the idea. I am just trying to draw your attention to some of the areas that can cause problems and need investigating before you buy into any village.

Just make sure you never buy into a village sight unseen (yes, it has been done!). Make a proper inspection, not only noting the available facilities, but also noting proximity to outside amenities such as shops, transport, medical centres, clubs, sporting facilities, restaurants, cinemas, libraries, churches et cetera. Also ask the management about village policies on things like pets, noise, long-term visitors, parking, conducting a business from your unit, alcohol on the premises, the right to continue residence if your health deteriorates, who carries insurance on the buildings and contents, how complaints are dealt with, residents' rights, how policies are arrived at, and the rights of management to change the rules.

In addition, speak with existing residents to get their overall impressions of living in the village, to find out if there are any quirky restrictions that may impact on your enjoyment of village life, and to find out what they think about the management and/ or owners.

Legislation

Retirement villages have sprung up like Topsy in recent years and operate in a semi-regulated environment. Most States do have specific retirement village Acts, but these pertain more to matters of tenure and the way villages are run, rather than to the financial aspects of village living.

In an effort to protect you from rashly entering into a retirement village contract, the laws in some States stipulate that prospective residents must be given certain key information 21 days before signing a contract. This is to give you time to digest it and investigate further. There would normally be a three-day cooling-off period as well if you wished to pull out of the contract, though you may incur some charges in doing so.

It's a lifestyle decision

You should not try to use standard investment criteria to determine whether or not to buy into a retirement village. The overriding consideration should be a question of lifestyle.

To stress the point, retirement villages are not good investments for residents. If you want a good return on your money put it into the share market or buy an investment property instead. Private retirement villages are designed to make a decent return for their developers, not for their residents.

The village exists to offer a service to its customers (the residents) for which the customers are obliged to pay – and there is nothing abnormal or wrong with that, so long as the price is fair and all conditions are understood and agreed to. Just treat it as a bonus if you manage to leave a retirement village with a small profit – but certainly don't expect it. The most important consideration about whether to move into a retirement village depends on whether you think you will be happy living there.

And also think, before you sign on the dotted line, that if you are looking at paying weekly service fees of say $250 or more in a serviced retirement village unit, you might just be happier staying at home and paying someone to come in and cook and clean for you for a similar or probably lesser sum.

For further information

Working out whether you should move into a retirement village or not, and then trying to find the right one are major decisions. It's likely you'll require some assistance, so a good starting point is the Commonwealth Department of Health and Aged Care, which has a section dealing with residential living requirements for seniors. It has an Aged Care Info line: 1800 020 103.

For more specific information about retirement villages, you can contact:

Association of Residents of Queensland Retirement Villages
10 Edenlea Retirement Village
Townsend Road
Buderim Qld 4556
Phone (07) 5476 8706

Retirement Village Residents Association
PO Box 280
Gymea NSW 2227
Phone: (02) 9524 8862

Seniors Information Service
45 Flinders St
Adelaide SA 5000
Phone (08) 8232 1441

The most common questions on retirement

I have had thousands of meetings with retirees and here are the most common questions I am asked.

'Should I take a lump sum or pension?'

The question of whether your employer offers you a lump sum or pension is an extremely important issue and you need to be very careful about how you handle it. Unfortunately, too often, invest-ment advisers recommend going for the lump sum for the simple reason that they often make no money if you go for the pension option. (As no sale of an investment product is made if you take the pension option, no commission is paid.)

The first step is to analyse your employer's pension scheme. Take a close look at how much it is and whether it is indexed to inflation. Be sure you understand what happens if you die. Is the pension *reversionary*, meaning does 100% or, more commonly, 66% go to your spouse for their lifetime? Equally, consider what happens if both you and your spouse die or are killed in an accident. Does your estate receive any benefit?

Looking back over the past decade or so, it seems to me (with hindsight) that many Australians would have been better off with a pension from their employer. With a pension you are usually guaranteed a fixed payment and when paid to public servants, they are effectively Government guaranteed.

There can be, however, some pretty good reasons *not* to take a pension, which could include that:

- Your life expectancy, and that of your spouse, is very low.
- The pension offered is very low, given the lump sum alternative.
- The pension is not linked to inflation.
- It isn't reversionary to your spouse if you die.
- You need a lump sum for a specific (and sensible) purpose.
- You want to be in full control of your own investments.

Most private enterprise schemes only offer a lump sum at retirement, but believe me, if offered, I'd be very tempted by a guaranteed monthly payment, linked to inflation and reversionary to my spouse. This would provide investment certainty, no hassles and a regular income. I like the sound of that, so don't throw the pension option away too quickly if you have it. And remember, a good 'each-way' bet may be to take a part pension and part lump sum.

'Should I buy my own pension?'

When your employer only offers you a lump sum you can then buy your own pension if you like. The main options are an annuity or an allocated pension.

Annuities

Annuities are offered by life insurance companies. They come in various types and the best known is probably a lifetime annuity that will pay you a fixed monthly amount depending upon how much money you have and the current interest rates. Interest rates were very high in 1990 and it was a great time to buy a lifetime annuity, conversely 1994 was a very poor year as they were at a cyclical low. From 1998 onwards, low interest rates have made these annuities less popular.

The old lifetime annuity was very unpopular – if you died you got nothing, on the other hand if you lived to 100 you 'won'. Modern annuities are more flexible, with 'term certain' annuities being where you nominate a minimum payment period, say, 10 years. If you died, for instance, after one year, your estate would receive payments for the next nine years.

You can also get annuities with payments linked to inflation and with a wide array of options. This flexibility is making annuities more attractive to retirees. A key tip with buying your own annuity is to shop around, as rates vary from one life insurance company to another.

Allocated pensions

Due to their greater flexibility, the most popular privately pur-chased pension has been the allocated pension. Their appeal is that you can rollover your Eligible Termination Payment (usually your super money) into an allocated pension and pay no lump sum tax. Once in the allocated pension, no tax is paid on invest-ment earnings.

There is both a minimum and maximum size pension you can take. The upper and lower limits are calculated by a formula that looks at the size of your investment in the allocated pension and your life expectancy. If, for instance, you had $100,000 and were 65, your minimum pension would be around $6,400 and your maximum would be just under $12,400.

The big advantage of an allocated pension is that you can not only nominate which investments you want (what percentage of shares, property and so on), you can also take out a lump sum if you wish (and pay the normal lump sum tax rates). On the pension you draw, there is also a 15% tax rebate. This means that you could be taking a pension of around $24,000 and have to pay no tax if this pension was your only source of income.

It all sounds pretty good, but an allocated pension is not always the best option. It all depends upon the size of your Eligible

Termination Payment, how it's made up, your age, personal situation, other assets and your tax planning. Clearly, you'll need professional help working this out.

Also, be aware that unlike an employer pension or a lifetime annuity, your allocated pension can run out of money. If you draw a higher pension than the returns your investments make, naturally you'll use up your capital. In addition, because you're entitled to make the investment decisions with an allocated pension (meaning, nominating in what assets your money is placed), poor decisions can also lose you capital.

'Should I rollover my money?'

Believe me, I have plenty of sympathy with people who tell me that the superannuation rules are too hard, that the system keeps on changing and they want their money out of it. But there are definite benefits of rolling over your Eligible Termination Payment (ETP) and staying in the super system.

- By rolling over (and remaining rolled over) you pay no lump sum tax on your ETP.
- Inside a rollover fund, you will pay a maximum rate of tax of only 15% on investment earnings. In an annuity or allocated pension you will pay no tax on investment earnings.
- Compared with investing in your own name, a *maximum* rate of tax of 15% is very attractive to most Australians.
- If you do choose to take your money out of the system, lump sum tax is much lower if you do it after age 55. At least try to leave your money rolled over until then.

These are the most common reasons for rolling over. However, due to your personal circumstances (involving things like excess benefits) you may actually be better off taking the money out of the superannuation environment. Whatever you do, seek good advice and be sure to weigh up the facts before committing yourself.

'How do I invest a large amount?'

Apart from a property sale or possibly an inheritance, for many Australians retirement is the first time that they have a large amount of cash to invest – and it can be pretty scary. With retirement money you get no second chances, so you must invest wisely.

I strongly suggest that you go over my 'Ten Keys to Successful Investing' in Chapter Eleven. Following these can't guarantee you success, but they will certainly put you on the right track.

Above all, please remember it's your money. Your future depends upon it, so I really want you to put in the time and effort to invest the money in a way that best suits you. This means doing your planning, budgeting and having a serious think about your attitude to risk. In the long run, the amount of investment risk you take will determine your return.

'How should I manage my money?'

Unfortunately, we all age and relatively simple money and investment decisions can get harder as we get older. It isn't a sensible option to pretend it won't happen to us so, basically, we have three choices:

- Increasingly pass responsibility over to your spouse, trusted family member or professional adviser.
- Consider purchasing a pension or annuity type product which pays you a regular income.
- Simplify your portfolio by holding a smaller number of investments or use balanced funds provided by professional managers.

Managing your own portfolio in retirement can be fun and providing you are happy to monitor your investments closely and keep detailed records, 'doing it yourself' can work. Just make sure you avoid the temptation to take a punt on speculative shares or property investments. Believe me, full-time investment professionals know that punters lose more often than they win. Set a long-term strategy and have the discipline to stick with it.

Most of you, though, are not budding professional investment managers and will want or need professional help in managing your money. Investment alone is complex enough, but add to this tax issues such as capital gains, franked dividends, lump sum tax, excess benefits and so on and it all gets pretty tricky.

While the majority of retirees will seek professional help, it's still really important that you understand the broad strategy, the level of risk and potential long-term returns from the portfolio suggested to you by your adviser.

The choice of money management is very personal, but, from my experience as an adviser, I find that having a simplified investment portfolio monitored by a competent, trustworthy adviser who has a good client reporting system is usually the best approach in the later years of your life.

'What does a typical retiree do?'

As you can imagine, different people do different things with their money. Some put it all in the bank, some buy property. My most valuable tip here is to diversify and spread your risk. We all like to think we know the 'best' investment, but why take unnecessary risk with retirement money?

A typical diversified retirement portfolio for a 65-year-old couple who own their own home could look something like this:

Cash	15%
Bonds and fixed interest	40%
Property securities	10%
Australian shares	25%
International shares	10%
Total	100%

Now, your investments are a very personal thing. I know retired clients who have 100% of their money in a Commonwealth Bank account and I also know retirees who keep 80% of their money in shares.

It all depends on how much risk you can sleep with at night but, do remember, the lower the risk you take, the lower your long-term returns.

'Why not put my money in the bank?'

Well, the advantage of this strategy is that providing you put it all in a strong bank, your chance of losing capital is just about as close as you can get to zero. Unfortunately though, your long-term financial prospects look pretty bleak. Let's say that you can earn 6% on your cash and that you pay a 20% average rate of tax. Let's also assume that inflation averages 4%.

In this example, the 6% you earn is 4.8% after tax. In other words, you are generating an after-tax return of 0.8% above inflation. Now, even if you could live off the 4.8% and not touch your capital, inflation still eats away at it.

To illustrate the corrosive effects of inflation, let's assume you have $100,000 in the bank and inflation is 4% p.a. Let's look at your nest egg's buying power every year over 20 years.

The buying power of $100,000 over 20 years after 4% inflation

Year	Buying power ($)
2001	100,000
2002	96,000
2003	92,160
2004	88,473
2005	84,934
2006	81,537
2007	78,275
2008	75,144
2009	72,138
2010	69,253
2011	66,483
2012	63,823
2013	61,270
2014	58,820
2015	56,467
2016	54,208
2017	52,040
2018	49,958
2019	47,960
2020	46,041

More depressing than this relentless erosion is the thought that even the interest income you earn each year from your bank deposit buys you increasingly less.

This is the main argument for investing in growth assets such as property and shares. Not only will your money grow in value over the long term, but so will the income you receive. Unlike interest returns, both rent and share dividends grow over time.

Sure, property and shares are more risky than cash but, funnily enough, over 20 years cash is a poor investment despite its low risk. Its buying power is ruined by tax and, in particular, inflation.

'Should I sell the house?'

It's human nature to think the grass is greener elsewhere, but only a few of my clients have successfully and happily moved to another suburb or more distant location. The key tip here is to rent where you would like to live before you sell your home and rebuy elsewhere. Often the 'lifestyle' advantages of moving to the beach simply don't happen – or they are overshadowed by living too far from friends and family.

Depending on how emotionally tied you are to the family home, the option of selling and buying something smaller, even in the same area, is quite valid. For a number of my clients this has meant a lower maintenance property, but importantly it has also freed up a sizeable amount of money which can provide a better lifestyle.

'How much should I leave to the kids?'

One of the things that we tend to do very poorly is estate planning (i.e. the management and preparation of our estate in anticipation of our death, to the maximum benefit of all concerned).

In particular, it frustrates me to see so many Australians with a valuable home and other assets living on a very restricted income in retirement due to a desire to pass all their existing wealth on to the kids – as distinct from dipping into some or all of it.

In planning your retirement, your attitude to this sometimes difficult issue should be one of your first priorities.

Let me put this in perspective. If a couple, both aged 65, own a home and have $300,000 to invest, they can basically set three broad objectives for their money:

- *Objective 1*. To preserve their capital and to pass it all to their children in today's dollars. (That is, to increase the $300,000 by inflation each year.)
- *Objective 2*. To preserve their capital and pass $300,000 on to their children without increasing it with inflation.
- *Objective 3*. To plan to spend all of it by the time they are 90.

Making Money

At that stage they will still own a home and will receive an age pension. At age 90, it is doubtful they will be taking too many world trips or buying the latest Paris fashions, in other words their regular living expenses will be modest.

Under each scenario, our imaginary couple could spend the following after-tax amounts, each year:

Objective 1	$11,000 per year
Objective 2	$16,250 per year
Objective 3	$19,000 per year

These figures assume the couple invest over the long term in a conservative, balanced portfolio appropriate to retirees. The portfolio would be comprised of cash, fixed interest, property securities and shares, assumed to be generating 4% income and 4% growth p.a., with inflation also at 4% p.a.

Now, I could top up these annual income figures with a part age pension but, to keep it simple, let's just focus on the principle of investment and using your capital. Do note, however, that under Objective 3 our couple would get the highest age pension over the years, as their capital would more significantly fall under the assets test applied by Centrelink.

The message here is simple. I don't see how most of us can live our lives to the full, have fun along the way and enjoy our family and friends if we aim for Objective 1 or, for many of us, Objective 2. You just need to have so much money to do it.

Don't get me wrong, however. I'm not trying to encourage you to leave nothing to your kids, I'm just urging you to be sensible. For most of us, after decades of raising our children, we quite reasonably want to give them the best financial advantages we can. What I am saying is that, unless you have significant wealth, it is difficult to have both a decent standard of living in retirement as well as preserve all of the assets that you have built up over a lifetime of work to leave to the children.

This is a delicate matter, certainly, and dealing with it may be one of those occasions when having a family conference is a good idea.

CHAPTER EIGHTEEN

Bankruptcy and Wills

There are many possibilities in life and very few certainties. On a less than cheerful note, one possibility is that you could go broke and one certainty is that you will die. Hopefully you will get through life without experiencing the first, but no one can escape the second. At least you may be able to reduce the trauma by being better informed in the case of bankruptcy and by having your estate in order when you die.

Bankruptcy

Bankruptcy is a legal status that can follow on from being insolvent, meaning not being able to meet your debts. It is covered under Commonwealth law by the *Bankruptcy Act*, so the provisions are the same in all States.

Bankruptcy is a legal status that applies only to individuals. Companies or businesses don't go bankrupt, but rather become 'insolvent' and are put into 'receivership' and a 'receiver' is brought in to take total control of the company's financial affairs.

Now, if you get into real trouble with your debts and bankruptcy is looming on the horizon, there are some basic steps to take which could head it off.

Inform your creditors

The first thing to do is to seek help from an accountant, a solicitor or a financial controller as soon as you realise you're in trouble. Then, discuss your financial situation with your creditors. This is absolutely critical and ideally should be done before you miss a repayment, as nothing gets a creditor offside so thoroughly as non-payment on the due date without explanation.

By revealing your financial problems sooner rather than later, you may be able to come to an agreement with your creditors where they accept a reduction in repayments and an extension of time to repay or accept a temporary halt to repayments altogether while you get your finances in order. Your creditors may have no problem with 'rescheduling' your debts, particularly if the cause of your insolvency is an unusual occurrence, say, an accident temporarily keeping you off work.

Honesty and good communication are the passwords here. If you don't speak up before missing a repayment it may be too late. Don't wait for the creditors to force the issue such as the bank foreclosing on your mortgage. You will be in a much better position to pay off your debts (and stay out of bankruptcy) if *you* take the first step without delaying.

Becoming bankrupt

Now, if it's apparent there is little chance of you being able to repay the money you owe or if your creditors won't reschedule or restructure the debt in any way, you can either become bankrupt voluntarily or your creditors can petition the Federal Court to declare you bankrupt. And to be declared bankrupt you need to be indebted for more than $2,000 (comprised of one or more debts).

No matter how it happens, once you become bankrupt, a bankruptcy trustee takes control of your estate. From the moment the bankruptcy trustee is appointed, all claims for payment by creditors have to be made through the trustee, whose responsibility it is to locate all your eligible assets and to make an equitable distribution of them between the creditors.

The appointment of a bankruptcy trustee is designed to protect both the creditors and the bankrupt. Having a trustee take control of a bankrupt's financial affairs theoretically means that the bankrupt will not be able to conceal any saleable assets from the creditors, nor will a particularly aggressive creditor be able to get more than their fair share of the disposable assets.

To become bankrupt voluntarily involves delivering a signed Debtor's Petition to the Official Receiver at the Insolvency and Trustee Services Australia and presenting with it a full statement of your affairs, nominating your assets, your debts, any summonses issued and your anticipated income for the next 12 months. Once the Official Receiver is satisfied your financial predicament is legitimate and your petition is accepted, you officially become bankrupt and a bankruptcy trustee is appointed. There are official and trustee fees involved in this process, but none to pay at this point – they are deducted once your estate is wound up – and take priority over any other debts.

Alternatively, a creditor or creditors can force you into bankruptcy. This process is quite involved and expensive.

- The creditors must firstly obtain a judgement on your debt from a court.
- The creditors then apply to the Official Receiver who issues a Bankruptcy Notice instructing you, the debtor, to pay the debt within a specified period (generally 21 days).
- If the debt is not paid by the due date, the creditors then must apply to the Federal Court to have you declared bankrupt.

At every stage in this process you have the opportunity to halt proceedings by paying the debts.

Restrictions placed on bankrupts

Once you are bankrupt there are a number of restrictions placed upon you.

- You can't be a director, a promoter, or a manager of a company without permission of the Federal Court.
- You aren't allowed to seek credit for more than $3,360 (indexed) without informing the potential creditor of your bankrupt status.
- You are unable to hold certain types of licences. For example, you can't hold a builder's licence for 10 years after declaring bankruptcy. Also be aware that the effect of bankruptcy on licensing varies from State to State.
- If asked, you must hand over your passport to the trustee and you cannot leave Australia without the permission of the trustee or the Federal Court.

But if your finances spin out of control it's not all bad news becoming bankrupt, and this is why some people choose the path voluntarily.

- Creditors stop pestering you – because all claims are handled by the trustee.
- Interest ceases to be added to debts outstanding once bankruptcy is established.
- Although most property of any value is taken from you as a bankrupt, some property is protected, such as household furniture, a

car worth less than $5,050 and tools of trade worth up to $2,600. This even applies to goods which might have been seized earlier by a bailiff – you may get them back.

- You are allowed to retain half of any income you earn over and above a trustee-determined threshold (which can be no less than 3.5 times the basic pension). The other half you are required to hand over to the bankruptcy trustee. Note that in cases of hardship, however, the Official Receiver does have the discretionary power to vary the level of contribution.
- Under bankruptcy, pensions, superannuation and benefits are usually protected from creditors.
- If you declare yourself bankrupt, you can choose your own bankruptcy trustee – either the Official Trustee or a registered trustee. The Official Trustee is an officer of the Insolvency and Trustee Services of Australia, a Commonwealth Government agency. Registered trustees are private accountants with the appropriate accreditations.

Now, please don't let me give you the impression that being bankrupt is no big deal or a rort enabling you to welsh on your responsibilities. It is not something to embrace casually. Despite legitimately providing you with some protection against further financial ruin, bankruptcy is restrictive, it deprives you of control over your affairs, it's invasive and rightly or wrongly it carries an eyebrow-raising stigma that lingers long after the bankruptcy (which remains on your credit record for seven years) has been discharged – which can be one of its nastiest characteristics.

Discharging bankruptcy

Bankruptcy is normally discharged automatically after three years from the date on which the statement of affairs is filed. However, if an objection has been lodged by the trustee, that can be extended to five or even eight years from the date of becoming bankrupt.

Some bankrupts may meet the criteria for an Early Discharge. As a bankrupt you may apply to the trustee for an Early Discharge six months after filing a statement of affairs. Alternatively, you can seek the annulment of the bankruptcy by order of the Federal Court, by paying your debts out in full or by coming to an agreement with your creditors to a payment proposal.

> **⊶ KEY THOUGHT**
>
> If you are in financial difficulties don't put your head in the sand – seek help from an accountant, a solicitor or the Insolvency and Trustee Service Australia and ask your creditors for their cooperation in your efforts to get your financial house in order. In many cases you will receive it but if you just stop making repayments and wait for your creditors to contact you, bankruptcy may be just around the corner.

Wills

You might not have to go through bankruptcy during your lifetime, but there's no avoiding death. And while there's also no way of avoiding the anguish it causes, it's cruel to exacerbate the suffering by not leaving behind a clear, current and valid will.

Around 20% of Australians who die every year do so without leaving a valid will – much too high a figure when you think how simple and inexpensive it is to prepare, and how much consternation is caused by dying without one.

What a will does

Simply, a will is a document stating what you want done with your possessions and property after your death. Anyone over the age of 18 is legally entitled to have a will and married people aged under 18 can have one too.

Broadly, a will should:

- provide primary directions for the distribution of your property following your death
- provide secondary directions in the event a beneficiary or beneficiaries die before you
- nominate guardians for any children under 18 or for any other dependants
- make provision for all people who are dependent on you – such as your partner, your children and elderly relatives
- revoke previous wills
- appoint an executor, as well as an alternative one in the event the first one can't or doesn't wish to do the job, or dies before you.

Making Money

Dying intestate

If you die without a valid will, known as dying 'intestate', the probate division of the Supreme Court will appoint an administrator to distribute your estate to your next of kin according to statutory priority laid down by the relevant State laws. To illustrate, let's look at the intestacy rules that apply in New South Wales where, if you die without a will, your estate will be divided (in descending priority), as follows.

- Where there is a spouse and no children, the entire estate goes to the spouse.
- Where there is a spouse and children:
  if the estate is worth less than $150,000, the entire estate goes to the spouse;
  if the estate is worth more than $150,000 (including the value of the matrimonial home), the spouse gets the first $150,000 plus all household effects, and the remainder of the estate is split 50/50 between the spouse and the children.
- Where there are children and no spouse, the estate is split equally between the children.
- Where there are no children and no spouse the parents of the deceased share the estate equally.
- Following this come other relatives. (There is a pecking order among them too.)
- If no relatives can be located, the estate goes to the State of New South Wales.

Note that in all the cases above, a de facto partner has the same rights as a spouse if the relationship has been in existence for at least two years.

If a married or de facto couple die at the same time and both are intestate, the older person is deemed for probate purposes to have died first. This means that before the younger person's estate is passed on to the beneficiaries, the younger person's estate firstly receives its statutory share of the older person's estate.

Bearing this in mind, let's look at an example of how dying without a will can really direct your assets to the wrong recipients and be nothing short of disastrous. We'll assume a 45-year-old divorced male – with three children – is killed with his 35-year-old female de facto partner in the same car crash. We will also assume he has assets worth $250,000, that both persons are intestate, and that probate is under New South Wales law.

Because the male is older, he is presumed to have died first and, therefore, the first $150,000 of his estate plus half of the remainder goes to her estate. This amount totals $200,000, leaving only $50,000 for his children. Because the female is also intestate, her estate, including the $200,000 from his estate, will go to her next of kin which could be her children (by another partner), parents, siblings, aunt or uncle. If she has no relatives, her estate will go to the Government. None of these recipients is very likely to be the one whom he would have wished 80% of his estate to go to – particularly as he has three children of his own! The 15 minutes it would have taken him to organise a will would have prevented such a travesty.

Who needs a will?

Anyone with an estate, a spouse or partner, children, a family and a desire for some, if not all, of their estate to go to a certain party or parties needs a will. And if there is no one in the family or no friend you wish to leave your estate to, you can always leave it to a charity, a foundation or an institution – for which you need a will.

Clearly, as circumstances change, your will needs revising. If you have separated, divorced, remarried or entered into a de facto relationship, you need to change your will, stating your new instructions. You may also need to change it if you have children, if any of your beneficiaries die or change their marital status, or if your executor dies.

Also be aware that divorce may automatically revoke part or all of your will. It ranges from total revocation in Tasmania (where you would die intestate if you hadn't written another one) to partial revocation in some States, to no effect at all in others. This is something you need to check.

Preparing a will

You can write your own will using a do-it-yourself kit. These are available from stationers, and cost as little as $5. Make sure you get one with instructions on how to fill it out and ensure you do it correctly – a badly written will may cause more grief for your beneficiaries than no will at all.

Making Money

For your will to be valid, there are two formal requirements you must meet, namely, it must be in writing, and it must be signed by you and by two witnesses. The witnesses (and their spouses) cannot be beneficiaries.

You can also have a solicitor draw up your will, which, if your affairs are simple, should cost you no more than $150. What you get for this is a document that's properly worded and better able to withstand a legal challenge from a party or parties who believe you may have short-changed them.

While drawing up your own will is certainly inexpensive, I recommend that you employ a solicitor to do it. This should ensure that all the legal requirements are complied with, that it is unambiguous, that it is free of technically incorrect terms, and that it is most likely to achieve the results you wish.

A solicitor can also advise you on the establishment of discretionary family trusts for certain beneficiaries, particularly for those who are especially dependent, vulnerable or hopeless with money. These trusts are not considered part of your estate and carry on independently after your death providing income to the nominated recipients. They are managed by a trustee and cannot be touched by other claimants against your estate.

The executor

In your will you need to appoint an executor, and *it's a choice you must make with care*. This is because it's the executor's job to administer your estate and to see your will is carried out as you intended. Your executor is responsible for ensuring that all legal requirements relating to the estate are properly dealt with, and that the funeral is carried out as wished. Most importantly, your executor has the final say in any dispute over the will, short of a legal challenge.

You can also give discretionary powers to your executor, enabling him or her to use their best judgement as to how parts of your estate are divided up. This saves you, for instance, having to list every single knick-knack you own and everyone you would like something to go to.

Anyone can be an executor, including a beneficiary, a solicitor or a professional trustee. So, who do you nominate? Well, clearly, given the responsibilities and powers an executor has, it's vital your executor be competent and, above all, trustworthy. An executor doesn't need prior experience and certainly not legal qualifications. What they do need is integrity and a genuine desire to see your last wishes properly fulfilled. My advice is to pick someone you know well and trust implicitly, preferably your spouse or partner, a close family member or friend. The person you nominate as executor doesn't have to accept the position, so it's best to ask first. You can also specify a fee in your will for executorial efforts if you wish.

In the event there is no one you consider suitable to be your executor you can nominate a professional to do the job, either a private trustee or the Public Trustee. A professional trustee will help you prepare your will for little or no charge, but in return for administering your estate will take a percentage of its worth following your death.

Trustee's fees are usually determined on a sliding scale, normally beginning at around 4% to 5% on the first $100,000 of the estate. This can be expensive, particularly if you are leaving a large estate, but trustees are the most beneficial when the estate is complicated and involves the long-term administration of a trust fund for your beneficiaries. Professional trustees are also very useful if there are some sharks among the beneficiaries.

⌐ KEY THOUGHT

Death is never easy for those left behind. Don't make it any harder on them by not having a valid, well-considered will. It's such a simple, inexpensive document to prepare and it's such a simple way to ensure your estate goes to the people you want it to go to. And if you don't have a will, you owe it to your family to get right on to it, today!

Two things you should know about estate planning

1. **Power of Attorney.** When doing your estate planning, I strongly advise you to think about having a power of attorney. This gives someone you trust the ability to act on your behalf. Now, a power of attorney can be a dangerous thing but the kind I recommend can only be used by the person or persons you nominate if you are incapacitated by an accident or illness. Remember, if you can't sign, your assets can't even be used to help you. Sure, your relatives could get a court order, but having a specific power of attorney is worth discussing with your solicitor.

2. **Testamentary Trusts.** Ask your lawyer about a testamentary trust. If something happens to you, this type of trust can mean that your children will receive income from your assets and earn up to the normal adult tax-free threshold of $6,000 each. This could make a huge difference to your family, so it's worth checking!

CHAPTER NINETEEN
Choosing an Adviser

A question I am often asked is 'How do I find an honest adviser who will work for me, and not for themselves?' Sadly, the investment and insurance industry has built up a reputation as being full of shonks flogging product to people for commission. The problem with this is that commission varies dramatically from product to product and, if your adviser is paid on this basis, there is always an uncertainty about whether the product recommended is the best product for you – or pays the most commission to the adviser.

Let's look at an older-style life insurance company savings plan, for example. After five years, it's likely to have a cash value of less than your total contributions. These plans usually take 10 years just to get back what you have put in, let alone getting in front. If the plan called for a $10 per week contribution, and instead you put that $10 per week into your mortgage, you'd be much better off.

So, why didn't the adviser recommend this course of action? The answer is painfully simple. By putting $10 a week into your mortgage, the adviser earns nothing. By selling you a long-term savings plan, the adviser would have made around $500. In this instance, the way the adviser is paid makes it very hard for them to give you the advice that's best for you.

So, what's the solution? Well, your money is really important to you, and a good adviser can really help, but you have to be tough and up-front with your concerns and questions.

My advice, if you need an adviser, is to do the obvious things. Ask family, friends and work colleagues for a referral. Keep an eye on the money sections of newspapers and see who the journalists talk to. Get a 'Registry of Financial Planners' from the Financial Planning Association by ringing 1800 337 301.

Once you have a name, make an initial appointment. At the meeting, ask the following questions.
■ *How long have you been giving advice?*
  This is most important. You can't beat experience. Also remember to ask how long they have been working for their current

employer. You don't want someone who switches jobs all the time.

- *What are your qualifications?*
  A degree in economics or business is a good start, but especially keep your eye out for ASIA (Associate of the Securities Institute of Australia) or DFP (Diploma of Financial Planning). The best advisers are likely to have the letters CFP (Certified Financial Planner) after their name.

- *Tell me about your company. Do you own part of it and who are the shareholders?*
  You need to know how long the company has been around and its background. I am always a keen student of who the company directors are – a solid group of directors makes me more comfortable. Also, if your adviser owns all or part of the company, they are not likely to leave too quickly.

- *What type of client do you specialise in?*
  Some advisers tend to deal with smaller clients, others with larger clients. If you are not the type of client the adviser wants, you won't get looked after well.

- *What resources does your company have in terms of investment research?*
  Investment is complicated. Your adviser will need technical support, so find out how strong this support is.

- *Do you give independent advice?*
  The company may be owned by a big institution, but still give independent advice, meaning they don't flog only their own products.

- *How do you charge?*
  I prefer 'fee for advice' advisers, meaning they charge you for their time and either don't take commission or brokerage, or give it back to you. If they do charge commission, make sure that they disclose this to you and the amount they get.

- *Do you hold a licence?*
  To give broad investment advice the adviser will need to hold an authority to operate under his or her company's licence. Have a look at the authority and also the company licence. You are looking for restrictions on the type of advice they can give. For example, many companies cannot give advice on direct share investments. While this should not be a major drama, you should know about it.

- *Do I get my advice in writing?*
  If you don't, leave straight away! Getting your advice in writing is essential, because this will help to protect you if things go wrong.
- *Describe your ongoing service. What does it cost?*
  You'll need ongoing advice. Find out how the adviser does this. I'd be very concerned if it's free. Free ongoing advice is usually worth what you pay for it – absolutely nothing!
- *Are you a member of the Financial Planning Association (FPA)?*
  In my admittedly biased opinion (I am a member and was its President in 1993–4), the FPA is the premier body for financial planners. Its Code of Ethics, Commission Disclosure Rules and Disputes Resolution system help to protect you.

Now, I know it's a pain asking these questions, but you must. Invest 20 minutes in getting satisfactory answers and while I can't promise that everything will be perfect, at least you'll be on the right track.

Also, while you are talking to the adviser, please be aware of the environment. Is it a professional workplace? Files lying everywhere always worries me. Does it feel efficient and comfortable? Were you greeted by the receptionist in an appropriate fashion? Did your adviser take phone calls during your meeting, or race out to get a cup of coffee – these are bad signs.

Also, be fair to the adviser; at the end of the meeting ask, 'Am I the sort of client you want? Please be honest about this or I'm sure we'll both be disappointed.' No point starting this important professional relationship if it does not suit both of you.

To finish on a positive note, there are now many good advisers but, in the final analysis, your money is your responsibility. Treat the job of finding the right adviser seriously.

CHAPTER TWENTY
The Internet

2001: A Space Odyssey or 2001: A Cyberspace Oddity?

The last year, the boom, then bust of so many Internet companies showed that even many of the so-called experts didn't have much of a grasp of online potential or reality.

There's no doubt about it though, the advent of the Internet has changed our lives forever: how we communicate, how we research, how we bank, how we shop, how we conduct business with other businesses and even how we date. It can be fun, educational and a useful and profitable tool but, for most of us, it has become and will remain *part* of our lives, not run our lives.

The Internet, according to some, is the modern equivalent of the printing press or the Industrial Revolution. It may well be, but I prefer to look at it as a technical *evolution*. Pundits also made the assertion that TV would mean the end of radio, and video would mean the end of cinemas. It didn't happen. Sure, you can bring up the morning paper online, check the news and sport, share prices, the entertainment section and even do the crossword, but this doesn't mean newspapers will become a thing of the past. It's a lifestyle thing. Sitting in front of a screen is a different experience to kicking back on the deck with a real paper. Shopping online is nothing like browsing in a real shop. Chatting online is not like a real conversation.

The uptake of this new technology in the past year or two has been phenomenal. No longer do you need to read statistics to see just how amazing that growth has been. I have friends who, until a short time ago, thought a keyboard was a place to hang their car keys and a hard drive was tackling Sydney to Brisbane without an overnight stop. Now they use home computers for e-mail, games and research. In fact, how many people do you know without e-mail, either at home or at work? Not many, probably. In private use there's a lot to explore and enjoy on the Internet – it's like having a library in your home. It can be used simply for banking, paying bills and buying shares or goods. In commercial use, business-to-business applications are time and cost effective and, despite the so-called 'tech-wreck', there are profits to be made for many businesses online.

What is the Internet?

Well firstly, the Internet is something that has introduced a whole lot of new terms into our vocabulary, such as 'e-mail', 'e-commerce', 'tech-wreck' and 'e-tail'. And there has been an influx of time-saving and irritating abbreviations like IT (Information Technology), B2B (business-to-business), B2C (business-to-consumer), 24 × 365 (twenty-four hours a day, year-round service), clicks 'n' bricks (a traditional retail outlet coupled with an online presence) and FAQs (frequently asked questions). Interestingly, the abbreviation www takes longer to say than 'World Wide Web'.

In simple terms, the Internet is just a whole bunch of computers that can connect to a whole bunch of other computers via a network. It's no more than a sophisticated network of phone lines where words and images are sent down the line instead of a voice.

Some people haven't embraced the Internet simply because they don't like or are scared of computers. Advances in technology have made them more user-friendly and they will become even more so when Internet and television merge, but for now, if you are technically challenged (like me), remember that to get a cold beer you don't need to know how the fridge works.

Hype and reality

Thankfully, a lot of hype about how wonderful and empowering the Internet is has died down and most online businesses that have survived are now taking a more realistic and sensible approach, treating e-commerce as a 'business' and not a way to get rich overnight.

The boom we saw in IT shares in early 2000 was driven by hype, fear and greed with very little 'dot-commonsense'. For a while it seemed as though the financial world had been taken over by young, high-flying executives on outrageous salaries who had more interest in alfresco lunches and fast cars than hard work.

The Internet hype was kicked along by the print media. In order to get Internet-related companies to spend money on advertising they had to surround the ads with articles worth reading, so a lot more coverage was given to e-commerce and start-up companies than they actually deserved.

For the latter half of 2000, we saw anti-hype and negativity that was almost as damaging for online ventures as the earlier hype and stupidity. The reality is, 2001 will see a few more dot com companies run out of cash, others grow organically and survive and others flounder and be picked up for a fraction of their value by big companies with deep pockets. With strict regulations now in place, listed companies have to disclose their financial position, so investors are far less likely to be swayed by any 'smoke and mirrors'.

E-mail

Electronic mail has to be IT's 'killer app' (to use another irritating abbreviation for an 'outstanding application of technology'). It's one of the most cost-effective and efficient ways to communicate and send/receive data. You can send several messages for the cost of a phone call and in far less time than it takes to write a traditional letter. It's a casual means of communicating – typing errors are par for the course – and e-mail protocol (good manners) demands that e-mails are answered pretty much as soon as they're read, which ensures a speedy response. Again you may find yourself up to your fingertips in abbreviations like '18r' (later), CU2NYT (see you tonight) or ;-) which is a wink (turn the book on its side).

Being able to send attachments is arguably the best part of e-mails. Whether it be photos of the family or documents and spreadsheets, there is no simpler, more effective way of transferring them. There have also been recent software developments, like Acrobat, that send data in a form that can't be altered by the receiver, which is ideal for contracts or other sensitive information. Another great advancement in e-mail technology is the ease with which you can access your mail when travelling, anywhere in the world.

There are also companies that offer free e-mail accounts, like Hotmail, that supply the service in the hope that you will be enticed by paid advertising that pops up when you log-in to check your mail. These types of e-mail accounts are terrific if you have members of the family that want their own personal addresses, rather than sharing yours, and when travelling (if your Internet Service Provider doesn't offer an easy-to-use retrieval service).

Increasingly however there has been an influx of nuisance

e-mails – chain letters, unsolicited junk e-mail and offers of get-rich schemes. Beware of these, especially as they are just another variation on old pyramid-selling operations. Be wary of any e-mail with something like 'Never have to worry about money again!' in the subject line, or a sender with an obscure e-mail address like zq10267@mail.www.yu. If enough people ignore unsolicited mail, it may eventually just go away.

Banking online

All the major banks are now online and it's a cost-effective and time-efficient way of checking your bank or loan balance, checking current interest rates, noting the effects of revised home loan payments, transferring funds from one account to another, applying for loans or credit cards, getting investment advice or paying bills directly from your account for things like telephone or energy supplies. It's a bit like having an ATM in your home without the cash withdrawal facility. Currently 8.6% of ANZ's customers have used online banking and the Big Four (Commonwealth, Westpac, ANZ and National) receive over half a million online visitors a month. Basically, the three biggest benefits offered by online banking are convenience, comparison (you can quickly check what each bank has to offer) and cost. Transaction fees for online banking are generally lower than for transactions made via an ATM or in a branch.

For example, here are some transaction fees on certain accounts (after exceeding the free transaction threshold) as at March 2001.

Institution	Branch	EFTPOS	ATM	Internet
ANZ	$2.50	$0.40	$0.65	$0.20
Commonwealth	$3.00	$0.40	$0.60	$0.40
National	$3.00	$0.60	$0.60	nil
St George	$2.15	$0.50	$0.50	$0.20
Westpac	$2.50	$0.50	$0.65	$0.25

Shopping online

Yes, there's stacks to buy on the Internet – wine, CDs, books, lingerie, flowers, real estate, second-hand goods, cars, travel – almost anything at all, apart from a haircut, and often at a discounted price.

Making Money

However, online shopping hasn't taken off as quickly as many predicted. The theory behind online shopping is sound. The vendors can afford to offer discounts because they are saving on office or shop rental, staff and sales commissions. The purchasers can save time and money by buying direct from their home or office computer. It sounds a simple and workable system, but I believe there are three main reasons why Internet shopping hasn't boomed yet.

Firstly, there's credit card security. While in most cases your transactions would be with creditable companies and your credit card details would be as safe as when you hand over your card in a shop, there is still a mental barrier to throwing your details into the wild and woolly world of cyberspace.

Secondly, what can appear to be a bargain may not be because of postage and handling charges or the currency exchange rate. A CD from an online store in the USA may look good value at, say, US$13.00 but our current peso-like exchange rate takes that to around A$26. Add in the freight and the price is around what you would pay in a retail outlet here and, in a traditional outlet, you can get it now, not have to wait a week or two.

Finally, I believe a lot of e-tailers ignored the fact that people actually enjoy traditional shopping! Call me old-fashioned, but I like to try on the shoes I want to buy, read the label on a bottle of wine and feel the tomatoes at the grocers. I also like interacting with real people, and being out and about in my community as well as getting a bit of exercise on the side.

Having said that, there are some e-tailers doing quite well, and some that will, given time. While Amazon (the world's biggest online book store) has lost millions of dollars due to capital outlay and has shed a lot of staff, the company still offers discounts on latest releases, an extensive back catalogue, interviews with authors, reviews, a gift certificate and an easy-to-use search engine. I noticed recently that Amazon will start charging publishers to have their books recommended in the promotional e-mails it sends to customers. According to the *Wall Street Journal* the fee could be as much as US$10,000 for each title. Amazon shares dropped 80% in 2000 but, with added revenue streams to their core business, this could be one stock worth watching.

Some Australian companies are also worth keeping an eye on. ColesMyer, for example, is committed to growing its online operation steadily and, while not in profit at the time of writing, had seen

350

growth of 28% and sales of $146 million in the six months to end January 2001. When you consider ColesMyer already pockets one in five retail dollars (through K-Mart, Target, Coles, Myer, Liquorland, Vintage Cellars, Bi-Lo, Officeworks etc.), it already has a huge customer base to work on. I also see an increase in online shopping for groceries, especially for people who are time-poor and can order from work to have it delivered that evening, and it must be a boon for people with disabilities.

Online shopping can also appeal to people challenged by distance or choice. There's a woman who lives in New York who buys her elderly mother's groceries on-line and gets them delivered to her mum's home in Sydney; and I know of expatriates in Third World countries who do their Christmas shopping online and have the presents gift-wrapped and delivered to their families and friends in Australia.

Credit card security

As a shopper on the Internet, the thought of sending a credit card number into cyberspace makes many people baulk; indeed some people simply refuse to do it. However, using your credit card on the Internet is no less secure than using it over the phone or fax. Indeed technically, sending it over the Internet is often more secure due to the encryption technologies now in place to code your number. The real danger of course lies in dealing with shonks at the other end who could load up your card with all sorts of bogus transactions. This is where you need to use your judgement, though my general advice on this is not to give your credit card number to anyone – be it over the Internet, by phone or even in person – unless you're confident you're dealing with someone reputable.

While credit card details sent over the Internet are generally secure, electronic mail is not as secure and I'd advise against sending any confidential information this way. With a secure web site, your details will be deleted as soon as the payment is processed. E-mail doesn't have this high level of technology, and there's more room for human error or carelessness. Most web sites offer a fax facility for payment as well.

Credit card companies don't advertise this widely, but in the unlikely event of someone getting your card number and using it, the same rules apply as if you lost it in the street. The important thing here is to report it immediately so the card can be cancelled and a new one issued. If you are still concerned, you can authorise your bank to pay the merchant by transferring funds from your account to theirs. The Commonwealth and St George banks are among those who provide this facility.

Sending money anywhere to buy from direct mail has its risks, so my advice is, only buy from a site you trust and that has a track record.

The stock exchange

The Australian Stock Exchange (ASX), as with others around the world, has built quite an impressive site. As you would expect, you get market news, price fluctuations, upcoming float information, simulated training, referrals to brokers and information on how to invest and so on, as well as a 'game' where you can buy a fictitious portfolio and follow it online. It's a great way to stick your toe in the share-market pond without getting it wet.

You'll also find discount stockbrokers who allow users to buy and sell by e-mail or direct through their web sites. ComSec (Commonwealth Bank Securities), for example, offers free market prices and information and brokerage from $16.30 for online trades up to $10,000. In February 2001, ComSec introduced a half-price offer ($8.15) for customers making more than fourteen trades a month in a bid to maintain its dominance in online broking. ComSec has over 600,000 customers, who account for about 8% of all trades conducted on the Australian Stock Exchange.

IT shares

I don't like the term 'tech-wreck' for the share-market crash that saw hundreds of online businesses bite the dust. It was more a much-needed 'tech-check', shaking out the online 'cowboys' who were out to make a short-term fortune. Yes, a lot of ordinary investors did lose their money as well but, as I've said in other parts of this book, if something seems too good to be true, it usually is.

At the time of the IT share-buying frenzy people were looking to buy into the dot com phenomenon, not looking at the dot com companies themselves. Unfortunately, a number of good online businesses, which could have grown organically to be successful, were also washed away when the tide turned on Internet companies. The negative reaction was almost as exaggerated as the hype that sent the shares skyrocketing in the first place.

The IT companies that will survive, and even thrive, in the future are either the ones with sound business plans and good management or those with extremely deep pockets (and these will be pretty easy to spot). With IT shares, my advice is still to tread carefully and to treat an online company as you would an ordinary business. Before investing, look at the company's track record as well as its projection, look at its business plan and the board of directors and senior management. Experience and expertise is a far better basis for investment than a great idea and a heap of enthusiasm.

There are two types of IT shares: software and hardware companies that make the content, and the communications companies that deliver it. The one thing that makes content companies successful is that they gain the market edge over their competition. The problem is, the competition may well come up with another earth-shattering 'killer app' that leapfrogs it ahead of the rest, only then in turn to be outdone by another operator.

While still competitive, a deliverer of content, like Telstra, is on far more solid ground. Apart from the Internet, they have a strong basis in other communications delivery through existing telephony, cable television or whatever. But, no matter what types of shares you invest in, it should be for the long term, not for a quick dollar.

E-commerce

E-commerce will become profitable for some companies, especially in the next four to eight years, not only because of advances in technology, but also because that's when there will be a new generation of consumers – today's generation of Nintendo and Game Boy warriors who have grown up 'pointing and clicking'.

There is a huge potential waiting for companies who learn how to use the online world for business. As I mentioned earlier in the chapter, business-to-business applications are efficient and cost-effective – invoicing, transferring documents, ordering stock can all be done at the click of a 'send' button.

The business-to-consumer sites are also sophisticated, as well as user-friendly, whether they are for banking, shopping or advice. I've mentioned a couple of companies that haven't met their projections, but here's one that has. In previous editions of *Making Money* I've followed the progress of an online travel company that began five years ago: The Great Barrier Reef Online Visitors Bureau. The site was set up by three people and built on a shoestring. These people were experts in the region and invited people to their part of the world, rather than sending travellers to a destination as traditional travel agents do. After three years the company was turning over a million dollars a year. Now, in early 2001, with a name change to Travel Online, it has more than 50 individual web sites and turns over a million dollars a month.

Travel is an industry particularly suited to the Internet. People who travel frequently are generally computer literate, time-poor and have a good disposable income. There are newsgroups where you can get advice and the experiences of other travellers, and travel is well-suited to advancing technology, like video streaming. Research has shown that the majority of travellers now use the Internet when planning a holiday, though most are still using it for looking, not booking. They get the information on a destination, then go to their local travel agency to fix up the details. However, according to Forrester Research, online travel sales will skyrocket to US$29 billion by 2003.

There are a number of lessons for any business from online travel e-commerce. Success could come from thinking a little laterally, becoming a specialist in a particular field or targeting the right consumer. If you were to open a traditional retail shop in a shopping mall that only sold, say, darts, I don't think your chances of survival would be good. But, remembering that the Internet consists of your computer connected to millions of other computers around the world, your target audience could become every darts player on the planet who owns a computer.

One big mistake many online businesses make is that they see the Internet only as a distribution mechanism. It is much more than that: it's a virtual world that you can actually 'move about' in. If you have a company that specialises in, say, vintage car parts, you can do a lot more than just put up a web page. You will find newsgroups for all types of cars in cyberspace – enthusiasts that chat, swap stories and give advice to each other. My advice to anyone with a specialist web site is to get out there in amongst your potential customers and sell yourself, 'work' the sites, let them get to know and trust you and, apart from the business, you can have a lot of fun meeting people with similar interests.

'Clicks 'n' bricks' is very much the buzz phrase at the moment and it simply means having a traditional business as well as an online operation. This makes a lot of sense, as the online presence may not have to be profitable in its own right if it is driving customers into the physical location.

So ... does your business need a web site?

Quite possibly, but carefully considering the following questions will help you decide.

- Why do you want a web site?
- Does your product suit the online environment?
- What is your potential market?
- How do you reach that market?

So many people, when asked why they are building a web site, answer along the lines of 'because everyone else has one'. This is not a sufficient reason to build a web site.

There are many other far more valid reasons such as:

- to make money
- to extend brand awareness
- to expand an existing customer base
- to increase existing customer loyalty
- to make the business more efficient
- to find out more about this new medium.

Let's take the last point. An important part of any business is investing in research and development, and if that's the sole reason for building a web site, it can be money well spent. As with any new venture, hands-on is the best way to learn, but also as always in business, do a business plan. Outline exactly what you want to achieve with a site, get quotes on how much it will cost to set up and maintain, and give yourself forward projections. Again, as with any new venture, make sure you have the energy and enthusiasm to stick to the plan.

There is a saying that came out of Silicon Valley in the USA: 'failure leads to success'. Now, this was probably penned by one of those highly paid executives that took a fall in the 'tech-wreck' to justify his previous position, but it is true. A lot of people tried to fly before the Wright Brothers took off and a lot of people had been chatting between two cans down a piece of string before Bell got the telephone to work.

Becoming an expert or specialist in your field is a key ingredient for success on the web, whether it be small or big business. Take the Nine Network and Microsoft. They have invested millions in the web site ninemsn.com.au. It will be successful, not because of the dollars backing the venture, but because of who they are and what they'll bring to the site. One partner is an expert in producing television programs and magazines, the other in producing the technology to make the content work. It's already the most popular site in Australia and, when interactive television becomes mainstream, they'll be in a fine position to take the high ground.

Interactive television

Interactive television – you will be able to choose what program you want to watch, when you want to watch it, and one day will even be able to chat live with overseas relatives in broadcast quality.

Imagine: it's Thursday night, you are watching the TV travel show 'Getaway'. You like the look of a segment on Bali. With a flick of the remote control you seamlessly turn over to the 'Getaway' web site where you will find every other story 'Getaway' has on Bali, in broadcast quality. You can check the weather forecast, currency exchange rate, duty free allowances and flight times. A red-hot deal flashes across the screen advertising a week at a Sheraton resort in Nusa Dua. You point the remote at the Sheraton icon and you get to see the hotel, pools, restaurants and rooms. You can then choose to book online (with your laser keyboard) or have a consultant ring you. There will be one standing by at the other end of the e-mail. All this from your lounge room!

How far in the future will this be a reality?

Well, technically it's here and, in a basic form, is being embraced by millions, particularly in the United Kingdom. Two Way TV in the UK broadcasts to seven million homes, that's as many as all homes with television in Australia. And here's another term that will become part of the language: 't-commerce' the term given to interactive shopping and trading via television. The big attractions for subscribers at present are sport, horse-tipping and two-way game shows. Two Way TV Australia is being trialled, but it may not have the same initial take-up since it will only be available to subscribers of cable TV.

Mobile phones/web phones

What do mobile phones have to do with the Internet? Quite a lot, for some people. Mobiles can be used, in conjunction with a laptop computer, to access the Internet wherever you are. And some believe that WAP (Wireless Application Protocol), as this is known, is the next 'killer app', although I'm not one of them. A number of phone companies, including Ericsson and Nokia, were working independently on this technology but decided to join together to build a common format that would allow Internet content to be transferred, without being customised, to mobile phones or personal organisers. Personally, while I admire the technology, I really can't see the majority of mobile phone owners needing to quickly access the stock exchange or airline departure details.

Now, I think mobile phones are terrific things, especially for tradespeople who need to be contacted on the job, on-the-road salespeople, people who are out of the office and also for personal use. But, what worries me is that they put people on a lead from which there is no escape. I've heard phones ring on the golf course, in cinemas, at school speech nights and even at a funeral. It does concern me that people are losing touch with the things that *do* matter – family, friends, hobbies and simple relaxation.

While the uptake hasn't been big (due mainly to competition in traditional telephony), web phones can also save you money when making STD and ISD phone calls. You don't need a computer or any special equipment for this, just your phone. You simply have to register with an Internet Service Provider (ISP) who will give you a Personal Identification Number (PIN) for future access. Next time you want to make a long-distance call you ring your local service provider (using your PIN), they connect with a service provider in the area you're calling via the Internet, and that ISP connects you to the number. This relatively inexpensive way of making long-distance calls works with tone-dial telephones, including public pay phones and mobile phones. Faxing via the Internet can also be done this way.

Making Money

Home offices

The Internet, particularly e-mail, has allowed for more and more people to work from home and there are great advantages. You can dress as you wish (I'm writing this in shorts and a T-shirt), you can take breaks when you want them, you can 'time-shift' (get in a swim or a game of golf and then work after hours) and there could be tax benefits in deductible items like electricity, telephone or a percentage of your rent or mortgage.

The one thing you need to run a successful home office is discipline – both the discipline to turn up at your desk each day and work, and the discipline to know when to knock off so work and home life don't get in each other's way. Another downside can be the 'tyranny of distance' – the isolation of not being able to interact with your colleagues. Having said that, I'm slightly envious of one person I know who works for clients in Australia and the UK from his home office in Vanuatu!

Cutting costs

For the home user, there are a couple of things you can do to cut costs using the Internet. If you're using it for research, you can find the pages you want, then go off-line by disconnecting. Those pages will stay on your hard disk for weeks; when you want to re-visit a site that has been stored or 'cached', just click 'work offline' and the site will appear. Alternatively, print out the pages and use the hard copy. With e-mail, you can collect your mail in a matter of minutes and then disconnect. Answer it off-line and send it next time you go online to check your mail again. It also saves time if you 'bookmark' your favourite sites. This keeps a record of a list of sites you like and instead of typing in the web address each time, you just click on the name of the site.

Making money

As I said earlier in the chapter, the anticipated rush to online shopping didn't happen, but it will still continue to be a growth area. A key reason many online businesses fail is the same one that bedevils many other businesses: lack of cash flow. No matter how much capital is invested in a venture, if sales don't happen, the business will go under and, the faster they burn their capital, the faster they disappear. The secret is to have a good business plan and to grow organically rather than overnight.

Now, if the primary reason to go online is to make money – terrific! But keep in mind you not only need to have a product people want, but you have to let people know where to find it. Sure, there's the potential to attract millions of customers into your online 'shop', but there's also a million other 'shops' out there trying to do the same.

So, just how do you get people to know you're open for business? Firstly, make sure your web address (Uniform Resource Locator, URL) is printed on all your business cards, stationery, signage and in other forms of advertising. Have a look at how many big companies include their URL in their TV and print advertising these days.

Next, and probably most importantly, have something worth-while on your site to reward the visitor and hopefully ensure that he/she keeps coming back.

Let's look at a hypothetical site for fishing gear. Fishing is the most popular sport in Australia, so if you sold tackle, it might make sense to have a web site. But it's a fact that you will need more bait than just a brochure showing rods and reels to hook a regular visitor. Sure, discounted gear will appeal to some, but think about what else your potential customers would want.

To get the person coming back the site could also have tide charts, a weather map, sunrise and sunset times, recommended bait for various types of fish, a bulletin board for anglers to boast of their catches or tell others where the big ones are biting, and even recipes telling you how to deal with the catch.

Now you have a site that people will trust, bookmark, visit regularly and then, hopefully, at some stage, buy their tackle from. Word of mouth will also make this site more and more popular.

If you're not doing things right, your customers will let you know. If your monthly 'hits' (people visiting the site) don't increase, you're obviously not rewarding the visitor. If they rise and continue to do so, you're on the right track. It's that simple.

Another important thing is to get your business listed on the world-wide search engines. These are facilities that list web sites by name and category. The user types in the subject they want and the search engine picks up on keywords and finds it. If, for example, your web site was built to advertise La Arrabbiata Italian restaurant in Carlton, Melbourne, you would have all pertinent words listed: 'Arrabbiata', 'Carlton', 'Melbourne', 'Italian food', 'Restaurant', 'Dining' etc.

Before even thinking of what to put on your web site, have a whiteboard session with your decision makers and staff, forget about the Internet for a moment and discuss the short-, medium- and long-term aims of the business generally and the business's image. This will help in your briefing to the web builder, as well as help you work out what you want your web site to do.

Building your own web site

The cost of a web site is akin to the proverbial length of a piece of string, ranging from next-to-nothing to literally millions, and again it pays to shop around.

To quickly deal with the 'next-to-nothing' option. There are software packages available that give templates for you to build your own site and most ISPs provide free space to house sites, usually up to around 5 megabytes. More often than not, however, do-it-yourself design can look like just that, which is fine for a personal site, but may not give the professionalism you seek for a business. You'll still be up for a few hundred dollars for the software and registering your domain name.

If you do decide to go further, it's worth doing properly. That doesn't mean it has to cost an arm and a leg, but it should have a solid foundation for future growth. It'll be money badly spent if your present (mediocre) site has to be rebuilt entirely a couple of years down the track.

It's important that your site reflects your company's personality, is functional and provides the user with a rewarding experience. For example, an international airline put up a web site in 1997, which consisted only of the head office address and the names of the board of directors. As a user going to that site I would want flight times and price schedules, seat availability, time zone differences, a weather map, details of in-flight entertainment, duty free allowances and any deals on offer. Many of these things don't require construction. There's no point trying to reinvent the wheel. Someone who has already built a weather map or a currency converter will usually be more than happy for you to simply link to theirs. After all, it's a way of getting more traffic to their site.

To give a ball-park figure of what you might expect to pay for a small but effective web site, allow around $1,000 for a home page and a couple of hundred dollars for each additional page. It will save a few dollars if you can explain to your chosen web builder how you want the site to look and feel and what you want to achieve.

For example, let's build a site for Clarrie's Camera Emporium. First, we need a home page. This then links to the cameras, film and accessories that Clarrie has to offer as well as deals and discounts.

Then, to make it more than an online brochure, let's put in some information on how to take better pictures, what film to use for what occasions and other photo tips. That will encourage a few people to return to the site. Now, what about a gallery of people's favourite, funniest or best baby pictures? That would be another reason for people to drop in to the site. The site is now even more rewarding because it is constantly changing. We also get the benefit of word of mouth, with people chosen for the gallery telling their friends to check out the site.

Next, why not have a competition, giving away a camera for the best photo? And, when people post their picture in, get them to include a stamped addressed envelope to return their snap, along with a voucher for free processing next time they want a film developed – a great enticement to get customers physically into the shop. See, now we've linked the clicks and the bricks with a 'call-to-action'!

And the costs for the site? For the information photo tips we can link to one of the major film manufacturers, so the only additional costs are the home page, the camera gear page, the gallery page and the maintenance/updating of the site, which, with a few lessons, Clarrie can learn to do himself.

There's also the possibility of having the camera prize donated in exchange for presenting its maker as the preferred brand on the web site. Later on, perhaps, this camera company may even become a paying advertiser on the site. So you can see that by applying some thought you can build a potentially profitable, interactive web site for relatively little outlay. Even if it's not initially profitable, it's good for Clarrie's image and branding.

A similar process can work for most businesses wanting to go online. For example, an online real-estate agency could pass on the cost of featuring a house to the vendors as part of the advertising budget, as well as getting additional revenue by featuring links to, say, a conveyancing solicitor, some lenders, selected builders, electricians, plumbers, architects, renovators and landscapers. This in turn gives these participants a value for money presence on the web. A renovator on his own probably doesn't need a web site, but parting with a couple of hundred dollars to be on someone else's site that is appealing to a similar target market may be a good investment.

Selling via e-mail is another very cheap option for people wanting to experiment with online commerce. Most retail outlets have regular customers. Strike up a conversation with them about your proposed e-mail club to let your valued customers know when you'll have specific items on special and see the reaction. My guess is, you'll be handed a heap of e-mail addresses. This is another simple example of clicks 'n' bricks. You email your customers letting them know of discounts to entice them into your shop.

When designing your web site, keep in mind two things:
- You are talking one-to-one with the customer.
- They are paying to visit your site.

In physical terms, they have driven to your shop or office and paid to park their car in a parking station. When they enter your shop they want friendly, efficient service and not to go away empty-handed.

So, when users get to your web site, they want a friendly welcoming home page that tells them where they are (who you are) and where they can go. In one 'click' (selecting an icon) they should be able to go to the area they want to look at. For the following flow chart, I've simplified ipac's web site navigation process.

From the Welcome Page, it's one 'click' to contact us or choose one of three areas: 'Financial Advice', 'Adviser Services' or our 'Strategic Partners'. If you go into 'Financial Advice', you are then only one click from 'Seminars', 'Growing Wealth', 'Your Retirement' and so on. And wherever you go in the site, you will still be only one click away from contacting us with an automatic pop-up e-mail.

Finally, the question of getting paid. Assuming users can buy things on your site, getting paid is technically no problem. You'll simply need a pay-by-credit-card facility on the site and, for those customers reluctant to send details down the line, a fax number or an address to which they can send their cheque.

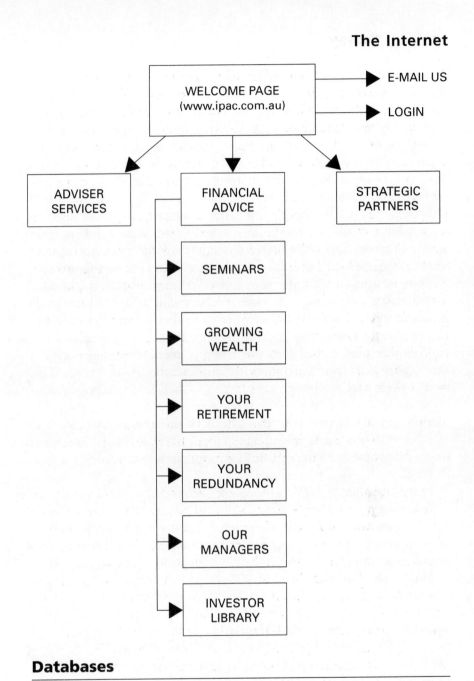

Databases

A database is a record of your customers and is a most important part of gaining an ongoing relationship with them. Very few people mind being put on a mailing list if they think they will benefit from getting information and discounts on products they are interested in.

Making Money

The advantages of using e-mail to contact customers are threefold. Firstly, there's no postage, advertising or printing costs, so it will be cheaper than advertising in a local paper. Secondly, because e-mail is relatively new, people are more likely to read it rather than discard something that comes in the post; and thirdly, and most importantly, it can be personalised so easily, enabling you to target people one-to-one. From your knowledge of your customer base, you can make e-mails personal and specific. If you had a hardware store, you could tell painters about discount paint offers or electricians about specials on insulated wiring. A bottle shop can separate wine drinkers from spirits drinkers and offer better specials than the ones on offer to walk-in shoppers. A bookshop may alert a John Grisham fan to new authors writing in a similar genre. A restaurant or club could offer a free bottle of wine and a rose for Valentine's Day bookings or promote a Melbourne Cup lunch. It just takes a little thought, but the important thing is to make sure the e-mail is welcome and not just another junk e-mail. Another thing to include in your e-mail is the facility for your customers to unsubscribe at any time. This makes them feel as though they aren't locked in to receiving your e-mails forever and, if people start dropping out, you'll be quickly alerted to the fact that you're not doing something right.

Which do you think would have more effect? A posted brochure, or an e-mail from Clarrie's Camera Emporium that read:

Hi Dave

Hope the Pentax 1200 is doing the job.

Just thought I'd let you know we've got a new wide-angle lens in for that model and for this month it's 25% off. We've also got a two-for-one processing offer on at the moment. Look forward to seeing you soon.

Happy snapping!

Clarrie

Advertising and cross-linking

While banner advertising has been less profitable than predicted, there are a number of ways of attracting advertisers to your site. Web sites are still an appealing medium for advertisers to use. Compared to other media the cost isn't huge and, placed properly, the ads can reach a target market.

Straight 'branding' can be important; it's certainly worked for companies like Coca Cola and Nike. If you had a web site for a sports store, a Nike logo on your home page says a lot about the type of store you are as well as promoting their brand. But, if you're the advertiser, you should make sure the ad makes the user 'do' something. 'Click here for the chance to win five new tyres' has far more appeal than 'Bob's tyres are the best'. This is sometimes referred to as 'pull' technology.

Television and print media use 'push' technology. You just sit there and information, entertainment and advertising is 'pushed' at you. You then either choose to ignore or absorb it. With online it's 'pull' technology. It's the viewer who decides what information they want to extract, which is why it's so important to get your content right. If it's pure information you want to get across, do it in an efficient and friendly manner. Remember the person accessing your information is paying for that privilege. They've already paid the price of a phone call to get there and while online they are paying their service provider.

The secret to the success of any web site is one-to-one interactivity. Unlike TV broadcasting, this is the ultimate in narrowcasting – communicating with an audience of one, and the audience must be able to communicate back. The perfect web site should be as personal as a phone call, but with the depth of a library.

Finally, consider 'cross-linking'. Placing reciprocal links with other sites in the same line of business can also pay dividends in raising your profile. If you had an online liquor outlet, surely wineries with web sites would want to link through to your site in return for you having a link to theirs.

Intranets

Here's another one of those techno-terms. An Intranet is basically a way of setting up an Internet site for your internal business workings that can't be accessed by the general public. Depending on your business, this can be a cost-effective and efficient way of transferring documents, data, conferencing, ordering stock, checking inventory, and leaving memos within the company.

Making Money

Domain names

If you want to build a web site, clearly you will need a web address (also known in technical terms as your 'domain name' or URL). You can register your address in Australia by contacting www.MelbourneIT.com.au, with registration costing $125 for two years. Within reason, you can register any name you like, so long as it's not already taken. Note, however, that your web address should reflect your business or company name, that generic terms like 'butcher' or 'baker' may be knocked back and, because of the growth in web sites, many of the best names may already be gone. You will also need an Internet Service Provider to host the site once it is named, as having a domain name without an ISP is like having a business name without a business premises. Your ISP can also arrange domain name registration for you, if you haven't already done it yourself.

As an alternative, your ISP may allow you to build a small site as *part of theirs* free of charge. However, the problem here is you'll end up with a domain name that's more cumbersome and harder to remember than the one you're likely to prefer. If Clarrie's Camera Emporium registered as part of OzEmail for example, the URL could be something like http://www.ozemail.com.au/~clarries-cameras.html, which doesn't exactly roll off the tongue. By registering its own address and paying the fee, the Camera Emporium could end up with a URL like www.clarriescameras.com.au, which is a lot easier to remember.

If you look at the sites listed at the end of the chapter, you'll see how all these entities have registered their own addresses. Web users really only have to remember the word between the 'www' and the 'com'.

Until recently, some people did well out of registering domain names, then waiting until someone else wanted that name and selling it to them. But this 'cybersquatting' is fast becoming a thing of the past due to regulation and benchmark court cases. Now, if you were to register a name like 'telstra-interactive.com.au' hoping Telstra may buy it from you one day, you'd be wasting your time. The courts would order you to hand over that name as only Telstra should be entitled to use it. At the time of writing, the Brisbane City Council had taken the owner of Brisbane.com to court saying the council was entitled to the domain. The outcome could have repercussions for people who own geographic domain names, especially those who are actually operating legitimate online businesses under that name.

Some web site do's and don'ts

These guidelines are somewhat technical, but may be useful to hand to a potential web builder. It's amazing how many web designers and builders think it's technology that impresses users rather than the content. When building a web site, keep these points in mind.

- Make sure the site is kept up to date. Would you buy clothes from a shop with last year's window display, or fish from a shop showing last week's catch?
- Provide contact details. You are dealing with people who may want to get in touch with you. Include your phone number, address and contact names.
- If your web site is for the local market, tell visitors immediately. If your market is global, gear up your site accordingly. It's annoying to fill out an order form and find at the bottom 'Available Canada only'. If you have a product that will sell internationally, provide clear freight details and costings.
- Don't supply broken links. Check your page frequently. It's frustrating to want to go somewhere only to find it doesn't happen.
- Don't use 'Under Construction' signs. All sites should always be under construction. The sign tells the user you're not ready, and if you're not ready, why put anything up?
- Don't use excessive and/or huge graphics. Sites can look great without going over the top. The 'keep it simple' philosophy is appreciated.

Tax

Yes, the Australian Taxation Office gets in everywhere. But it does have quite a useful site. It has areas for business, individuals, accountants and students as well as an instalment calculator and facilities for non-English-speaking visitors. It's there to help you with the latest TaxPack and answers to FAQs on all areas of taxation, particularly the GST. You can also lodge your Business Activity Statements online.

Making Money

Sex

Well, I'm sure that heading has more interest for most people than the last! A lot has been reported in the media about the seedy side of the web and it's a fact: there are sex sites on the Internet – and sex sells. According to US surveys on successful commercial sites, the most profitable were, in descending order, sex, travel and computer software. The positive benefit to all Internet users has been that, because the sex sites have been making money, they have been the forerunners in developing new technology that we can all use. In fact, some online companies recommend that their executives monitor the porn sites to keep abreast (pardon the pun) of new applications. These sites have been the leaders in one-to-one video technology and forming symbiotic relationships with their competitors. The previously mentioned 'push' and 'pull' technologies (apologies again) comes into play here. Because users have different objectives and tastes when visiting these sites, one site may direct a visitor to an opposition site that specialises in whatever that user wants, and receive a fee for doing so. This area is not a hotchpotch collection of sleazy backyard operators, but a sophisticated and highly thought-out online industry.

There are two things that should be pointed out with sex sites, however: firstly, they don't just pop up, you have to go looking for them, just as you would for information on diabetes or cauliflowers; and secondly, you can censor access to such sites by using software such as Cyberpatrol, Cybersitter and Net Nanny which is readily available on the Internet.

The future

In many ways the future is already here, with facilities being trialled and used by the minority that will soon become part of our everyday lives. These developments include interactive television, e-cash, online auctions, satellite Internet access, cable modems, Digital Subscriber Lines, bandwidth improvement, compression, WAP technology and so on.

It's an exciting time we're living in. For a moment think back a few decades. We didn't have colour television, automatic teller machines, mobile phones, fax machines, VCRs, CDs or even McDonalds. And the next decade will unveil many more significant changes.

The Internet is here to stay and I really don't believe anyone will be able to do without it in future. Check out www.lehmans.com. This is a company that sells *only* non-electrical devices and has been 'serving the Amish and others without electricity with products for simple, self-sufficient living since 1955 – preserving the past for future generations'. If you can flog a hand-cranked ice-cream maker online, surely any business should at least think about the potential of the Internet!

In the previous edition of *Making Money*, I paraphrased President J.F. Kennedy and ended the chapter with, 'Ask not what you can do with the Internet, but what the Internet can do for you'. I think we now know enough about the Internet to answer that.

The Internet can be used for banking, shopping, trading shares, streamlining business transactions or adding value and profit to your existing business. But, again, the over-hyped and greedy dot com companies that failed did so because they didn't fully understand the medium or the consumer. The Internet is far, far more than just a commercial entity. It's a place for gaining information (and mis-information), for communication and for fun. The ability to play backgammon or Scrabble with someone halfway round the world may be enough for some users. The most important thing though is to use it, not to let it use you.

Some useful sites

Here's a list of some sites you may like to check out:
Australian Stock Exchange – www.asx.com.au
Commonwealth Bank – www.commbank.com.au
National Australia Bank – www.national.com.au
Westpac – www.westpac.com.au
ANZ – www.anz.com.au
Cannex – www.cannex.com.au
Telstra White Pages – www.whitepages.com.au
Telstra Yellow Pages – www.yellowpages.com.au
Travel Online – www.travelonline.com
NineMSN – www.ninemsn.com.au
Australian Taxation Office – www.ato.gov.au
Amazon – www.amazon.com
David Jones – www.davidjones.com.au
Woolworths – www.woolworths.com.au

Making Money

ColesMyer – www.colesmyer.com.au
Australian Financial Review – www.afr.com.au
The Age – www.theage.com.au
The Australian – www.theaustralian.com.au
Sydney Morning Herald – www.smh.com.au
Your Mortgage magazine – www.yourmortgage.com.au
ipac securities – www.ipac.com.au
Yahoo (Australia and New Zealand) – www.yahoo.com.au
Excite Search Engine – www.excite.com.au
Hotmail – www.hotmail.com
Domain registration (Australia) – www.MelbourneIT.com.au
Domain registration (USA) – www.internic.net
Amish online shopping – www.lehmans.com

CHAPTER TWENTY-ONE

The Lessons of the Past – 1998

Given how much happened in 2000, 1998 may seem like a previous generation, but I don't want you to forget history. Believe me, there is much money to be saved and made by studying it. Even so, you're probably wondering what on earth I am going on about in this chapter. Well, given that even the memories of professional investors rapidly fade, let alone those of part-time or first-time investors, 1998 was a year I want you to think about, and remember.

Sure, we've had 1987 (the market crash), 1994 (when investors lost money in all mainstream asset classes except cash) and even the Great Depression of the 1930s, which are all highly instructive in terms of market behaviour, but 1998 is a bit closer to home and you can learn some really valuable lessons from it.

Firstly, some facts. The returns from the various investment classes over the 12 months to 31 December 1998 were as follows:

Australian shares	11.6%
International shares	32.3%
Australian fixed interest	9.5%
International fixed interest	10.8%
Australian property trusts	18.0%
Cash	5.1%

In other words it looked like a pretty reasonable year when compared to average, annual long-term returns. Not spectacular, certainly, but nothing like the disaster of 1994, when investment returns were as follows:

Australian shares	−8.7%
International shares	−8.0%
Australian fixed interest	−4.7%
International fixed interest	−3.0%
Australian property trusts	−5.6%
Cash	5.4%

Making Money

1994 was the worst year I can find in decades, and the returns highlight this. But there are two points I want to make. Firstly, while very long-term investment charts are a pretty reliable guide to the future, they do tend to disguise some of the short-term euphoria and complete panic that happen during the course of most years. Secondly, you'll never become a decent investor if you let your heart rule your investment decision-making processes. Let me use 1998 to highlight these points.

The pretty mild-looking returns in 1998 disguise an astoundingly turbulent year, one of the wildest I can remember. Despite the fact that having a strong understanding of the performance of investments over hundreds of years – including the impact of wars, plagues and the occasional depression – has made me fairly emotionally stable when it comes to the whole fear/greed cycle that drives most of our investment decisions (fear of losing money, greed when markets are rising), and also having a completely cynical view that neither I nor anyone else has the faintest clue about what markets will do in the short term, I've got to admit that my determination to maintain my long-term investment strategy was sorely tested.

It was an innocuous enough start to the year, and rather than using the benefit of hindsight, let's look at how I was feeling in my first newspaper column for 1998, published in the *Sydney Morning Herald* and the Melbourne *Age* during the week starting 24 January 1998. It carried the headline 'Setting Strategies for the Long Term'.

When it comes to the economic outlook for 1998 you can take your pick from a smorgasbord of predictions. Inflation, disinflation or even deflation. Asia recovers, or collapses. Trying to accurately forecast trends for 1998 is made incredibly difficult by the unresolved situation in Asia, plus the fact that we are smack bang in the middle of the shift to the information era. One of my colleagues at ipac securities, Arun Abey, expresses this rather nicely:

In over 20 years of economic and investment market research, never before have I witnessed such a paucity of analysis capable of providing a sensible explanation of the present, let alone the future.

At the heart of this is a massive technological revolution, spawned by the continued rise in the power and cost decreases in the now ubiquitous microchip. Technological revolutions are not new. What is new is one based on knowledge and information which is not especially capital intensive, is easily transportable, is all-pervasive and difficult to control even by totalitarian governments.

Globalisation of investment and trade is not new. But the scale of it, now covering the vast majority of the world's population, and the role played by powerful multinational companies, are new.

Change is not new, but the pace and extent of it is. Whole industries and professions now may rise and fall in about 20 years. Word processing didn't exist 20 years ago. It has now peaked and is about to decline rapidly as voice-activated systems take over.

Given the global volatility of currencies and sharemarkets, the nearly universal lack of job security and the potential threat that one scenario, deflation, poses to the value of assets such as property, one would be forgiven for thinking that most of us would batten down the hatches, curtail spending and eliminate as quickly as possible any credit card or other non-tax-deductible debts, such as a mortgage on a primary residence.

But, quite extraordinarily, while the global economic outlook is uncertain, many individuals seem to be concentrating on growing debt rather than assets. Lending statistics released this week and reported in Tuesday's *Herald* [19 January], show nearly $1 billion in new unsecured lending, which mainly sits on our credit cards for the year to November 1997. Apparently we used our home to secure over $900 million in personal loans in November alone and this, plus a 16% rise in the use of fixed rate personal loans, saw an overall increase of 39% in the use of personal finance products.

Now, an unabashed optimist would argue that the majority of this money is being borrowed to negatively gear some high-quality investment assets, but even my rose-coloured glasses can't convince me of that. Hopefully, quite a bit of this surge in personal borrowings against a home is being done to consolidate high-interest loans and convert existing personal debt into a lower interest package that can be paid off more quickly. This is rational and indeed an appropriate course of action, but it is of considerable concern to me that rising values in select parts of the Australian property market, rising share values and the success of the Telstra float for over a million share investors have boosted our confidence to extend personal debt for a holiday, pool, car or new electronic toy.

The 1990s, apart from the rather nasty investment blip in 1994 where you lost money on just about all the major asset classes except cash, has been a sunny period for investors. Australian shares as measured by the

Making Money

All Ordinaries Accumulation Index delivered a healthy return of some 12.5% p.a., or nearly 10% p.a. in real terms. International shares, as measured by the MSCI index, delivered a similar return. Large commercial, retail and industrial property, as measured by the Australian Property Trust Accumulation Index, provided an average return of some 13% p.a. Thanks to the strong returns from fixed interest in the period 1990 to 1993, this asset class returned an average of just over 13 and only cash, as measured by the SBC Bank Bill index, looked pretty sad at an average of around 6.5% p.a., but then again even this was a much better real return (the return in excess of inflation) than could be historically expected on such a safe investment.

My greatest fear for 1998 is not that the global economy will plummet into a complete meltdown. It won't. European and Anglo-Saxon economies are actually in much better shape than they were 10 years ago. Asia at present can do nothing right, but this has been pretty much priced into the markets. My fear is that the mixed messages from economists and politicians will distract us from setting a long-term investment strategy and sticking to it.

January is always an excellent time to set a budget and to revisit short-, medium- and long-term plans and my tips for 1998 are:

- Jot down your assets and liabilities. Hopefully your net wealth (assets less liabilities) grew in 1997. Increasing your net wealth is obviously a good thing, but be careful about the unrealised growth in the value of your assets. This can disappear just as quickly as it came. If, for example, your property grows in value on paper by $50,000 but your loans increased by $30,000, you could argue that you are $20,000 better off. But be careful – you have $50,000 unrealised gains which can disappear, but $30,000 in debts which won't.
- Analyse your cashflow. Be very careful about running a deficit budget and covering the hole with credit card debt or personal loans. Running deficit budgets didn't work for our Government and it won't work for you either.
- Set up a disciplined investment plan. Don't try to time the market. It's a mug's game. As the old saying goes, 'It's time *in* the market, not timing, that counts.'
- You must diversify. Holding a couple of properties and a couple of shares is a silly strategy given the pace of global change. Diversification into a global portfolio of quality assets can be done today with $100 a month via a professional fund manager. Holding a limited number of traditional blue chip stocks is no longer a logical strategy in a time of dramatic

change. Some blue chip stocks of the past, such as Burns Philp, can be overrun by this new era.
- Above all, don't let the volatility that looks set to continue in 1998 distract you from your longer term goals.

The one constant, the ageing of our population, continues at a cracking pace. And about the only thing I can guarantee in the future is that unless you've got a very healthy pot of money put aside when you choose to, or are forced to, stop work, your quality of life is going to dive as rapidly as the Indonesian rupiah. But unlike the rupiah, your lifestyle won't ever recover.

As usual, forecasters had the normal mixed views about what would happen over the year, but I was fairly calm. Then in June 1998 the first major shock of the year came along – the Aussie dollar collapsed by around 20% against major currencies. Recession was predicted, and in a recession you're better off holding cash, but again I was fairly relaxed. This is my column from the *Sydney Morning Herald* and the *Age* in the week starting 13 June 1998.

The frenzy over the fall of the Australian dollar over the last couple of weeks provides some interesting insights into investor behaviour. Against the US dollar and most European currencies, the Aussie had declined by around 20% in the last 12 months. But recent events which then saw our dollar fall below 60 cents against the US currency seem to have caused investors to go into action mode.

Our banks are suddenly swamped with people wanting to switch their variable loan to a fixed rate loan. Clients of financial planners are asking about switching into international funds, stockbrokers are being asked by their clients for companies with a strong component of their income coming from overseas, and those thinking about a European holiday at Christmas are buying English pounds and deutschmarks, or otherwise planning a local camping holiday.

This is all quite rational behaviour, but why is it that we have to wait until a major panic comes along to do things that are basically common-sense? Let's face it, the Australian dollar is totally unpredictable over short-term periods. But over the last two decades its long-term trend is all too clear. Our purchasing power in a global context has dropped markedly. It's rather sad to say you don't need to go back far to find a time when the Australian dollar actually allowed us to travel to a European,

Making Money

American or Japanese destination without feeling impoverished. The damage to the dollar (mainly due to governments wilfully running large deficit budgets, our previous poor track record in controlling inflation and our inefficient work practices) has seen it travelling about as well as the *Titanic*.

Now, this did not suddenly become obvious last week, but the general inability of investors to have anything vaguely resembling a strategic plan for managing their money becomes painfully obvious in times such as this.

If you want to be a financially independent Australian, you have to hold approximately 35% to 40% of your investment assets in offshore investments. No, this is not a sudden rush of wisdom brought on by the dollar falling below 60 cents. Prior to deregulation in 1983, international investment was all too hard. There were no Australian-based international fund managers readily available to retail investors with a couple of thousand dollars. And even if you did want to send a cheque to London or New York to make an investment with a manager based there, firstly you needed to get written approval from the Australian Tax Office.

But after deregulation in 1983, international investment became simple. Whether the dollar is trading at US$1.40 or US58 cents, the principle of international diversification is frighteningly obvious. Australia's economic output is less than 1% of the world's. Our sharemarket is less than 1.5% of global markets. Equally, our market is strongly commodity based.

You don't need to be the Albert Einstein of investment to work out that leaving all your assets in 1% or less of the globe is a pretty dopey strategy. Even better, it's hard to see how, in the long run, the strategy of having a decent chunk of your wealth in quality offshore assets can fail to protect you. Firstly, you obtain genuine diversification in all the major global economies. Secondly, you have exposure to different companies, both in the scale and variety of their operations as compared to local investments. Thirdly, you are exposed to many different currencies.

Sure, if the Aussie dollar rises strongly over a sustained period, you would lose by holding offshore investments if you sold out. But this is not exactly the most obvious scenario for the dollar. More importantly, it is vitally important to remember that we spend around 35 to 40 cents in each dollar on imported items. While it is impossible to hedge our spending patterns exactly, it makes a lot of sense to me that if 35% to 40% of my spending is on imported goods and services, holding 35% to 40% of my investment assets in a broad basket of foreign assets will at least give me a realistic chance of maintaining my standard of living in both a local and global context.

If you are wondering whether you should rush out to do this tomorrow, the answer is no. I've got no idea if the dollar will go to 55 cents or back to 65 cents, but one thing history has taught me is that when things seem best, we get our biggest crashes and when things seem worst, we get our biggest recoveries. So my advice is to go back to your strategic plan to build or maintain your wealth and make sure that you have a solid core of offshore assets, or at least a plan to get there over time.

In terms of how to do this, please forget about the Swiss villa, unless you are filthy rich. Like a ski chalet, this is a lifestyle asset, not an investment. The only sensible ways to get offshore exposure are via Australian listed companies with a high level of offshore business activity, hence offshore assets and revenue, or with an international share fund, which, in my view, is the best way to go. International share funds are run by our major banks and insurance companies as well as by fund management groups such as BT, Rothschild, Jardine Fleming and County. They hold many companies spread across many economies. Get hold of a prospectus from a few of these groups or go and see a financial planner.

The good news is that international funds are getting far more cost-effective – many have zero entry fees these days and the ongoing fees are dropping. Also, the minimum investment levels have dropped and you'll find funds that will accept lump sums of $1,000, or $100 per month on a regular basis. The fact that a bit over $3 a day will get you a globally diversified portfolio has not been picked up by many Australians. However, it's an opportunity you should not miss.

On another point, the current media hype is all about rising interest rates and how now is a good time to lock your mortgage into a fixed rate. I have no problem with this, because we are at or close to the bottom of the interest rate cycle, but let's not get too excited about media speculation that rates could rise by 2%, 3% or even 5%. The consequences of a big rise are very simple. We would drop rapidly into a recession, unemployment would explode and our share and property markets would fall dramatically. If on the other hand our dollar keeps falling we actually make our export and tourism industries even more competitive.

So you choose. A potentially falling dollar? Or the next recession, which would hit us at just about the time the Federal Liberal Government needs to run for re-election?

A Reserve Bank-inspired recession? I don't think so.

Making Money

The recession headlines soon went away and by July 1998, the Dow Jones Index (USA) was thundering along at 9,000-plus and the Australian All Ordinaries Index was at 2,800. But then things started to get really exciting as the Russian collapse came on top of the Asian crisis. 'The World Will End'-type headlines were the theme of the day and, while my heart was racing (should I panic and sell everything?), writing helped me remain disciplined, as my following column of the week starting 5 September 1998 shows.

Life is never dull, but this is getting ridiculous. On Monday night (our time) we get the second-biggest points fall in the Dow Jones in history, then on Tuesday night this was followed up with the second-biggest points rise in history. I'm not sure whether brokers, fund mangers and investors are on Viagra and Prozac, or are switching from one to the other on a daily basis. But the question on everyone's lips is 'What is going to happen next?' If you are serious about working out the answer to this, you'd do better to ask a psychologist than an economist or analyst, because the market is being swept up and down on a tide of emotion. Were listed global companies worth 7% less on Monday than they were on Sunday, and were they worth 4% more on Tuesday? I think not.

What the markets are trying to work out is exactly what effect the Russian crisis will have, how it will relate to Asia, what impact this will have on Japan, what it means for German banks which have lent heavily into Russia, and what the whole lot means for the earnings outlook of companies worldwide.

About the only certainty is short-term uncertainty. The markets will continue to 'roll with the punches'. In other words, emotions – the key driving force behind short-term movement in the sharemarket – are very brittle, and new pieces of bad news such as a drop in corporate earnings or a spread of the Asian/Russian flu to new countries will have a devastating effect. Equally, pieces of good news such as signs of support for Russia, new fiscal initiatives in Japan or confident statements about the strength of the US economy will see a sharp recovery in share prices.

In other words, trying to pick short-term movements is all very silly, because the factors that will cause market movements over the coming weeks and months are as yet quite unpredictable.

This is all a bit depressing, but if we forget day-to-day share traders for a second and consider the fate of the great majority of share owners who have been quietly purchasing shares with surplus income, things become clearer.

The Lessons of the Past – 1998

Over the centuries, one consistent feature of sharemarkets is that during boom times values become extremely optimistic. They price in every piece of good news imaginable. Sooner or later something happens (usually a war or unexpected crisis such as Asia and Russia) to dampen the prospects for corporate profitability, and the markets tumble. Then, of course, they price in every piece of bad news imaginable and become overly pessimistic. The reality is usually somewhere in between.

As I said in this column two months ago, at above 9,000 the Dow Jones index was relying on a very strong growth story, and if all the positive predictions came true, the index could go even higher. But if corporate earnings were flat, the market was overpriced.

Certainly no bad news, let alone the current drama, was factored into prices with the Dow Jones at 9,000. If new share-market investors are a bit disillusioned with the present market volatility, my advice is to get used to it. Even in the low inflationary period from the late 1920s to the 1970s we had 11 market corrections. The most impressive of these was 1929 to 1932 when the market fell 84%, but other downturns included 45% between February 1937 and April 1938, 17% between July 1956 and December 1957 and 28% between December 1968 and May 1970.

For those who are already fully invested in local and international share markets (by this I mean that if your plan is to have 40% in shares and you currently hold 40%, you are fully invested), my advice is to go along for the ride, but do remember to stick with your discipline. As share values fall, they are likely to drop below your 40% target, which is a signal for you to top up with a few purchases to keep you at your target level. (The same applies in reverse when share values boom – this simple discipline forces you to buy at lower prices and sell at higher prices.)

For people who for one reason or another are holding cash, this is an excellent chance to at least start to build up some market exposure. Despite some of the more interesting 'the end of the world is nigh' headlines, this is about the only thing that won't happen. Sure, more bad news can drive markets lower – much lower – just as good news will drive them higher. But the highest probability is that things will be neither that good nor that bad. What presents itself as an interesting opportunity is that, at the moment, for the first time in the last couple of years, the market is actually priced on the basis of quite a bit of bad news.

If you want to make money in the short term, you'll need to find someone with a much better crystal ball than mine, but if it's long-term wealth creation you're on about, then shares and well-located property are the foundation to your plans. But as history shows, these growth assets, while spectacularly effective over 10- and 20-year time frames, can be extremely volatile in the short and medium term.

Personally, while I wouldn't be selling shares in the current market unless some extraneous factor forced me to do so, this is certainly an opportunity to top up the portfolio. As far as I can tell, people are still using the telephone, doing their banking, buying food, enjoying a cup of coffee, maintaining and renovating their homes, and it is these simple things that are the lifeblood of many listed companies.

And as I gaze upwards I can report confidently that the sky, despite rumours to the contrary, is not falling.

For a change, my advice that this was a great chance to build up market exposure was spot on, as was my final comment about the sky not falling. By November things had calmed down a bit, and in my column of the week starting 7 November 1998, I recapped my emotional roller-coaster of a year, and reflected that my investment discipline had saved me from major losses:

I tend to cop a bit of flak over my view that the typical investor, let alone so-called experts, will, if they follow their instincts, only end up with a small fortune if they start with a very big one. This is certainly a pretty cynical view of the incompetence of the human race when it comes to making money, but you've got to admit that the facts do support my position. Despite the case that shares this century have given an average total return of some 7% p.a. above inflation, and that our most common investment, our home, has grown at an average rate of around 2% above inflation (depending upon where you live), you'd think that our current generation of retirees would be rolling in money. But a bit of a look at average retiree income and the number of people on an age pension shows conclusively that this is not the case. Australian Bureau of Statistics numbers show that only 3.4% of retirees aged above 65 have an annual income of $36,000 or more (the rest have less). This amount translates into around $550 a week in the hand, which is typically what many working Australians would regard as a reasonable level of retirement income.

The next generation of Australian retirees, we so-called baby boomers, are far more aware of the retirement funding issue and thankfully there are some good signs. Compulsory superannuation is forcing many of us to save more, and the banks report that the vast majority of people with a mortgage are paying more than the minimum monthly amount and are therefore effectively saving on a regular basis.

This is good stuff, and demonstrates that maybe we aren't quite as hopeless as I thought. But the reason these two strategies work is because we are not relying on our instincts about what property and share markets will do on a day-to-day basis. With increased mortgage repayments and compulsory super we have made, or have been forced to make, a disciplined decision to save and, barring an end-of-the-world scenario, disciplined saving is pretty much a guaranteed strategy.

But how good are we at picking markets? Well, I have been using the market gyrations of the last few months as a test of how effective following my instincts would be as a method for making money. Like most keen investors I read a variety of newspapers and magazines each week and follow any economic or investment news on the TV with avid interest. But what I've tried to do since 1 July this year is to jot down what strategy I would apply to my portfolio if I took a 'trading approach' to investment, rather than a long-term 'asset allocation' approach. My diary looks like this:

1–15 July   Having panicked and sold out of the market in late June, the share market rises from low 2,600s to early 2,800s. Most of the bad news may be over. Time to jump back in?

16–31 July Horrible news about Russia. Will Japanese banks fall over? Will the Japanese sell US bonds to fund banking sector? Possible deflationary spiral? Go to cash!

1–15 Aug. Think I got that right. Market hits lows of mid-2,500s, but I suspect more bad news to come. Got this bit right, as in late August market falls below 2,500.

1–30 Sept. Dreadful headlines. Hold cash, build up stocks of canned food, dig large hole in backyard in case the world comes to an end.

1–15 Oct. Despite bounce in the market at the end of September to just above 2,600, I am still terrified. Keep holding cash.

16–31 Oct. Market starts rising. Moves from mid-2,400s to mid-2,600s. Bits of good news in the papers. Japanese seem committed to sorting out the banking sector. US growth numbers look pretty strong. Buy back into the market. Fill in hole in backyard.

Making Money

All this proved to me is that my emotions are about the worst investment guide I could possibly use. As the bad news rolled out, my confidence fell and 'sell' was my primary belief. As markets rose, my confidence rose, but I wouldn't have bought back in until the rise was well under way.

The upshot of this is that in the period from 1 July to 31 October, my portfolio would have been mainly in cash. Market volatility was quite extreme, but in one of those quirks of fate, the All Ordinaries Index at 31 October was slightly above its level at 1 July. As usual, my trading decision would have been appalling due to being influenced by the two main human emotions when it comes to investment – fear and greed. The fear of losing money as markets fall, and greed cutting in as markets rise.

At the moment I am feeling pretty positive with the better global and economic business news, but no doubt the next unexpected shock will soon change all that. So I will stick with my boring old regular savings habit and disciplined asset allocation strategy.

Sure, at times I'll be terrified that the world is about to collapse, but it's worth remembering that there is as much risk being out of the market as being in it.

Looking back from the relative safety of June 2001, I can now laugh at my diary entry for the week of 1–30 September. To end my experiences in 1998, this was my last column for the year:

Christmas is coming, this is my last column of 1998, and what a year it has been. Today, to say we are living in interesting times is an understatement.

Moving at breakneck speed towards a global economy and the information era is one thing at a business level, but it is important not to forget that we are also changing rapidly in our attitudes and expectations. Successful investors in 1999 and beyond will pay close attention to both of these trends. We are living longer, retiring earlier and have an extremely high set of material expectations. Exactly how we are going to fund these dreams, as I have been speculating in this column throughout the year, is a complete mystery to me. But for the record, let me once again note that if you are hoping that any government in future decades will fund our expensive tastes, just forget it. A recent OECD report shows that as a percentage of the working population, the over-65-year-olds comprised 13.9% in 1960, 16% in 1990 and are projected to be 16.7% in 2000,

18.6% in 2010, 25.7% in 2020 and a pretty terrifying 33% in 2030.

This puts me at the age of 74 in 2030, hopefully in decent health, and still enjoying a bit of golf and our excellent Australian red wine. While I'm no mathematician, you don't need to be a genius to work out that if about 5 million of us ageing baby boomers want the younger generation to fund our lifestyle, we'd have a better chance of winning the lottery next week.

On a positive note, awareness of this issue is slowly creeping into our minds. To my amusement, a straw poll of under-30-year-olds that we did last year highlighted it. One hundred per cent of them answered 'no' to the question 'Will the Government pay for your retirement?' This was looking pretty good, until we asked the next question: 'What are you doing about it?' Ninety per cent said 'absolutely nothing' and the other 10% planned to marry someone rich – which, I've got to admit, is one of the oldest and most effective strategies for financial security.

The changing economy has also caused many Australians much angst. This newspaper reported earlier this year that some 3.3 million Australians had received a redundancy payment in the last 10 years. Job security has gone forever and the responsibility for getting and keeping a job had been shifted from the employer to the employee. Those with a flexible attitude and an ability to learn new skills love this environment. It means change and new challenges. But those who have a hankering for the days when we joined the bank at 16 and retired at 65 with a gold watch quite understandably find the whole situation threatening.

As we and the economy change, our attitudes to investment have changed. Only two decades ago our investment choices were basically a bank account or property. Shares were for the rich, and offshore investment, prior to deregulation in 1983, was all too hard. But today we can invest overseas via an international fund with $1,000, or in the case of some funds, with $100 a month.

Today, over 40% of adult Australians own shares, and dinner party conversations have switched from property to how our Telstra stocks are performing. In fact, it's been the year of the stocks starting with 'T'. Telstra and TAB, along with the banks and Newscorp, have really driven our market. Shareholders with a high exposure to stocks starting with 'B', such as the old favourites BHP and Burns Philp, are licking their wounds and hoping for better days. This is one of the key messages for the new century. Traditional diversification strategies, such as owning two properties in the same area or even two shares, are quite pathetic at a time when things are changing so rapidly.

Making Money

With a long-term view, I'm quite confident that share-market indexes will move up. But I'm much less confident about the fate of individual stocks. While the 'average' return will be positive, some companies will fail to adjust and will therefore collapse. Other companies that do adapt, are in the right industry (such as Telstra), or are companies targeting the new growth areas are likely to do very well. But to participate in what is going to be a period of vast opportunities and major threats, investors will have to build up share portfolios that are diversified over many countries, including sectors and individual stocks. Not to do so would be foolhardy, in particular given the fact that you can get this level of diversification, at a very realistic cost, for around $100 a month.

Our old favourite, property, has also changed. For decades, increases in value would sweep the country. Sure, some areas did better than others, but in general property was pretty good. Today it can still be good, but in low-job-growth areas it has been terrible. As the significant fall in Canberra property values showed us, when jobs contract in a low-inflationary climate, property has few friends.

Maybe I'm more sensitive to them, but it seems to me that investment scams have exploded in size and complexity. There is no doubt that many Australians are feeling uncertain about the future in terms of their job prospects. Retirees with fixed interest portfolios are really feeling the pinch of falling interest rates, and investment scams offering high interest rates or the prospect of rapid wealth are attractive to both groups.

Interestingly, the scams have expanded from the usual pyramid schemes and get-rich-quick systems to assets we usually regarded as 'safe'. The sale of ridiculously overpriced property via seminar selling and 'free flights' reached a frenzy in the last 12 months and, despite all the warnings, people are still buying without doing any independent research which would so easily point out how overpriced some of this property is.

Anyway, it has been a fascinating year and I've got a very strong feeling in my bones that 1999 won't be dull. Some investments that we never expected to fail will, and some we've never heard of will do very well. We'll get a few global shocks that we didn't expect and also good news that we didn't expect.

But the world will continue and the imperative for working Australians to get their financial act together is high.

Well, enough of this for 1998. I hope your Christmas brings you together with family and friends, but don't put the turkey on your credit card unless you can pay it off in January.

As you can see, in any year much can happen. But it's worth sharing the emotional roller-coaster of 1998 with you, for it reinforces just about every belief I have about money. Let me conclude by summarising these beliefs.

1. No one knows what markets will do in the short term.
2. Wealth is created not by *where* you invest but by the fact that you *do invest* in something sensible.
3. Saving is more important than investing. If you save on a regular basis, even if you bury it under your rose bushes, at least you'll have something.
4. Quality shares and quality property have done well for centuries. Despite short-term disasters they will continue to do so.
5. Set a savings and investment discipline and stick to it, regardless of newspaper headlines.
6. While it is hard to make the decision to buy, quality assets are only ever cheap in a time of economic disaster.
7. Above all, don't sell your quality assets during times of panic.

Look, I'm pretty confident that the sun will rise and set and the tides will rise and fall for many centuries to come. But while investment is far less predictable than this on a weekly, monthly or even yearly cycle, over the decades people who spend less than they earn, save on a regular basis, and buy quality assets will be a lot richer than 'market timers', gamblers, lottery hopefuls, those who can't get their act together, or those who spend their lives saying, 'I'll get started tomorrow'.

Conclusion

There are well over 100,000 words in this book and, in writing this conclusion, I've been thinking about which are the most important in terms of helping you to be financially successful. And, you know, I reckon the important stuff – the things that really make a difference – are pretty much commonsense.

If all you remember are just the following words, I think you'll do well.

- Think about what you want your life to be like. Set yourself simple, achievable financial goals in the short, medium and long term. Plan to consistently spend less than you earn and to put these savings into buying and paying off your home and building superannuation. Once your home is paid off, put your normal mortgage repayments into investments such as shares and property.

- Always remember that risk equals return and never make an investment without really understanding it. Avoid 'get rich' schemes. Plan to minimise your tax, but stay away from tax schemes of dubious merit. Think about your retirement plans early in your life and, when you do retire, plan to make the most of your money. Remember, your estate planning will impact on the life you lead in retirement.

- Above all, never forget that your money is no good to you if you forget to enjoy it. Money is important, but health, family and friends are more important. Money only provides choice about how you lead your life.

Money preoccupies much of our lives, and I'd love to see every Australian with a plan to become *financially* independent. No, we won't all get there, but those with a plan will have a much better chance than those without. I hope this book helps you to build that plan and puts you firmly on the road to financial security, independence and wealth.

Appendix

The table on the following page provides the yearly percentage returns for the main investment classes over the calendar years 1983 to 2000, as well as the annualised average returns* for the period.

The real significance of these figures lies in showing just how variable investment returns can be in the short term, and just how worthwhile they can also be when averaged out over the long term.

Once again I urge you – invest for the long term. You may strike a few bad years along with the good, but overall the good ones should outnumber the bad and you're bound to come out on top.

* An 'annualised return' is an average annual return calculated on the assumption that an initial investment is held and not sold, and that all dividends and/or interest payments are reinvested. It's a compounded return, giving a more accurate picture of long-term investment performance than a simple average annual return (where each year's investment returns are simply added up and then divided by the number of years).

Calendar-year market returns (%), 1983–2000

Year	Aust. shares	Aust. fixed interest	Int'l shares	Int'l fixed interest	Aust. listed property	Cash	CPI inflation
1983	66.80	14.33	32.26	14.93	50.23	13.56	8.62
1984	−2.26	12.02	14.35	15.15	10.07	12.40	2.60
1985	44.06	8.07	70.75	55.80	5.25	15.44	8.18
1986	52.22	18.92	45.62	25.13	35.42	18.12	9.77
1987	−7.86	18.60	7.01	13.78	5.75	15.33	7.14
1988	17.88	9.36	4.14	13.34	16.06	12.84	7.60
1989	17.40	14.40	26.15	18.83	2.35	18.37	7.83
1990	−17.52	19.10	−15.09	13.51	8.70	16.24	6.85
1991	34.24	24.75	19.96	18.14	20.08	11.20	1.51
1992	−2.31	10.41	4.58	9.62	6.99	6.92	0.28
1993	45.36	16.32	24.21	14.31	30.12	5.39	1.95
1994	−8.67	−4.69	−8.04	−3.02	−5.57	5.34	2.55
1995	20.19	18.64	26.05	19.89	12.74	8.06	5.05
1996	14.60	11.90	6.24	10.67	14.49	7.57	1.52
1997	12.23	12.23	41.64	10.65	20.31	5.63	−0.25
1998	11.63	9.54	32.34	10.80	17.95	5.14	1.58
1999	16.10	−1.22	17.19	0.30	−4.97	5.01	1.80
2000	4.80	12.08	2.19	10.36	17.92	6.27	5.80
Annualised 18-year returns	**15.67**	**12.27**	**17.89**	**14.59**	**13.91**	**10.39**	**4.42**

Aust. shares — Aust. All Ordinaries Accum. Index and S&P/ASX 300 Accum. Index
Aust. fixed interest — UBSWA All Maturities Composite Bond Index
Int'l shares — MSCI World Ex Australia in A$ (unhedged)
Int'l fixed interest — JPM Global Government Bond (hedged) ex Aust.

Aust. listed property — Aust. Property Trust Accum. Index
Cash — UBSWA Bank Bill Index (90 Day Bank Bill used for period 1984–87)
CPI — Consumer Price Index

(Source: ipac securities.)

Australian median home prices, 2000–2001
($000's)

		March 2000	March 2001
Sydney	Established dwellings	360	360
Rest of NSW	All dwellings	179	170
Melbourne	Established dwellings	216	217
Rest of VIC	All dwellings	137	133
Brisbane	Established dwellings	182	185
Rest of QLD	All dwellings	150	146
Perth	Established dwellings	191	192
Rest of WA	All dwellings	178	150
Adelaide	Established dwellings	167	161
Rest of SA	All dwellings	110	115
Hobart	All dwellings	151	131
Rest of TAS	All dwellings	105	92
Canberra	Established dwellings	200	189
All Capital Cities	Established dwellings	240	237
All Other Areas	Established dwellings	152	145

Notes: Median dwelling prices have been obtained from a census of all dwellings financed by Commonwealth Bank loan approvals.

The median price is the middle value of dwelling prices. That is, 50% are above and 50% are below the median price.

All prices rounded to nearest $1,000.

(*Source*: Housing Industry Association/Commonwealth Bank.)

Index

Index

Index

Index

Index

Index

Index

Index